CANADIAN
EDITION

Essentials of
Negotiation

Roy J. Lewicki
The Ohio State University

Bruce Barry
Vanderbilt University

David M. Saunders
Queen's University

Kevin Tasa
McMaster University

McGraw-Hill
Ryerson
Connect. Learn. Succeed.

Essentials of Negotiation
Canadian Edition

The Internet addresses listed in the text were accurate at the time of publication. The inclusion of a Web site does not indicate an endorsement by the authors or McGraw-Hill Ryerson, and McGraw-Hill Ryerson does not guarantee the accuracy of information presented at these sites.

ISBN-13: 978-0-07-097996-3
ISBN-10: 0-07-097996-0

1 2 3 4 5 6 7 8 9 10 TCP 1 9 8 7 6 5 4 3 2 1

Printed and bound in Canada

Care has been taken to trace ownership of copyright material contained in this text; however, the publisher will welcome any information that enables them to rectify any reference or credit for subsequent editions.

Vice President, Editor in Chief: Joanna Cotton
Executive Sponsoring Editor: Kim Brewster
Developmental Editor: Lori McLellan
Marketing Manager: Cathie Lefebvre
Copy Editor: Catharine Haggert
Production Coordinator: Michelle Saddler
Composition: S R Nova Pvt Ltd., Bangalore, India
Interior Design: Word & Image Design Studio
Cover Design: Word & Image Design Studio
Cover Image Credit: antishock/Shutterstock
Printer: Transcontinental Printing

National Library of Canada Cataloguing in Publication
Essentials of negotiation/Roy J. Lewicki ... [et al.]. – Canadian ed.

Includes bibliographical references and index.
ISBN 978-0-07-097996-3

1. Negotiation in business–Textbooks. 2. Negotiation–Textbooks. I. Lewicki, Roy J.

HD58.6.E87 2010   658.4'052   C2010-906707-X

We dedicate this book to all negotiation and mediation professionals who try to make the world a better place.

About the Authors

Roy J. Lewicki is the Dean's Distinguished Teaching Professor and Professor of Management and Human Resources at the Max M. Fisher College of Business, The Ohio State University. He has authored or edited 24 books, as well as numerous research articles. Professor Lewicki has served as the president of the International Association of Conflict Management, and received the first David Bradford Outstanding Educator award from the Organizational Behavior Teaching Society for his contributions to the field of teaching in negotiation and dispute resolution.

Bruce Barry is Professor of Management and Sociology at Vanderbilt University. His research on negotiation, influence, power, and justice has appeared in numerous scholarly journals and volumes. Professor Barry is a past president of the International Association for Conflict Management and a past chair of the Academy of Management Conflict Management Division.

David M. Saunders is Dean of the School of Business at Queen's University, Canada. He has coauthored several articles on negotiation, conflict resolution, employee voice, and organizational justice. He has taught at Duke University, People's University in Beijing, China, and at McGill University in Montreal and Tokyo. Professor Saunders is currently Chair of the Canadian Federation of Business School Deans, a member of the Board of Directors of AACSB International, and member of the Board of Trustees of the European Foundation for Management Development (EFMD).

Kevin Tasa is Associate Professor of Organizational Behaviour at the DeGroote School of Business, McMaster University. His research on decision making, goal setting, and group cognition has been published in top management journals. He has received teaching awards for his courses on negotiation and organizational behaviour, and has also served as the Director of the MBA program at McMaster.

Contents in Brief

Table of Contents

Preface to the First Canadian Edition

Welcome to the first Canadian Edition of *Essentials of Negotiation*. This book represents our response to many faculty and students who asked for a relatively short, concise, and still comprehensive overview of the field of negotiation. The objective of this volume is to provide readers with the core concepts of negotiation in a succinct manner. This need was prompted by many faculty requesting a book for use in shorter academic courses, executive education programs, or as an accompaniment to other resource materials for courses in negotiation, labour relations, conflict management, human resource management, and the like.

This Canadian edition was greatly influenced by a group of anonymous reviewers, who commented on the U.S.-based version, and provided invaluable advice regarding content that would be relevant for Canadian readers. We thank each reviewer for their contributions and hope this edition meets the needs of Canadian students and instructors of negotiation. We also thank the group of anonymous reviewers who examined the first draft of the Canadian edition. These reviewers provided guidance that ranged from Canadian negotiation examples to judgments about the coverage of specific topics. For example, Chapter 8, Disputes and Third-Party Help, is unique to the Canadian edition and is a response from reviewers to add coverage of topics such as mediation and arbitration.

Overview of This Book

For the instructor or reader who is not familiar with prior American versions of *Essentials of Negotiation*, a brief overview is in order. The first four chapters introduce the reader to "Negotiation Fundamentals." The first chapter introduces the field of negotiation and conflict management, describes the basic problem of interdependence with other people, and briefly explores the challenges of managing that interdependence. Chapters 2 and 3 then present the two core strategic approaches to negotiation: the basic dynamics of competitive (win-lose) bargaining (Chapter 2) and the basic dynamics of integrative (win-win) negotiation (Chapter 3). Chapter 4 describes the fundamental preparation that negotiators must do to get ready for a negotiation: selecting the strategy, framing the issues, defining negotiation objectives, and planning the steps one will pursue to achieve those objectives. We encourage readers to think of the first four chapters as the basic building blocks of any negotiation.

The next 7 chapters explore *advanced topics* on critical negotiation sub-processes. In Chapter 5, we discuss how a negotiator's perceptions, cognitions, and emotions tend to shape (and often bias) the way the negotiator views and interprets bargaining interaction. Chapter 6 examines two central elements. First, we examine the processes by which negotiators effectively communicate their interests, positions, and goals, and make sense of the other party's communications. We then look at the way communication patterns impact three major concerns that are critical to effective negotiations—trust, reputations, and fairness. Next, Chapter 7 focuses on the related issues of power and persuasion in negotiation. The chapter begins by exploring the key sources of power available to most negotiators, and then moves to the way negotiators actually exert influence—how they use the tools of communication and power to bring about desired attitude and behaviour changes in the other party. In Chapter 8, we discuss disputes, and how parties can use third-party help to get negotiations back on track when things stall.

In Chapter 9 we discuss whether there are, or should be, accepted ethical standards to guide negotiations. We identify the major ethical dimensions raised in negotiation, describe the ways negotiators tend to think about these choices, and provide a framework for making informed ethical decisions. In Chapter 10, we examine how negotiations change when there are multiple parties at the table—such as negotiating within groups and teams—attempting to achieve a collective agreement or group consensus. In Chapter 11, we examine how different languages and national culture changes the "ground rules" of negotiation. This chapter discusses some of the factors that make international negotiation different, and how national culture affects the rhythm and flow of negotiation.

Finally, in Chapter 12, we include a single-chapter section called *reflection*, in which we tie together the whole book at a broad level. We look back at the broad perspective we have provided, and suggest 10 best practices for those who wish to continue to improve their negotiation skills.

There are several other changes worth noting in this new Canadian edition:

Addition of **Learning Objectives** to most chapters and a **Chapter Summary and Key Learning Points** to replace Chapter Summaries.

LEARNING OBJECTIVES

The main purpose of this chapter is to provide an overview of distributive situations and the strategies you can use to negotiate your way through them. After reading the chapter you should be able to:

1. Recognize distributive bargaining situations,

2. Understand the importance of goals and targets, reservation points, and alternatives,

3. Understand the varied tactical approaches used in distributive situations, and

4. Recognize and defend yourself from hardball tactics used by others.

What comes to mind when most people think about negotiation? Images probably include arguments over points of view and competitive behaviour intended to beat the other side. While many people are attracted to this type of negotiation and look forward to learning and sharpening an array of hard-bargaining skills, others are repelled by it and would rather walk away than negotiate this way. They argue that competitive bargaining is old-fashioned, needlessly confrontational, and destructive. In many cases this is true, especially when relationships matter a great deal and the potential exists to create value for both sides. Nevertheless, there are many situations negotiators face where resources are limited, one party's gain is [...] best approach is to focus on [...] limited resources.

Distributive bargaining is [...] or win-lose, bargaining. In a dis[...] the goals of one party are usu[...] conflict with the goals of th[...] fixed and limited, and both p[...] share. One important strategy [...] fully—one party tries to give [...] only when it provides a strateg[...]

Chapter Summary and Key Learning Points

In this chapter we examined the basic structure of competitive or distributive bargaining situations and some of the strategies and tactics used in distributive bargaining. We worked through the example of Alex and John negotiating the sale of John's business unit. Recall that Alex's reservation point was $310,000 and John's was $275,000. Although they don't know it because reservation points are confidential, they are negotiating to see who claims most of the $35,000 value. If they agreed to a selling price of $281,000, would you consider that a good deal? You would probably say it is a better deal for Alex, and you would probably be right. However, it is also important to remember that both sides are better off because the sale price is superior to each party's reservation points. Alex claimed more value than John, but to John's credit, he didn't agree to a deal that made him worse off.

"Negotiation Points" boxes that can be used to emphasize the pedagogical value of certain key points in the text.

Negotiation Point

1.3

The Importance of Aligning Perceptions

Having information about your negotiation partner's perceptions is an important element of negotiation success. When your expectations of a negotiated outcome are based on faulty information, it is likely that the other party will not take you seriously. Take, for example, the following story told to one of the authors:

At the end of a job interview, the recruiter asked the enthusiastic MBA student, "And what starting salary were you looking for?"

The MBA candidate replied, "I would like to start in the neighbourhood of $125,000 per year, depending on your benefits package."

The recruiter said, "Well, what would you say to a package of five weeks' vacation, 14 paid holidays, full medical and dental coverage, company matching retirement fund up to 50 percent of your salary, and a new company car leased for your use every two years . . . say, a red Corvette?"

The MBA sat up straight and said, "Wow! Are you kidding?"

"Of course," said the recruiter. "But you started it."

Tables and figures elaborate on concepts discussed.

TABLE 3.1 | Refocusing Questions to Reveal Win-Win Options

Expanding the Pie
1. How can both parties get what they want?
2. Is there a resource shortage?
3. How can resources be expanded to meet the demands of both sides?

Logrolling
1. What issues are of higher and lower priority to me?
2. What issues are of higher and lower priority to the other negotiator?
3. Are there any issues of high priority to me that are of low priority for and vice versa?
4. Can I "unbundle" an issue—that is, make one larger issue into two o that can then be logrolled?
5. What are things that would be inexpensive for me to give and valuab negotiator to get that might be used in logrolling?

Nonspecific Compensation
1. What are the other negotiator's goals and values?
2. What could I do that would make the other negotiator happy and sim me to get my way on the key issue?
3. What are things that would be inexpensive for me to give and valuab negotiator to get that might be used as nonspecific compensation?

---

doesn't know this) and has no idea of her resistance point ($310,000). This information—what Alex knows or infers about John's positions—is represented in Figure 2.1.

FIGURE 2.1 | The Situation between Alex and John

Seller's Bargaining Range (John)

Buyer's Bargaining Range (Alex)

$270K — $275K — $280K — $285K — $290K — $295K — $300K — $305K — $310K

$270K Alex's Opening Offer
$275K John's Resistance Point
$280K Alex's Target Point
$300K John's Asking Price
$310K Alex's Resistance Point

The figure also illustrates another important concept, the spread between the resistance points, called the **bargaining zone**, or *zone of potential agreement*. In this

---

Key Terms and Margin Definitions highlight important terms relevant to negotiation.

chilling effect
the tendency for parties to advocate extreme positions on the belief that an arbitrator will develop a solution near the middle

final offer arbitration
a type of arbitration where the arbitrator must choose between one of the last offers put forth by the parties

tion each side has a clear incentive to shape the arbitrator's judgment by presenting offers that are self-serving. When each side presumes that the arbitrator will develop a solution that falls in the middle they are more likely to advocate extreme positions. This behaviour is known as the **chilling effect**.

A second type of arbitration, known as **final offer arbitration**, was developed to try and encourage parties to formulate less extreme positions. The key difference between traditional arbitration and final offer arbitration is that in final offer arbitration the arbitrator must choose one of the proposals put forth by a disputant. The arbitrator is not permitted to formulate a settlement that falls in the middle or create the arbitrator's own terms for a desired outcome.

The major advantages of arbitration are:

1. the negotiation or dispute ends with a final solution,
2. the solution is usually binding, meaning that parties usually cannot choose whether to follow the solution or not,
3. the solution is often seen as credible because arbitrators tend to be perceived as wise, fair, and impartial, and
4. the costs of prolonging the dispute are avoided.

There are also some disadvantages to arbitration, including:

1. by placing control over the outcome in another person's hands, each party takes a risk that the solution is one that they cannot live with,
2. parties may not like the outcome and issues may remain outstanding,
3. in comparison to mediation, which we discuss next, there is less commitment to an arbitrator decision. When parties feel less committed to a decision, they

Addition of a completely new chapter (**Chapter 8: Disputes and Third Party Help**) to boost coverage of topics such as mediation and arbitration in Canada.

8 CHAPTER

Disputes and Third-Party Help

LEARNING OBJECTIVES

The main purpose of this chapter is to provide an overview of

In the introductory chapter we observed that a frequent consequence of interdependent relationships is conflict. Conflict has many sources; it can result from the strongly divergent needs of the two parties or from misperceptions and misunderstandings. Conflict can occur when the two parties are working toward the same goal and generally

Significant reduction of the material on Power and addition of all-new material on Persuasion (**Chapter 7** is now called Power and Persuasion).

Summary of Power

In closing our discussion of power we wish to stress two key points. First, while we have presented many vehicles for attaining power in this chapter, it must be remembered that power can be highly elusive and fleeting in negotiation. Almost anything can be a source of power if it gives the negotiator a temporary advantage over the other party (e.g., a BATNA or a piece of critical information). Second, power is only the capacity to influence; using that power and skilfully exerting influence on the other requires a great deal of sophistication and experience. We now turn our attention to power's complement—persuasion.

Persuasion

During negotiations, actors frequently need to convince the other party that they have offered something of value, their offer is reasonable, and they cannot offer more. If you have power, this can generally be done in an easier and quicker fashion

Merging of the former Chapter 6 (Communication) and Chapter 9 (Relationships). The new **Chapter 6** is called Communication Processes and Outcomes.

How to Improve Communication in Negotiation   119

How to Improve Communication in Negotiation

Given the many ways that communication can be disrupted and distorted, we can only marvel at the extent to which negotiators can actually understand each other. Failures and distortions in perception, cognition, and communication are the paramount contributors to breakdowns and failures in negotiation. Research consistently demonstrates that even those parties whose goals are compatible or integrative may fail to reach agreement or may reach suboptimal agreements because of the misperceptions of the other party or because of breakdowns in the communication process.

Three main techniques are available for improving communication in negotiation: the use of questions, listening, and role reversal.

Chapter 10: Multiparty and Team Negotiations now includes all-new material focusing on Team Negotiations.

Team Negotiation

Team negotiation occurs when more than one person joins together to jointly represent one of the parties at the negotiation table. Although it is often possible for just one person to do the negotiation, there is usually a benefit to a group working together. Do teams actually provide benefits in comparison to individuals acting alone? Research comparing the effects of teams versus individuals has shown that when at least one of the parties at the negotiation table is a team, more value tends to be created. One of the reasons this happens is teams tend to share more information than individuals acting alone. Thus, teams often facilitate the integrative dimension of negotiations. However, teams are not necessarily better at claiming value. Although they may not be better in distributive situations, it should also be pointed out that teams are not necessarily worse.

■ Instructor and Student Support

Integrated Learning System

Great care was used in the creation of the supplemental materials to accompany *Essentials of Negotiation*, Canadian Edition. Whether you are a seasoned faculty member or a newly minted instructor, you will find the support materials to be comprehensive and practical.

Instructor and Student Online Learning Centres—www.mcgrawhill.ca/olc/lewicki
This Online Learning Centre is a text Web site that follows the textbook material chapter-by-chapter. Students will find custom quizzes for chapter content and a searchable glossary. Instructors will find downloadable supplements, including the Instructor's Manual, Computerized Test Bank, and PowerPoint® Presentations.

WebCT/BlackBoard
McGraw-Hill Ryerson offers a range of flexible integration solutions for WebCT and BlackBoard platforms. Contact your local McGraw-Hill *i*Learning Sales Specialist for more information.

iLearning Sales Specialist
Your Integrated Learning Sales Specialist is a McGraw-Hill Ryerson representative who has the experience, product knowledge, training, and support to help you assess and integrate any of the above-noted products, technology, and services into your course for optimum teaching and learning performance. Whether it's how to use our test bank software, helping your students improve their grades, or how to put your entire course online, your *i*Learning Sales Specialist is there to help. Contact your local *i*Learning Sales Specialist today to learn how to maximize all McGraw-Hill Ryerson resources!

iLearning Services Program
McGraw-Hill Ryerson offers a unique *i*Services package designed for Canadian faculty. Our mission is to equip providers of higher education with superior tools and resources required for excellence in teaching. For additional information, visit www.mcgrawhill.ca/highereducation/iservices/.

McGraw-Hill Ryerson's National Teaching and Learning Conference Series
The educational environment has changed tremendously in recent years, and McGraw-Hill Ryerson continues to be committed to helping you acquire the skills you need to succeed in this new milieu. Our innovative Teaching and Learning Conferences Series brings faculty from across Canada together with 3M Teaching Excellence award winners to share teaching and learning best practices in a collaborative and stimulating environment. Pre-conference workshops on general topics, such as teaching large classes and technology integration, will also be offered. We will also work with you at your own institution to customize workshops that best suit the needs of your faculty at your institution.

■ Acknowledgements

We would like to thank the following instructors whose comments and suggestions throughout the review and development process greatly added to the value of this first Canadian edition:

Carolyn Gaunt, Cambrian College
Glenna Urbshadt, British Columbia Institute of Technology
Michael Gulycz, Seneca College of Applied Arts and Technology
Davar Rezania, Grant MacEwan University
Frank Maloney, George Brown College
Emma Pavlov, York University
Geoffrey Leonardelli, University of Toronto
Regis Yaworski, Georgian College of Applied Arts and Technology
Maurice Mazerolle, Ryerson University
Ian Sakinofsky, Ryerson University
Steve Harvey, Bishop's University
Robert Oppenheimer, Concordia University
Donald Hill, Langara College
Fernando Olivera, University of Western Ontario
Jane Deighan, Southern Alberta Institute of Technology
Debbie Gamracy, Fanshawe College
Sean MacDonald, University of Manitoba
Tammy Towill, Capilano University
Chris Bell, York University
Tom Arhontoudis, George Brown College

Also, this book could not have been completed without the assistance of many other people. We would specifically like to thank the following people:

- Many of our colleagues in the negotiation and dispute resolution field, whose research efforts have made the growth of this field possible, and who have used earlier editions and told us what they liked and did not like;

- The staff of McGraw-Hill Ryerson, especially Kim Brewster, Executive Editor; Lori McLellan, Developmental Editor; Margaret Henderson, Manager, Editorial & Design Services; and Michelle Saddler, Production Editor for their ongoing confidence and patience as we completed the work;

- Anthony Celani and Navin Chadha, for their research assistance;

- Cat Haggert, for her excellent work in editing this volume; and

- Our families, who continue to provide us with the time and support that we require to finish this project.

Thank you one and all!

Roy J. Lewicki
Bruce Barry
David M. Saunders
Kevin Tasa

CHAPTER 1

The Nature of Negotiation

On 1 April 2003, Air Canada filed for bankruptcy protection. While under protection from creditors, two prominent bidders attempted to gain control of the airline. The first bidder, Cerberus Capital Management, was ultimately rejected due to concerns about whether pension agreements would be affected. The second bidder, Trinity Time Investments, backed by businessman Victor Li, initially offered $650 million in exchange for chairmanship and a board veto. As negotiations progressed, changes to the pension plan once again emerged as an issue, ultimately leading to the bid being withdrawn. Eighteen months after filing for bankruptcy protection, Air Canada accepted an $850 million financing package from Deutsche Bank. The deal was accepted only after last-minute talks between CEO Robert Milton and Canadian Auto Worker union president Buzz Hargrove succeeded in persuading the union to make concessions on cost-cutting demanded by the buyer.

Janet and Jocelyn are roommates. They share a one-bedroom apartment in a big city where they are both working. Janet, an accountant, has a solid job with a good company, but she has decided that it is time to go back to school to get her MBA. She has enrolled in an evening MBA program and is now taking classes. Jocelyn works for an advertising company and is on the fast track. Her job not only requires a lot of travel, but also requires a lot of time socializing with clients. The problem is that when Janet is not in evening class, she needs the apartment to be quiet to get her work done. However, when Jocelyn is at the apartment, she talks a lot on the phone, brings friends home for dinner, and is either getting ready to go out for the evening or coming back in very late (and noisily!). Janet has had enough of this disruption and is about to confront Jocelyn.

On 3 May 2003, 250 crab fisherman from Shippagan, New Brunswick, set fire to four fishing boats and a processing plant. Their violent protest was a response to federal government changes that transferred some of their crab quotas to neighbouring lobstermen and aboriginal groups. The Fisheries Minister at the time, Robert Thibault, ordered a reduction of the crab quota from 24,300 to 18,700 tonnes, and transferred much of the excess to fishermen and aboriginals in outlying regions. The federal government noted that it was trying to balance competing concerns. On one hand, they argued that transferring crab rights to aboriginal communities is a good way to create employment in much needed areas. On the other hand, the government was also concerned about dwindling fish and crab stocks. The changes announced by the government were designed to help cod fishermen and lobstermen recover lost income created by reduced quotas in those areas by allowing them to fish for crab, which is still relatively abundant. How should each side respond to the outburst?

Finally, consider the case of the Pontiac Silverdome, the former home of football's Detroit Lions. The 88,000 seat stadium, built in 1975 at a cost of $55.7 million, set an indoor attendance record in 1987 when it hosted a mass by Pope John Paul II. In 2002 the Detroit Lions moved to a new football stadium in downtown Detroit and the Silverdome lost its most important tenant. In the fall of 2009, Toronto businessman Andreas Apostolopoulos spotted an auction ad in the back of a newspaper describing the upcoming auction of the Silverdome. Not expecting to win, he submitted a bid of $583,000, or approximately 1% of the original cost. In a surprise outcome, even to Mr. Apostolopoulos, his bid was chosen as the winner. Now he must decide what to do with an aging stadium located in a region with high unemployment and reduced tax rolls. Future negotiations are sure to follow.

These are all examples of negotiation—negotiations that are about to happen, are in the process of happening, or have happened in the past and created consequences for the present. And they all serve as examples of the problems, issues, and dynamics that we will address throughout this book.

People negotiate all the time. Friends negotiate to decide where to have dinner. Children negotiate to decide which television program to watch. Businesses negotiate to purchase materials and to sell their products. Lawyers negotiate to settle legal claims before they go to court. The police negotiate with terrorists to free hostages. Nations negotiate to open their borders to free trade. Negotiation is not a process reserved only for the skilled diplomat, top salesperson, or ardent advocate for an organized lobby; it is something that everyone does, almost daily. Although the stakes are not usually as dramatic as bankruptcy proceedings or violent protests, sometimes people negotiate for major things like a new job, other times for relatively minor things, such as who will wash the dishes.

Negotiations occur for several reasons: (1) to agree on how to share or divide a limited resource, such as land, or property, or time; (2) to create something new that neither party could do on his or her own; or (3) to resolve a problem or dispute between the parties. Sometimes people fail to negotiate because they do not recognize that they are in a negotiation situation. By choosing options other than negotiation, they may fail to achieve their goals, get what they need, or manage their problems as smoothly as they might like to. People may also recognize the need for negotiation but do poorly because they misunderstand the process and do not have good negotiating skills. After reading this book, we hope you will be thoroughly prepared to recognize negotiation situations, understand how negotiation works, know how to plan, implement, and complete successful negotiations, and, most importantly, be able to maximize your results.

■ Becoming a Better Negotiator

Before we begin to dissect the complex social process known as negotiation, we need to say several things about how we will approach this subject and how you can use this book to improve your negotiation skills.

First, our insights into negotiation are drawn from three sources. The first is our experience as negotiators ourselves and the rich number of negotiations that occur every day in our own lives and in the lives of people around the world. The second source is the media—television, radio, newspaper, magazine, and Internet—that report on actual negotiations every day. We will use quotes and examples from the media to highlight key points, insights, and applications throughout the book. Finally, the third source is the wealth of social science research that has been conducted on numerous aspects of negotiation. There is a massive and still-growing collection of good research in the field of negotiations, and a primary purpose of this book is to help you understand the theory and process of effective negotiations that has emerged (and is emerging) from all that careful study. This research has been conducted in the fields of economics, psychology, political science, communication, labour relations, law, sociology, and anthropology. We draw from all these research traditions in our approach to negotiation. When we need to acknowledge the authors of a major theory or set of research findings, we will use an endnote; complete references for that work can be found in the bibliography at the end of the book.

Second, we need to highlight the importance of practice, reflection, and analysis. As you progress through this book we are certain you will come to realize that the skills you are learning are appropriate in some situations but not others. Sometimes it is better to open a negotiation with an aggressive first offer, and sometimes it is better to continue gathering information before putting an offer on the table. How do you decide what to do? The answer will have to wait until the next chapter. However, our main point right now is that to master the skill of knowing when and how to make opening offers, you need to experiment with different approaches, reflect on how your counterpart responds, and assess whether or not your approach needs to be modified. Trying to become a better negotiator without practice, reflection, and analysis would be like learning to read music without practicing an instrument; valuable knowledge, to be sure, but probably not your goal.

Third, we offer a few words of encouragement. Despite the widespread perception to the contrary, good negotiators are made, not born. Even if your natural instinct is to run away from negotiation situations, you experience sweaty palms just thinking about the process, or you have extremely low confidence in your ability to negotiate, don't worry. Our experience as negotiation researchers and teachers consistently shows that even the most nervous and shy person has the ability to increase their confidence and ability through careful study and practice. It may also surprise you that in our classrooms even seasoned executives often fail to reach optimal deals when the situation presents itself. Experienced negotiators are not necessarily better, partly because the real world contains so few sources of accurate feedback that can help someone improve their skills. The barriers to reaching optimal deals are many, and after reading this book you will be in a much better position to overcome those barriers, help your counterparts see the barriers differently, and make all parties involved better off.

Finally, many people assume that negotiation is all about the give-and-take process used to reach an agreement. While that give-and-take process is extremely important, negotiation is a very complex social process. Many of the most important factors that shape a negotiation result do not occur during the negotiation, they occur *before* the parties start to negotiate, or shape the context *around* the negotiation. Although the back and forth process of negotiations is usually more exciting than careful planning and preparation, we urge you to keep in mind that outcomes are often largely determined by factors that exist externally.

The purpose of the rest of this chapter is to provide an overview of key negotiation concepts and introduce the rest of the chapters that follow. After defining the main characteristics of negotiation situations, we will introduce the topics of interdependence, mutual adjustment, value claiming and creating, and conflict. Although each of these topics is addressed in more detail later on, gaining a basic understanding of them now will help you appreciate the more subtle aspects that follow.

■ Characteristics of a Negotiation Situation

negotiation
decision-making situations in which two or more interdependent parties attempt to reach agreement

What do we mean by negotiation? We will use the term **negotiation** to refer to decision-making situations in which two or more interdependent parties attempt to reach agreement. We negotiate whenever we cannot achieve our objectives single-handedly.[1]

Negotiation situations have fundamentally the same characteristics, whether they are peace negotiations between countries at war or business negotiations between buyer and seller or labour and management. Those who have written extensively about negotiation argue that there are several characteristics common to all negotiation situations.[2]

1. There are two or more parties—that is, two or more individuals, groups, or organizations. Although people can "negotiate" with themselves—as when someone debates whether to spend a Saturday afternoon studying, playing tennis, or going to the football game—we consider negotiation as a process *between* individuals, within groups, and between groups.

2. There is a conflict of needs and desires between two or more parties—that is, what one wants is not necessarily what the other one wants—and the parties must search for a way to resolve the conflict. For example, couples face negotiations over vacations, management of their children, budgets, and automobiles.

3. The parties negotiate by *choice!* That is, they negotiate because they think they can get a better deal by negotiating than by simply accepting what the other side will voluntarily give them or let them have. Negotiation is largely a voluntary process. We negotiate because we think we can improve our outcome or result, compared with not negotiating or simply accepting what the other side offers. It is a strategy pursued by choice; seldom are we required to negotiate. There are times to negotiate and times not to negotiate (see Negotiation Point 1.1 for examples of when we should not negotiate). Our experience is that most individuals in Western culture do not negotiate enough. We assume a price or situation is non-negotiable and don't even bother to ask or to make a counteroffer!

4. When we negotiate we expect a "give-and-take" process that is fundamental to the definition of negotiation itself. We expect that both sides will modify or move away from their opening statements, requests, or demands. Although both parties may at first argue strenuously for what they want—each pushing the other side to move first—ultimately both sides will modify their opening

Negotiation Point

1.1

When You Shouldn't Negotiate

There are times when you should avoid negotiating. In these situations, stand your ground and you'll come out ahead.

When you'd lose the farm:

If you're in a situation where you could lose everything, choose other options rather than negotiate.

? ✳ When you're sold out:

When you're running at capacity, don't deal. Raise your prices instead.

When the demands are unethical:

Don't negotiate if your counterpart asks for something you cannot support because it's illegal, unethical, or morally inappropriate. When your character or your reputation is compromised, you lose in the long run.

When you don't care:

If you have no stake in the outcome, don't negotiate. You have everything to lose and nothing to gain.

When you don't have time:

When you're pressed for time, you may choose not to negotiate. If the time pressure works against you, you'll make mistakes, and you may fail to consider the implications of your concessions. When under the gun, you'll settle for less than you could otherwise get.

When they act in bad faith:

Stop the negotiation when your counterpart shows signs of acting in bad faith. If you can't trust their negotiating, you can't trust their agreement. In this case, negotiation is of little or no value. Stick to your guns and cover your position, or discredit them.

When waiting would improve your position:

Perhaps you'll have a new technology available soon. Maybe your financial situation will improve. Another opportunity may present itself. If the odds are good that you'll gain ground with a delay, wait.

When you're not prepared:

If you don't prepare, you'll think of all your best questions, responses, and concessions on the way home. Gathering your reconnaissance and rehearsing the negotiation will pay off handsomely. If you're not ready, just say "no."

Source: J. C. Levinson, M. S. A. Smith, and O. R. Wilson, Guerrilla Negotiating: Unconventional Weapons and Tactics to Get What You Want (New York: John Wiley, 1999), pp. 22–23. This material is used by permission of John Wiley & Sons, Inc.

position to reach an agreement. This movement may be toward the "middle" of their positions, called a compromise. Truly creative negotiations may not require compromise, however; instead the parties may invent a solution that meets the objectives of *all* parties. Of course, if the parties do NOT consider it a negotiation, then they don't necessarily expect to modify their position and engage in this give and take.

5. The parties prefer to negotiate and search for agreement rather than to fight openly, have one side dominate and the other capitulate, permanently break off contact, or take their dispute to a higher authority to resolve it. Negotiation occurs when the parties prefer to invent their own solution for resolving the conflict, when there is no fixed or established set of rules or

procedures for how to resolve the conflict, or when they choose to bypass those rules. Organizations and systems invent policies and procedures for addressing and managing those procedures. Video rental stores have a policy for what they should charge if a rental is kept too long. Normally, people just pay the fine. They might be able to negotiate a fee reduction, however, if they have a good excuse for why the video is being returned late. Similarly, criminal lawyers negotiate or plea-bargain for their clients who would rather be assured of a negotiated settlement than take their chances with a judge and jury in the courtroom. Similarly, the courts may prefer to negotiate as well to clear the case off the docket and assure some punishment.

tangibles
the price or the terms of agreement

intangibles
the underlying psychological motivations that may directly or indirectly influence the parties during a negotiation

6. Successful negotiation involves the management of **tangibles** (e.g., the price or the terms of agreement) and also the resolution of **intangibles**. Intangible factors are the underlying psychological motivations that may directly or indirectly influence the parties during a negotiation. Some examples of intangibles are (1) the need to "win," beat the other party, or avoid losing to the other party; (2) the need to look "good," "competent," or "tough" to the people you represent; (3) the need to defend an important principle or precedent in a negotiation; and (4) the need to appear "fair" or "honourable" or to protect one's reputation. Intangibles are often rooted in personal values and emotions. Intangible factors can have an enormous influence on negotiation processes and outcomes; it is almost impossible to ignore intangibles because they affect our judgment about what is fair, or right, or appropriate in the resolution of the tangibles.

◼ Interdependence

One of the key characteristics of a negotiation situation is that the parties need each other to achieve their preferred objectives or outcomes. That is, either they *must* coordinate with each other to achieve their own objectives, or they *choose* to work together because the possible outcome is better than they can achieve by working on their own. When the parties depend on each other to achieve their own preferred outcome they are *interdependent*. The Air Canada bankruptcy story that opened this chapter is a good illustration of this point. The deal between Deutsche Bank and Air Canada could not be formulated in isolation; the unions agreed to cost-cutting measures only after they were convinced that the survival of the airline was at risk without those concessions.

independent
parties are able to meet their own needs without the help and assistance of others

dependent
parties must rely on others for what they need

interdependent
parties are characterized by interlocking goals

Most relationships between parties may be characterized in one of three ways: independent, dependent, or interdependent. **Independent** parties are able to meet their own needs without the help and assistance of others; they can be relatively detached, indifferent, and uninvolved with others. **Dependent** parties must rely on others for what they need. Since they need the help, benevolence, or co-operation of the other, the dependent party must accept and accommodate to that provider's whims and idiosyncrasies. For example, if an employee is totally dependent on an employer for a job and salary, the employee will have to either do the job as instructed and accept the pay offered, or do without. **Interdependent** parties, however, are characterized by interlocking goals—the parties need each other to accomplish their objectives. For instance, in a project management team, no single person could complete a complex project alone. The time limit is usually too short, and no individual has all the skills or knowledge to complete it. For the group to accomplish its goals, each person needs to rely on the other project team members to contribute their time, knowledge, and resources and to synchronize their efforts. Note that having interdependent goals does not mean that everyone wants or needs exactly the same thing. Different project team members may need different things, but they must work together for each to accomplish their goals. This mix of convergent and conflicting goals characterizes many interdependent relationships.

Types of Interdependence Affect Outcomes

The interdependence of people's goals and the *structure* of the situation in which they are going to negotiate strongly shape negotiation processes and outcomes. When the goals of two or more people are interconnected so that only one can achieve the goal, such as running a race in which there will be only one winner, the situation is competitive. This is also known as a zero-sum, or distributive, situation, in which "individuals are so linked together that there is a negative correlation between their goal attainments."[3] Zero-sum, or **distributive situations** are also present when parties are attempting to divide a limited or scarce resource, such as a pot of money, a fixed block of time, and the like. To the degree that one person achieves his or her goal, the other's goal attainment is blocked. In contrast, when parties' goals are linked so that one person's goal achievement helps others to achieve their goals, it is a mutual-gains situation, also known as a non-zero-sum or **integrative situation**, where there is a positive correlation between the goal attainments of both parties. If one person is a great music composer and the other is a great writer of lyrics, they can create a wonderful musical hit together. The music and words may be good separately, but fantastic together. To the degree that one person achieves his or her goal, the other's goals are not necessarily blocked, and may in fact be significantly enhanced. The strategy and tactics that accompany each type of situation are discussed later in this chapter and much more extensively in Chapters 2 and 3.

Alternatives Shape Interdependence

We noted at the beginning of this section that parties choose to work together because the possible outcome is better than what may occur if they do not work together. Evaluating interdependence therefore also depends heavily on the desirability of *alternatives* to working together. Roger Fisher, William Ury, and Bruce Patton, in their popular book *Getting to Yes: Negotiating Agreement without Giving In*, stress that "whether you should or should not agree on something in a negotiation depends entirely upon the attractiveness to you of the best available alternative."[4] They call this alternative a **BATNA (Best Alternative to a Negotiated Agreement)** and suggest that negotiators need to understand their own BATNA and the other party's BATNA. The value of a person's BATNA is always relative to the possible settlements available in the current negotiation. A BATNA may offer independence, dependence, or interdependence with someone else. A student who is a month away from graduation and has only one job offer at a salary far lower than he hoped has the choice of accepting that job offer or unemployment; there is little chance that he is going to influence the company to pay him much more than their starting offer. A student who has two offers has a choice between two future interdependent relationships. Remember that every possible interdependency has an alternative, although

distributive situation
when the goals of two or more people are zero-sum so that one can gain only at the other's expense

integrative situation
when parties' goals are linked, but not zero-sum, so that one person's goal achievement does not block the goal achievement of another

BATNA (Best Alternative to a Negotiated Agreement)
the best alternative to a negotiated agreement, which may be saying "no" and walking away

Negotiation Point

1.2

The Used Car

"Hey, Paul, would you come on over to my place a little before three?" Orlo asked his neighbour during a phone call. "I've got someone coming over to look at the old Cadillac, and I need some competition . . . just act interested."

When the prospect showed up, he saw two men poking around under the hood. Orlo greeted him, and introduced him to Paul who glanced up and grunted. After a quick tour of the car, the prospect was obviously interested.

"You mind if I take it for a spin?" he ventured. Orlo looked at Paul. Paul shrugged his shoulders, "Sure. Remember, I was here first." The prospect returned, impressed with the roominess and comfortable ride. "OK, how much do you want?"

Orlo quoted the price listed in the newspaper, and Paul objected, "Hey!"

The prospect stuck out his hand. "I'll take it!"

Orlo looked sheepishly at Paul and shook the now-buyer's hand.

After the new owner left, Paul said, "I can't believe that he paid you that much for that old car!"

Source: Leigh Steinberg, Winning with Integrity (New York: Random House, 1998), p. 47.

the alternative might not be a very good one; negotiators can always say "no" and walk away. See Negotiation Point 1.2 for a lesson on how one party manipulates the perception of his possible BATNA to get the other to agree. We will further discuss the role and use of BATNAs throughout the rest of the book.

■ Mutual Adjustment

When parties are interdependent, they have to find a way to resolve their differences. Both parties can influence the other's outcomes and decisions, and their own outcomes and decisions can be influenced by the other.[5] This mutual adjustment continues throughout the negotiation as both parties act to influence the other.[6] It is important to recognize that negotiation is a process that transforms over time, and mutual adjustment is one of the key causes of the changes that occur during a negotiation.[7] The effective negotiator needs to understand how people will adjust and readjust, and how the negotiations might twist and turn, based on one's own moves and the others' responses.

Mutual Adjustment and Concession Making

Negotiations often begin with statements of opening positions. Each party states its most preferred settlement proposal, hoping that the other side will simply accept it, but not really believing that a simple "yes" will be forthcoming from the other side. If the proposal isn't readily accepted by the other, negotiators begin to defend their own initial proposals and critique the others' proposals. Each party's rejoinder usually suggests alterations to the other party's proposal and perhaps also contains changes to his or her own position. When one party agrees to make a change in his or her

dilemma of honesty
how much of the truth to tell the other party

position, a concession has been made.[8] Concessions restrict the range of options within which a solution or agreement will be reached. Deciding how to use concessions as signals to the other side and attempting to read the signals in the other's concessions are not easy tasks, especially when there is little trust between negotiators. Two of the dilemmas that all negotiators face, identified by Harold Kelley,[9] help explain why this is the case. The first dilemma, the **dilemma of honesty**, concerns how much of the truth to tell the other party. (The ethical considerations of these dilemmas are discussed in Chapter 9.) On the one hand, telling the other party everything about your situation may give that person the opportunity to take advantage of you. On the other hand, not telling the other person anything about your needs and desires may lead to a stalemate. Just how much of the truth should you tell the other party?

dilemma of trust
how much of what the other party tells them should negotiators believe

Kelley's second dilemma is the **dilemma of trust**: how much of what the other party tells them should negotiators believe? If you believe everything the other party says, then he or she could take advantage of you. If you believe nothing that the other party says, then you will have a great deal of difficulty in reaching an agreement. How much you should trust the other party depends on many factors, including the reputation of the other party, how he or she treated you in the past, and a clear understanding of the pressures on the other in the present circumstances. Sharing and clarifying information is not as easy as it first appears.

The search for an optimal solution through the processes of giving information and making concessions is greatly aided by trust and a belief that you're being treated honestly and fairly. Two efforts in negotiation help to create such trust and beliefs—one is based on perceptions of outcomes and the other on perceptions of the process. Outcome perceptions can be shaped by managing how the receiver views the proposed result. Perceptions of the trustworthiness and credibility of the process can be enhanced by conveying images that signal fairness and reciprocity in proposals and concessions (see Negotiation Point 1.3). When one party makes several proposals that are rejected by the other party and the other party offers no proposal, the first party may feel improperly treated and may break off negotiations. When people make a concession, they trust the other party and the process far more if a concession is returned. In fact, the belief that concessions will occur in negotiations appears to be almost universal. During training seminars, we have asked negotiators from more than 50 countries if they expect give-and-take to occur during negotiations in their culture; all have said they do. This pattern of give-and-take is not just a characteristic of negotiation, it is also essential to joint problem solving in most interdependent relationships.[10] Satisfaction with negotiation is as much determined by the process through which an agreement is reached as with the actual outcome obtained. To eliminate or even deliberately attempt to reduce this give-and-take—as some legal and labour-management negotiating strategies have attempted[11]—is to short-circuit the process, and it may destroy both the basis for trust and any possibility of achieving a mutually satisfactory result.

■ Value Claiming and Value Creation

Earlier, we identified two types of interdependent situations—zero-sum and non-zero-sum. Zero-sum, or *distributive situation*, are ones where there can be only one winner or where the parties are attempting to get the larger share or piece of a fixed

Negotiation Point

1.3

The Importance of Aligning Perceptions

Having information about your negotiation partner's perceptions is an important element of negotiation success. When your expectations of a negotiated outcome are based on faulty information, it is likely that the other party will not take you seriously. Take, for example, the following story told to one of the authors:

At the end of a job interview, the recruiter asked the enthusiastic MBA student, "And what starting salary were you looking for?"

The MBA candidate replied, "I would like to start in the neighbourhood of $125,000 per year, depending on your benefits package."

The recruiter said, "Well, what would you say to a package of five weeks' vacation, 14 paid holidays, full medical and dental coverage, company matching retirement fund up to 50 percent of your salary, and a new company car leased for your use every two years . . . say, a red Corvette?"

The MBA sat up straight and said, "Wow! Are you kidding?"

"Of course," said the recruiter. "But you started it."

resource, such as an amount of raw material, money, time, and the like. In contrast, non-zero-sum, or *integrative* or *mutual gains situation*, are ones where many people can achieve their goals and objectives.

The structure of the interdependence shapes the strategies and tactics that negotiators employ. In distributive situations negotiators are motivated to win the competition and beat the other party or to gain the largest piece of the fixed resource that they can. To achieve these objectives, negotiators usually employ win-lose strategies and tactics. This approach to negotiation—called distributive bargaining—accepts the fact that there can only be one winner given the situation and pursues a course of action to be that winner. The purpose of the negotiation is to *claim value*—that is, to do whatever is necessary to claim the reward, gain the lion's share, or gain the largest piece possible.[12] An example of this type of negotiation is purchasing a used car or buying a used refrigerator at a yard sale. We fully explore the strategy and tactics of distributive bargaining, or processes of claiming value, in Chapter 2, and some of the less ethical tactics that can accompany this process in Chapter 9.

In contrast, in integrative situations the negotiators should employ win-win strategies and tactics. This approach to negotiation—called integrative negotiation—attempts to find solutions so both parties can do well and achieve their goals. The purpose of the negotiation is to *create value*—that is, to find a way for all parties to meet their objectives, either by identifying more resources or finding unique ways to share and coordinate the use of existing resources. An example of this type of negotiation might be planning a wedding so that the bride, groom, and both families are happy and satisfied, and the guests have a wonderful time. We fully explore the strategy and tactics of integrative, value creating negotiations in Chapter 3.

It would be simple and elegant if we could classify all negotiation problems into one of these two types and indicate which strategy and tactics are appropriate for each problem. Unfortunately, *most actual negotiations are a combination of claiming and creating value processes*. The implications for this are significant:

1. *Negotiators must be able to recognize situations that require more of one approach than the other*: those that require predominantly distributive strategy and tactics, and those that require integrative strategy and tactics. Generally, distributive bargaining is most appropriate when time and resources are limited, when the other is likely to be competitive, and when there is no likelihood of future interaction with the other party. Every other situation should be approached with an integrative strategy.

2. *Negotiators must be versatile in their comfort and use of both major strategic approaches*. Not only must negotiators be able to recognize which strategy is most appropriate, but they must be able to use both approaches with equal versatility. There is no single "best," "preferred," or "right" way to negotiate; the choice of negotiation strategy requires adaptation to the situation. Moreover, if most negotiation issues or problems have components of both claiming and creating values, then negotiators must be able to use both approaches in the same deliberation.

3. *Negotiator perceptions of situations tend to be biased toward seeing problems as more distributive/competitive than they really are*. Accurately perceiving the nature of the interdependence between the parties is critical for successful negotiation. Unfortunately, most negotiators do not accurately perceive these situations. People bring baggage with them to a negotiation: past experience, personality, moods, habits, and beliefs about how to negotiate. These elements dramatically shape how people perceive an interdependent situation, and these perceptions have a strong effect on the subsequent negotiation. Moreover, research has shown that people are prone to several systematic biases in the way they perceive and judge interdependent situations. While we discuss these biases extensively in Chapter 5, the important point here is that the predominant bias is to see interdependent situations as more distributive or competitive than they really are. As a result, there is a tendency to assume a negotiation problem is more zero-sum than it may be and to overuse distributive strategies for solving the problem. As a consequence, negotiators often leave unclaimed value at the end of their negotiations because they failed to recognize opportunities for creating value.

The tendency for negotiators to see the world as more competitive and distributive than it is, and to underuse integrative, creating-value processes, suggests that many negotiations yield suboptimal outcomes. At the most fundamental level, successful coordination of interdependence has the potential to lead to synergy, which is the notion that "the whole is greater than the sum of its parts." There are numerous examples of synergy. In the business world, many research-and-development joint ventures are designed to bring together experts from different industries, disciplines, or problem orientations to maximize their innovative potential beyond what each company can do individually. Examples abound of new technologies in the areas of medicine, communication, computing, and the like. In these situations, interdependence was created between two or more of the parties, and the creators of these enterprises, who successfully applied the negotiation skills discussed throughout this book, enhanced the potential for successful value creation.

In summary, while value is often created by exploiting common interests, differences can also serve as the basis for creating value. The heart of negotiation is exploring both common and different interests to create this value and employing such interests as the foundation for a strong and lasting agreement. Differences can be seen as insurmountable, however, and in that case serve as barriers to reaching agreement. As a result, negotiators must also learn to manage conflict effectively to manage their differences while searching for ways to maximize their joint value.

■ Conflict

A potential consequence of interdependent relationships is conflict. Conflict can result from the strongly divergent needs of the two parties or from misperceptions and misunderstandings. Conflict can occur when the two parties are working toward the same goal and generally want the same outcome or when both parties want very different outcomes. Regardless of the cause of the conflict, negotiation can play an important role in resolving it effectively. In this section, we will define conflict, discuss the different levels of conflict that can occur, and review the functions and dysfunctions of conflict.

Conflict may be defined as a "sharp disagreement or opposition, as of interests, ideas, etc." and includes "the perceived divergence of interest, or a belief that the parties' current aspirations cannot be achieved simultaneously."[13] Conflict results from "the interaction of interdependent people who perceived incompatible goals and interference from each other in achieving those goals."[14]

Levels of Conflict

One way to understand conflict is to distinguish it by level. Four levels of conflict are commonly identified:

1. *Intrapersonal or intrapsychic conflict*. These conflicts occur within an individual. Sources of conflict can include ideas, thoughts, emotions, values, predispositions, or drives that are in conflict with each other. We want an ice cream cone badly, but we know that ice cream is very fattening. We are angry at our boss, but we're afraid to express that anger because the boss might fire us for being insubordinate. The dynamics of intrapsychic conflict are traditionally studied by various subfields of psychology: cognitive psychologists, personality theorists, clinical psychologists, and psychiatrists. Although we will occasionally delve into the internal psychological dynamics of negotiators (e.g., in Chapter 5), this book generally doesn't address intrapersonal conflict.

2. *Interpersonal conflict*. A second major level of conflict is between individuals. Interpersonal conflict occurs between workers, spouses, siblings, roommates, or neighbours. Most of the negotiation theory in this book is drawn from studies of interpersonal negotiation and directly addresses the management and resolution of interpersonal conflict.

3. *Intragroup conflict*. A third major level of conflict is within a group—among team and work group members and within families, classes, living units, and tribes. At the intragroup level, we analyze conflict as it affects the ability of the group to make decisions, work productively, resolve its differences, and continue to achieve its goals effectively.

4. *Intergroup conflict*. The final level of conflict is intergroup—between organizations, ethnic groups, warring nations, or feuding families or within splintered, fragmented communities. At this level, conflict is quite intricate

because of the large number of people involved and the multitudinous ways they can interact with each other. The violent protest by the New Brunswick crab fishermen is an example of intergroup conflict. Not only were the crab fishermen battling the federal government, they were indirectly battling neighbouring lobstermen and aboriginal groups, who stood to benefit from the change in federal policy. Negotiations at this level are also the most complex. Because these conflicts are so difficult to handle without assistance, we devote a whole chapter (Chapter 8) to approaches to handling disputes and the use of third parties in the process.

Functions and Dysfunctions of Conflict

Most people initially believe that conflict is bad or dysfunctional. This belief has two aspects: first, that conflict is an indication that something is wrong, broken, or dysfunctional, and, second, that conflict creates largely destructive consequences. Deutsch and others[15] have elaborated on many of the elements that contribute to conflict's destructive image:

1. *Competitive, win-lose goals.* Parties compete against each other because they believe that their interdependence is such that goals are in opposition and both cannot simultaneously achieve their objectives. Competitive goals lead to competitive processes to obtain those goals.[16]

2. *Misperception and bias.* As conflict intensifies, perceptions become distorted. People come to view things consistently with their own perspective of the conflict. Hence, they tend to interpret people and events as being either with them or against them. In addition, thinking tends to become stereotypical and biased—parties endorse people and events that support their position and reject outright those who oppose them.

3. *Emotionality.* Conflicts tend to become emotionally charged as the parties become anxious, irritated, annoyed, angry, or frustrated. Emotions overwhelm clear thinking, and the parties may become increasingly irrational as the conflict escalates.

4. *Decreased communication.* Productive communication declines with conflict. Parties communicate less with those who disagree with them and more with those who agree. The communication that does occur is often an attempt to defeat, demean, or debunk the other's view or to strengthen one's own prior arguments.

5. *Blurred issues.* The central issues in the dispute become blurred and less well defined. Generalizations abound. The conflict becomes a vortex that sucks in unrelated issues and innocent bystanders. The parties become less clear about how the dispute started, what it is "really about," or what it will take to solve it.

6. *Rigid commitments.* The parties become locked into positions. As the other side challenges them, parties become more committed to their points of view and less willing to back down from them for fear of losing face and looking foolish. Thinking processes become rigid, and the parties tend to see issues as simple and "either/or" rather than as complex and multidimensional.

7. *Magnified differences, minimized similarities.* As parties lock into commitments and issues become blurred, they tend to see each other—and each other's positions—as polar opposites. Factors that distinguish and separate them from

each other become highlighted and emphasized, while similarities that they share become oversimplified and minimized. This distortion leads the parties to believe they are further apart from each other than they really may be, and hence they may work less hard to find common ground.

8. _Escalation of the conflict._ As the conflict progresses, each side becomes more entrenched in its own view, less tolerant and accepting of the other, more defensive and less communicative, and more emotional. The net result is that both parties attempt to win by increasing their commitment to their position, increasing the resources they are willing to spend to win, and increasing their tenacity in holding their ground under pressure. Both sides believe that by adding more pressure (resources, commitment, enthusiasm, energy, etc.), they can force the other to capitulate and admit defeat. As most destructive conflicts reveal, however, nothing could be further from the truth! Escalation of the conflict level and commitment to winning can increase so high that the parties will destroy their ability to resolve the conflict or ever be able to deal with each other again.

These are the processes that are commonly associated with escalating, polarized, "intractable" conflict. However, conflict also has many productive aspects.[17] Figure 1.1 outlines some productive aspects of conflict. From this perspective, conflict is not simply destructive or productive, it is both. The objective is not to eliminate conflict but to learn how to manage it to control the destructive elements while enjoying the productive aspects. Negotiation is a strategy for productively managing conflict.

FIGURE 1.1 | Functions and Benefits of Conflict

- Discussing conflict makes organizational members more aware and able to cope with problems. Knowing that others are frustrated and want change creates incentives to try to solve the underlying problem.
- Conflict promises organizational change and adaptation. Procedures, assignments, budget allocations, and other organizational practices are challenged. Conflict draws attention to those issues that may interfere with and frustrate employees.
- Conflict strengthens relationships and heightens morale. Employees realize that their relationships are strong enough to withstand the test of conflict; they need not avoid frustrations and problems. They can release their tensions through discussion and problem solving.
- Conflict promotes awareness of self and others. Through conflict, people learn what makes them angry, frustrated, and frightened and also what is important to them. Knowing what we are willing to fight for tells us a lot about ourselves. Knowing what makes our colleagues unhappy helps us to understand them.
- Conflict enhances personal development. Managers find out how their style affects their subordinates through conflict. Workers learn what technical and interpersonal skills they need to upgrade themselves.
- Conflict encourages psychological development—it helps people become more accurate and realistic in their self-appraisals. Through conflict, people take others' perspectives and become less egocentric. Conflict helps people believe they are powerful and capable of controlling their own lives. They do not simply need to endure hostility and frustration but can act to improve their lives.
- Conflict can be stimulating and fun. People feel aroused, involved, and alive in conflict, and it can be a welcome break from an easygoing pace. It invites employees to take another look and to appreciate the intricacies of their relationships.

Source: Reprinted with the permission of Lexington Books, an imprint of The Rowman and Littlefield Publishing Group, from Working Together to Get Things Done: Managing for Organizational Productivity by Dean Tjosvold. Copyright © 1986 by Lexington Books.

In this chapter, we have set the groundwork for a thorough and detailed examination of the negotiation process. We began with examples to introduce the variety of negotiations that occur daily and to discuss how we will present material in this book. Our discussion and these examples led us to explore four key elements of the negotiation process: managing interdependence, engaging in mutual adjustment, creating or claiming value, and managing conflict. Each of these elements is foundational to understanding how negotiation works.

1. Managing interdependence is about the parties understanding the ways they are dependent on each other for attaining their goals and objectives.

2. Mutual adjustment introduces the ways parties begin to set goals for themselves in a negotiation and adjust to goals stated by the other party to emerge with an agreement that is satisfactory to both.

3. Claiming and creating value are the processes by which parties handle negotiation opportunities to share or "win" a scarce resource or to enhance the resource so both sides can gain.

4. Finally, managing conflict helps negotiators understand how conflict is functional and dysfunctional. It involves some basic strategies to maximize the benefits of conflict and limit its costs.

These four processes are central to any negotiation, and they serve as the foundation for our expanded treatment of this subject. Next, we provide an overview of our broader approach by introducing the overall organization and chapters in the book.

Overview of the Chapters in This Book

The book is organized into 12 chapters that are divided into three distinct sections. The first section, which we call the fundamentals of negotiation, includes the first four chapters. Chapters 2 and 3 explore the basic strategy and tactics of distributive bargaining and integrative negotiation, which we briefly introduced earlier. Chapter 4 explores how parties can plan and prepare a negotiation strategy and effectively anticipate their encounter with the other negotiator. Although this might seem out of sequence—rarely will an expert negotiate and then plan—we feel it is important to understand the terms and concepts in Chapters 2 and 3 before learning about the planning process. Therefore, we encourage you to think of the first 4 chapters as the basic building blocks of any negotiation.

The next 7 chapters explore advanced topics on critical negotiation sub-processes. In Chapter 5, we discuss how a negotiator's perceptions, cognitions, and emotions tend to shape (and often bias) the way the negotiator views and interprets bargaining interaction. Chapter 6 examines two central elements. First, we examine the processes by which negotiators effectively communicate their interests, positions, and goals, and make sense of the other party's communications. We then look at the way communication patterns impact three major concerns that are critical to effective negotiations—trust, reputations, and fairness. Next, Chapter 7 focuses on the related issues of power and persuasion in negotiation. The chapter begins by exploring the key sources of power available to most negotiators, and then moves to the way negotiators actually exert influence—how they use the tools of communication and power to bring about desired attitude and behaviour changes in the other party. In Chapter 8 we discuss disputes, and how parties can use third-party help to get negotiations back on track when things stall.

In Chapter 9 we discuss whether there are, or should be, accepted ethical standards to guide negotiations. We identify the major ethical dimensions raised in negotiation, describe the ways negotiators tend to think about these choices, and provide a framework for making informed ethical decisions. In Chapter 10 we examine how negotiations change when there are multiple parties at the table attempting to achieve a collective agreement or group consensus, such as negotiating within groups and teams. In Chapter 11 we examine how different languages and national culture changes the "ground rules" of negotiation. This chapter discusses some of the factors that make international negotiation different, and how national culture affects the rhythm and flow of negotiation.

Finally, in Chapter 12 we include a single-chapter section called reflection, in which we tie together the whole book at a broad level. We look back at the broad perspective we have provided, and suggest ten best practices for those who wish to continue to improve their negotiation skills.

Key Terms

BATNA (Best Alternative to a Negotiated Agreement), p. 7
Dependent, p. 6
Dilemma of honesty, p. 9
Dilemma of trust, p. 9
Distributive situation, p. 7
Independent, p. 6
Intangibles, p. 6
Integrative situation, p. 7
Interdependent, p. 6
Negotiation, p. 4
Tangibles, p. 6

CHAPTER 2

Strategy and Tactics of Distributive Bargaining

LEARNING OBJECTIVES

The main purpose of this chapter is to provide an overview of distributive situations and the strategies you can use to negotiate your way through them. After reading the chapter you should be able to:

1. Recognize distributive bargaining situations,

2. Understand the importance of goals and targets, reservation points, and alternatives,

3. Understand the varied tactical approaches used in distributive situations, and

4. Recognize and defend yourself from hardball tactics used by others.

What comes to mind when most people think about negotiation? Images probably include arguments over points of view and competitive behaviour intended to beat the other side. While many people are attracted to this type of negotiation and look forward to learning and sharpening an array of hard-bargaining skills, others are repelled by it and would rather walk away than negotiate this way. They argue that competitive bargaining is old-fashioned, needlessly confrontational, and destructive. In many cases this is true, especially when relationships matter a great deal and the potential exists to create value for both sides. Nevertheless, there are many situations negotiators face where resources are limited, one party's gain is the other party's loss, and the best approach is to focus on claiming the majority of those limited resources.

Distributive bargaining is sometimes called competitive, or win-lose, bargaining. In a distributive bargaining situation, the goals of one party are usually in fundamental and direct conflict with the goals of the other party. Resources are fixed and limited, and both parties want to maximize their share. One important strategy is to guard information carefully—one party tries to give information to the other party only when it provides a strategic advantage. Meanwhile, it is highly desirable to get information from the other party to improve negotiation power. Distributive bargaining is basically a competition over who is going to get the most of a limited resource, which is often money. Whether or not one or both parties achieve their objectives will depend on the strategies and tactics they employ.[1]

There are three reasons why every negotiator should be familiar with distributive bargaining. First, negotiators face some interdependent situations that are distributive, and to do well in them they need to understand how they work.

Second, because many people use distributive bargaining strategies and tactics almost exclusively, all negotiators need to understand how to counter their effects. Third, every negotiation situation has the potential to require distributive bargaining skills when at the "claiming value" stage.[2] Understanding distributive strategies and tactics is important and useful, but negotiators need to recognize that these tactics can also be counterproductive and costly. Often they cause the negotiating parties to focus so much on their differences that they ignore what they have in common.[3] These negative effects notwithstanding, *distributive bargaining strategies and tactics are quite useful when a negotiator wants to maximize the value obtained in a single deal, when the relationship with the other party is not overly important, and when they are at the claiming value stage of negotiations.*

■ The Distributive Bargaining Situation

To describe how the distributive bargaining process works, we will walk through an actual negotiation between the owner of a growing business and a property developer. The central facts of the case are real; however, certain details have been changed for illustrative purposes.

A few years ago, Alexandra (who prefers to be called Alex) started a small fashion design company out of her basement in a suburb of Montreal. The business had grown substantially and she could no longer continue operating from her home—she needed to find a new location. Her search for a suitable unit was going nowhere when, as luck would have it, she noticed a new business development only a few blocks from her home. She excitedly called the number on the sign and was put in touch with John, the developer of the property. Their initial conversation revealed several things. First, the unit was big enough for Alex's needs, even leaving a bit of room for growth. Second, the unit would be ready for occupancy in about four weeks—just enough time to get organized for the move. And third, the developer was looking to sell the unit, not lease it, which was exactly what Alex had in mind. With these issues cleared up over the phone, Alex and John agreed to meet in person the next day to discuss the possible sale of the unit.

Notice the distributive nature of the upcoming meeting between Alex and John. Alex wishes to pay as little as possible for the property while John hopes she will pay a large sum. Thus, it appears to be a classic fixed-sum situation with competing goals between the two parties. To do well in situations like this, negotiators are advised to pay close attention to several important concepts. We will introduce these concepts gradually as we continue to progress through Alex's negotiation with John.

They met the next day at the construction site to take a tour and begin talking numbers. As they walked around John casually made the first offer, suggesting that the selling price was $300,000. This was $20,000 more than Alex hoped to pay, but $10,000 less than the amount she considered her maximum affordable price. These numbers represent key points in the analysis of any distributive bargaining situation. Alex's preferred price is the **target point**, the point at which a negotiator would like to conclude negotiations. The target is also sometimes referred to as a

target point
the point at which a negotiator would like to conclude negotiations

resistance point
a negotiator's bottom
line, or the point
at which they are
indifferent to a deal

negotiator's *aspiration*. The price beyond which Alex will not go is the **resistance point**, a negotiator's bottom line—the most he or she will pay as a buyer (for a seller, it's the smallest amount they will settle for). It is also sometimes referred to as a *reservation price*. Finally, the asking price is the initial price set by the seller; Alex might decide to counter John's asking price with her initial offer—the first number she will quote to the seller.

How does Alex decide on her initial offer? There are many ways to answer this question. Fundamentally, however, to make a good initial offer Alex must understand something about the process of negotiation. In Chapter 1, we discussed how people expect give-and-take when they negotiate, and Alex needs to factor this into her initial offer. If Alex opened the negotiation at her target point ($280,000) and then had to make a concession, this first concession would have her moving away from her target point to a price closer to her resistance point. If she really wants to achieve her target, she should make an initial offer that is lower than her target point to create some room for making concessions. At the same time, the starting point cannot be too far from the target point. If Alex made the first offer too low (e.g., $200,000), John might break off negotiations, believing her to be unreasonable or foolish. Although judgments about how to determine first offers can often be quite complex and can have a dramatic influence on the course of negotiation, let us stay with the simple case for the moment and assume that Alex decided to offer $270,000 as a reasonable first offer; this price is less than her target point and well below her resistance point. In the meantime, remember that although this illustration concerns only price, all other issues or agenda items for the negotiation have starting, target, and resistance points.

Both parties to a negotiation should establish their starting, target, and resistance points before beginning a negotiation. Starting points are often in the opening statements each party makes (i.e., the seller's listing price and the buyer's first offer). The target point is usually learned or inferred as negotiations get under way. People typically give up the margin between their starting points and target points as they make concessions. The resistance point, the point beyond which a person will not go and would rather break off negotiations, is not known to the other party and should be kept secret.[4] One party may not learn the other's resistance point even after the end of a successful negotiation. After an unsuccessful negotiation, one party may infer that the other's resistance point was near the last offer the other was willing to consider before the negotiation ended.

DILBERT ©UFS. Reprinted by permission.

The parties' starting and resistance points are usually arranged in reverse order, with the resistance point being a high price for the buyer and a low price for the seller. Thus, continuing the illustration, Alex would have been willing to pay up to $310,000 for the unit John asked $300,000 for. Alex can speculate that John may be willing to accept something less than $300,000 and might well regard $290,000 as a desirable figure. What Alex does not know (but would dearly like to) is the lowest figure that John would accept. Is it $290,000? $285,000? Alex assumes it is $275,000 (and for now we will assume this is accurate). John, for his part, initially knows nothing about Alex's position but soon learns her starting point when she offers $270,000. John may suspect that Alex's target point is not too far away (in fact it is $280,000, but John doesn't know this) and has no idea of her resistance point ($310,000). This information—what Alex knows or infers about John's positions—is represented in Figure 2.1.

FIGURE 2.1 | The Situation between Alex and John

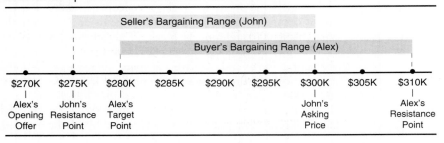

The figure also illustrates another important concept, the spread between the resistance points, called the **bargaining zone**, or *zone of potential agreement*. In this area the actual bargaining takes place, for anything outside these points will be summarily rejected by one of the two negotiators. When the buyer's resistance point is above the seller's—she is minimally willing to pay more than he is minimally willing to sell for, as is true in this example—there is a *positive bargaining zone*. When the reverse is true—the seller's resistance point is above the buyer's, and the buyer won't pay more than the seller will minimally accept—there is a *negative bargaining zone*. If, in the example, John would minimally accept $300,000 and Alex would maximally pay $280,000, then a negative bargaining range would exist. Negotiations that begin with a negative bargaining range are likely to stalemate. They can be resolved only if one or both parties are persuaded to change their resistance points or if someone else forces a solution upon them that one or both parties dislike. However, because negotiators don't begin their deliberations by talking about their resistance points (they're discussing initial offers and demands instead), it is often difficult to know whether a positive zone exists until the negotiators get deep into the process. Both parties may realize that there is no overlap in their resistance points only after protracted negotiations have been exhausted; at that point, they will have to decide whether to end negotiations or re-evaluate their resistance points, a process described in more detail later on.

Target points, resistance points, and initial offers all play an important role in distributive bargaining. Target points influence both negotiator outcomes and negotiator satisfaction with their outcomes, opening offers play an important role in influencing negotiation outcomes (see below), and resistance points play a very important role as a warning for the possible presence of hardball tactics (see below).[5]

bargaining zone
the space between the resistance points of each negotiator

The Role of Alternatives to a Negotiated Agreement

In addition to opening bids, target points, and resistance points, a fourth factor may enter the negotiations: an alternative outcome that can be obtained by completing a deal with someone else. In some negotiations, the parties have only two fundamental choices: (1) reach a deal with the other party, or (2) reach no settlement at all. In other negotiations, however, one or both parties may have the possibility of an alternative deal with another party. Thus, in the case of Alex and John, Alex may continue searching for a unit and find another she is willing buy. Similarly, if John waits long enough he will presumably find another interested buyer. If Alex picks a different unit to buy, speaks to the owner of that unit, and negotiates the best price that she can, that price represents her alternative.

Recall from Chapter 1 that negotiators need to ensure they have a clear understanding of their *best alternative to a negotiated agreement*, or BATNA.[6] Having a number of alternatives can be useful, but it is really one's *best* alternative that will influence the decision to close a deal or walk away. Understanding the BATNA and making it as strong as possible provide a negotiator with more power in the current negotiation because the BATNA clarifies what he or she will do if an agreement cannot be reached. Classic advice to home purchasers is to "fall in love with three houses, not just one." This is solid advice—when good alternatives are available, negotiators are less likely to take unnecessary risks. In addition, negotiators who have stronger BATNAs will have more power throughout the negotiation and accordingly should be able to achieve more of their goals.

Alternatives are also important because they give negotiators the power to walk away from any negotiation when the emerging deal is not very good. The number of realistic alternatives that negotiators have will vary considerably from one situation to another. In negotiations where they have many attractive alternatives, they can set their goals higher and make fewer concessions. In negotiations where they have no attractive alternative, such as when dealing with a sole supplier, they have much less bargaining power. Good distributive bargainers identify their realistic alternatives before starting discussions with the other party so they can properly gauge how firm to be in the negotiation.[7] Good bargainers also try to improve their alternatives while the negotiation is underway. If Alex's negotiations with John extend over a period of time, she should keep her eye on the market for other, possibly better, alternatives. She may also continue to negotiate with the owner of the existing alternative unit for a better deal. Both courses of action involve efforts by Alex to maintain and expand her bargaining power by improving the quality of her alternatives.[8]

Settlement Point

The fundamental process of distributive bargaining is to reach a settlement within a positive bargaining zone. The objective of both parties is to obtain as much of the bargaining zone as possible—that is, to reach an agreement as close to the other party's resistance point as possible.

Both parties in distributive bargaining know that they might have to settle for less than what they would prefer (their target point), but they hope that the agreement will be better than their own resistance point. For agreement to occur, both parties must believe that the settlement, although perhaps less desirable than they would prefer, is the best that they can get. This belief is important, both for reaching agreement and for ensuring support for the agreement after the negotiation concludes. Negotiators who do not think they got the best agreement possible, or who believe that they lost something in the deal, may try to get out of the agreement later or find other ways to recoup their losses. If Alex thinks she got the short end of the deal, she could make life miserable and expensive for John by making extraneous claims later—claiming that the unit had hidden damages, and so on. Another factor that will affect satisfaction with the agreement is whether the parties will see or deal with each other again. If John is selling all the units and moving on to other developments, then Alex may be unable to contact him later for any adjustments and should therefore ensure that she evaluates the current deal very carefully (good advice in any situation, but especially the case here).

Fundamental Strategies

The primary objective in distributive bargaining is to maximize the value of the current deal. In the current example, the buyer has four fundamental strategies available:

1. To push for a settlement close to the seller's (unknown) resistance point, thereby yielding the largest part of the settlement range for the buyer. The buyer may attempt to influence the seller's view of what settlements are possible by making extreme offers and small concessions.

2. To convince the seller to change his resistance point by influencing the seller's beliefs about the value of the unit (e.g., by telling him that the unit is overpriced), and thereby increase the bargaining range.

3. If a negative settlement range exists, to convince the seller to reduce his resistance point to create a positive settlement zone or to change her own resistance point to create an overlap. Thus, John could be persuaded to accept a lower price, or Alex could decide she has to pay more than she wanted to.

4. To convince the seller to believe that this settlement is the best that is possible—not that it is all he can get, or that he is incapable of getting more, or that the buyer is winning by getting more. The distinction between a party believing that an agreement is the best possible (and not the other interpretations) may appear subtle and semantic. However, in getting people to agree it is important that they feel as though they got the best possible deal. Ego satisfaction is often as important as achieving tangible objectives (recall the discussion of tangibles and intangibles in Chapter 1).

In all these strategies, the buyer is attempting to influence the seller's perceptions of what is possible through the exchange of information and persuasion. Regardless of the general strategy taken, two tasks are important in all distributive bargaining situations: (1) discovering the other party's resistance point, and (2) influencing the other party's resistance point.

Discovering the Other Party's Resistance Point

Information is the life force of negotiation. The more you can learn about the other party's target, resistance point, motives, feelings of confidence, and so on, the more able you will be to strike a favourable agreement (see Negotiation Point 2.1). At the same time, you do not want the other party to have certain information about you. Your resistance point, some of your targets, and confidential information about a weak strategic position or an emotional vulnerability are best concealed.[9]

2.1

The Piano

When shopping for a used piano, Orvel Ray answered a newspaper ad. The piano was a beautiful upright in a massive walnut cabinet. The seller was asking $1,000, and it would have been a bargain at that price, but Orvel had received a $700 tax refund and had set this windfall as the limit that he could afford to invest. He searched for a negotiating advantage.

He was able to deduce several facts from the surroundings. The piano was in a furnished basement, which also contained a set of drums and an upright acoustic bass. Obviously the seller was a serious musician, who probably played jazz. There had to be a compelling reason for selling such a beautiful instrument.

Orvel asked the first, obvious question, "Are you buying a new piano?"

The seller hesitated. "Well, I don't know yet. See, we're moving out of the province, and it would be very expensive to ship this piano clear across the country."

"Did they say how much extra it would cost?" Orvel queried.

"They said an extra $300 or so."

"When do you have to decide?"

"The packers are coming this afternoon."

Now Orvel knew where the seller was vulnerable. He could ship the piano cross-country, or sell it for $700 and still break even. Or he could hold out for his asking price and take his chances. "Here's what I can do: I can give you $700 in cash, right now," Orvel said as he took seven $100 bills out of his pocket and spread them on the keyboard. "And I can have a truck and three of my friends here to move it out of your way by noon today."

The seller hesitated, then picked up the money. "Well, I suppose that would work. I can always buy a new piano when we get settled."

Orvel left before the seller could reconsider. By the time the group returned with the truck, the seller had received three other offers at his asking price, but because he had accepted the cash, he had to tell them that the piano had already been sold.

If the seller had not volunteered the information about the packers coming that afternoon, Orvel might not have been able to negotiate the price.

Source: From J. C. Levinson, M. S. A. Smith, and O. R. Wilson, Guerrilla Negotiating (New York: John Wiley, 1999), pp. 15–16.

Alternatively, you may want the other party to have certain information—some of it factual and correct, some of it contrived to lead the other party to believe things that are favourable to you. Because each side wants to obtain some information and to conceal other information, and because each side knows that the other also wants to obtain and conceal information, communication can become complex. Information is often conveyed in a code that evolves during negotiation. People answer questions with other questions or with incomplete statements; to influence the other's perceptions, however, they must establish some points effectively and convincingly.

Influencing the Other Party's Resistance Point

Central to planning the strategy and tactics for distributive bargaining is locating the other party's resistance point and the relationship of that resistance point to your own. Keep in mind that by definition, a resistance point is the point at which the person is indifferent to a deal; beyond that point they prefer no deal. The resistance point is established by the value expected from a particular outcome, which in turn is the product of the worth and costs of an outcome. Alex sets her resistance point based on the amount of money she can afford to pay (in total or in monthly mortgage payments), the estimated market value or worth of the unit, and other factors in the bargaining mix (e.g., closing date). A resistance point will also be influenced by the cost an individual attaches to delay or difficulty in negotiation (an intangible) or in having the negotiations aborted. If Alex, who had set her resistance point at $310,000, were faced with the choice of paying $315,000 or continuing to operate the business from home, she might well re-evaluate her resistance point. The following factors are important in attempting to influence the other person's resistance point: (1) the value the other attaches to a particular outcome, (2) the costs the other attaches to delay or difficulty in negotiations, and (3) the cost the other attaches to having the negotiations aborted.

A significant factor in shaping the other person's understanding of what is possible—and therefore the value he or she places on particular outcomes—is the other's understanding of your own situation. Therefore, when influencing the other's viewpoint, you must also deal with the other party's understanding of your value for a particular outcome, the costs you attach to delay or difficulty in negotiation, and your cost of having the negotiations aborted.

To explain how these factors can affect the process of distributive bargaining, we will make four major propositions.[10]

1. *The higher the other party's estimate of your cost of delay or impasse, the stronger the other party's resistance point will be.* If the other party sees that you need a settlement quickly and cannot defer it, he or she can seize this advantage and press for a better outcome. Expectations will rise and the other party will set a more demanding resistance point. The more you can convince the other that your costs of delay or aborting negotiations are low (that you are in no hurry and can wait forever), the more modest the other's resistance point will be.

2. *The higher the other party's estimate of his or her own cost of delay or impasse, the weaker the other party's resistance point will be.* The more a person needs a settlement, the more modest he or she will be in setting a resistance point. Therefore, the more you can do to convince the other party that delay or aborting negotiations will be costly, the more likely he or she will be to establish a modest resistance point. In contrast, the more attractive the other party's alternatives, the more likely he or she will be to set a high resistance point. If negotiations are unsuccessful, the other party can move to an attractive alternative. In the earlier example, we mentioned that both Alex and John have satisfactory alternatives.

3. *The less the other party values an issue, the lower their resistance point will be.* The resistance point may soften as the person reduces how valuable he or she considers that issue. If you can convince the other party that a current negotiating position will not have the desired outcome or that the present position is not as attractive as the other believes, then he or she will adjust their resistance point.

4. *The more the other party believes that you value an issue, the lower their resistance point may be.* The more you can convince the other that you value a particular issue the more pressure you put on the other party to set a more

modest resistance point with regard to that issue. Similarly, if you know that a position is important to the other party you can expect the other to resist giving up on that issue, and there may be less possibility of a favourable settlement in that area. As a result, you may need to lower your expectations to a more modest resistance point.

■ Tactical Tasks

Within the fundamental strategies of distributive bargaining there are four important tactical tasks concerned with targets, resistance points, and the costs of terminating negotiations for a negotiator to consider: (1) assess the other party's target, resistance point, and cost of terminating negotiations; (2) manage the other party's impression of the negotiator's target, resistance point, and cost of terminating negotiation; (3) modify the other party's perception of his or her own target, resistance point, and cost of terminating negotiation; and (4) manipulate the actual costs of delaying or terminating negotiations. Each of these tasks is discussed in more detail below.

Assessing the Other Party's Target, Resistance Point, and Costs of Terminating Negotiations

An important first step for a negotiator is to obtain information about the other party's target and resistance points. The negotiator can pursue two general routes to achieve this task: obtain information indirectly about the background factors behind an issue (indirect assessment) or obtain information directly from the other party about their target and resistance points (direct assessment).

Indirect Assessment An individual sets a resistance point based on many potential factors. For example, how do you decide how much rent or mortgage payment you can afford each month? How do you decide what a condo or used car is really worth? There are lots of ways to go about doing this. Indirect assessment means determining what information an individual likely used to set target and resistance points and how he or she interpreted this information. For example, in labour negotiations, management may infer whether or not a union is willing to strike by how hard the union bargains or by the size of its strike fund. The union decides whether or not the company can afford a strike based on the size of inventories, market conditions for the company's product, and the percentage of workers who are members of the union. In a real-estate negotiation, how long a piece of property has been on the market, how many other potential buyers actually exist, how soon a buyer needs the property for business or living, and the financial health of the seller will be important factors. An automobile buyer might view the number of new cars in inventory on the dealer's lot, refer to newspaper articles about automobile sales, read about a particular car's popularity in consumer buying guides (i.e., the more popular the car, the less willing she may be to bargain on the price), or consult reference guides to find out what a dealer pays wholesale for different cars. See Negotiation Point 2.2 for more detail on the power of information in automobile purchases.

2.2

Buying a New Car

Not so long ago, Canadian automobile dealerships were able to keep their wholesale costs hidden. People buying new cars could see the sticker price, or manufacturer's suggested retail price (MSRP), posted clearly in car windshields. The basic strategy for most buyers was to try and negotiate a discount off of this price. In contrast, today information is much more freely available. Organizations such as Car Cost Canada (http://carcostcanada.com) and the Automobile Protection Association (http://www.apa.ca) can provide information on dealer wholesale prices and hidden rebates for a small fee.

To illustrate, an imported mid-sized sedan was recently listed with a MSRP of $42,550 (including the base price, freight charge, A/C tax, and an optional package). Years ago, a consumer might try to haggle for hours to knock $1000 off this price, and leave the dealership convinced they received a good deal. Armed with better information, today's consumer would feel differently. The wholesale price on the car is actually $39,000, which means there is a markup of more than $3500. In addition, the information purchased by the consumer would reveal a hidden factory-to-dealer rebate of $2500 on the car. This rebate costs the dealer nothing, and in many cases they are not obligated to reveal these rebates to consumers. When the rebate is factored in, the actual cost to the dealer is $36,500. With this knowledge, paying approximately $41,500 for the car doesn't sound like such a good deal.

Direct Assessment In bargaining, the other party does not usually reveal accurate and precise information about his or her targets, resistance points, and expectations. Sometimes, however, the other party will provide accurate information. When pushed to the absolute limit and in need of a quick settlement, the other party may explain the facts quite clearly. If company executives believe that a wage settlement above a certain point will drive the company out of business, they may choose to state that absolute limit very clearly and go to considerable lengths to explain how it was determined. Similarly, a condo buyer may tell the seller his absolute maximum price and support it with an explanation of income and other expenses. In these instances, the party revealing the information believes that the proposed agreement is within the settlement range—and that the other party will accept the offered information as true rather than see it as a bargaining ploy. An industrial salesperson may tell the purchaser about product quality and service, alternative customers who want to buy the product, and the time required to manufacture special orders.

Most of the time, however, the other party is not so forthcoming, and the methods of getting direct information are more complex. In international diplomacy, various means are used to gather information. Sources are cultivated, messages are intercepted, and codes broken. In labour negotiations, companies have been known to recruit informers or bug union meeting rooms, and unions have had their members collect papers from executives' wastebaskets. In real estate negotiations, sellers have entertained prospective buyers with abundant alcoholic beverages in the hope that tongues will be loosened and information revealed.[11] Additional approaches include provoking the other party into an angry outburst or putting the other party under pressure designed to cause him or her to make a slip and reveal valuable information. Negotiators will also simulate exasperation and angrily stalk out of negotiations in the hope that the other, in an effort to avoid a deadlock, will reveal what they really want.

Manage the Other Party's Impressions

An important tactical task for negotiators is to control the information sent to the other party about your target and resistance points, while simultaneously guiding him or her to form a preferred impression of them. Negotiators need to screen information about their positions and to represent them as they would like the other to believe them. Generally speaking, screening activities are more important at the beginning of negotiation, and direct action is more useful later on. This sequence also allows time to concentrate on gathering information from the other party, which will be useful in evaluating resistance points, and on determining the best way to provide information to the other party about one's own position.

Screening Activities The simplest way to screen a position is to say and do as little as possible. "Silence is golden" when answering questions; words should be invested in asking the other negotiator questions instead. Reticence reduces the likelihood of making verbal slips or presenting any clues that the other party could use to draw conclusions. A look of disappointment or boredom, fidgeting and restlessness, or probing with interest all can give clues about the importance of the points under discussion. Concealment is the most general screening activity.

Another approach, available when group negotiations are conducted through a representative, is calculated incompetence. With this approach, constituents do not give the negotiating agent all the necessary information, making it impossible for him or her to leak information. Instead, the negotiator is sent with the task of simply gathering facts and bringing them back to the group. This strategy can make negotiations complex and tedious, and it often causes the other party to protest vigorously at the negotiator's inability to divulge important data or to make agreements. Lawyers, real estate agents, and investigators frequently perform this role. Representatives may also be limited, or limit themselves, in their authority to make decisions. For example, a man buying a car may claim that he must consult his wife before making a final decision.

When negotiation is carried out by a team—as is common in diplomacy, labour–management relations, and many business negotiations—channelling all communication through a team spokesperson reduces the inadvertent revelation of information (team negotiations are discussed more extensively in Chapter 10). In addition to reducing the number of people who can actively reveal information, this allows members of the negotiating team to observe and listen carefully to what the other party is saying so they can detect clues and pieces of information about their position. Still another screening activity is to present a great many items for negotiation, only a few of which are truly important to the presenter. In this way, the other party has to gather information about so many different items that it becomes difficult to detect which items are really important. This tactic, called the "snow job" or "kitchen sink," may be considered a hardball tactic (discussed later in this chapter) if carried to an extreme.[12]

Direct Action to Alter Impressions Negotiators can take many actions to present facts that will directly enhance their position or make it appear stronger to the other party. One of the most obvious methods is *selective presentation*, in which negotiators reveal only the facts necessary to support their case. Negotiators can also use selective presentation to lead the other party to form the desired impression of their resistance point or to create new possibilities for agreement that are more favourable than those that currently exist. Another approach is to explain or interpret known facts to present a logical argument that shows the costs or risks to oneself if the other party's proposals are implemented. An alternative is to say, "If you were in my shoes, here is the way these facts would look in light of the proposal you have presented."

Displaying *emotional reaction* to facts, proposals, and possible outcomes is another form of direct action negotiators can take to provide information about what is important to them. When Buzz Hargrove was president of the Canadian Autoworkers Union, he responded to a contract offer from an employer as follows: "Quite frankly, this is a ****ing insult to our union. We have not signed an agreement anywhere with any major employer anywhere close to this, not even in the same ballpark." Researchers Neil Fassina at the University of Manitoba and Glen Whyte of the University of Toronto examined the effect of these types of responses to opening offers. They found that negotiators who respond to a counterpart's offer with an obvious verbal and nonverbal display of displeasure do tend to claim more value. However, counterparts on the other end of "the flinch," as the technique is sometimes called, are more likely to view the relationship in a negative light. To temper this effect, Fassina and Whyte conducted a second study and found that negotiators who used a less intense negative reaction claimed just as much value as those who used the intense reaction. They also found that the negative relationship costs were suppressed.[13] Thus, it appears that letting a negotiation counterpart see your negative reaction to an offer, as long as it isn't too intense, increases the likelihood that you will claim more value.

Modify the Other Party's Perceptions

A negotiator can alter the other party's impressions of his or her own objectives by making outcomes appear less attractive or by making the cost of obtaining them appear higher. The negotiator may also try to make demands and positions appear more attractive or less unattractive to the other party.

There are several approaches to modifying the other party's perceptions. One approach is to interpret for the other party what the outcomes of his or her proposal will really be. A negotiator can explain logically how an undesirable outcome would result if the other party really did get what he or she requested. This may mean highlighting something that has been overlooked. Another approach to modifying the other's perceptions is to conceal information. An industrial seller may not reveal to a purchaser that certain technological changes are going to reduce the cost of producing the products significantly. A seller of real estate may not tell a prospective buyer that in three years a proposed highway will isolate the property being sold from attractive portions of the city. Concealment strategies may carry with them the ethical hazards mentioned earlier.

Manipulate the Actual Costs of Delay or Termination

Negotiators have deadlines. A contract will expire. Agreement has to be reached before an important meeting occurs. Someone has to catch a plane. Extending negotiations beyond a deadline can be costly, particularly to the person who has the deadline, because that person has to either extend the deadline or go home empty-handed. At the same time, research and practical experience suggest that a large majority of agreements in distributive bargaining are reached when the deadline is near.[14] In addition, time pressure in negotiation appears to reduce the demands of the other party,[15] and when a negotiator represents a constituency, time pressure appears to reduce the likelihood of reaching an agreement.[16] Manipulating a deadline or failing to agree by a particular deadline can be a powerful tool in the hands of the person who does not face deadline pressure. In some ways, the ultimate weapon in negotiation is to threaten to terminate negotiations, denying both parties the possibility of a settlement. One side then will usually feel this pressure more acutely than the other, and so the threat is a potent weapon. There are three ways to manipulate the costs of delay in negotiation: (1) plan disruptive action, (2) form an alliance with outsiders, and (3) manipulate the scheduling of negotiations.

Disruptive Action One way to encourage settlement is to increase the costs of not reaching a negotiated agreement. In one instance, a group of unionized food-service workers negotiating with a restaurant rounded up supporters, had them enter the restaurant just prior to lunch, and had each person order a cup of coffee and drink it leisurely. When regular customers came to lunch, they found every seat occupied.[17] In another case, people dissatisfied with automobiles they purchased from a certain dealer had their cars painted with large, bright yellow lemons and signs bearing the dealer's name, then drove them around town in an effort to embarrass the dealer into making a settlement. Public picketing of a business, boycotting a product or company, and locking negotiators in a room until they reach agreement are all forms of disruptive action that increase the costs to negotiators for not settling and thereby bring them back to the bargaining table. Such tactics can work, but they may also produce anger and escalation of the conflict.

Alliance with Outsiders Another way to increase the costs of delay or terminating negotiations is to involve other parties in the process who can somehow influence the outcome. Individuals who are dissatisfied with the practices and policies of businesses or government agencies form task forces, political action groups, and protest organizations to bring greater collective pressure on the target. For example, professional schools within universities often enhance their negotiation with higher management on budget matters by citing required compliance with external accreditation standards to substantiate their budget requests.

Schedule Manipulation The negotiation scheduling process can often put one party at a considerable disadvantage. Businesspeople going overseas to negotiate with customers or suppliers often find that negotiations are scheduled to begin immediately after their arrival, when they are still suffering from the fatigue of travel and jet lag. Alternatively, a host party can use delay tactics to squeeze negotiations into the last remaining minutes of a session to extract concessions from the visiting party.[18] Automobile dealers likely negotiate differently with a customer half an hour before quitting time on Saturday than at the beginning of the workday on Monday. Industrial buyers have a much more difficult negotiation when they have a short lead time because their plants may have to sit idle if they cannot secure a new contract for raw materials in time.

The opportunities to increase or alter the timing of negotiation vary widely across negotiation domains. In some industries it is possible to stockpile raw materials at relatively low cost or to buy in large bulk lots; in other industries, however, it is essential that materials arrive at regular intervals because they have a short shelf life (as many manufacturing firms move to just-in-time inventory procedures, this becomes increasingly true).

◼ Positions Taken during Negotiation

Effective distributive bargainers need to understand the process of taking positions during bargaining, including the importance of the opening offer and the opening stance, and the role of making concessions throughout the negotiation process.[19] At the beginning of negotiations, each party takes a position, and then one party will typically change his or her position in response to information from the other party or in response to the other party's behaviour. Below we will return to the negotiation between Alex and John to illustrate the power of opening offers and the concession-making process that usually follows.

Opening Offers

When negotiations begin, the negotiator is faced with a perplexing problem. What should the opening offer be? Will the offer be seen as too low or too high by the other negotiator and be contemptuously rejected? Recall that John casually made an opening offer of $300,000 and Alex did not call off the discussion. Imagine how different things might look if Alex had pre-empted John's opening offer and made an offer herself of $270,000. What effect would this have on John? When a classroom of negotiation students is asked whether they prefer to make the opening offer or wait to hear what their counterpart proposes, a wide majority tend to favour waiting and making a counteroffer. Many are surprised to hear that the best advice is usually to make the first offer. Why would we suggest this?

anchoring effect
the observation that people who make decisions under uncertain conditions are influenced by initial starting numbers

The power of first offers comes from the **anchoring effect**, which is based on the observation that people making decisions under uncertain conditions are influenced by initial starting numbers. Research by Adam Galinsky and Thomas Mussweiler suggests that making the first offer in a negotiation is advantageous because it can anchor a negotiation, especially when information about alternative negotiation outcomes is not considered. Negotiators can dampen the "first offer effect" by the other negotiator, however, by concentrating on their own target and focusing on the other negotiator's resistance point.

So, Alex's attempt to anchor John on $270,000 is likely to lead to a lower selling price than if she had waited for John to make the first offer. As long as opening offers are not too outrageous, research indicates that negotiators who make exaggerated opening offers get higher settlements than do those who make low or modest opening offers.[20] There are at least two reasons that an ambitious opening offer is advantageous.[21] First, it gives the negotiator room for movement and therefore allows him or her time to learn about the other party's priorities. Second, an ambitious opening offer acts as a metamessage and may create, in the other party's mind, the impression that (1) there is a long way to go before a reasonable settlement will be achieved, (2) more concessions than originally intended may have to be made to bridge the difference between the two opening positions, and (3) the other may have incorrectly estimated his or her own resistance point.[22] Two disadvantages of an ambitious opening offer are that (1) it may be summarily rejected by the other party, and (2) it communicates an attitude of toughness that may be harmful to long-term relationships. The more exaggerated the offer, the greater is the likelihood that it will be summarily rejected by the other side. Therefore, negotiators who make exaggerated opening offers should also have viable alternatives they can employ if the opposing negotiator refuses to deal with them.

Opening Stance

A second decision to be made at the outset of distributive bargaining concerns the stance or attitude to adopt during the negotiation. Will you be competitive (fighting to get the best on every point) or moderate (willing to make concessions and compromises)? Some negotiators take a belligerent stance, attacking the positions, offers, and even the character of the other party. In response, the other party may mirror the initial stance, meeting belligerence with belligerence. Even if the other party does not directly mimic a belligerent stance, he or she is unlikely to respond in a warm and open manner. Some negotiators adopt a position of moderation and understanding, seeming to say, "Let's be reasonable people who can solve this problem to our mutual satisfaction." Even if the attitude is not mirrored, the other's response is likely to be constrained by such a moderate opening stance.

It is important for negotiators to think carefully about the message that they wish to signal with their opening stance and subsequent concessions because there is a tendency for negotiators to respond "in kind" to distributive tactics in negotiation.[23] That is, negotiators tend to match distributive tactics from the other party with their own distributive tactics, so negotiators should make a conscious decision about what they are signalling to the other party with their opening stance and subsequent concessions.

To communicate effectively, a negotiator should try to send a consistent message through both the opening offer and stance.[24] A reasonable bargaining position is usually coupled with a friendly stance, and an exaggerated bargaining position is usually coupled with a tougher, more competitive stance. When the messages sent by the opening offer and stance are in conflict, the other party will find them confusing to interpret and answer.

Initial Concessions

An opening offer is usually met with a counteroffer, and these two offers define the initial bargaining range. Sometimes the other party will not counteroffer but will simply state that the first offer (or set of demands) is unacceptable and ask the opener to come back with a more reasonable set of proposals. For example, John might have responded to Alex's $270,000 offer by saying, "That's quite a bit lower than I had in mind. Maybe we need to keep looking at the unit before we begin talking numbers." In any event, after the first round of offers, the next question is, what movement or concessions are to be made? Negotiators can choose to make none, to hold firm and insist on the original position, or they can make some concessions. Note that it is not an option to escalate one's opening offer, that is, to set an offer further away from the other party's target point than one's first offer. This would be uniformly met with disapproval from the other negotiator. If concessions are to be made, the next question is, how large should they be? Note that the first concession conveys a message, frequently a symbolic one, to the other party about how you will proceed.

Opening offers, opening stances, and initial concessions are elements at the beginning of a negotiation that parties can use to communicate how they intend to negotiate. An exaggerated opening offer, a determined opening stance, and a very small opening concession signal a position of firmness; a moderate opening offer, a co-operative opening stance, and a reasonable initial concession communicate a basic stance of flexibility. By taking a firm position, negotiators attempt to capture most of the bargaining range for themselves so that they maximize their final outcome or preserve maximum manoeuvring room for later in the negotiation. Firmness can also create a climate in which the other party may decide that concessions are so meagre that he or she might as well capitulate and settle quickly rather than drag things out. Paradoxically, firmness may actually shorten negotiations.[25] There is also the very real possibility, however, that firmness will be reciprocated by the other. One or both parties may become either intransigent or disgusted and withdraw completely.

There are several good reasons for adopting a flexible position.[26] First, when taking different stances throughout a negotiation, one can learn about the other party's targets and perceived possibilities by observing how he or she responds to different proposals. Negotiators may want to establish a co-operative rather than a combative relationship, hoping to get a better agreement. In addition, flexibility keeps the negotiations proceeding; the more flexible one seems, the more the other party will believe that a settlement is possible.

Role of Concessions

Concessions are central to negotiation. Without them, negotiations would not exist. If one side is not prepared to make concessions, the other side must capitulate or the negotiations will deadlock. People enter negotiations expecting concessions. Negotiators are less satisfied when negotiations conclude with the acceptance of their first offer, likely because they feel they could have done better.[27] Good distributive bargainers will not begin negotiations with an opening offer too close to their own resistance point, but rather will ensure that there is enough room in the bargaining range to make some concessions. Research suggests that people will generally accept the first or second offer that is better than their target point,[28] so negotiators should try to identify the other party's target point accurately and avoid conceding too quickly to that point (see Negotiation Point 2.3. for guidelines on how to make concessions).

Negotiators also generally resent a take-it-or-leave-it approach; an offer that may have been accepted had it emerged as a result of concession making may be rejected when it is thrown on the table and presented as a *fait accompli*. This latter approach, called Boulwarism,[29] has been illustrated many times in labour relations.

Negotiation Point

2.3

Twelve Guidelines for Making Concessions

Donald Hendon, Matthew Roy, and Zafar Ahmed (2003) provide the following 12 guidelines for making concessions in negotiation:

1. Give yourself enough room to make concessions.

2. Try to get the other party to start revealing their needs and objectives first.

3. Be the first to concede on a minor issue but not the first to concede on a major issue.

4. Make unimportant concessions and portray them as more valuable than they are.

5. Make the other party work hard for every concession you make.

6. Use trade-offs to obtain something for every concession you make.

7. Generally, concede slowly and give a little with each concession.

8. Do not reveal your deadline to the other party.

9. Occasionally say "no" to the other negotiator.

10. Be careful trying to take back concessions even in "tentative" negotiations.

11. Keep a record of concessions made in the negotiation to try to identify a pattern.

12. Do not concede "too often, too soon, or too much."

Source: D. W. Hendon, M. H. Roy, and Z. U. Ahmed, "Negotiation Concession Patterns: A Multicountry, Multiperiod Study." American Business Review 21 (2003), pp. 75–83.

In the past, some management leaders objectively analyzed what they could afford to give in their upcoming contract talks and made their initial offer at the point they intended for the agreement (i.e., they set the same opening offer, target point, and resistance point). They then insisted there were no concessions to be made because the initial offer was fair and reasonable based on their own analysis. Unions bitterly fought these positions and continued to resent them years after the companies abandoned this bargaining strategy.

There is ample data to show that parties feel better about a settlement when the negotiation involved a progression of concessions than when it didn't.[30] Rubin and Brown suggest that bargainers want to believe they are capable of shaping the other's behaviour, of causing the other to choose as he or she does.[31] Because concession making indicates an acknowledgment of the other party and a movement toward the other's position, it implies recognition of that position and its legitimacy. The intangible factors of status and recognition may be as important as the tangible issues themselves. Concession making also exposes the concession maker to some risk. If the other party does not reciprocate, the concession maker may appear to be weak. Thus, not reciprocating a concession may send a powerful message about firmness and leaves the concession maker open to feeling that his or her esteem has been damaged or reputation diminished.

A reciprocal concession cannot be haphazard. If one party has made a major concession on a significant point, it is expected that the return offer will be on the same item or one of similar weight and somewhat comparable magnitude. To make an additional concession when none has been received (or when the other party's concession was inadequate) can imply weakness and can squander valuable manoeuvring room. After receiving an inadequate concession, negotiators may explicitly state what they expect before offering further concessions: "That is not sufficient; you will have to concede X before I consider offering any further concessions."

To encourage further concessions from the other side, negotiators sometimes link their concessions to a prior concession made by the other. They may say, "Since you have reduced your demand on X, I am willing to concede on Y." A powerful form of concession making involves wrapping a concession in a package, sometimes described as "logrolling."[32] For example, "If you will move on A and B, I will move on C and D." Packaging concessions also leads to better outcomes for negotiators than making concessions singly on individual issues.[33]

Pattern of Concession Making

The pattern of concessions a negotiator makes contains valuable information, but it is not always easy to interpret. When successive concessions get smaller, the obvious message is that the concession maker's position is getting firmer and that the resistance point is being approached. This generalization needs to be tempered, however, by noting that a concession late in negotiations may also indicate that there is little room left to move. When the opening offer is exaggerated, the negotiator has considerable room available for packaging new offers, making it relatively easy to give fairly substantial concessions. When the offer or counteroffer has moved closer to a negotiator's target point, giving a concession the same size as the initial one may take a negotiator past the resistance point. The pattern of concession making is also important. Consider a pattern of concessions Alex and John might have gone through. Assume that they started from opening positions of $270,000 for Alex and $300,000 for John. Alex makes three concessions, each worth $4,000, to leave her at a current position of $282,000. In contrast, John makes four concessions, worth $4,000, $3,000, $2,000, and $1,000, to leave him at $290,000. They both then tell their counterparts they have conceded about all that they can. John is more likely to be believed when he makes this assertion because he has signalled through the pattern of his concession making that there is not much left to concede. When Alex claims to have little left to concede, her counterpart is less likely to believe her because the pattern of concessions (three concessions worth the same amount) suggests that there is plenty left to concede, even though Alex has actually conceded more than John.[34] Note that we have not considered the words spoken by Alex and John as these concessions were made. Behaviours and words are interpreted by the other party when we negotiate; it is important to signal to the other party with both our actions and our words that the concessions are almost over.

Final Offers

Eventually a negotiator wants to convey the message that there is no further room for movement—that the present offer is the final one. A good negotiator will say, "This is all I can do" or "This is as far as I can go." Sometimes, however, it is clear that a simple statement will not suffice; an alternative is to use concessions to convey the point. A negotiator might simply let the absence of any further concessions convey the message in spite of urging from the other party. The other party may not recognize at first that the last offer was the final one and might volunteer a further concession to get the other to respond. Finding that no further concession occurs, the other party may feel betrayed and perceive that the pattern of concession–counter concession was violated. The resulting bitterness may further complicate negotiations.

One way negotiators may convey the message that an offer is the last one is to make the last concession more substantial. This implies that the negotiator is throwing in the remainder of the negotiating range. The final offer has to be large enough to be dramatic yet not so large that it creates the suspicion that the negotiator has been holding back and that there is more available on other issues in the bargaining mix.[35] A concession may also be personalized to the other party ("I went to my boss and got a special deal just for you"), which signals that this is the last concession the negotiator will make.

Closing the Deal

After negotiating for a period of time, and learning about the other party's needs, positions, and perhaps resistance point, the next challenge for a negotiator is to close the agreement. Several tactics are available to negotiators for closing a deal;[36] choosing the best tactic for a given negotiation is as much a matter of art as science.

Provide Alternatives Rather than making a single final offer, negotiators can provide two or three alternative packages for the other party that are more or less equivalent in value. People like to have choices, and providing a counterpart with alternative packages can be a very effective technique for closing a negotiation. This technique can also be used when a task force cannot decide on which recommendation to make to upper management. If in fact there are two distinct, defensible possible solutions, then the task force can forward both with a description of the costs and benefits of each.

Assume the Close Salespeople use an assume-the-close technique frequently. After having a general discussion about the needs and positions of the buyer, often the seller will take out a large order form and start to complete it. The seller usually begins by asking for the buyer's name and address before moving on to more serious points (e.g., price, model). When using this technique, negotiators do not ask the other party if he or she would like to make a purchase. Rather, they act as if the decision to purchase something has already been made so they might as well start to get the paperwork out of the way.[37]

Split the Difference Splitting the difference is perhaps the most popular closing tactic. The negotiator using this tactic will typically give a brief summary of the negotiation ("We've both spent a lot of time, made many concessions, etc.") and then suggest that, because things are so close, "why don't we just split the difference?" While this can be an effective closing tactic, it does presume that the parties started with fair opening offers. A negotiator who uses an exaggerated opening offer and then suggests a split-the-difference close is using a hardball tactic (see below).

Exploding Offers An exploding offer contains an extremely tight deadline to pressure the other party to agree quickly. For example, a person who has interviewed for a job may be offered a very attractive salary and benefits package, but also be told that the offer will expire in 24 hours. The purpose of the exploding offer is to convince the other party to accept the settlement and to stop considering alternatives. This is particularly effective in situations where the party receiving the exploding offer is still in the process of developing alternatives that may or may not turn out to be viable (such as the job candidate who is still interviewing with other firms). People can feel quite uncomfortable about receiving exploding offers, however, because they feel as if they're under unfair pressure. Exploding offers appear to work best for organizations that have the resources to make an exceptionally attractive offer early in a negotiation to prevent the other party from continuing to search for a potentially superior offer.

Sweeteners Another closing tactic is to save a special concession for the close. The other negotiator is told, "I'll give you X if you agree to the deal." For instance, when selling a condo the owner could agree to include the previously excluded curtains, appliances, or light fixtures to close the deal. To use this tactic effectively negotiators need to include the sweetener in their negotiation plans or they may concede too much during the close.

■ Hardball Tactics

We now turn to a discussion of hardball tactics in negotiation. Many popular books of negotiation discuss using hardball negotiation tactics to beat the other party.[38] Such tactics are designed to pressure negotiators to do things they would not otherwise do, and their presence usually disguises the user's adherence to a decidedly distributive bargaining approach. It is not clear exactly how often or how well these tactics work, but they work best against poorly prepared negotiators. They also can backfire, and there is evidence that very adversarial negotiators are not effective negotiators.[39] Many people find hardball tactics offensive and are motivated for revenge when such tactics are used against them. Many negotiators consider these tactics out-of-bounds for any negotiation situation.[40] We do not recommend the use of any of the following techniques. In fact, it has been our experience that these tactics do more harm than good in negotiations. They are much more difficult to enact than they are to read, and each tactic involves risk for the person using it, including harm to reputation, lost deals, negative publicity, and consequences of the other party's revenge. It is important that negotiators understand hardball tactics and how they work so they can recognize and understand them if hardball tactics are used against them.

Dealing with Typical Hardball Tactics

The negotiator dealing with a party who uses hardball tactics has several choices about how to respond. A good strategic response to these tactics requires that the negotiator identify the tactic quickly and understand what it is and how it works. Most of the tactics are designed either to enhance the appearance of the bargaining position of the person using the tactic or to detract from the appearance of the options available to the other party. How best to respond to a tactic depends on your goals and the broader context of the negotiation (With whom are you negotiating? What are your alternatives?). No one response will work in all situations. We now discuss four main options that negotiators have for responding to typical hardball tactics.[41]

Ignore Them Although ignoring a hardball tactic may appear to be a weak response, it can in fact be very powerful. It takes a lot of energy to use some of the hardball tactics described below, and while the other side is using energy to play these games, you can be using your energy to work on satisfying your needs. Not responding to a threat is often the best way of dealing with it. Pretend you didn't hear it. Change the subject and get the other party involved in a new topic. Call a break and, upon returning, switch topics. All these options can deflate the effects of a threat and allow you to press on with your agenda while the other party is trying to decide what trick to use next.

Discuss Them Fisher, Ury, and Patton suggest that a good way to deal with hardball tactics is to discuss them—that is, label the tactic and indicate to the other party that you know what she is doing.[42] Then offer to negotiate the negotiation process itself, such as behavioural expectations of the parties, before continuing on to the substance of the talks. Propose a shift to less aggressive methods of negotiating. Explicitly acknowledge that the other party is a tough negotiator but that you can be tough too. Then suggest that you both change to more productive methods that can allow you both to gain. Fisher, Ury, and Patton suggest that negotiators separate the people from the problem and then be hard on the problem, soft on the people. It doesn't hurt to remind the other negotiator of this from time to time during the negotiation.

Respond in Kind It is always possible to respond to a hardball tactic with one of your own. Although this response can result in chaos, produce hard feelings, and be counterproductive, it is not an option that should be dismissed out of hand. Once the smoke clears, both parties will realize that they are skilled in the use of hardball tactics and may recognize that it is time to try something different. Responding in kind may be most useful when dealing with another party who is testing your resolve or as a response to exaggerated positions taken in negotiations.

Co-Opt the Other Party Another way to deal with negotiators who are known to use aggressive hardball tactics is to try to befriend them before they use the tactics on you. This approach is built on the theory that it is much more difficult to attack a friend than an enemy. If you can stress what you have in common with the other party and find another element upon which to place the blame (the system, foreign competition), you may then be able to sidetrack the other party and thereby prevent the use of any hardball tactics.

Typical Hardball Tactics

We will now discuss some of the more frequently described hardball tactics and their weaknesses.

Good Cop/Bad Cop The good cop/bad cop tactic is named after a police interrogation technique in which two officers (one kind, the other tough) take turns questioning a suspect. The use of this tactic in negotiations typically goes as follows: The first interrogator (bad cop) presents a tough opening position, punctuated with threats, obnoxious behaviour, and intransigence. The interrogator then leaves the room to make an important telephone call or to cool off—frequently at the partner's suggestion.

While out of the room, the other interrogator (good cop) tries to reach a quick agreement before the bad cop returns and makes life difficult for everyone. A more subtle form of this tactic is to assign the bad cop the role of speaking only when the negotiations are headed in a direction that the team does not want; as long as things are going well, the good cop does the talking. Although the good cop/bad cop tactic can be somewhat transparent, it often leads to concessions and negotiated agreements.[43]

"Mr. Mosbacher, are you expecting anything via U.P.S.?"

This tactic has many weaknesses. As mentioned above, it is relatively transparent, especially with repeated use. It can be countered by openly stating what the negotiators are doing. A humorously delivered statement like "You two aren't playing the old good cop/bad cop game with me, are you?" will go a long way to deflating this tactic even if both of the other parties deny it self-righteously. The good cop/bad cop tactic is also much more difficult to enact than it is to read; it typically alienates the targeted party and frequently requires negotiators to direct much more energy toward making the tactic work smoothly than toward accomplishing the negotiation goals. Negotiators using this tactic can become so involved with their game playing and acting that they fail to concentrate on obtaining their negotiation goals.

Lowball/Highball Negotiators using the lowball (highball) tactic start with a ridiculously low (or high) opening offer that they know they will never achieve. The theory is that the extreme offer will cause the other party to re-evaluate his or her own opening offer and move closer to or beyond their resistance point. The risk of using this tactic is that the other party will think negotiating is a waste of time and will stop negotiating. Even if the other party continues to negotiate after receiving a lowball (highball) offer, it takes a very skilled negotiator to be able to justify the extreme opening offer and to finesse the negotiation back to a point where the other side will be willing to make a major concession toward the outrageous bid.

The best way to deal with a lowball (highball) tactic is not to make a counter-offer, but to ask for a more reasonable opening offer from the other party. The reason that requesting a reasonable opening offer is important is because this tactic works in the split second between hearing the other party's opening offer and the delivery of your first offer. If you give in to the natural tendency to change your opening offer because it would be embarrassing to start negotiations so far apart, or because the other party's extreme opening makes you rethink where the bargaining zone may lie, then you have fallen victim to this tactic. When this happens, you have been "anchored" by the other party's extreme first offer.

Good preparation for the negotiation is a critical defence against this tactic, which is something to keep in mind as you read Chapter 4 on planning for negotiation. Proper planning will help you know the general range for the value of the item under discussion and allow you to respond verbally with one of several different strategies: (1) insisting that the other party start with a reasonable opening offer and refusing to negotiate further until he or she does; (2) stating your understanding of the general market value of the item being discussed, supporting it with facts and figures, and by doing so, demonstrating to the other party that you won't be tricked; (3) threatening to leave the negotiation, either briefly or for good, to demonstrate dissatisfaction with the other party for using this tactic; and (4) responding with an extreme counteroffer to send a clear message you won't be anchored by an extreme offer from the other party.

Bogey Negotiators using the bogey tactic pretend that an issue of little or no importance to them is quite important. Later in the negotiation, this issue can then be traded for major concessions on issues that are actually important to them. This tactic is most effective when negotiators identify an issue that is quite important to the other side but of little value to themselves. For example, a seller may have a product in the warehouse ready for delivery. When negotiating with a purchasing agent, the seller may ask for large concessions to process a rush order for the client. The seller can reduce the size of the concession demanded for the rush order in exchange for concessions on other issues, such as the price or the size of the order. Another example of a bogey is to argue as if you want a particular work assignment or project (when in fact you don't prefer it) and then, in exchange for large concessions from the other party, accept the assignment you actually prefer (but had pretended not to).

This tactic is fundamentally deceptive, and as such it can be a difficult tactic to enact. Typically, the other party will negotiate in good faith and take you seriously when you are trying to make a case for the issue that you want to bogey. This can lead to the very unusual situation of both negotiators arguing against their true wishes (the other party is asking for large concessions on other issues to give you the bogey issue you really don't want, and you are spending time evaluating offers and making arguments for an issue you know you do not want). It can also be very difficult to change gracefully and accept an offer in completely the opposite direction. If this manoeuvre cannot be done, however, then you may end up accepting a suboptimal deal—the bogey may be something you do not really want, and perhaps the other party doesn't either.

Although the bogey is a difficult tactic to defend against, being well prepared for the negotiation will make you less susceptible to it. When the other party takes a position completely counter to what you expected, you may suspect that a bogey tactic is being used. Probing with questions about why the other party wants a particular outcome may help you reduce the effectiveness of a bogey. Finally, you should be very cautious about sudden reversals in positions taken by the other party, especially late in a negotiation. This may be a sign that the bogey tactic has been in use. Again, questioning the other party carefully about why the reverse position is suddenly acceptable and not conceding too much after the other party completely reverses a position may significantly reduce the effectiveness of the bogey.

The Nibble   Negotiators using the nibble tactic ask for a proportionally small concession (for instance, 1 to 2 percent of the total profit of the deal) on an item that hasn't been discussed previously to close the deal. Herb Cohen describes the nibble as follows: After trying many different suits in a clothing store, tell the clerk that you will take a given suit if a tie is included for free.[44] The tie is the nibble. Cohen claims that he usually gets the tie. In a business context, the tactic occurs like this: After a considerable amount of time has been spent in negotiation, when an agreement is close, one party asks to include a clause that hasn't been discussed previously and that will cost the other party a proportionally small amount. This amount is too small to lose the deal over, but large enough to upset the other party. This is the major weakness with the nibble tactic—many people feel that the party using the nibble did not bargain in good faith (as part of a fair negotiation process, all items to be discussed during the negotiation should be placed on the agenda early). Even if the party claims to be very embarrassed about forgetting this item until now, the party who has been nibbled will not feel good about the process and will be motivated to seek revenge in future negotiations.

According to Landon, there are two good ways to combat the nibble.[45] First, respond to each nibble with the question "What else do you want?" This should continue until the other party indicates that all issues are in the open; then both parties can discuss all the issues simultaneously. Second, have your own nibbles prepared to offer in exchange. When the other party suggests a nibble on one issue, you can respond with your own nibble on another.

Intimidation   Many tactics can be gathered under the general label of intimidation. What they have in common is that they all attempt to force the other party to agree by means of an emotional ploy, usually anger or fear. For example, the other party may deliberately use *anger* to indicate the seriousness of a position.

Another form of intimidation includes increasing the appearance of *legitimacy*. When legitimacy is high, set policies or procedures are in place for resolving disputes. Negotiators who do not have such policies or procedures available may try to invent them and then impose them on the other negotiator while making the process appear legitimate. For example, policies that are written in manuals or preprinted official forms and agreements are less likely to be questioned than those that are delivered verbally;[46] long and detailed loan contracts that banks use for consumer loans are seldom read completely.[47] The greater the appearance of legitimacy, the less likely the other party will be to question the process being followed or the contract terms being proposed.

Finally, *guilt* can also be used as a form of intimidation. Negotiators can question the other party's integrity or the other's lack of trust in them. The purpose of this tactic is to place the other party on the defensive so that they are dealing with the issues of guilt or trust rather than discussing the substance of the negotiation.

To deal with intimidation tactics, negotiators have several options. Intimidation tactics are designed to make the intimidator feel more powerful than the other party and to lead people to make concessions for emotional rather than objective reasons (e.g., a new fact). When making any concession, it is important for negotiators to understand why they are doing so. If one starts to feel threatened, assumes that the other party is more powerful (when objectively he or she is not), or simply accepts the legitimacy of the other negotiator's "company policy," then it is likely that intimidation is having an effect on the negotiations.

If the other negotiator is intimidating, then discussing the negotiation process with him or her is a good option. You can explain that your policy is to bargain in a fair and respectful manner, and that you expect to be treated the same way in return. Another good option is to ignore the other party's attempts to intimidate you, because intimidation can only influence you if you let it. While this may sound too simplistic, think for a moment about why some people you know are intimidated by authority figures and others are not—the reason often lies in the perceiver, not the authority figure.

Another effective strategy for dealing with intimidation is to use a team to negotiate with the other party. Teams have at least two advantages over individuals in acting against intimidation. First, people are not always intimidated by the same things; while you may be intimidated by one particular negotiator, it is quite possible that other members on your team won't be. The second advantage of using a team is that the team members can discuss the tactics of the other negotiators and provide mutual support if the intimidation starts to become increasingly uncomfortable.

Aggressive Behaviour A group of tactics similar to those described under intimidation includes various ways of being aggressive in pushing your position or attacking the other person's position. Aggressive tactics include a relentless push for further concessions ("You can do better than that"), asking for the best offer early in negotiations ("Let's not waste any time. What is the most that you will pay?"), and asking the other party to explain and justify his or her proposals item by item or line by line ("What is your cost breakdown for each item?"). The negotiator using these techniques is signalling a hard-nosed, intransigent position and trying to force the other side to make many concessions to reach an agreement.

When faced with another party's aggressive behaviour tactics an excellent response is to halt the negotiations to discuss the negotiation process itself. Negotiators can explain that they will reach a decision based on needs and interests, not aggressive behaviour. Again, having a team to counter aggressive tactics from the other party can be helpful for the same reasons discussed above under intimidation tactics. Good preparation and understanding of both one's own and the other party's needs and interests together make responding to aggressive tactics easier because the merits to both parties of reaching an agreement can be highlighted.

Snow Job The snow job tactic occurs when negotiators overwhelm the other party with so much information that he or she has trouble determining which facts are real or important, and which are included merely as distractions. Governments use this tactic frequently when releasing information publicly. Rather than answering a question briefly, they release thousands of pages of documents from hearings and transcripts that may or may not contain the information that the other party is seeking. Another example of the snow job is the use of highly technical language to hide a simple answer to a question asked by a non-expert. Any group of professionals—such as engineers, lawyers, or computer network administrators—can use this tactic to overwhelm ("snow") the other party with so much information and technical language that the non-experts cannot make sense of the answer. Frequently, in order not to be embarrassed by asking "obvious" questions, the recipient of the snow job will simply nod his or her head and passively agree with the other party's analysis or statements.

Negotiators trying to counter a snow job tactic can choose one of several alternative responses. First, they should not be afraid to ask questions until they receive an answer they understand. Second, if the matter under discussion is in fact highly technical, then negotiators may suggest that technical experts get together to discuss the technical issues. Finally, negotiators should listen carefully to the other party and identify consistent and inconsistent information. Probing for further information after identifying a piece of inconsistent information can work to undermine the effectiveness of the snow job. For example, if one piece of incorrect or inconsistent information is discovered in the complete snow job package, the negotiator can question the accuracy of the whole presentation (e.g., "Since point X was incorrect, how can I be sure that the rest is accurate?"). Again, strong preparation is very important for defending effectively against the snow job tactic.

In this chapter we examined the basic structure of competitive or distributive bargaining situations and some of the strategies and tactics used in distributive bargaining. We worked through the example of Alex and John negotiating the sale of John's business unit. Recall that Alex's reservation point was $310,000 and John's was $275,000. Although they don't know it because reservation points are confidential, they are negotiating to see who claims most of the $35,000 value. If they agreed to a selling price of $281,000, would you consider that a good deal? You would probably say it is a better deal for Alex, and you would probably be right. However, it is also important to remember that both sides are better off because the sale price is superior to each party's reservation points. Alex claimed more value than John, but to John's credit, he didn't agree to a deal that made him worse off.

As you prepare for, and navigate through, distributive situations, there are a number of things you should keep in mind. We conclude the chapter by summarizing some of the most important.

1. Preparation is key. This advice is so important that we devote a whole chapter (Chapter 4) to it.

2. Analyze your target, reservation point, and BATNA before you negotiate.

3. Focus on trying to determine your counterpart's target, reservation point, and BATNA.

4. If you are prepared, and it is possible, make the opening offer. Even if it is not possible to make the opening offer, remember that anchoring is a powerful tool that influences final outcomes.

5. Use concessions symbolically. Decreases in concession size indicate that you are approaching your limits. You should also remember not to make unilateral concessions; if you concede, make sure your counterpart knows they are expected to concede as well.

6. Watch for hardball tactics and don't be swayed by them. Remember, for most tactics the best defence is preparation. Keeping your cool and signalling that you know what you are doing go a long towards minimizing the effect of hardball tactics.

Key Terms

Anchoring effect, p. 30
Bargaining zone, p. 20

Resistance point, p. 19
Target point, p. 18

Strategy and Tactics of Integrative Negotiation

LEARNING OBJECTIVES

In this chapter we provide an overview of integrative negotiations and the strategies you can use to create value. After reading the chapter you should be able to:

1. Recognize integrative bargaining situations,

2. Know the key steps in the integrative bargaining process, and

3. Understand key strategies and tactics that facilitate value creation.

Do you remember the 2004–2005 National Hockey League (NHL) season? Probably not, for reasons that have nothing to do with whether or not you are a fan of the game or completely indifferent. Due to a labour dispute between the team owners and the National Hockey League Players' Association (NHLPA), a lockout created the first cancellation of a full season of any professional sports league in North America. The estimated financial losses for team owners was $273 million, and negotiations continued on and off for a period of 310 days.[1] There were numerous issues at stake, including minimum salaries, playoff bonuses, reducing the schedule of games, free agency, and revenue sharing.[2] In retrospect, the parties now seem to agree that the central barrier to agreement was whether there should be a salary cap, which is a maximum ceiling each team would be allowed to pay its players. The player's union opposed the salary cap because even though the cap applies to the team as a whole, it would result in downward pressure on individual player salaries over time.[3]

Recall the characteristics from Chapter 2 that identified a negotiation as distributive. These included things like a single negotiation issue and a win-lose structure. At first glance, the story of the lost NHL season appears to be distributive. The salary cap issue takes the general form of a win-lose situation—the team owners want a cap and the players do not want one. In this chapter we move beyond these simple win-lose situations to explore situations where the goals of the parties are not mutually exclusive. If one side achieves its goals, the other is not precluded from achieving its goals as well. One party's gain is not at the other party's expense. The fundamental structure of an integrative negotiation situation is such that it allows both sides to achieve their objectives.[4] Although the situation may initially appear to the parties to be win-lose, discussion and mutual exploration will often suggest alternatives where both parties can gain.

Unfortunately, the process of discovering joint gains is often quite difficult to do. The story of the lost NHL season can be used to highlight some of the barriers to creating integrative agreements. Therefore, we will return to the story in several places in this chapter as we elaborate on the process and tactics associated with integrative negotiations.

◼ An Overview of the Integrative Negotiation Process

Past experience, biased perceptions, and the truly distributive aspects of bargaining make it remarkable that integrative agreements occur at all. But they do, largely because negotiators work hard to overcome inhibiting factors and search assertively for common ground. Those wishing to achieve integrative results find that they must manage both the *context* and the *process* of the negotiation to gain the co-operation and commitment of all parties. Key contextual factors include creating a free flow of information, attempting to understand the other negotiator's real needs and objectives, emphasizing commonalities between parties, and searching for solutions that meet the goals and objectives of both parties. Below we explain in more detail each of these contextual elements.

Creating a Free Flow of Information

Effective information exchange promotes the development of good integrative solutions.[5] Research shows that the failure to reach integrative agreements is often linked to the failure to exchange enough information to allow the parties to identify integrative options.[6] For the necessary exchange to occur, negotiators must be willing to reveal their true objectives and to listen to each other carefully. In short, negotiators must create the conditions for a free and open discussion of all related issues and concerns. Willingness to share information is not a characteristic of distributive bargaining situations, in which the parties may distrust one another, conceal and manipulate information, and attempt to learn about the other purely for their own competitive advantage.

Attempting to Understand the Other Negotiator's Real Needs and Objectives

Negotiators differ in their values and preferences. What one side needs and wants may or may not be the same as what the other party needs and wants. One must understand the other's needs before helping to satisfy them. When negotiators are aware of the possibility that the other's priorities are not the same as their own, this can stimulate the parties to exchange more information, understand the nature of the negotiation better, and achieve higher joint profits.[7] Similarly, integrative agreements are facilitated when parties exchange information about their priorities for particular issues, but not necessarily about their positions on those issues.[8] Throughout the process of sharing information about preferences and priorities, negotiators must make a true effort to understand what the other side really wants to achieve. This is in contrast to distributive bargaining, where negotiators either make no effort to understand the other side's needs and objectives or do so only to challenge, undermine, or even deny the other party the opportunity to have those needs and objectives met. The communicative aspects of information flow and understanding, while critical to integrative negotiation, also require that Kelley's dilemmas of trust and honesty be managed (see Chapter 1).[9] In addition, negotiators may differ in their ability to differentiate needs and interests from positions, as when one party knows and applies a truly integrative process while the other party is unskilled or naive about negotiations. In such situations, the more experienced party may need to assist the less experienced party in discovering his or her underlying needs and interests.

Emphasizing the Commonalities between the Parties and Minimizing the Differences

To sustain a free flow of information and the effort to understand the other's needs and objectives, negotiators may need a different outlook or frame of reference (see Chapter 5 for a discussion of framing). Individual goals may need to be redefined as best achieved through collaborative efforts directed toward a collective goal. Sometimes the collective goal is clear and obvious. For example, politicians in the same party may recognize that their petty squabbles must be put aside to ensure the party's victory at the polls. Managers who are quarrelling over cutbacks in their individual department budgets may need to recognize that unless all departments sustain appropriate budget cuts, they will be unable to change an unprofitable firm into a profitable one. At other times, the collective goal is neither so clear nor so easy to keep in sight. For example, one of the authors worked as a consultant to a company that was closing a major manufacturing plant while simultaneously opening several other plants in different parts of the country. The company was perfectly willing to transfer employees to new plants and let them take their seniority up to the time of their move with them; the union agreed to this arrangement. However, conflict developed over the transfer issue. Some employees were able to transfer immediately, whereas others—those who were needed to close and dismantle the old plant—could not. Because workers acquired seniority in the new plants based on the date they arrived, those who stayed to close the old plant would have comparatively less seniority once they arrived at the new plants. The union wanted everyone to go at the same time to avoid this inequity. This was unworkable for management. In the argument that resulted, both parties lost sight of the larger goal—to transfer all willing employees to the new plants with their seniority intact. Only by constantly stressing this larger goal were the parties able to maintain a focus on commonalities that eventually led to a solution; management allowed the workers to select their new jobs in advance and transferred their seniority to those jobs when the choice was made, not when the physical move actually occurred.

Searching for Solutions that Meet the Needs and Objectives of Both Sides

The success of integrative negotiation depends on the search for solutions that meet the needs and objectives of both sides. In this process, negotiators must be firm but flexible—firm about their primary interests and needs, but flexible about how these needs and interests are met.[10] When the parties are used to taking a combative, competitive orientation toward each other, they are generally concerned only with their own objectives. In such a competitive interaction, a low level of concern for the other's objectives may cause two forms of behaviour. First, negotiators may work to ensure that what the other obtains does not take away from one's own accomplishments. Second, negotiators may attempt to block the other from obtaining his or her objectives because of a strong desire to win or to "defeat the opponent." In contrast, successful integrative negotiation requires both negotiators not only to define and pursue their own goals, but also to be mindful of the other's goals and to search for solutions that satisfy both sides. Outcomes are measured by the degree to which they meet both negotiators' goals. They are not measured by determining whether one party is doing better than the other. If the objective of one party is simply to get more than the other, integrative negotiation is difficult at best; if both strive to get more than the other, integrative negotiation may be impossible.

Recognizing Integrative Situations

By now you will probably recognize that distributive and integrative situations call for different approaches in negotiation behaviour and style. So, how do you recognize the type of situation you are faced with? The following factors, or clues, usually indicate that an integrative approach is called for:

- the negotiation includes more than one issue
- it is possible to add more issues to the mix
- the negotiation is likely to recur over time
- the parties have varying preferences across the issues

Each factor does not need to be present for a situation to be integrative. Our key point is you should look for signs that these factors are present, and if they are, an integrative approach is likely called for.

At least two, and perhaps all, of these factors were visible in the situation between the NHL team owners and the player's union. First, there were several issues to be negotiated; the salary cap issue was fundamentally important, but it was not the only one that had to be dealt with. And second, the parties had different preferences across some of the issues to be negotiated. When the parties differ on the extent to which they value each, or some, of the issues to be negotiated, it is possible for them to trade-off low value issues in exchange for high value issues.

In summary, integrative negotiation requires a process fundamentally different than distributive bargaining. Negotiators must attempt to probe below the surface of the other party's position to discover his or her underlying needs. They must create a free and open flow of information and use their desire to satisfy both sides as a guide to structure their dialogue. If negotiators do not have this perspective—if they approach the problem and their "opponent" in win-lose terms—integrative negotiation cannot occur.

Key Steps in the Integrative Negotiation Process

So, assuming your initial analysis of the situation indicates that an integrative approach is called for, what do you do? Before we can begin to answer this question, we need to clarify the distinction between *creating* value and *claiming* value. When we talk of claiming value, we are referring to a process whereby a negotiator carves out their share of a finite set of resources. This is also called distributive negotiation, and by now should be quite familiar to you. When we talk of creating value, we refer to a process where parties with conflicting yet compatible interests trade low-priority issues for higher-priority issues. It is extremely important for you to keep in mind that in integrative situations, negotiators can create value, as well as claim it.

The relationship between creating and claiming value is shown graphically in Figure 3.1. The goal of creating value is to push the claiming value line towards the upper right-hand side of Figure 3.1. When this is done to the fullest extent possible, the line is called the *Pareto efficient frontier*, and it contains a point where "there is no agreement that would make any party better off without decreasing the outcomes to any other party."[11] One way to conceptualize integrative negotiation is that it is the process of identifying Pareto efficient solutions. Any time you find yourself in an integrative situation, one of your goals should be to create a deal that falls on the Pareto efficient frontier.

FIGURE 3.1 | Creating and Claiming Value and the Pareto Efficient Frontier

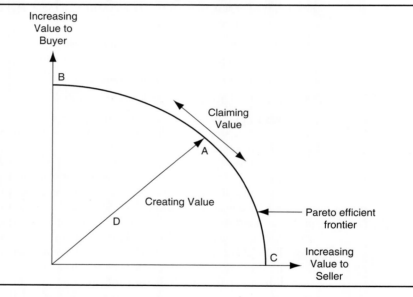

We say, "one of your goals," because this isn't the only thing you should consider. To elaborate, consider the four deals (A, B, C, and D) listed in Figure 3.1. Deal A is one that falls on the Pareto efficient frontier and is equally divided between the buyer and seller. Thus, this deal creates all the value possible and the two sides have equally claimed their share of "the pie." Deals B and C also fall on the Pareto efficient frontier. Are they as good as deal A? Although each deal has created as much value as possible, in both cases one of the parties has claimed all the value that has been created. In deal B, the seller is unlikely to celebrate their efforts at creating value because the buyer has taken it all from them.

To put this in perspective, we briefly return to the story of the lost NHL season introduced earlier. Let's assume there were only three issues to be addressed (salary cap, minimum salaries, and sharing of revenue between teams), and consider a possible deal from the perspective of the player's union (or NHLPA). In an ideal world, the union would like no salary cap, a minimum salary that is reasonably high (like a minimum wage), and equal revenue sharing between teams to ensure league stability. Imagine a situation where to end the strike and get back to work, the players agreed to a deal in which there was a salary cap, the minimum salary was within an acceptable range, and revenue sharing was not equal, but instead based on a complicated formula that guaranteed at least some revenue sharing.

Is this a good deal? It largely depends on how each party prioritizes the issues and assesses these priorities quantitatively (which we discuss in more detail in the following chapter). Deals can fall anywhere along or below the efficient frontier. Knowing what we know about how contentious the negotiation was between the team owners and the NHLPA, there is a very good chance that the actual deal that was agreed to fell below the curve (see point D in the figure). Deals in the zone below the curve are "good" deals, because they exceed the resistance points of both sides; but they are not "great" deals, because they do not reach the efficient frontier. This is sometime referred to as *leaving money on the table* because value that could have potentially been created was not. Unfortunately, in our experience, most negotiators settle for outcomes that exceed their reservation prices, and therefore make them better off, but fail to reach deals that create all the value that was possible.

An understanding of the Pareto efficient frontier produces two additional insights. First, there is a tension between value creating and value claiming. This tension, sometimes called **the negotiator's dilemma**, was described by Lax and Sebenius several decades ago as follows: "No matter how much creative problem solving enlarges the pie, it must still be divided; value that has been created must be claimed." This should make clear that your desire to be a co-operative value creator should not be your exclusive focus. It is important, to be sure, but you must always remember to claim your share as well.

The second insight is that processes to create value should precede those to claim value for two reasons: (1) processes that create value are effective when done collaboratively and without a focus on "who gets what," and (2) claiming value involves distributive bargaining processes that need to be introduced carefully into integrative negotiation or they may harm the relationship and derail progress. With these insights in mind, we now turn to the major steps of the integrative negotiation process.

Understand the Situation Fully—Identify Interests and Needs

Many writers on negotiation—most particularly, Roger Fisher, William Ury, and Bruce Patton in their popular book, *Getting to Yes*—have stressed that a key to achieving an integrative agreement is the ability of the parties to understand and satisfy each other's *interests*.[12] Identifying interests is a critical step in the integrative negotiation process. **Interests** are the underlying concerns, needs, desires, or fears that motivate a negotiator to take a particular position. Fisher, Ury, and Patton explain that while negotiators may have difficulty satisfying each other's specific positions, an understanding of the underlying interests may permit them to invent solutions that meet their interests. In this section, we will first define interests more completely and then discuss how understanding them is critical to effective integrative negotiation.

the negotiator's dilemma
there is a tension between behaviours that are competitive and behaviours that are co-operative

interests
the underlying concerns, needs, desires, or fears that motivate a negotiator to take a particular position

An example reveals the essence of the difference between interests and positions:

> Consider the story of two men quarrelling in a library. One wants the window open and the other wants it closed. They bicker back and forth about how much to leave it open: a crack, halfway, three-quarters of the way. No solution satisfied them both. Enter the librarian. She asks one why he wants the window open. "To get some fresh air." She asks the other why he wants it closed. "To avoid the draft." After thinking a minute, she opens wide a window in the next room, bringing in fresh air without a draft.[13]

This is a classic example of negotiating over positions and failing to understand underlying interests. The positions are "window open" and "window closed." If they continue to pursue positional bargaining, the set of possible outcomes can include only a victory for the one who wants the window open, a victory for the one who wants it shut, or some compromise in which neither gets what he wants. Note that a compromise here is more a form of lose-lose than win-win for these bargainers because one party believes he won't get enough fresh air with the window partially open and the other believes that any opening is unsatisfactory. The librarian's questions transform the dispute by focusing on *why* each man wants the window open or closed: to get fresh air, to avoid a draft. Understanding these interests enables the librarian to invent a solution that meets the interests of both sides—a solution that was not at all apparent when the two men were arguing over their positions.

In this description, the key word is *why*—why they want what they want. When two parties begin negotiation, they usually expose their position or demands. In distributive bargaining, negotiators trade positions back and forth, attempting to achieve a settlement as close to their targets as possible. However, in integrative negotiation, both negotiators need to pursue the other's thinking and logic to determine the factors that motivated them to arrive at their goals. The presumption is that if both parties understand the motivating factors for the other, they may recognize possible compatibilities in interests that permit them to invent new options that both will endorse.

Types of Interests   Lax and Sebenius have suggested that several types of interests may be at stake in a negotiation and that each type may be intrinsic (the parties value it in and of itself) or instrumental (the parties value it because it helps them derive other outcomes in the future).[14]

Substantive interests relate to the focal issues under negotiation—economic and financial issues such as price or rate, or the substance of a negotiation such as the division of resources (they are like the tangible issues discussed in Chapter 1). These interests may be intrinsic or instrumental or both; we may want something because it is intrinsically satisfying to us and/or we may want something because it helps us achieve a long-range goal. Thus, the job applicant may want $40,000 both because the salary affirms his intrinsic sense of personal worth in the marketplace and because it instrumentally contributes toward paying off his education loans.

Process interests are related to the way a dispute is settled. One party may pursue distributive bargaining because he enjoys the competitive game of wits that comes from nose-to-nose, hard-line bargaining. Another party may enjoy negotiating because she believes she has not been consulted in the past and wants to have some say in how a key problem is resolved. In the latter case, the negotiator may find the issues under discussion less important than the opportunity they allow her to voice her opinions.[15] Process interests can also be both intrinsic and instrumental. Having a voice may be intrinsically important to a group—it allows them to affirm their legitimacy and worth and highlights the key role they play in the organization; it can also be instrumentally important, in that if they are successful in gaining voice in this negotiation, they may be able to demonstrate that they should be invited back to negotiate other related issues in the future.

Relationship interests indicate that one or both parties value their relationship with each other and do not want to take actions that will damage it. Intrinsic relationship interests exist when the parties value the relationship both for its existence and for the pleasure or fulfillment that sustaining it creates. Instrumental relationship interests exist when the parties derive substantive benefits from the relationship and do not wish to endanger future benefits by souring it.

Finally, Lax and Sebenius point out that the parties may have *interests in principle*.[16] Certain principles—concerning what is fair, what is right, what is acceptable, what is ethical, or what has been done in the past and should be done in the future—may be deeply held by the parties and serve as the dominant guides to their action. These principles often involve intangible factors (see Chapter 1). Interests in principles can also be intrinsic (valued because of their inherent worth) or instrumental (valued because they can be applied to a variety of future situations and scenarios).

Some Observations on Interests We have several observations about interests and types of interests in negotiation:

1. *There is almost always more than one type of interest underlying a negotiation.* Parties will often have more than substantive interests about the issues.[17] They can also care deeply about the process, the relationship, or the principles at stake. Note that interests in principles effectively cut across substantive, procedural, and relationship interests as well, so the categories are not exclusive.

2. *Parties can have different types of interests at stake.* One party may care deeply about the specific issues under discussion while the other cares about how the issues are resolved—questions of principle or process. Bringing these different interests to the surface may enable the parties to see that they care about very different things and that there is a need to invent solutions that address the interests of both sides.

3. *Interests can change.* Like positions on issues, interests can change over time. What was important to the parties last week—or even 20 minutes ago—may not be important now. Interaction between the parties can put some interests to rest, but it may raise others. Thus, the parties must constantly be attentive to changes in their own interests and the interests of the other side. When one party begins speaking about things in a different way—when the language or emphasis changes—the other party should look for a change in interests.

4. *Surfacing interests.* There are numerous ways to surface interests. Sometimes people are not even sure about their own interests. Negotiators should not only ask themselves "What do I want from this negotiation?" but also "Why do I want that?" "Why is that important to me?" "What will achieving that help me do?" and "What will happen if I don't achieve my objective?" Listening to your own inner voices—fears, aspirations, hopes, desires—is important to bring your own interests to the surface.

The same dialogue is essential in clarifying the other party's interests. Asking probing questions and paying careful attention to the other party's language, emotions, and nonverbal behaviour are essential keys to the process. You might also want to distinguish between intrinsic interests—which need to be satisfied as ends in themselves—and instrumental interests—which help one get other outcomes. In both cases, once these interests are understood, it may be possible to invent a variety of ways to address them. The result is a mutually satisfactory solution.

5. *Surfacing interests is not always easy or to one's best advantage.* Critics of the "interests approach" to negotiation have identified the difficulty of defining interests and taking them into consideration. Provis suggests that it is often difficult to define interests and that trying to focus on interests alone often oversimplifies or conceals the real dynamics of a conflict.[18] In some cases parties do not pursue their own best objective interests but instead focus on one or more subjective interests, which may mislead the other party. Thus, a car buyer may prefer a fast, flashy car (his subjective interest) even though his objective interest is to buy a safe, conservative one.

6. *Focusing on interests can be harmful.* There are situations where focusing on interests can impede negotiations. For instance, with a group of negotiators whose consensus on a particular issue is built around a unified position rather than a more generalized set of interests, a focus on interests may not help to achieve a solution. If a coalition is held together by a commitment to pursue a specific objective in negotiation, then encouraging the chief negotiator to discuss interests rather than push for the specific objective is clearly encouraging him or her to deviate from the coalition's purpose.

Generate Alternative Solutions

The search for alternatives is the creative phase of integrative negotiation. Once the parties have attempted to understand each other's interests, they need to generate a variety of alternative solutions. The objective is to create a list of options or possible solutions to the problem; evaluating and selecting from among those options will be their task in the final phase.

Several techniques have been suggested to help negotiators generate alternative solutions. Five different methods for achieving integrative agreements have been proposed and are discussed next.[19] Each method refocuses the issues under discussion and requires progressively more information about the other side's true needs. Solutions move from simpler, distributive agreements to more complex and comprehensive, integrative ones, and there are several paths to finding joint gain.[20] We suggest that parties begin with the easiest and least costly method and progress to the more costly approaches only if the simpler ones fail.

Each approach will be illustrated by the example of two partners in a successful enterprise, Business Consulting Firm, Samantha and Emma, that employs eight other non-partner consultants. The partners are deciding where to locate their new office; half their clients are downtown and half are in the suburbs. There are two possible locations that they are considering leasing. Samantha prefers the downtown location. It has less floor space but is a more prestigious address. While its offices are smaller, its location is equidistant from where both partners live. Emma prefers the location in the suburbs. It has more floor space and larger offices, and it is newer. It is also located closer to Emma's house, but farther from Samantha's. A compromise solution—stay in the current location—is possible, but Samantha and Emma want to determine whether other solutions better meet the needs of the consulting firm.

Expand the Pie Many negotiations begin with a shortage of resources, and it is not possible for both sides to satisfy their interests or obtain their objectives under the current condition. A simple solution is to add resources—expand the pie—in such a way that both sides can achieve their objectives. For instance, the Business Consulting Firm could lease offices both downtown and in the suburbs to serve both sets of its clients. A projected expansion of the business could pay for both leases. In expanding the pie, one party requires no information about the other party except her interests; it is a simple way to solve resource shortage problems. In addition, the approach assumes that simply enlarging the resources will solve the problem. Thus, leasing both locations would be a very satisfactory solution if Samantha and Emma liked both locations and wanted to expand their business. However, expanding the pie would not be a satisfactory solution if their disagreement was based on other grounds—if, for example, they had different visions about the future of the firm—or if the whole firm had to gather for meetings frequently. In addition, to the extent that the negotiation increases the costs of a person or organization not directly involved in the negotiation (e.g., the employees in this example), the solution may be integrative for the negotiators but problematic for other stakeholders.[21]

logroll
the process of exchanging low priority issues for issues of higher priority

Logroll Successful **logrolling** requires the parties to find more than one issue in conflict and to have different priorities for those issues.[22] The parties then agree to trade off among these issues so that one party achieves a highly preferred outcome on the first issue and the other person achieves a highly preferred outcome on the second issue. If the parties do in fact have different preferences on different issues and each party gets his or her most preferred outcome on a high-priority issue, then each should receive more and the joint outcomes should be higher.[23] For instance, the Business Consulting Firm could lease the downtown location and give Emma the bigger office. Samantha would get her preferred location, which is more important to her, and Emma would receive better working space, which is more important to her.

Logrolling is frequently done by trial and error—as part of the process of experimenting with various packages of offers that will satisfy everyone involved. The parties must first establish which issues are at stake and then decide their individual priorities on these issues. If there are already at least two issues on the table, then any combination of two or more issues may be suitable for logrolling. Research suggests that negotiators reach better agreements as the number of issues being negotiated increases.[24] If it appears initially that only one issue is at stake, the parties may need to engage in "unbundling" or "unlinking," which is the process of separating a single issue into two or more issues so that the logrolling may begin.[25] Additional issues of concern may also be generated through the brainstorming processes described below.

Finally, logrolling may be effective when the parties can combine two issues, but not when the parties take turns in successive negotiations—that is, when one party gets what he wants this time, while the other gets what she wants next time. Research by Mannix, Tinsley, and Bazerman shows that when parties do not expect to negotiate with the other person in the future, they are less likely to employ logrolling over time and hence may reach a suboptimal agreement in the current negotiation.[26]

Use Nonspecific Compensation A third way to generate alternatives is to allow one person to obtain his objectives and pay off the other person for accommodating his interests. The payoff may be unrelated to the substantive negotiation, but the party who receives it nevertheless views it as adequate for agreeing to the other party's preferences. Such compensation is "nonspecific" because it is not directly related to the substantive issues being discussed. For instance, the Business Consulting Firm could decide to lease in the suburbs and give Samantha all new office furniture. In this case Emma gets her preferred location, while Samantha receives new office furniture as nonspecific compensation for agreeing to the new office location.

For nonspecific compensation to work, the person doing the compensating needs to know what is valuable to the other person and how seriously she is inconvenienced (i.e., how much compensation is needed to make her feel satisfied). Emma might need to test several different offers (types and amounts of compensation) to find out how much it will take to satisfy Samantha. This discovery process can turn into a distributive bargaining situation, as Samantha may choose to set very high demands as the price for locating in the suburbs while Emma tries to minimize the compensation she will pay.

Cut the Costs for Compliance Through cost cutting, one party achieves her objectives and the other's costs are minimized if she agrees to go along. For instance, the Business Consulting Firm could decide to lease in the suburbs and provide Samantha with a travel subsidy and a new company car and reserved parking space. In this case Emma gets her preferred location, while Samantha's costs for agreeing to the new office location are reduced.

Unlike nonspecific compensation, where the compensated party simply receives something for agreeing, cost cutting is designed to minimize the other party's costs for agreeing to a solution. The technique is thus more sophisticated than logrolling or nonspecific compensation because it requires a more intimate knowledge of the other party's real needs and preferences (the party's interests, what really matters to him, how his needs can be specifically met).

bridge solution
inventing new options
to build agreement

Find a Bridge Solution When the parties are able to invent new options that meet all their respective needs they have created a **bridge solution**. For instance, the Business Consulting Firm could decide to expand the number of partners in the firm and lease a larger space downtown, with new office furniture for everyone and a prestigious street address.

Successful bridging requires a fundamental reformulation of the problem so that the parties are not discussing positions but, rather, they are disclosing sufficient information to discover their interests and needs and then inventing options that will satisfy those needs.[27] Bridging solutions do not always remedy all concerns; Emma may not enjoy the commute and Samantha may not be convinced about growing the firm, but both have agreed that working together is important to them, and they have worked to invent a solution that meets their most important needs. If negotiators fundamentally commit themselves to a win-win negotiation, bridging solutions are likely to be highly satisfactory to both sides.

The successful pursuit of these five strategies requires a meaningful exchange of information between the parties. The parties must either volunteer information or ask each other questions that will generate sufficient information to reveal win-win options. A series of refocusing questions that may reveal these possibilities is presented in Table 3.1.[28]

TABLE 3.1 | Refocusing Questions to Reveal Win-Win Options

Expanding the Pie
1. How can both parties get what they want?
2. Is there a resource shortage?
3. How can resources be expanded to meet the demands of both sides?

Logrolling
1. What issues are of higher and lower priority to me?
2. What issues are of higher and lower priority to the other negotiator?
3. Are there any issues of high priority to me that are of low priority for the other negotiator, and vice versa?
4. Can I "unbundle" an issue—that is, make one larger issue into two or more smaller ones that can then be logrolled?
5. What are things that would be inexpensive for me to give and valuable for the other negotiator to get that might be used in logrolling?

Nonspecific Compensation
1. What are the other negotiator's goals and values?
2. What could I do that would make the other negotiator happy and simultaneously allow me to get my way on the key issue?
3. What are things that would be inexpensive for me to give and valuable for the other negotiator to get that might be used as nonspecific compensation?

Cost Cutting
1. What risks and costs does my proposal create for the other negotiator?
2. What can I do to minimize the other negotiator's risks and costs so that he or she would be more willing to agree?

Bridging
1. What are the other negotiator's real underlying interests and needs?
2. What are my own real underlying interests and needs?
3. What are the higher and lower priorities for each of us in our underlying interests and needs?
4. Can we invent a solution that meets the relative priorities, underlying interests, and needs of both negotiators?

■ Section Summary

Our discussion of the basic approaches to generating alternative solutions may give the impression that if negotiators simply invent enough different options, they will find a solution to solve their problem rather easily. Although identifying options sometimes leads to a solution, solutions are usually attained through hard work and pursuit of several related processes: information exchange, focusing on interests rather than positions, and firm flexibility.[29] Information exchange allows parties to maximize the amount of information available. Focusing on interests allows parties to move beyond opening positions and demands to determine what the parties really want—what needs truly must be satisfied. Finally, firm flexibility allows parties to be firm with regard to what they want to achieve (i.e., interests) while remaining flexible on the means by which they achieve it. Firm flexibility recognizes that negotiators have one or two fundamental interests or principles, although a wide variety of positions, possible solutions, or secondary issues may get drawn into the negotiations. Thus, among the many viable alternatives that will satisfy a negotiator, the important ones directly address the top priorities. Negotiators need to be able to signal to the other side the positions on which they are firm and the positions on which they are willing to be flexible.

Evaluate and Select Alternatives

The final stage in the integrative negotiation process is to evaluate the alternatives generated during the previous phase and to have all parties agree on one of the alternatives. When the challenge is a reasonably simple one, the evaluation and selection steps may be effectively combined into a single step. For those uncomfortable with the integrative process, though, we suggest a close adherence to a series of distinct steps: definitions and standards, alternatives, evaluation, and selection. Following these distinct steps is also a good idea for those managing complex problems or a large number of alternative options. Negotiators will need to weigh or rank-order each option against clear criteria. If no option or set of options appears suitable and acceptable, this is a strong indication that the problem was not clearly defined (return to definitions), or that the standards developed earlier are not reasonable, relevant, and/or realistic (return to standards). Finally, the parties will need to engage in some form of decision-making process in which they debate the relative merits of each negotiator's preferred options and come to agreement on the best options. The following guidelines should be used in evaluating options and reaching a consensus.[30]

Narrow the Range of Solution Options   Examine the list of options generated and focus on those that one or more negotiators strongly support. This approach is more positive than allowing people to focus on negative, unacceptable criteria and options. Solutions that are not strongly advocated by at least one negotiator should be eliminated at this time.

Evaluate Solutions on the Basis of Quality, Standards, and Acceptability
Solutions should be judged on two major criteria: how good they are, and how acceptable they will be to those who have to implement them. Negotiators will evaluate the quality dimension by determining what is best, what is most rational, what is most logical. To the degree that parties can support their arguments with statements of hard fact, logical deduction, and appeals to rational criteria, their arguments will be more compelling in obtaining the support of others. Fisher, Ury, and Patton suggest that the parties appeal to **objective standards** for making decisions.[31] This suggests that the parties are more likely to accept a solution they perceive as fair and equitable to all concerned than one that seems biased. Thus, the parties should search for precedents, arbitration decisions, or other objectively fair outcomes and processes that can be used as benchmarks for legitimizing the fairness of the current settlement. These criteria may be different from what the negotiators judge to be most rational or the best solution. Those evaluating the solution options may also have to be prepared to make trade-offs to ensure that the criteria of both quality and acceptability are met.

objective standards
objectively fair outcomes or processes that can be used to benchmark settlements

Agree to the Criteria in Advance of Evaluating Options Ideally, negotiators should agree to the criteria for evaluating potential integrative solutions early in the process.[32] Negotiators can use these criteria when they have to narrow the choice of options to a single alternative—for example, one candidate for a new job—or to select the option most likely to succeed. If the parties first debate criteria and determine which ones are most important, they will be able to decide on criteria independent of the consideration of any particular candidate or option. Then, when they consider the individual candidates or options, they will pick the best one based on these criteria, not on the individual preferences of one side or the other. If the parties agree, they may revise their criteria later to improve their choice, but they should do so only with the agreement of all negotiators. In fact, it is not a bad idea to check criteria periodically and determine whether each negotiator places the same priority on them as before. Discussion of alternatives frequently leads negotiators to revise their preferences, as well as their estimates of the probability of success and the cost of particular options.

Be Willing to Justify Personal Preference People often find it hard to explain why they like what they like, or dislike what they dislike. When asked, "Why do you like that?" the reply is often, "I don't know, I just do." Moreover, negotiators gain little by pressing opponents to justify themselves—doing so usually just makes them angry and defensive; they may feel that a simple statement of preference is not viewed as sufficient. For example, if the topic under negotiation is what to have for dinner, and one party states that she hates clam chowder, no amount of persuasive effort is likely to induce her to eat clam chowder. Instead, the parties would be more productive if they accepted this information and attempted to explore other options for dinner. Yet personal preferences often have a deep-seated rationale—recall our discussion of how interests, values, and needs underlie positions. Thus, inquiries from one party about the other party's preferences may be an effort to probe behind a position and identify underlying interests and needs. If the other party elicits a little defensiveness in response to a why question, the negotiator should explain that the intent is to probe for possible underlying interests that might facilitate a collaborative settlement rather than to challenge one's perspective.

Be Alert to the Influence of Intangibles in Selecting Options One party may favour an option because it helps satisfy an intangible—gaining recognition, looking strong or tough to a constituency, feeling like a winner, and so on. Intangibles or principles can serve as strong interests for a negotiator. Intangibles can lead the negotiator to fight harder to attain a particular solution if that option satisfies both tangible and intangible needs. Some parties may be uncomfortable with discussing intangibles, or even be unaware of their nature and power in the negotiation process. It is often good practice to help the other party identify those intangibles and make them public as part of the evaluation process. The other party is likely to prefer options that satisfy those intangibles, and to the degree that you can accept them, agreeing to those options may be important concessions.

Use Subgroups to Evaluate Complex Options Small groups may be particularly helpful when several complex options must be considered or when many people will be affected by the solution. Groups of six to eight people, composed of representatives from each faction, side, or subgroup, will be able to work more effectively than a large group. Group processes in negotiation are discussed in more detail in Chapter 10.

Take Time Out to Cool Off Even though the parties may have completed the hardest part of the process—generating a list of viable options—they may become upset if communication breaks down, they feel their preferences are not being acknowledged, or the other side pushes too hard for a particular option. If the parties become angry, they should take a break. They should make their dissatisfaction known and openly discuss the reasons for it. The parties should feel that they are back on an even emotional keel before continuing to evaluate options. Finally, they should work as hard as possible to keep discussions on the specifics of the proposals, not on the people advocating them. The parties should depersonalize the discussion as much as possible so that the options for settlement are not associated with the people who advocated them.

Explore Different Ways to Logroll Earlier we discussed a variety of ways to invent options. The strategy of logrolling is effective not only in inventing options but also as a mechanism to combine options into negotiated packages. Neale and Bazerman identify a variety of approaches in addition to simply combining several issues into a package.[33] Three of these, in particular, relate to the matters of outcome, probabilities, and timing—in other words, *what* is to happen, the *likelihood* of it happening, and *when* it happens.

1. **Exploit Differences in Risk Preference** People have different tolerances for risk, and it may be possible to create a package that recognizes differences in risk preferences.[34] For instance, suppose two entrepreneurs are discussing a future business venture. One has little to risk at the moment and everything to gain in the future; the other has a lot on the line now that he does not want to risk losing if the future is bad. If the entrepreneurs simply agree to split profits in the future, the one with a large amount of current risk may feel vulnerable. Logrolling around these interests can create a solution that protects one entrepreneur's current investment first while providing long-term profits for the other entrepreneur as well.

2. **Exploit Differences in Expectations** As with differences in risk, differences in expectations about the likelihood of future events can permit the parties to invent a solution that addresses the needs of both. For example, the entrepreneur with a lot to lose now may also have pessimistic expectations about the future of the joint venture, whereas the entrepreneur with little to lose may be more optimistic about it. The optimist may thus be willing to gamble more on the future profitability and payout, whereas the pessimist may be willing to settle for a smaller but more assured payment. It is also possible to use contingent contracts to manage different expectations about the future.[35] Contingent contracts adjust as circumstances unfold. For instance, one can include changing oil prices into a contract and adjust delivery fees based on quarterly oil prices.

3. **Exploit Differences in Time Preferences** Negotiators may have different time preferences—one may be concerned about meeting short-term needs while the other may be interested in the long-term rewards of their relationship.[36] Parties with short-term interests will need immediate gratification, whereas parties who look for long-term rewards may be willing to make immediate sacrifices to ensure a future payoff. Parties with different time preferences can invent solutions that address both their interests.

Keep Decisions Tentative and Conditional Until All Aspects of the Final Proposal Are Complete Even though a clear consensus may emerge about the solution option(s) that will be selected, the parties should talk about the solution in conditional terms—a sort of "soft bundling." Maintaining a tentative tone allows negotiators to suggest changes or revise the final package throughout this stage. Points agreed upon in earlier discussions are not firm until the entire package is determined. Parties do not have to feel that because they closed an earlier option they have burned bridges behind them; rather, nothing should be considered final until everything is final. For instance, when buying a house recently one of the authors of this text returned to an earlier discarded option and chose to renovate an older home rather than to pay more for an already renovated house.

Minimize Formality and Record Keeping until Final Agreements Are Closed Negotiators typically do not want to lock themselves into specific language or written agreements until they are close to a consensus. They want to make sure they will not be firmly held to any comments recorded in notes or transcripts. In general, the fewer the written records during the solution-generating phase, the better. In contrast, when the parties are close to consensus, one side should write down the terms of the agreement. This document may then be used as a "single text," to be passed from party to party as often as necessary until all sides agree to the phrasing and wording of their agreement.[37]

We strongly urge groups to avoid the apparent expediency of voting on final agreements or packages. This accomplishes only the relative disenfranchisement of the losing party and makes it more likely that "losers" will be less committed than "winners" to the implementation of the negotiated outcome.

Strategies that Facilitate Successful Integrative Negotiation

Successful integrative negotiation can occur if the parties are predisposed to finding a mutually acceptable joint solution. Realistically, however, there is no guarantee that your counterpart will act co-operatively. For many reasons, your counterpart will often display behaviours that are competitive, antagonistic, and secretive. Don't be surprised or afraid of this possibility; there are many things you can do to increase the likelihood that the people you negotiate with act in a manner more consistent with integrative negotiation. In this section, we identify some of the key strategies and tactics you can use to make this more likely.

Create a Common Objective or Goal

When the parties believe they are likely to benefit more from working together than from competing or working separately, the situation offers greater potential for successful integrative negotiation. Three types of goals—common, shared, and joint—may facilitate the development of integrative agreements.

common goal
a goal that all parties share equally

A **common goal** is one that all parties share equally, each one benefiting in a way that would not be possible if they did not work together. A town government and an industrial manufacturing plant may debate the amount of taxes the plant owes, but they are more likely to work together if the common goal is to keep the plant open and employ half the town's workforce.

shared goal
a goal that both parties work toward but that benefits each party differently

A **shared goal** is one that both parties work toward but that benefits each party differently. For example, partners can work together in a business but not divide the profits equally. One may receive a larger share of the profit because he contributed more experience or capital investment. Inherent in the idea of a shared goal is that parties will work together to achieve some output that will be divided among them. The same result can also come from cost cutting, by which the parties can earn the same outcome as before by working together, but with less effort, expense, or risk. This is often described as an "expandable pie" in contrast to a "fixed pie" (see Chapter 5).

joint goal
a goal that involves individuals with different personal goals agreeing to combine them in a collective effort

A **joint goal** is one that involves individuals with different personal goals agreeing to combine them in a collective effort. For example, people joining a political campaign can have different goals: One wants to satisfy personal ambition to hold public office, another wants to serve the community, and yet another wants to benefit from policies that will be implemented under the new administration. All will unite around the joint goal of helping the new administration get elected.

The key element of an integrative negotiation situation is the belief that all sides can benefit. Whether the sides attain the same outcome or different outcomes, all sides must believe that they will be better off by working in co-operation than by working independently or competing.

Share Information

Earlier in the chapter we discussed the importance of information exchange. Although most people are reluctant to share information in negotiation, preferring to keep their priorities a secret, integrative deals cannot be made without at least some sharing of information. Imagine for a second how difficult it would be to exchange low priority issues for high priority issues if you do not know how your counterpart prioritizes the issues. Many people fear information sharing because they are worried about saying too much and exposing themselves to being exploited. What information can you safely share with a counterpart?

In general, there are three types of information you can share that are not risky and will increase the chances of creating value. These three types of information are: (1) information about your underlying interests, (2) information about your priorities and preferences, and (3) information about your interpretation of key facts.

1. **Underlying Interests** In this chapter we have emphasized the importance of interests, particularly as they relate to value creation. Truthfully revealing your underlying needs as they relate to the negotiation is a major predictor of success in integrative negotiations.

2. **Priorities and Preferences** If there are three issues to be negotiated, is it a good idea to let your counterpart know how you rank the three issues in terms of importance? Newcomers to negotiation are often surprised to learn that the answer is *yes*. Remember, logrolling is almost impossible unless information about priorities is discovered.

3. **Interpretation of Key Facts** Very often, negotiators will benefit from discussion of information about their interpretation of the quality of issues. For example, how do they interpret the market value of a parcel of land being negotiated? How likely do they think interest rates are to go up or down? The key issue here is to make sure you seek clarification on how to value a particular resource.

Build Trust

A healthy by-product of information sharing is that it tends to build trust. When a negotiator reveals something about their relevant interests or priorities, they are perceived to be more trustworthy.

Although there is no guarantee that trust will lead to collaboration, there is plenty of evidence to suggest that mistrust inhibits collaboration. People who are interdependent but do not trust each other will act tentatively or defensively. Defensiveness means that they will not accept information at face value but instead will look for hidden, deceptive meanings. When people are defensive, they withdraw and withhold information. Defensive people also attack the other party's statements and position, seeking to defeat their position rather than to work together. Either of these responses is likely to make the negotiator hesitant, cautious, and distrustful of the other, undermining the negotiation process.[38]

Generating trust is a complex, uncertain process; it depends in part on how the parties behave and in part on the parties' personal characteristics. When people trust each other, they are more likely to share information and to communicate accurately their needs, positions, and the facts of the situation.[39] In contrast, when people do not trust each other, they are more likely to engage in positional bargaining, use threats, and commit themselves to tough positions.[40] As with defensiveness, mistrust is likely to be reciprocated and to lead to unproductive negotiations. To develop trust effectively, each negotiator must believe that both she and the other party choose to behave in a co-operative manner; moreover, each must believe that this behaviour is a signal of the other's honesty, openness, and a similar mutual commitment to a joint solution (see Chapter 6 for more discussion of trust in negotiation).

Make Multiple Offers Simultaneously

The process of making and receiving offers tends to differ between distributive and integrative negotiations. Firstly, we recommend that you avoid the tendency to negotiate on an issue-by-issue basis. Doing so reduces the likelihood that tradeoffs can be discovered. Secondly, we recommend making multiple offers at the same time. What does it mean to make multiple simultaneous offers?

The basic idea behind **multiple simultaneous offers** is to present your counterpart with more than one package offer, ensuring that each package offer is of equal value to yourself. For example, you might tell your counterpart that you are going

multiple simultaneous offers presenting more than one package offer, ensuring that each package offer is of equal value to yourself

to make not one, but two (or three) offers. Then, say that package 1 includes a selling price of $300,000 and a closing date of June 1st, and package 2 includes a selling price of $310,000 and a closing date of July 1st. By doing so, you send a message to your counterpart that you are both flexible and prepared.

Sometimes a counterpart will respond with a multiple package offer of their own. By studying their counteroffer and comparing it to your original offer, you are more likely to be able to discern which issues are weighted higher and lower by each of you. Sometimes a counterpart will be too surprised or confused to respond accordingly. Even if they fail to come back with a counteroffer you can still ask them which of your offers comes closest to matching their preferences. You can also acquire information by asking them which offer is farthest from their preferences. Either way, the purpose is to use the process to learn about their underlying preferences and interests.

A final word of advice is in order. Be sure to develop multiple simultaneous offers that are close to your target point and not your reservation point. Be ambitious. The last thing you want is for your counterpart to listen to your offers and respond by saying, "I'll take the second one. Where do I sign?"

The Motivation and Commitment to Work Together

For integrative negotiation to succeed, the parties must be motivated to collaborate rather than to compete. They need to be committed to reaching a goal that benefits both of them rather than to pursuing only their own ends. They must adopt interpersonal styles that are more congenial than combative, more open and trusting than evasive and defensive, more flexible (but firm) than stubborn (but yielding). Specifically, they must be willing to make their own needs explicit, to identify similarities, and to recognize and accept differences. They must also tolerate uncertainties and unravel inconsistencies.

It might appear that for successful integrative negotiation to occur, each party should be just as interested in the objectives and problems of the other as he is in his own—that each must assume responsibility for the other's needs and outcomes as well as for his own. This is an *incorrect* interpretation; in fact, such behaviour is more likely to be dysfunctional than successful. Parties who are deeply committed to each other and each other's welfare often do not achieve the best solution.[41] As close as the parties may feel to each other, it is unlikely that they will completely understand each other's needs, objectives, and concerns, and thus they can fall into the trap of not meeting each other's objectives while thinking they are.[42] Parties strongly committed to each other are likely to yield more than they would otherwise; the result is that they may arrive at a joint outcome that is less satisfactory than one they would have reached had they remained firm in pursuing their own objectives.

Parties in negotiation maximize their outcomes when they assume a healthy, active self-interest in achieving their own goals while also recognizing that they are in a collaborative, problem-solving relationship.[43] Maximizing outcomes may also be negatively correlated with one party's ability to punish the other party. De Dreu, Giebels, and van de Vliert showed that even co-operatively motivated negotiators have less trust, exchange less information about preferences and priorities, and achieve agreements of lower joint profit when they can punish the other party than when they do not have this capability.[44]

Motivation and commitment to problem solving can be enhanced in several ways:

1. The parties can learn that they share a common fate; to quote Ben Franklin, "If we do not hang together, we will surely hang separately."

2. The parties can demonstrate to each other that there is more to be gained by working together (to increase the payoffs or reduce the costs) than by working separately. The parties can emphasize that they may have to work together after the negotiations are over and will continue to benefit from the relationship they have created. In spite of these efforts, competitive and contentious behaviour may persist.

3. The parties can engage in commitments to each other before the negotiations begin; such commitments have been called **pre-settlement settlements**[45] and are distinguished by three major characteristics:

   a. The settlement results in a firm, legally binding, written agreement between the parties (it is more than a "gentlemen's agreement").

   b. The settlement occurs in advance of the parties undertaking full-scale negotiations, but the parties intend that the agreement will be replaced by a more clearly delineated long-term agreement that is to be negotiated.

   c. The settlement resolves only a subset of the issues on which the parties disagree and may simply establish a framework within which the more comprehensive agreement can be defined and delineated.

pre-settlement settlements
commitments made by negotiating parties before negotiations begin

Try Post-settlement Settlements

Sometimes, instead of agreeing to commitments upfront, negotiators reach a settlement and try to agree upon improvements to that settlement afterwards. This process is called a **post-settlement settlement**.[46] How does this work? If you negotiate an agreement that you are not 100% satisfied with, you can suggest to your counterpart to continue discussing further improvements to the existing agreement. Emphasize to your counterpart that these discussions are informal and will not affect the current agreement unless they result in a better agreement than the original. Also reiterate that if either of you are not satisfied with these discussions you can rely on your existing agreement. This will help reassure your counterpart that you are not trying to force last-minute concessions. If both sides end up discovering additional value, then agree to share that value. In this way, everybody wins.

post-settlement settlement
negotiators reach a settlement and try to agree upon improvements to that settlement afterwards

Use Clear and Accurate Communication

Another precondition for high-quality integrative negotiation is clear and accurate communication. First, negotiators must be willing to share information about themselves.[47] They must be willing to reveal what they want and, more important, must be willing to state why they want it in specific, concrete terms, avoiding generalities and ambiguities. Second, the other negotiators must understand the communication. At a minimum, they must understand the meaning they each attach to their statements; hopefully, the parties each interpret the basic facts in the same way, but if they don't, then they should reconcile them. Others at the negotiation can frequently identify ambiguities and breakdowns in communication. If someone on a bargaining team makes a confusing statement, others can address it and try to clarify it. When one person on the other side does not grasp a difficult point, someone else from the same side will often be able to find the words or illustrations to bring out the meaning. Mutual understanding is the responsibility of both sides. The communicator must be willing to test whether the other side has received the message that was intended. Similarly, the listener must engage in active listening, testing to make sure that what he or she received and understood is the message that the sender intended.

Multiple communication channels, such as opportunities for the two sides to communicate in addition to during "formal negotiations," will help negotiators clarify the formal communication or exchange information if the formal channels break down. Conversations over coffee breaks, separate meetings between chief negotiators outside the formal sessions, and off-the-record contacts between key subordinates are all alternatives to the formal channel. The negotiators must exercise care, however, to make sure that the multiple messages and contacts are consistent. Sending conflicting messages during integrative negotiation can confuse the other party at best, and threaten or anger at worst.

When there are strong negative feelings or when one or more parties are inclined to dominate, negotiators may create formal, structured procedures for communication. Under these circumstances, negotiators should follow a procedure that gives everyone a chance to speak. For example, most rules for debates limit statements to five minutes, and similar rules are often adopted in contentious open meetings or public hearings. In addition, the parties may agree to follow a previously agreed-on agenda so that everyone can be heard and their contributions noted. Other ways to ensure effective communication processes in negotiation are covered extensively in Chapter 6.

An Understanding of the Dynamics of Integrative Negotiation

It is possible for negotiators to have "traditional" views of negotiation that lead them to assume that the distributive bargaining process is the only way to approach negotiations. Several studies indicate that training in integrative negotiation enhances the ability of the parties to successfully pursue the process. For example, Weingart, Hyder, and Prietula demonstrated that training negotiators in integrative tactics— particularly in how to exchange information about priorities across issues and preferences within issues, and how to set high goals—significantly enhanced the frequency of integrative behaviours and led the parties to achieve higher joint outcomes.[48] This study also found that using distributive tactics, such as strongly trying to persuade the other of the validity of one's own views, was negatively related to joint outcomes. In addition, Lowenstein, Thompson, Gentner, and their colleagues have found that analogical training appears to be an especially powerful way to learn about integrative negotiation.[49] Analogical learning involves the direct comparison of different negotiation examples to identify and understand the underlying principles and structure of the negotiation.

In this chapter we examined the basic structure of integrative bargaining situations and some of the strategies and tactics used in integrative bargaining. Our primary objective was to increase the chances you will recognize integrative negotiation opportunities when they are present and be better able to respond accordingly. Let's briefly return to the story of the NHL lockout discussed in the chapter opening.

After 310 days the NHL and the NHLPA reached a settlement on a six-year collective bargaining agreement. As we mentioned at the outset, a key issue in the dispute was the salary cap. In the end, the settlement included a team payroll cap of $39 million for the 2005–06 season, and the cap would be adjusted on a year-to-year basis according to revenue. Although this issue was a critical factor that led to the lockout, it was not the only issue under consideration. For example, the final agreement included the following: (1) rookie salaries would be capped at $850,000 per season, (2) players under contract had their pay cut by 24% immediately, (3) no player could account for 20% of a team's payroll, and (4) a new drug-testing policy was put in place.

By most expert accounts, the final agreement favoured team owners and the league and did little to improve the bargaining position of the players. Thus, to use the terminology we have introduced in the book, the creation of a long-term contract that improved the future viability of the league *created value*. However, it also appears that team owners and the league *claimed* the majority of the value that was created.

As you prepare for, and navigate through, integrative situations, there are a number of things you should keep in mind. The following points are some of the most important.

1. Preparation is key. Yes, this is the same point we mentioned in the previous chapter (it's that important).

2. When the situation contains integrative potential, adopt a co-operative orientation. Share and ask for information, attempt to understand your counterpart's needs and interests, and search for solutions that reconcile the needs and interests of all parties.

3. Become familiar with the different ways of inventing options, such as expanding the pie and logrolling.

4. Do not negotiate on an issue-by-issue basis, instead try to negotiate packages. When making offers, try to create multiple offers and present them simultaneously.

5. Don't forget about claiming. Negotiators who work hard to create value shouldn't lose sight of the fact that value must also be claimed.

Key Terms

Bridge solution, p. 54
Common goal, p. 60
Interests, p. 49
Joint goal, p. 60
Logroll, p. 53
Multiple simultaneous offers, p. 61

The negotiator's dilemma, p. 49
Objective standards, p. 56
Post-settlement settlement, p. 63
Pre-settlement settlements, p. 63
Shared goal, p. 60

Negotiation: Planning and Strategy

LEARNING OBJECTIVES

The main purpose of this chapter is to provide a useable framework that will assist negotiators as they get ready to negotiate. After reading this chapter you should be able to:

1. Formulate appropriate goals for negotiation purposes,

2. Understand the basic steps of the planning process, and

3. Consider some strategic choices that flow from the planning process.

Experienced negotiators with a history of success often point to preparation as one of the most important factors contributing to their positive outcomes. Although most of us would agree that preparation is essential, a surprisingly common error is to either under-prepare or not prepare at all. Why do people so frequently commit this error? Sometimes, people downplay the importance of preparation because they just want to hear what the other party has to say. While it may be comforting to think you can simply walk away if you don't like the other side's offer, the truth is that walking away becomes very difficult if you don't anticipate and analyze your own limits. A poorly prepared negotiator needlessly surrenders initiative and power to the other side.

People also downplay the importance of preparation because they think it takes too much time. As any experienced negotiator will tell you, it actually saves time. When you know your limits, your alternatives, and have analyzed these from your counterpart's perspective, you are less likely to drag on the discussion and more likely to quickly walk away if necessary. In short, less time is required in face-to-face negotiation when you are prepared.

Finally, and perhaps most importantly, people often don't know how to properly prepare for a negotiation. Preparation goes beyond creating a wish list and thinking about your minimum fall-back position. There are several elements to consider when preparing to negotiate—and the analysis of your own perspective and priorities is only one element. A diligent negotiator considers their own perspective, the perspective of their counterpart, characteristics of the situation, and the relationship between all the parties involved.

In this chapter we begin to build a roadmap for this important process. The techniques apply whether you are getting ready for a labour negotiation, a negotiation with a supplier, a customer, or even a family member. We conclude the chapter with a discussion of how the planning process can guide your choice of negotiation strategy and some advice on different approaches you may choose.

■ Goals—The Focus that Drives a Negotiation

The first step in developing and executing a negotiation is to determine one's goals. Negotiators must anticipate what goals they want to achieve in a negotiation and focus on how to achieve those goals. As noted in Chapter 1, negotiators must consider substantive goals (e.g., money or a specific outcome), intangible goals (e.g., winning, beating the other party, or getting a settlement at any cost), and procedural goals such as shaping the agenda or simply having a voice at the table. Effective preparation requires a thorough, thoughtful approach to these goals; negotiators should specify their goals and objectives clearly. This includes listing all goals they wish to achieve in the negotiation, determining the priority among these goals, identifying potential multi-goal packages, and evaluating possible trade-offs among multiple goals.

Direct Effects of Goals

Four aspects of how goals affect negotiation are important to understand:

1. Wishes are not goals, especially in negotiation. Wishes may be related to interests or needs that motivate goals (see Chapter 3), but they are not goals themselves. A wish is a fantasy, a hope that something might happen; a goal is a specific, focused target that one can realistically plan to achieve.

2. Goals are often linked to the other party's goals. The linkage between the two parties' goals defines an issue to be settled (see the discussion of issues later in this chapter) and is often the source of conflict. To illustrate with a simple example that many people can relate to: A car purchaser's goal is to get a car cheaply, and the dealer's goal is to sell it at the highest possible price; thus, the "issue" is the price the purchaser will pay for the car.

3. There are boundaries or limits to what goals can be (see the discussion of walkaways and alternatives later in this chapter). If what we want exceeds these limits (i.e., what the other party is capable of or willing to give), we must either change our goals or end the negotiation. Goals must be attainable. If my goal—"to buy this car at a cheap price"—isn't possible because the dealer won't sell the car "cheaply" (notice that "cheaply" is an ambiguous goal at this point), I'm going to have to either change my goal or find another car to buy (perhaps from a different dealer).

4. Effective goals must be concrete, specific, and measurable. The less concrete and measurable our goals are, the harder it is to (1) communicate to the other party what we want, (2) understand what the other party wants, and (3) determine whether an offer on the table satisfies our goals. "To get a car cheaply" or "to agree on a price so that the loan payment does not use all of my paycheque" is not a very clear goal. What do I mean by "use up my paycheque"? Is this every week's paycheque or only one cheque a month? Do I want the payment to be just under 100 percent of the paycheque, or about 50 percent, or perhaps even 25 percent? The negotiator has to determine exactly how big a payment can comfortably come out of his or her paycheque at present interest rates and add to that what is available for a down payment

to be able to negotiate exactly what he or she is willing to pay a month. But as you can see, even this figure is not totally clear.

Goals can also be intangible or procedural. In the car purchase example, intangible goals might include enhancing reputation among one's friends by owning and driving a sports car; maintaining an image as a shrewd, pennywise negotiator; or paying any price to ensure convenient, reliable transportation. In other negotiations, intangible goals might include maintaining a reputation as a tough but principled negotiator, establishing a precedent for future negotiations, or conducting the negotiations in a manner that is fair to all sides and assures each party fair treatment.

Which of these many criteria should we use? The answer depends on you: your specific objectives and your priorities among multiple objectives. Trade-offs will be inevitable and can cloud your perspective while negotiating, so you have to clearly remember what you wanted to achieve when the negotiation started.

Indirect Effects of Goals

Simple and direct goals can often be attained in a single negotiation session and with a simple negotiating strategy. Too often, though, we limit our negotiations to pursuing short-term goals, and downplay the long-term impact of our negotiations. This short-term thinking affects our choice of strategy; in developing and framing our goals, we may ignore the present or future relationship with the other party in favour of a simplistic concern for achieving only the substantive outcome. As an example, suppose your beloved aging grandmother decides she is too old to drive and asks you whether you want to buy her car. She says she knows nothing about cars and simply wants a "fair price." While you may be able to strike a very favourable deal on the price, if she or other family members discover that you took advantage of her age and ignorance about cars, the long-term consequences for you may be very negative!

Other negotiation goals—those that are complex or difficult to define—may require initiating a sequence of negotiation episodes. In these cases, progress will be made incrementally, and it may depend on establishing a strong relationship with the other party. Examples here include a substantial increase in one's line of credit with a bank or credit union or the establishment of a privileged status with an important trading partner. Such relationship-oriented goals should motivate the negotiator toward a strategy choice in which the relationship with the other party is valued as much as (or even more than) the substantive outcome.

Understanding the Flow of Negotiations: Stages and Phases

Before we explore the specific planning processes for negotiation, it is important to understand the typical steps or flow in a negotiation to anticipate how negotiations are likely to evolve and why planning is so important.

Several researchers have studied the flow of negotiations over time—often by classifying the type of communication parties use at various points in the process. This work has confirmed that negotiation, like communication in problem-solving groups and in other forms of ritualistic social interaction, proceeds through distinct phases or stages.[1]

Leonard Greenhalgh has articulated a stage model of negotiation that is particularly relevant for integrative negotiation. He suggests that there are seven key steps to an ideal negotiation process (see Figure 4.1):

FIGURE 4.1 | Phases of Negotiation

Phase 1	Phase 2	Phase 3	Phase 4	Phase 5	Phase 6	Phase 7
Preparation →	Relationship building →	Information gathering →	Information using →	Bidding →	Closing the deal →	Implementating the agreement

Source: Reprinted with the permission of The Free Press, an imprint of Simon & Schuster Adult Publishing Group, from Managing Strategic Relationships: The Key to Business Success by Leonard Greenhalgh. Copyright © 2001 by Leonard Greenhalgh.

Preparation: deciding what is important, defining goals, thinking ahead about how to work with the other party.

Relationship building: getting to know the other party, understanding how you and the other party are similar and different, and building commitment toward achieving a mutually beneficial set of outcomes. Greenhalgh argues that this stage is extremely critical to satisfactorily moving the other stages forward.

Information gathering: learning what you need to know about the issues, about the other party and their needs, about the feasibility of possible settlements, and about what might happen if you fail to reach agreement with the other side.

Information using: at this stage, negotiators assemble the case they want to make for their preferred outcomes and settlement, one that will maximize the negotiator's own needs. This presentation is often used to "sell" the negotiator's preferred outcome to the other.

Bidding: the process of making moves from one's initial, ideal position to the actual outcome. Bidding is the process by which each party states their "opening offer" and then makes moves in that offer toward a middle ground.

Closing the deal: the objective of this stage is to build commitment to the agreement achieved in the previous phase. Both the negotiator and the other party have to assure themselves that they reached a deal they can be happy with, or at least accept.

Implementing the agreement: determining who needs to do what once the agreement is reached. Not uncommonly parties discover that the agreement is flawed, key points were missed, or the situation has changed and new questions exist. Flaws in moving through the earlier phases arise here, and the deal may have to be reopened or issues settled by mediators, arbitrators, or the courts.

Greenhalgh argues that this model is largely prescriptive—that is, this is the way people ought to negotiate—and he creates a strong case for why this is so. However, examination of the actual practice of negotiators shows that they frequently deviate from this model. One reason is differences in national culture. For example, Canadian and American negotiators typically view the process more in "win-lose," or distributive, terms; they don't do much relationship building or planning, and they move directly to bidding, closing, and implementation. In contrast, Asian negotiators spend a great deal of time on relationship building and truncate the steps toward the end of the negotiation process.[2] Another reason negotiations deviate from the prescriptive model is that few people are familiar with it. Despite these barriers, you can still use the model to organize the process. Even though one party rarely has complete control over the process, it is recommended that negotiators encourage their counterparts to follow the phases recommended by Greenhalgh. You never know, they might actually agree.

▪ Getting Ready: The Planning Process

The foundation for success in negotiation is not in the game playing or the dramatics. The dominant force for success in negotiation is in the planning that takes place prior to the dialogue. Effective planning also requires hard work on the following points:

- defining the issues
- assembling issues and defining the bargaining mix
- defining interests
- defining limits and alternatives
- defining one's own objectives (targets) and opening bids (where to start)
- assessing constituents and the social context in which the negotiation will occur
- analyzing the other party
- planning the issue presentation and defence
- defining protocol—where and when the negotiation will occur, who will be there, what the agenda will be, and so on

The remainder of this chapter discusses each of these steps in detail (see also a summary of the planning guide in Table 4.1 that may be used to plan one's own

TABLE 4.1 | Negotiation Planning Guide

1. What are the issues in the upcoming negotiation?

2. Based on a review of ALL the issues, what is the "bargaining mix"? (Which issues do we have to cover? Which issues are connected to other issues?)

3. What are my interests?

4. What are my limits—what is my walkaway? What is my alternative?

5. Defining targets and openings—where will I start, what is my goal?

6. Who are my constituents and what do they want me to do?

7. Who are the opposing negotiators and what do they want?

8. What overall strategy do I want to select?

9. What protocol needs to be followed in conducting this negotiation?

negotiation). The list represents the collective wisdom of several sources,[3] each of which has its own list of key steps, which often vary in order.

Before commencing this discussion, we want to note four things:

- First, we assume that a single planning process can be followed for both a distributive and an integrative process. Although we have highlighted the differences between them in the last two chapters, we believe that with the exception of the specific tactics negotiators intend to use, one comprehensive planning process can be used for either form of negotiation.

- Second, at this point in the book, we have concentrated on distributive and integrative processes and the differences between them. However, there are several "structural" factors surrounding a negotiation that may also affect the strategizing and planning processes. These structural factors include the number of issues, length of the negotiation, "rules" that govern or limit how we negotiate, number of parties at the table or having an influence on the negotiation, and the broader network of relationships among parties at the table and decision makers away from the table.[4]

- Third, we assume that negotiations will be conducted primarily one to one— that is, you and another individual negotiator. This is the simplest model to understand and plan for. However, it is not uncommon for negotiations to have two sides and multiple parties on each side, or multiple parties represented at the table, or multiple groups and organizations.

- Finally, while we describe these steps in a relatively linear fashion; complete and up-to-date planning will require a certain degree of shuttling back and forth between steps to assure alignment of strategy and plan. For example, information often cannot be obtained and accumulated simply and straightforwardly, and information discovered in some of the later steps may force a negotiator to reconsider and re-evaluate earlier steps. As a result, the first iteration through the planning process should be tentative, and the negotiator should be flexible enough to modify and adjust previous steps as new information becomes available.

1. Defining the Issues

This step itself usually begins with an analysis of what is to be discussed in the negotiation. Some negotiations may only consist of a single issue—for example, the price of an item, such as the price of a coffee table being purchased at a yard sale or the price of a used car. Other negotiations are more complex. Thus, the purchase of one company by another may include a large number of questions such as price, transfer of inventory, executives and workers who will be retained, transferred, or laid off, and new headquarters location.

The number of issues in a negotiation, together with the relationship between the negotiator and the other party, is often the primary determinant of whether one uses a distributive or integrative strategy. Single-issue negotiations tend to dictate distributive negotiations because the only real negotiation issue is the price or "distribution" of that issue. In contrast, multiple-issue negotiations lend themselves more to integrative negotiations because parties can use processes such as logrolling to create issue "packages" that are mutually beneficial.

For instance, in the sale of a house, both parties may begin by believing that price is the only issue, but quickly realize that other issues are equally central: financing the purchase, date of sale, or date of occupancy. They might also identify other issues, such as appliances to be included, repair of a broken fence, or payment for the fuel oil left in the storage tank. During the purchase process, the buyer's lawyer, banker, or real estate agent might draw up a list of other things to consider: taxes to pay, escrow amounts for undiscovered problems, or a written statement that the seller must leave the house in "broom-clean" condition. Note that it does not take long to generate a fairly detailed list. In any negotiation, a complete list of the issues at stake is best derived from the following sources:

1. An analysis of all the possible issues that need to be decided.

2. Previous experience in similar negotiations.

3. Research conducted to gather information (e.g., reading a magazine article on how to buy a house).

4. Consultation with experts in that industry (real estate agents, bank loan officers, lawyers, accountants, or friends who have bought a house recently).

Similarly, even in multiple-issue negotiations, the opportunity to create value may be lost in competitive dynamics that minimize trust and information sharing and that treat each issue in a distributive manner. This is discussed further in the next section.

2. Assembling the Issues and Defining the Bargaining Mix

The next step in planning is to assemble all the issues that have been defined into a comprehensive list. The combination of lists from each side in the negotiation determines the bargaining mix. In generating a list of issues, negotiators may feel that they put too much on the table at once or raise too many issues. This may happen if the parties do not talk frequently or if they have lots of business to transact. As we noted in Step 1, however, introducing a long list of issues into a negotiation often makes success more, rather than less, likely—provided that all the issues are real. Large bargaining mixes allow many possible components and arrangements for settlement, thus increasing the likelihood that a particular package will meet both parties' needs and therefore lead to a successful settlement. At the same time, large bargaining mixes can lengthen negotiations because they present so many possible combinations of issues to consider, and combining and evaluating all these mixes makes valuing the deal very complex.[5]

After assembling issues on an agenda, the negotiator next must prioritize them. Prioritization includes two steps:

1. *Determine which issues are most important and which are less important.* Once negotiation begins, parties can easily be swept up in the rush of information, arguments, offers, counteroffers, trade-offs, and concessions. For those who are not clear in advance about what they want and what they can do without, it is easy to lose perspective and agree to suboptimal settlements, or to get distracted by long debates over points that are relatively unimportant. When negotiators do not have priorities, they may be more likely to yield on those points aggressively argued by the other side rather than to yield based on their own priorities.

    Priorities can be set in a number of ways. One simple way is for the negotiator to rank-order the issues by asking "What is most important?" "What is second most important?" and "What is least important?" An even simpler process is to group issues into categories of high, medium, or low importance. When the negotiator represents a constituency, it is important to involve that group in setting priorities. Priorities can be set for both interests and more specific issues. A third, more precise method is to award a total of 100 points to the total package of issues, and then to divide the points among the issues in proportion to each issue's relative importance. If the negotiator has confidence in the relative weighting of points across the issues, then trading off and "packaging" possible settlements together becomes more systematic.[6]

It is also important to set priorities (and possibly assign points) for both tangible and intangible issues. Intangible issues are often difficult to discuss and rank-order, yet if they remain subjective and not quantified, negotiators may overemphasize or underemphasize them.

Finally, negotiators may also wish to specify a bargaining range for each issue in the mix. Thus, not only would a "best possible" and "minimally acceptable" package be specified, but also a target and minimally acceptable level would be specified for each issue in the mix.

2. *Determine whether the issues are linked together or separate.* If the issues are separate, they can be easily added or subtracted; if connected, then settlement on one will be linked to settlement on the others and making concessions on one issue will inevitably be tied to some other issue. The negotiator must decide whether the issues are truly connected—for instance, whether the price he will pay for the house is dependent on what the bank will loan him—as opposed to simply being connected in his own mind for the sake of achieving a good settlement.

3. Defining Interests

After defining the issues, the negotiator must proceed to define the underlying interests and needs. As we extensively discussed in Chapter 2, *positions*—an opening bid or a target point—are what a negotiator wants. *Interests* are why she wants them. A target point of $135,000 for a condo would be a position; this is what the negotiator hopes to pay. The interest would be "to pay a fair market price, and one I can afford, for that two bedroom condominium." Although defining interests is more important to integrative negotiation than to distributive bargaining, even distributive discussions can benefit from one or both parties identifying the key interests. If issues help us define what we want, then understanding interests requires us to ask *why* we want it. Asking "why" questions usually brings critical values, needs, or principles that we want to achieve in the negotiation to the surface.[7] Interests may be

- substantive, that is, directly related to the focal issues under negotiation
- process-based, that is, related to how the negotiators behave as they negotiate
- relationship-based, that is, tied to the current or desired future relationship between the parties

Interests may also be based on the intangibles of negotiation, including principles or standards to which the parties wish to adhere, the informal norms by which they will negotiate, and the benchmarks they will use to guide them toward a settlement, to achieve a fair or reasonable deal, or to get the negotiation concluded quickly.

4. Knowing Limits and Alternatives

What will happen if the other party refuses to accept some proposed items for the agenda or states issues in such a way that they are unacceptable? Good preparation requires that you establish two clear points: your *resistance point* and your *alternatives*.

A *resistance point* is the place where you decide that you should absolutely stop the negotiation rather than continue because any settlement beyond this point is not minimally acceptable. If you are the seller, your resistance point is the least you will take for the item you have for sale; if you are the buyer, your resistance point is the most you will pay for the item.

Setting resistance points as a part of planning is critical. Most of us have been involved in buying situations where the item we wanted wasn't available, but we allowed ourselves to be talked into a more expensive model. Moreover, some competitive situations generate intense pressures to escalate the price. For example, in an auction, if there is a bidding war with another person, one may pay more than was planned. Gamblers, analogously, may encounter a losing streak and end up losing more money than they had planned. Clear resistance points help keep people from agreeing to deals that they later realize weren't very smart.

On the other hand, *alternatives* are other agreements negotiators could achieve and still meet their needs. Alternatives are very important in both distributive and integrative processes because they define whether the current outcome is better than another possibility. In any situation, the better the alternatives, the more power you have because you can walk away from the current negotiation and still know that your needs and interests can be met. In the house-purchase example, the more a buyer has researched the real estate market and understands what other comparable houses are available, the more she knows that she can walk away from this negotiation and still have acceptable housing choices. See Negotiation Point 4.1 for a current example of the power of resistance points and strong alternatives.

5. Setting Targets and Openings

After negotiators have defined the issues, assembled a tentative agenda, and consulted others as appropriate and necessary, the next step is to define two other key points: the specific *target point* where one realistically expects to achieve a settlement and the *asking price*, representing the best deal one can hope to achieve.

There are numerous ways to set a target. One can ask, "What is an outcome that I would be comfortable with?" "At what point would I be generally satisfied?" "What have other people achieved in this situation?" Targets may not be as firm and rigid as resistance points or alternatives; one might be able to set a general range or a class of several outcomes that would be equally acceptable.

Similarly, there are numerous ways to set an opening bid. An opening may be the best possible outcome, an ideal solution, something even better than was achieved last time. It is easy to get overly confident, however, and to set an opening that is so unrealistic that the other party immediately laughs, gets angry, or walks away before responding. While openings are usually formulated around a "best possible" settlement, it is also easy to inflate them to the point where they become self-defeating because they are too unrealistic in the eyes of the other negotiator or observers with a more realistic perspective.

Negotiation Point

4.1

How to Survive the Dragons' Den

The Dragons' Den is one of the Canadian Broadcasting Corporation's (CBC) highest-rated television programs, offering entrepreneurs the opportunity to pitch their ideas to wealthy investors (called the Dragons) hoping that at least one of them provides enough investment capital to help build their businesses. Entrepreneurs Joseph Iuso and Brian Crozier were given such an opportunity when all five Dragons offered them 1 million dollars to purchase 40% of their already flourishing online internet banking service company UseMyBank Services Inc., which is a far greater stake in the company than the entrepreneurs originally sought (i.e., 1 million dollars for 5% of the company). Convinced that the entrepreneurs would have difficulty acquiring this capital elsewhere, the Dragons stood firm on their offer, expecting that it would be accepted. Contrary to these expectations, Iuso and Crozier made Dragons' Den history by being the first entrepreneurs to turn down a 1 million dollar offer. Although appearing to be a questionable decision, Iuso and Crozier made this decision with an understanding of their resistance point, 1 million dollars for a 5% share of the company, and of the existence of other alternatives that the Dragons did not believe existed. Crozier notes "we have the luxury of not needing the money desperately."

Source: D. Parkinson, "They snubbed the Dragons' Den: Young company's rejection of TV show's terms highlights pitfalls in the race to raise capital." The Globe and Mail, 6 May 2010, Sect. E, p. 1.

Target Setting Requires Positive Thinking about One's Own Objectives When approaching a negotiation, negotiators often attempt to become aware of the other party—how they behave, what they will probably demand, and how it feels dealing with them. It is possible to devote too much attention to the other party—that is, to spend too much time trying to discern what the other negotiator wants or how to meet those demands. If negotiators focus attention on the other party to the exclusion of themselves, they may plan their entire strategy as a reaction to the other's anticipated conduct. Reactive strategies are likely to make negotiators feel threatened and defensive and lessen their flexibility and creativity. In contrast, by defining realistic, optimistic, and pessimistic targets for oneself, negotiators can take a proactive stance in which they are aware of the range of possible outcomes. This permits them to be flexible in what they will accept and improves the likelihood of arriving at a mutually satisfactory outcome.

Target Setting Often Requires Considering How to Package Several Issues and Objectives Most negotiators have a mixture of bargaining objectives, so they must consider the best way to achieve satisfaction across multiple issues. To package issues effectively, negotiators need to understand the definition of the issues, bargaining mix, and the other's bargaining mix. Negotiators can then propose package settlements that will help them achieve their targets on key issues.

It is possible to evaluate packages the same way as evaluating individual issues—by defining optimistic, realistic, and pessimistic packages.[8] When packages involve intangible issues, or issues for which it is difficult to specify definite targets, it is harder to evaluate and compare the packages explicitly.

Target Setting Requires an Understanding of Trade-offs and Throwaways

The discussion of packaging raises another possible challenge: What if the other party proposes a package that puts issues A, B, and C in one's optimistic range, puts item D in the realistic range, puts E at the pessimistic point, and does not even mention item F, which is part of one's own bargaining mix? Is item F a throwaway item that can be ignored? If it is not a throwaway item, is it relatively unimportant and worth giving up to lock in agreement on A, B, and C in the optimal range? Now suppose the other party has proposed two packages, the one described above and a second one that places items A and E in the optimistic range, items B and F in the realistic range, and C at the pessimistic point, while it ignores D. Would the first or the second package be more attractive?

Negotiators may want to consider giving away "something for nothing" if such an item can be part of the transaction. Even if an issue is unimportant or inconsequential to you, it may be valuable or attractive to the other party. Awareness of the actual or likely value of such concessions can considerably enrich the value of what one offers to the other party at little or no cost to oneself. Using the house example again, the seller may have eight months left on a parking-lot pass for the same lot that the buyer wants to use. Because the money the seller paid for the pass is non-refundable, the pass will be worthless to the seller once she leaves the area, but the buyer could see the pass as a valuable item.

To evaluate these packages, negotiators need to have some idea of what each item in the bargaining mix is worth in terms that can be compared across issues. The negotiator needs some way of establishing trade-offs. This may be difficult to do because different items or issues will be of different value to the negotiator and will often be measured in different terms.

As mentioned earlier, it may be desirable to find a common dimension such as dollar value or a scale of utility points to compare issues in the bargaining mix or to compare tangibles with intangibles, so that one can evaluate all items in the mix on a common dimension. Even if the fit is not perfect, any guide is better than none. Moreover, if intangibles are a key part of the bargaining mix, negotiators must know the point at which they are willing to abandon the pursuit of an intangible in favour of substantial gains on tangibles. In labour relations, for example, most issues included in the bargaining mix are converted into dollar equivalents for easier comparison and evaluation of alternative packages. However, not everything is easy to convert into money or points. Moreover, these points are only meaningful to the party establishing them, and only for as long as the points reflect the basic values and targets of the negotiator in that situation.

6. Assessing Constituents and the Social Context of the Negotiation

When people are negotiating for themselves—for example, buying a used racing bicycle or exercise machine—they can determine the bargaining mix on their own. But when people negotiate in a professional context, there may be more than two parties. First, there may be more than two negotiators at the table. Multiple parties at the table often lead to coalitions of negotiators who align with each other to win the negotiation. Second, negotiators also have constituents—bosses, superiors who make the final decision, or other parties who will evaluate and critique the solution achieved. Moreover, there may be observers of the negotiation who also watch and critique the negotiation. When one has a constituent or observers, other issues arise, such as who conducts the negotiation, who can participate in the negotiation, and who has the ultimate power to ratify negotiated agreements. Finally, negotiation occurs in a context of rules—a social system of laws, customs, common business practices, cultural norms, and political cross-pressures.

One way to assess all the key parties in a negotiation is to complete a "field analysis." Imagine that you are the captain of a soccer team, about to play a game on the field (see Figure 4.2). Assessing constituents is the same as assessing all the parties who are in the soccer stadium:

1. Who is, or should be, on the team on your side of the field? Perhaps it is just the negotiator (a one-on-one game). But perhaps you want other help: a lawyer, accountant, or other expert assistance; someone to coach you, give you moral support, or listen closely to what the other side says; a recorder or note taker.

2. Who is on the other side of the field? This is discussed in more detail in the next section.

3. Who is on the sidelines and can affect the play of the game? Who are the negotiation equivalents of owners and managers? This includes your direct superior or the person who must approve or authorize the agreement reached. Most importantly, these considerations directly affect how decisions will be made about what is acceptable or unacceptable to those on each side.

4. Who is in the stands? Who is watching the game, is interested in it, but can only indirectly affect what happens? This might include senior managers, shareholders, competitors, financial analysts, the media, or others. When multiple parties enter the negotiation—whether they are parties on the sidelines who are active in the negotiation or "interested parties" who may be impacted by the settlement—negotiations will become more complex.

5. What is going on in the broader environment in which the negotiation takes place? A number of "context" issues can affect negotiation:

   - What is the history of your relationship with the other party, and how does it affect the overall expectations they bring to this negotiation?

   - What kind of a relationship is expected or desired for the future, and how do these expectations affect the current negotiation?

   - How often do you expect to negotiate in the future—that is, how many rounds of negotiation will there be? Multi-round negotiations create issues of managing precedents, negotiating trades across time, and assuring that current agreements are enacted and monitored.

   - What are the deadlines or time limits? To extend the game metaphor, games have a finite time period that is broken down into periods or segments. Are there similar constraints that bound this negotiation?

   - What are the "rules of the game" by which this agreement will be managed? Is there a set of fixed rules, such as a legal structure that will bind and enforce contracts? What are the common and acceptable practices in the legal system in which the deal is being done? Is the rule

FIGURE 4.2 | A Field Analysis of Negotiation

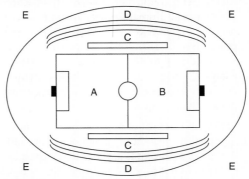

A.   The direct actors (who is on the field on our side?)

B.   The opposition actors (who is on the field on their side?)

C.   Indirect actors (who is on the sidelines?)

D.   Interested observers (who is in the stands?)

E.   Environmental factors (what is going on in the broad environment of the game—outside the stadium, but shaping and defining what happens in the stadium?)

structure itself negotiable so that you can make up your own rules about how certain problems and situations will be handled? Will one party try to impose rules unilaterally, and what can the other side do? Finally, is there a forum in which certain negotiations should take place—a public space, a private office, a lawyer's office, a courthouse—and are there dispute resolution mechanisms in place to guide how you should behave if both sides cannot agree?[9]

- What is common and acceptable practice in the ethical system in which the deal is being done? How will you decide if one party "cheats"; are there clear rules about what is and is not fair?

- What is common and acceptable practice given the culture in which the negotiation is conducted?

7. Analyzing the Other Party

Earlier in this section we discussed the importance of assigning priorities to one's own goals and objectives. Gathering information about the other party is also a critical step in preparing for negotiation. Learning the other's issues, preferences, priorities, interests, alternatives, and constraints is almost as important as determining one's own. If negotiators have not had the opportunity to meet with people from the other side, then they should find a way to start to see the negotiation from the other party's perspective or to gather information to learn about their issues, interests, and priorities. Negotiators might call the other party and speak to them prior to the formal meeting, or try to take their perspective and anticipate what they might want. It may also be possible to speak to others who know the other party or to people who have been in their situation before. The goal is to understand how they are approaching the negotiation and what they are likely to want. By comparing this assessment against your own, one can begin to define areas where there may be strong conflict (both parties have a high priority for the same thing), simple trade-offs (both parties want the same group of things but in differing priorities), or no conflict at all (both parties want very different things and both can easily have their objectives and interests met).

What information does one party need about the other party to prepare effectively? Several key pieces of background information will be of great importance, including their:

- resources, issues, and bargaining mix
- interests and needs
- resistance point and alternative(s)
- targets and objectives
- reputation and negotiation style
- constituents, social structure, and authority to make an agreement
- likely strategy and tactics

In theory, it would be extremely useful to have as much of this information as possible before negotiations occur. In reality, it may not be possible to obtain this information before the negotiation starts. If this is the case, the negotiator should plan to collect as much of this information as possible during the opening stages of the actual deliberations.

The Other Party's Resources, Issues, and Bargaining Mix The more information one can gather about the other through initial research the better. Which data are most relevant will depend on the issues and likely elements in the bargaining mix. An analysis of the other party's business history or previous negotiations, successful and otherwise, might provide useful clues. Financial data about the other party might be obtained through channels such as financial statements, the Internet, newspapers, files, company biographies, stock reports, and public records of legal judgments. One might investigate the other party's inventories. Sometimes one can learn a great deal simply by visiting the other party or speaking to his or her friends and peers. Another way to learn is to ask questions of people who have done business with the other party.[10] Even a general sense of how able the other party is at addressing and meeting our issues or needs and what issues they will bring to the bargaining table will help to predict how the process is likely to unfold.

The Other Party's Interests and Needs In addition to learning about the party's major issues and resources, one also needs to get information about his or her current interests and needs. This information may be obtained through a variety of routes:

- conducting a preliminary interview, including a broad discussion of what the other party would like to achieve in the upcoming negotiations (focus on broad interests, not just issues)
- anticipating the other party's interests (as if you were "in their shoes")
- asking others who know or have negotiated with the other party
- reading how the other party portrays himself or herself in the media

The importance of the issues or interests, along with the nature of the past relationship with the other party, will influence the depth to which one probes to get information. Although it does take time and effort to get information, the results are usually more than worth the investment because valuable information can often be gathered through a phone call or a visit.

The Other Party's Limits and Alternatives We also need to get a sense of the other party's limits and alternatives. How far can they go? What is the maximum they can give us? And what will they do if this negotiation does not succeed? Understanding the other party's limits and alternatives is important because it will give us some information about how far we can "push" them. How good are their alternatives? If the other party has a strong and viable alternative, she or he will probably be confident in negotiation, set high objectives, and be willing to push hard for those objectives. In contrast, if the other party has a weak alternative, then she or he will be more dependent on achieving a satisfactory agreement with you, and be less likely to push as hard.

Bear in mind that in a distributive negotiation, the other party may be less likely to disclose this information, and/or may misrepresent their limits and alternatives to pressure us into a deal that is better for them. In an integrative negotiation, there should be more openness between the parties, which should lead to more accurate disclosure of limits and alternatives.

The Other Party's Targets and Openings After negotiators have obtained information about the other side's issues, bargaining mix, and interests, they also need to understand his or her goals. People often think stereotypically about the other party's interests and targets; they use their own targets and values as a guide and assume that others are like themselves and want similar things. A manager who is always after a bigger paycheque may be surprised to learn that some of his subordinates are more interested in having a challenging job, schedule flexibility, or increased leisure time than they are in maximizing their salary.

How can one understand and appraise the other party's targets? Although speculation about another's objectives is seldom sufficient, most people do not gather information systematically—and they should. One of the best ways to get this information is directly from the other party. Because information about the other party's targets is so important to the strategy formulation of both parties, professional negotiators will often exchange information about targets or opening proposals days or even weeks before negotiations begin.

The Other Party's Constituents, Authority, and Social Structure As in planning Step 6, it is important to understand the broader social context in which the negotiation will occur for the other party. Who will they bring to the table? Who are they accountable to? What rules or procedures are they likely to follow? This analysis can be quite simple for purchasing a used computer, but quite complex in a large multinational negotiation.

The most direct impact of the broader social context is on the other negotiator's ability to make binding agreements. When negotiators represent others, their power to make agreements may be restricted in many ways. Sometimes a constituency stipulates that negotiators cannot make any binding agreements; often negotiators can only present proposals from the constituency or collect information and take it back to their superiors.

There are many reasons for limiting a negotiator's authority. Negotiators without decision authority cannot be won over by a persuasive presentation to commit their constituency to something they do not want. They cannot give out sensitive information carelessly. Although these limitations may be helpful to a negotiator, they can also be frustrating. The other party might ask, "Why should I speak with this person, if she cannot make a decision and may not even be well informed about what I want?" Negotiation under these circumstances can seem like an exercise in futility. When a negotiator always has to check things out with those he represents, the other party may refuse to continue until someone who has the power to answer questions and make decisions is brought to the table. Negotiating teams should think seriously about sending in a negotiator with limited authority. Although that person will not be able to make unauthorized decisions, the limited authority may frustrate the other party and create an unproductive tension in the negotiating relationship.

More broadly, the negotiator needs to know how the other party's organization makes decisions to support or ratify an agreement. Is there a senior executive who will dictate the decision? Will people vote? Or is the decision by consensus? How decisions are made can have dramatic implications for who needs to be directly influenced on the other side.

The Other Party's Reputation and Style As noted earlier, the other party's past negotiating behaviour is a good indication of how he or she will behave in the future. Even if a bargainer has had no previous experience with the other person, speaking to those who have dealt with that person in the past can be very valuable. Has the other party acted distributively or integratively?

This kind of information is an important determinant of how to approach the other party in the negotiation. Whether or not they have a reputation for being co-operative or competitive may affect the strategy pursued in the next negotiation. On the other hand, there is a potential danger in drawing conclusions from this information. Assuming that the other party will act in the future as he or she has been described as acting in the past is just that—an assumption. People can act differently in different circumstances at different times. Although gathering information about the other party's past behaviour is a reasonable starting point for making assumptions, keep in mind that people do change over time. One author on negotiation notes:

> Assumptions are potential hurdles that can move us in the wrong direction ... The reality of negotiation is that we must and should make assumptions about the opposing party ... The important thing to remember is that your assumptions are just that. They are no better than poorly educated guesses at best. Don't fall in love with your assumptions. Check them out; they are neither right nor wrong until proven so.[11]

One's impression of the other party's reputation may be based on several factors:

1. how the other party's predecessors have negotiated with you in the past,
2. how the other party has negotiated with you in the past, either in the same or in different contexts, or
3. how the other party has negotiated with others in the past.

The Other Party's Strategy and Tactics Finally, it is also helpful to gain information about the other party's intended strategy and tactics. Although it is unlikely the other party will reveal his or her strategy outright—particularly if she or he is intending to use distributive tactics—one can infer this information from data collected during preparation. Information collected about issues, objectives, reputation, style, alternatives, and authority may indicate a great deal about what strategy the other party intends to pursue. As we have noted before, negotiators will have to gather this information on an emergent basis as the negotiation unfolds; if their expectations have been incorrect, it will be necessary to recalibrate their strategic response.

8. Presenting Issues to the Other Party

One important aspect of negotiations is to present a case clearly and to provide ample supporting facts and arguments; another is to refute the other party's arguments with counterarguments.

Because of the breadth and diversity of issues that can be included in negotiations, it is not possible to specify all the procedures that can be used to assemble information. There are, however, some good general guides that can be used. A negotiator can ask these questions:

1. What facts support my point of view? What substantiates or validates this information as factual?
2. Whom may I consult or talk with to help me elaborate or clarify the facts? What records, files, or data sources exist that support my arguments?

3. Have these issues been negotiated before by others under similar circumstances? Can I consult those negotiators to determine what major arguments they used, which ones were successful, and which were not?

4. What is the other party's point of view likely to be? What are his or her interests? What arguments is the other party likely to make? How can I respond to those arguments and seek more creative positions that go further in addressing both sides' issues and interests?

5. How can I develop and present the facts so they are most convincing? What visual aids, pictures, charts, graphs, expert testimony, and the like, can be helpful or make the best case?

9. What Protocol Needs to Be Followed in this Negotiation?

A negotiator should consider a number of elements of protocol or process:

- *What agenda should we follow?* We briefly mentioned this issue in Step 6, in assessing the social structure. A negotiator may unilaterally draw up a firm list of issues well before the initial negotiation meeting. This process is valuable because it forces negotiators to think through their positions and decide on objectives. The unilateral list of issues constitutes a preliminary agenda for negotiation. It is what the negotiator wants to discuss, and the *order* or *priority* in which he wants to discuss them (e.g., least versus most important issue first).

  While the negotiator may propose agendas unilaterally, this approach has a potential risk. If the negotiator's list differs from a preset agenda or the other side's preferred list, the negotiator may bring issues to the table that the other party is unprepared to discuss or may define priorities that cannot be achieved realistically. For this reason, many professional negotiators such as labour negotiators and diplomats often exchange and negotiate the agenda in advance. They want to agree on what issues will be discussed on the agenda before engaging in the substantive discussion of those issues.

- *Where should we negotiate?* Negotiators are more comfortable on their home turf—their own office, building, or city. They know the space, they feel comfortable and relaxed, they have direct access to all the amenities— secretaries, research information, expert advice, computers, and so on. In cross-cultural negotiations (see Chapter 11), language and cultural differences may come into play, and the parties may have to travel across many time zones, stay in unfamiliar locations, eat unfamiliar food, and deal with similar potential problems. If negotiators want to minimize the advantage that comes with home turf, then they need to select neutral territory in which neither party will have an advantage. In addition, negotiators can choose the degree of formality of the environment. Formal deliberations are often held in board or conference rooms or hotel meeting rooms; informal deliberations can be held in restaurants, cocktail lounges, or private airline clubs.

- *What is the time period of the negotiation?* If negotiators expect long, protracted deliberations, they might want to negotiate the time and duration of sessions. When do we start? How long do we meet? When do we need to end? When can we call for coffee breaks or time to caucus with our team?

- *What might be done if negotiation fails?* What will happen if we deadlock? Will we go to a third-party neutral? Might we try some other techniques?

- *How will we keep track of what is agreed to?* Many negotiators don't consider the importance of recording exactly what was discussed and agreed to. Being a recording secretary may be perceived as a tedious and uninteresting job. Experienced negotiators know that this role is critical, however. First, the person with the best notes often becomes the "memory" of the session, as her or his notes are later consulted to determine what was said and discussed. Second, the person with the best notes may also volunteer to draft the initial agreement; this person may have some latitude in how the agreement is stated and what points are emphasized or deemphasized. Finally, if the agreement is highly technical or complex, one certainly wants to have the agreement reviewed by experts and specialists—lawyers, financial analysts, accountants, engineers, and so on.

  In new bargaining relationships, discussions about these procedural issues should occur *before* the major substantive issues are raised. The ease or difficulty of resolving these procedural issues can be used as litmus tests to determine how the negotiation on the larger substantive issues will proceed. If the negotiator enjoys success in these procedural negotiations, it may be easier to reach agreement later on the substantive issues.

- *How do we know whether we have a good agreement?* Finally, do we have a process in place for assuring that once the negotiation has concluded, we can systematically evaluate how the deal compares with (1) our initial plan, and (2) our sense of the best we can do given the other party and all of the structural and procedural constraints?

■ Strategy—Moving from Planning to Action

strategy
the overall plan to accomplish one's goals in a negotiation and the action sequences that will lead to the accomplishment of those goals

Once a negotiator has completed the planning process, they then move to the important next sequence: selecting and developing a strategy. Experts on business strategy define **strategy** as "the pattern or plan that integrates an organization's major targets, policies, and action sequences into a cohesive whole."[12] Applied to negotiations, strategy refers to the overall plan to accomplish one's goals in a negotiation and the action sequences that will lead to the accomplishment of those goals.

Strategy versus Tactics

tactics
short-term, adaptive moves designed to enact or pursue broad (or higher-level) strategies

How are strategy and tactics related? Although the line between strategy and tactics may seem fuzzy, one major difference is that of scale, perspective, or immediacy.[13] **Tactics** are short-term, adaptive moves designed to enact or pursue broad (or higher-level) strategies, which in turn provide stability, continuity, and direction for tactical behaviours. For example, your negotiation strategy might be integrative, designed to build and maintain a productive relationship with the other party while using a joint problem-solving approach to the issues. In pursuing this strategy, appropriate tactics include describing your interests, using open-ended questions and active listening to understand the others' interests, and inventing options for mutual gain. Tactics are subordinate to strategy; they are structured, directed, and driven by strategic considerations. In Chapters 2 and 3, we outlined the strategies of distributive bargaining and integrative negotiation, along with the associated tactics that are likely to accompany each strategy.

Unilateral versus Bilateral Approaches to Strategy

A unilateral choice is one that is made without the active involvement of the other party. Unilaterally pursued strategies can be wholly one-sided and intentionally ignorant of any information about the other negotiator. However, any reasonable strategy should also include processes for gaining information about the other party, and incorporating that information into the choice of a negotiation strategy is always useful. Therefore, while we are going to initially describe strategies as unilateral in nature, they should clearly evolve into ones that fully consider the impact of the other's strategy on one's own.

The Dual Concerns Model as a Vehicle for Describing Negotiation Strategies

The dual concerns model was developed to describe the basic orientation people take toward conflict.[14] This model proposes that individuals in conflict have two levels of related concerns: a level of concern for their own outcomes, and a level of concern for the other's outcomes. Savage, Blair, and Sorenson propose a similar model for the choice of a negotiation strategy. They propose that a negotiator's unilateral choice of strategy is reflected in the answers to two simple questions: (1) How much concern does the actor have for achieving the substantive outcomes at stake in this negotiation (substantive goals)? and (2) How much concern does the negotiator have for the current and future quality of the relationship with the other party (relationship goals)? The answers to these questions result in the mix of alternative strategies presented in Figure 4.3.[15]

FIGURE 4.3 | The Dual Concerns Model

		Substantive outcome important?	
		Yes	**No**
Relational outcome important?	**Yes**	Collaboration	Accommodation
	No	Competition	Avoidance

Alternative Situational Strategies The power of this model lies in requiring the negotiator to determine the relative importance and priority of the two dimensions in the desired settlement. As Figure 4.3 shows, answers to these two questions suggest at least four types of initial strategies for negotiators: competition, collaboration, accommodation, and avoidance. A strong interest in achieving only substantive outcomes—getting this deal, winning this negotiation, with little or no regard for the effect on the relationship or on subsequent exchanges with the other party—tends to support a competitive (distributive) strategy. A strong interest in achieving only the relationship goals—building, preserving, or enhancing a good relationship with the other party—suggests an accommodation strategy. If both substance and relationship are important, the negotiator should pursue a collaborative (integrative) strategy. Finally, if achieving neither substantive outcomes nor an enhanced relationship is important, the party might be best served by avoiding negotiation. Each of these different strategic approaches also has different implications for negotiation planning and preparation.[16] We discuss both non-engagement and engagement strategies next.

The Non-engagement Strategy: Avoidance Avoidance may serve a number of strategic negotiation purposes. In fact, there are many reasons why negotiators might choose not to negotiate:

- If one is able to meet one's needs without negotiating at all, it may make sense to use an avoidance strategy.

- It simply may not be worth the time and effort to negotiate (although there are sometimes reasons to negotiate in such situations; see the section on accommodation, below).

- The decision to negotiate is closely related to the desirability of available alternatives—the outcomes that can be achieved if negotiations don't work out. In Chapter 2, we discussed the role that resistance points play in defining a strategy and the possibility that alternative deals are available; in Chapters 2 and 3, we explored the key role of a BATNA in evaluating the value of a particular agreement. A negotiator with very strong alternatives has considerable power because he or she doesn't need this negotiation to succeed to achieve a satisfactory outcome. Having weak alternatives puts negotiators at a disadvantage. The presence of an alternative can influence the decision about whether to avoid negotiation in two ways. First, the negotiator with a strong alternative may wish to avoid negotiation strictly on efficiency grounds—it is simply quicker and easier to take the alternative than to get involved in a negotiation. But having a weak alternative may also suggest avoiding negotiation—once negotiations begin, the pressure of the negotiation process may lead to a poor outcome, which the negotiator may feel obligated to accept because the alternative is also very poor.

Active-Engagement Strategies: Competition, Collaboration, and Accommodation Competition and collaboration were described extensively in the last two chapters. Competition is described throughout this book as distributive, or win-lose, bargaining, and collaboration as integrative, or win-win, negotiation.

Accommodation is as much a win-lose strategy as competition, although it has a decidedly different image—it involves an imbalance of outcomes, but in the opposite direction ("I lose, you win" as opposed to "I win, you lose"). As Figure 4.3 shows, an accommodative strategy may be appropriate when the negotiator considers the relationship outcome more important than the substantive outcome. In other words, the negotiator wants to let the other win, keep the other happy, or not endanger the relationship by pushing hard to achieve some goal on the substantive issues. This strategy is often used when the primary goal of the exchange is to build or strengthen the relationship (or the other party) and the negotiator is willing to sacrifice the outcome. An accommodative strategy may also be necessary if the negotiator expects the relationship to extend past a single negotiation episode. The idea is that if "I lose and you win" this time, over multiple negotiations in the relationship the win-lose accounts will balance. In any long-term social relationship, it is probably healthy for one negotiator or the other to accept a suboptimal outcome in a given negotiation while expecting reciprocal accommodation (tit for tat) from the other negotiator in the future. Such reciprocity has been called the glue that holds social groups together.[17]

How do these three strategies—competition, collaboration, and accommodation—differ? Table 4.2[18] summarizes the three types of strategies (distributive, integrative, and accommodative), and compares and contrasts them across a number of different dimensions.

In addition to their positive characteristics, as described in the table, each of these three negotiation strategies also has certain predictable drawbacks if applied blindly, thoughtlessly, or inflexibly:

- Distributive strategies tend to create "we-they" or "superiority-inferiority" patterns and may lead to distortions in judgment regarding the other side's contributions and efforts, as well as to distortions in perceptions of the other side's values, needs, and positions (see the discussion of framing biases in Chapter 5).

- If a negotiator pursues an integrative strategy without regard to the other's strategy, then the other may manipulate and exploit the collaborator and take advantage of the good faith and goodwill being demonstrated. Blind pursuit of an integrative process can also lead negotiators to cease being accountable to their constituencies in favour of pursuit of the negotiation process for its own sake. For example, negotiators who approach the process with an aggressive "we can solve any problem" attitude may produce an agreement that is unacceptable to their constituency (e.g., their companies), which will then be rejected and force the negotiator to resume negotiations.

- Accommodative strategies may generate a pattern of constantly giving in to keep the other happy or to avoid a fight. This pattern establishes a precedent that is hard to break. It could also lead the other to a false sense of well-being due to the satisfaction that comes with the "harmony" of a good relationship, which may completely ignore all the giveaways on substance. Over time, this imbalance is unlikely to persist, but efforts to stop the giving or restore the balance may be met with surprise and resentment.

It is also useful to remember that in presenting these strategies we are describing pure forms that do not capture the mixture of issues and motivations that actually characterize the evolution of most actual negotiation strategies. Just as most conflicts are neither purely competitive nor purely co-operative, most negotiation strategies reflect a variety of goals, intentions, and situational constraints that tend to make any "pure" strategy difficult to follow.[19]

TABLE 4.2 | Characteristics of Different Engagement Strategies

Aspect	Competition (Distributive Bargaining)	Collaboration (Integrative Negotiation)	Accommodative Negotiation
Payoff structure	Usually a fixed amount of resources to be divided	Usually a variable amount of resources to be divided	Usually a fixed amount of resources to be divided
Goal pursuit	Pursuit of own goals at the expense of those of others	Pursuit of goals held jointly with others	Subordination of own goals in favour of those of others
Relationships	Short-term focus; parties do not expect to work together in the future	Long-term focus; parties expect to work together in the future	May be short-term (let the other win to keep the peace) or long-term (let the other win to encourage reciprocity in the future)
Primary motivation	Maximize own outcome	Maximize joint outcome	Maximize others' outcome or let them gain to enhance relationship
Trust and openness	Secrecy and defensiveness; high trust in self, low trust in others	Trust and openness, active listening, joint exploration of alternatives	One party relatively open, exposing own vulnerabilities to the other
Knowledge of needs	Parties know own needs but conceal or misrepresent them; neither party lets the other know real needs	Parties know and convey real needs while seeking and responding to needs of the other	One party is overresponsive to other's needs so as to repress own needs
Predictability	Parties use unpredictability and surprise to confuse other side	Parties are predictable and flexible when appropriate, trying not to surprise	One party's actions totally predictable, always catering to other side
Aggressiveness	Parties use threats and bluffs, trying to keep the upper hand	Parties share information honestly, treat each other with understanding and respect	One party gives up on own position to mollify the other
Solution search behaviour	Parties make effort to appear committed to position, using argumentation and manipulation of the other	Parties make effort to find mutually satisfying solutions, using logic, creativity, and constructiveness	One party makes effort to find ways to accommodate the other
Success measures	Success enhanced by creating bad image of the other; increased levels of hostility and strong in-group loyalty	Success demands abandonment of bad images and consideration of ideas on their merit	Success determined by minimizing or avoiding conflict and smoothing all hostility; own feelings ignored in favour of harmony
Evidence of unhealthy extreme	Unhealthy extreme reached when one party assumes total zero-sum game; defeating the other becomes a goal in itself	Unhealthy extreme reached when one subsumes all self-interest in the common good, losing self-identity and self-responsibility	Unhealthy extreme reached when abdication to other is complete, at expense of personal and/or constituent goals
Key attitude	Key attitude is "I win, you lose"	Key attitude is "What's the best way to address the needs of all parties?"	Key attitude is "You win, I lose"
Remedy for breakdown	If impasse occurs, mediator or arbitrator may be needed	If difficulties occur, a group dynamics facilitator may be needed	If behaviour becomes chronic, party becomes negotiationally bankrupt

Source: Adapted and expanded from Robert W. Johnston, "Negotiation Strategies: Different Strokes for Different folks," Personnel 59 (March–April 1982), pp. 38–39. Used with permission of the author.

Planning is a critically important activity in negotiation. As we noted at the outset, however, negotiators frequently fail to plan for a variety of reasons. Effective planning allows negotiators to design a road map that will guide them to agreement. While this map may frequently need to be modified and updated as discussions with the other side proceed and as the world around the negotiation changes, working from the map is far more effective than attempting to work without it. A negotiator who carefully plans will make an effort to do the following:

1. Understand the key issues that must be resolved in the upcoming negotiation.

2. Assemble all the issues together and understand the complexity of the bargaining mix.

3. Understand and define the key interests at stake that underlie the issues.

4. Define the limits (points where we will walk away) and alternatives (other deals we could do if this deal does not work out).

5. Clarify the targets to be achieved and the opening points—where we will begin the discussion.

6. Understand my constituents and what they expect of me.

7. Understand the other party in the negotiation—their goals, issues, strategies, interests, limits, alternatives, targets, openings, and authority.

8. Plan the process by which I will present and "sell" my ideas to the other party (and perhaps to my own constituency).

9. Define the important points of protocol in the process—the agenda, who will be at the table or observing the negotiation, where and when we will negotiate, and so on.

When negotiators are able to consider and evaluate each of these factors, they will know what they want and will have a clear sense of direction on how to proceed; in other words, they will be in a better position to formulate the right strategy. This sense of direction, and the confidence derived from it, is a very important factor in affecting negotiating outcomes.

Key Terms

Strategy, p. 84

Tactics, p. 84

Perception, Cognition, and Emotion

The basic building blocks of all social encounters include perception (how we make sense of our environment), cognition (how we process information) and emotion (internal affective states). Each of these factors can play a role in shaping negotiation interactions and outcomes, often in subtle and difficult-to-observe ways. A working knowledge of how humans perceive and process information is important to understanding why people behave the way they do during negotiations.

Consider the case of the Dionne quintuplets, the first set of quintuplets to ever survive childbirth. Born in rural Ontario in 1934, they were swiftly removed from the family home by the provincial government and placed in a public viewing facility (known as Quintland), where they were observed by more than 3 million visitors before returning home almost a decade later.[1] A book by Canadian writer Pierre Burton documents their painful upbringing, which he calls a sideshow, and the difficult and tragic transition to adulthood. A trust fund with millions of dollars was created to support the girls, but, under mysterious circumstances, the money vanished.[2]

By 1998 there were only three quintuplets remaining alive. At that time, they were living together in Montreal on a pension of only $700 per month, and had been negotiating with the Ontario government for financial support for more than three years. In February 1998 the government made what it called a "take it or leave it" offer of $2000 per month per sister for the rest of their lives. Tied to this offer was a condition that if the sisters went public the offer would be withdrawn. In somewhat of a surprise move, the media-shy sisters did go public, announcing they hoped for "justice, not charity," an inquiry into their treatment and the handling of the trust fund, as well as financial restitution.

The government, led by then-Premier Mike Harris, initially stated the offer was final. Then, they announced that the offer would be back on the table. In the face of massive public support for the sisters, the government was forced to continue negotiations with the sisters and their lawyer. After one week of intense negotiations, a settlement of $4 million was reached. In addition, the premier travelled to Montreal to issue a personal apology to the remaining sisters. Newspaper reports at the time revealed that the premier was actively involved in the negotiations and the aggressive stance came directly from him.

What does this story have to do with perception, cognition, and emotion? The answer is: a great deal. We will return to the story of the Dionne quintuplets throughout the chapter to illustrate several key points.

■ Perception

Perception Defined

perception
the process by which individuals connect to their environment by ascribing meaning to messages and events

Negotiators approach each situation guided by their perceptions of past situations and current attitudes and behaviours. **Perception** is the process by which individuals connect to their environment by ascribing meaning to messages and events. Perception is strongly influenced by the perceiver's current state of mind, role, and comprehension of earlier communications.[3] Other parties' perceptions, the environment, and the perceiver's own dispositions are also important influences on one's ability to interpret with accuracy what the other party is saying and meaning. We will now examine in more detail how perceptions are created and how they affect what happens in negotiation.

Perception is a "sense-making" process; people interpret their environment so that they can respond appropriately (see Figure 5.1). Environments are typically complex—they present a large number and variety of stimuli, each having different properties such as magnitude, colour, shape, texture, and relative novelty. This complexity makes it impossible to process all the available information, so perception becomes selective, tuning in on some stimuli while tuning out others. As a result, there are a number of perceptual "shortcuts" that allow people to process information more readily. Unfortunately, the perceptual efficiencies that result may come at the expense of accuracy.

FIGURE 5.1 | The Perceptual Process

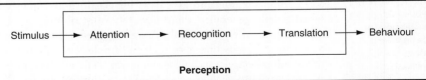

Perceptual Distortion

In any given negotiation, the perceiver's own needs, desires, motivations, and personal experiences may create a predisposition about the other party. This is cause for concern when it leads to biases and errors in perception and subsequent communication. We will discuss four major perceptual errors: stereotyping, halo effects, selective perception, and projection. Stereotyping and halo effects are examples of perceptual distortion by generalization: small amounts of perceptual information are used to draw large conclusions about individuals. Selective perception and projection are, in contrast, forms of distortion that involve anticipating certain attributes and qualities in another person. The perceiver filters and distorts information to arrive at a consistent view.

stereotyping
when one individual assigns attributes to another solely on the basis of the other's membership in a particular social or demographic category

Stereotyping is a very common distortion of the perceptual process. It occurs when one individual assigns attributes to another solely on the basis of the other's membership in a particular social or demographic category. Stereotypes are formed about a wide variety of different groups, for example, the younger generation, males or females, Italians or Germans, or people of different races, religions, or sexual orientations. In each case, stereotypes tend to be formed in the same way. People assign an individual to a group based on one piece of perceptual information (e.g., the individual is young or old); then they assign a broad range of other characteristics of the group to this individual (e.g., "Old people are conservative; this person is old and therefore is conservative" or "Young people are disrespectful; this person is young and therefore is disrespectful"). There may be no factual basis for the conclusion that this particular older individual is conservative; the conclusion is based on the generalization of qualities that have been attributed—accurately or not—to the larger group. Applying other traits associated with the category to this particular individual further compounds the error.

The government's initial response to the Dionne sisters highlights this point. As leader of the Progressive Conservative party of Ontario, Mike Harris moved the party away from its politically centrist roots to a more conservative ideological basis. Part of this philosophy was the view that people should not rely on government handouts. Observers at the time noted the government was perceiving the Dionne sisters in the same way it perceived welfare recipients—as liabilities on the public purse.

Once formed, stereotypes are often highly resistant to change. The simple process of using a single criterion—even an arbitrary one—to divide people into groups encourages group members to begin to define themselves as "we" and the other group as "they" and then to make evaluative comparisons between them. Individuals are more likely to resort to stereotyping under certain conditions. Examples include time pressure, cognitive stress, and mood,[4] as well as when conflicts involve values, ideologies, and direct competition for resources among groups.[5]

halo effects
when people generalize about a variety of attributes based on the knowledge of one attribute of an individual

Halo effects in perception are similar to stereotypes. Rather than using a person's group membership as a basis for classification, however, halo effects occur when people generalize about a variety of attributes based on the knowledge of one attribute of an individual.[6] A smiling person is judged to be more honest than a frowning or scowling person, for example, even though there is no consistent relationship between smiling and honesty. Halo effects may be positive or negative. A good attribute may be generalized so that people are seen in a very positive light, whereas a negative attribute has the reverse effect. The more prominent the attribute is in influencing the overall judgment about an individual, the more likely that it will be used to cast further information into a perspective consistent with the initial judgment. Halo effects are most likely to occur in perception (1) when there is very little experience with a person along some dimension (and hence generalization occurs about that person from knowledge of him or her in other contexts),

(2) when the person is well known, and (3) when the qualities have strong moral implications.[7]

Halo effects and stereotypes are common hazards in negotiation. Negotiators are apt to form rapid impressions of each other based on very limited initial information, such as appearance, group membership, or initial statements. Negotiators tend to maintain these judgments as they get to know each other better, fitting each piece of new information into some consistent pattern. Finally, the mere suggestion that the other party can be viewed in moral terms—for example, honest or dishonest, ethical or unethical—is likely to affect the perception of a wide variety of their other attributes.[8]

selective perception
when the perceiver singles out certain information that supports or reinforces a prior belief and filters out information that does not confirm that belief

Selective perception occurs when the perceiver singles out certain information that supports or reinforces a prior belief and filters out information that does not confirm that belief. Selective perception has the effect of perpetuating stereotypes or halo effects: After forming quick judgments about individuals on the basis of limited information, people may then filter out further evidence that might disconfirm the judgment. An initial smile from the other party, which leads the negotiator to believe that he or she is honest or co-operative, might also lead the negotiator to downplay any of that party's statements that demonstrate an intention to be crafty or competitive. If the negotiator perceives the same initial smile as a smirk, then the negotiator may downplay the other party's offers to establish an honest and co-operative relationship. In both cases, the negotiator's own biases—the predisposition to view the smile as honest or dishonest—are likely to affect how the other party's behaviour is perceived and interpreted.

projection
when people assign to others the characteristics or feelings that they possess themselves

Projection occurs when people assign to others the characteristics or feelings that they possess themselves. Projection usually arises out of a need to protect one's own self-concept—to see oneself as consistent and good. Negotiators may assume that the other party would respond in the same manner they would if positions were reversed. For instance, if a negotiator is really bothered by delays in negotiations but needs to tell the other party that there will be an unavoidable delay, the negotiator may expect the other party to exhibit frustration at the announcement. While it is possible that the other party will be frustrated, it is also possible that he or she will welcome the delay as an opportunity to complete work on a different project, and that any frustration was only a projection from the negotiator's mind.

Framing

frame
the subjective mechanism through which people evaluate and make sense out of situations, leading them to pursue or avoid subsequent actions

A key issue in perception and negotiation is framing. A **frame** is the subjective mechanism through which people evaluate and make sense out of situations, leading them to pursue or avoid subsequent actions.[9] Framing has become a popular concept among social scientists who study cognitive processes, decision making, persuasion, and communication. The popularity of framing has come with the recognition that often two or more people who are involved in the same situation or in a complex problem see it or define it in different ways.[10] For example, two people walk into a room full of people and see different things: One (the extrovert) sees a great party; the other (the introvert) sees a scary and intimidating unfriendly crowd. Because people have different backgrounds, experiences, expectations, and needs, they frame people, events, and processes differently.

Frames are important in negotiation because "people can encounter the same dispute and perceive it in very different ways as a result of their backgrounds, professional training, or past experiences."[11] A frame is a way of labelling these different individual interpretations of the situation. Management theorist Mary Parker Follett, who was one of the first to write about integrative negotiation, observed that parties who arrive at a joint agreement achieve unity "not from giving in [compromise] but from 'getting the desires of each side into one field of vision.'"[12] Thus, frames emerge and converge as the parties talk about their preferences and priorities; they allow the parties to begin to develop a shared or common definition of the issues related to a situation and a process for resolving them.

"Now, when we explain this to Mom and Dad, let's make sure we give it the right spin."

© 1998; Reprinted courtesy of Bunny Hoest and Parade Magazine.

How parties frame and define a negotiating issue or problem is a clear reflection of what they define as critical to negotiating objectives, what their expectations and preferences are for certain possible outcomes, what information they seek and use to argue their case, the procedures they use to try to present their case, and the manner in which they evaluate the outcomes actually achieved.[13] Understanding framing dynamics helps negotiators consciously elevate the framing process, thereby better controlling it; negotiators who understand how they are framing a problem may understand more completely what they are doing, what the other party is doing, and how to have more control over the negotiation process. Finally, both current theory and a stream of supportive empirical research show that frames may be malleable and, if so, can be shaped or reshaped as a function of information and communication during negotiation. In the next few pages, we will describe frames in more detail and illustrate with examples how knowledge of framing can assist you in your negotiations.

Frames in Negotiation

One of the ways framing affects negotiations is by influencing how negotiators interpret available options. Our understanding of framing has its origins in the classic decision making research by Tversky and Kahneman.[14] To illustrate, in one study they presented a group of participants with the following problem:

> The country is preparing for the outbreak of an unusual new disease that is expected to kill six hundred people. Two alternative programs are being considered. Which would you favour?

The participants were split into two groups. One group was given the following two choices:

1. If Program A is adopted, two hundred people will be saved.
2. If Program B is adopted, there is a one-third probability that all will be saved and a two-thirds probability that none will be saved.

In this group, 76% chose Program A and 24% chose Program B. A second group was also presented with two choices:

1. If Program A is adopted, four hundred people will die.
2. If Program B is adopted, there is a one-third probability that no one will die and a two-thirds probability that all will die.

In this group, only 13% chose Program A and 87% chose Program B. What makes this result so interesting is the fact that the choices presented to both groups had the same probability of saving lives. In contrast, the way the choices were *framed* was different. The first group's choices were framed in terms of lives saved, while the second group's choices were framed in terms of lives lost.

This type of frame, often referred to as a *gain/loss frame*, affects human behaviour and choice largely through its effect on people's risk preferences. To understand this process more fully, we need to introduce the concept of a reference point. According to Kahneman and Tversky, a **reference point** is an arbitrary point used to evaluate an alternative as either a gain or a loss. In the new disease problem, participants who were asked to focus on lives saved tended to look at the problem from a perspective that focused on gains. Thus, the choices they made tended to be risk averse. In contrast, the group with the reference point that focused on lives lost tended to make choices that were risk seeking, largely because they looked at the situation from a perspective of losses.

Framing effects are quite common in negotiation situations. Just imagine what it would be like to be an entrepreneur faced with the choice to sell or not sell the business you started from scratch. If a professional and independent evaluator appraised the value of the business at one million dollars, how would you react under these two scenarios? In scenario one, you had the business appraised one year ago and were told it was worth $800,000. In scenario two, you also had the business appraised one year ago, but this time the value was $1.2 million. Would this affect how you negotiated today?

Chances are, it would. In scenario one the value has increased $200,000 (placing you in a gain frame), while in scenario two the value has decreased by the same amount (placing you in a loss frame). Even though the current appraised value of your business is one million dollars, previous values are likely to affect how you feel about offers as you are negotiating. Being in a loss frame is likely to make you more risk seeking. In this case, you might reject a reasonable offer solely because you tell yourself "I'm not taking a loss on the sale."

Framing effects might also have played a role in the Dionne quintuplets situation. If the government's ideology was so opposed to using public money for purposes of restitution, then any amount of money paid to the sisters would be a loss. Because loss frames are associated with risky behaviour, it is plausible that the government placed its reference point at "paying nothing" and took the risky option of taking a hard line.

reference point
an arbitrary point used to evaluate an alternative as either a gain or a loss

Remember that framing effects can affect your counterpart's behaviour as well as your own. You should be on the lookout for signs that your counterpart is adopting either a gain or a loss frame. For example, in a labour-management negotiation the way outcomes are framed can determine subsequent concessionary behaviour. If you are representing management, you should couch your proposals in terms of what the other side stands to gain. You might also want to emphasize the inherent risk in the negotiation situation. Watch out for telltale signs of negative frames, such as your counterpart's use of negative language or mention of losses. Remember, you have the ability to influence the way they perceive the situation.

To this point, we have emphasized the impact of gain and loss frames. Although this particular type of frame is common and frequently encountered, there are other types of frames you should watch for. The following are examples of other frame types:

1. *Outcome frame*—a party's predisposition to achieving a specific result or outcome from the negotiation. To the degree that a negotiator has a specific, preferred outcome he or she wants to achieve, the dominant frame may be to focus all strategy, tactics, and communication toward getting that outcome. Parties who have a strong outcome frame are more likely to engage primarily in distributive (win-lose or lose-lose) negotiations than in other types of negotiations.

2. *Aspiration frame*—a predisposition toward satisfying a broader set of interests or needs in negotiation. Rather than focusing on a specific outcome, the negotiator tries to ensure that his or her basic interests, needs, and concerns are met. Parties who have a strong aspiration frame are more likely to be primarily engaged in integrative (win-win) negotiation than in other types.

3. *Process frame*—how the parties will go about resolving their dispute. Negotiators who have a strong process frame are less likely than others to be concerned about the specific negotiation issues but more concerned about how the deliberations will proceed, or how the dispute should be managed. When the major concerns are largely procedural rather than substantive, process frames will be strong.

4. *Identity frame*—how the parties define "who they are." Parties are members of a number of different social groups—gender (male), religion (Roman Catholic), ethnic origin (Italian-Canadian), place of birth (Calgary), current place of residence (Montreal), and the like. These are only a few of the categories people can use to define themselves and distinguish themselves from others.

In summary, value differences between the parties, differences in personality, power differences, and differences in the background and social context of the negotiators may lead the parties to adopt different frames. As an example, see Negotiation Point 5.1.

The Frame of an Issue Changes as the Negotiation Evolves The definition of issues at stake in a negotiation may change as the discussion evolves. Rather than focus only on the dominant frames that parties hold at the beginning of a negotiation, it is also important to consider patterns of change (transformation) that occur as parties communicate with each other. For example, one classic study of legal

5.1

Chinese Negotiation Frames

While skilled negotiators know that their and their opponents' negotiation frames are shaped through experience and culture, few stop to critically examine the cultural elements that shape others' perceptions about conflict. For example, Catherine Tinsley of Georgetown University has identified the five concepts from Chinese culture that those attempting to negotiate in China should recognize:

- *Social linkage.* The Chinese believe that people should be viewed in the context of their larger social groups rather than as isolated individuals.

- *Harmony.* Because people are inherently imbedded in their social network, peaceful coexistence is highly valued.

- *Roles.* To maintain social harmony, people must understand and abide by the requirements of their role in the relationship network. Roles specify duties, power, and privileges while specifying where in the relational hierarchy an individual falls.

- *Reciprocal obligations.* Each role specifies the obligations that people expect to fulfill and receive within the social network. These obligations persist over time, solidifying the relational network across generations.

- *Face.* The value the Chinese place on saving "face" is central to their perception of social interaction. Face is lost if an individual acts in a manner that is inconsistent with his or her role or fails to fulfill reciprocal obligations. Face is so valued that the threat of losing it is the primary force that ensures fulfillment of obligations and, consequently, continuance of the relational hierarchy.

Negotiators approaching discussions with the Chinese would do well to consider the perspective on conflict that these cultural realities have created. For example, individual negotiators often rely on the power of their personal network to achieve desired ends. This perspective, which Tinsley called the "relational bargaining frame," encourages parties to augment their power by both soliciting the support of powerful people and arguing for the social legitimacy of their position. While those from a more individualistic culture might reject out of hand the argument that a proposed settlement would be unpopular, such an argument would have great power in the more collectivist Chinese culture. Similarly, parties in the relational frame would be more likely to solicit outside opinions. A powerful strategy might be to encourage parties to align their positions to be compatible with the goals of a greater social collective.

Source: C. H. Tinsley, "Understanding Conflict in a Chinese Cultural Context," in R. Bies, R. Lewicki, and B. Sheppard (eds.), *Research on Negotiation in Organizations 6*, pp. 209–25 (Stamford CT: JAI, 1997).

disputes suggested that these disputes tend to be transformed through a process of "naming, blaming, and claiming."[15] *Naming* occurs when parties in a dispute label or identify a problem and characterize what it is about. *Blaming* occurs next, as the parties try to determine who or what caused the problem. Finally, *claiming* occurs when the individual who has the problem decides to confront, file charges, or take some other action against the individual or organization that caused the problem.

Frames are shaped by conversations that the parties have with each other about the issues in the bargaining mix. Although both parties may approach the discussion with initial frames that resemble the categories described earlier, the ongoing interaction between them shapes the discussion as each side attempts to argue from his or her own perspective or counter-argue against the other's perspective. At least four factors can affect how the conversation is shaped:

1. Negotiators tend to argue for *stock issues*, or concerns that are raised every time the parties negotiate. For example, wage issues or working conditions may always be discussed in a labour negotiation; the union always raises them, and management always expects them to be raised and is ready to respond. Negotiations over stock issues can be restructured to include more or fewer issues, increasing the likelihood that a resolution can be found.[16]

2. Each party attempts to make the *best possible case* for his or her preferred position or perspective. One party may assemble facts, numbers, testimony, or other compelling evidence to persuade the other party of the validity of his or her argument or perspective. Early in a negotiation it is not uncommon for the parties to "talk past each other," with each trying to impose a certain perspective as the dominant conversation rather than listening to the other's case and trying to refute it. Each party is interested in controlling the conversation by controlling the focus; however, each party's argument eventually begins to shift as they both focus on either refuting the other's case or modifying their own arguments on the basis of the other's arguments.[17]

3. Frames may define major *shifts and transitions* in a complex overall negotiation. In diplomatic negotiations, successful bargaining has been described as a two-stage process called "formula/detail."[18] One article described this process as follows: "Parties first seek a compromise that establishes some formula or framework of broad objectives and principles. Then they draw out a number of detailed points of agreement. The framework defines the subset of points that is debatable, while the detail phase permits the debate and packaging of specific issues to construct a settlement acceptable to both sides."[19] Some have described the formula-detail model in three stages: (1) diagnosis, in which the parties recognize the need for change or improvement, review relevant history, and prepare positions; (2) formula, in which the parties attempt to develop a shared perception of the conflict, including common terms, referents, and fairness criteria; and (3) detail, in which the parties work out operational details consistent with the basic formula.[20]

4. Finally, *multiple agenda items* operate to shape issue development. Although parties usually have one or two major objectives, priorities, or core issues, there are often a number of lesser or secondary items. When brought into the conversation, these secondary concerns often transform the conversation about the primary issues. In a careful analysis of teacher negotiations in two school districts, one researcher showed how issues became transformed throughout a negotiation.[21] For instance, an issue of scheduling was reframed as an issue of teacher preparation time, and an issue on the cost of personal insurance became transformed into an issue about the extent of insurance benefits.

One of the most important aspects of framing as issue development is the process of reframing, or the manner in which the thrust, tone, and focus of a conversation change as the parties engage in it. Reframing is a dynamic process that may occur many times in a conversation. It comes as parties challenge each other, as they present their own case or refute the other's, or as they search for ways to reconcile seemingly incompatible perspectives. Reframing can also occur as one party uses metaphors, analogies, or specific cases to illustrate a point, leading the other to use the metaphor or case as a new way to define the situation. Reframing may be done intentionally by one side or the other, or it may emerge from the conversation as one person's challenges fuel the other's creativity and imagination. In either case, the parties often propose a new way to approach the problem.

Summary of Framing Framing is about focusing, shaping, and organizing the world around us—making sense of complex realities and defining them in ways that are meaningful to us. We discussed the different type of frames that exist and their importance for understanding strategic choices in negotiation. We can offer the following prescriptive advice about problem framing for the negotiator:

- *Frames shape what the parties define as the key issues and how they talk about them.* To the degree that the parties have preferences about the issues to be covered, outcomes to be achieved, or processes to be addressed, they should work to ensure that their own preferred frames are accepted and acknowledged by the others.
- *Both parties have frames.* When the frames match, the parties are more likely to focus on common issues and a common definition of the situation; when they do not match, communication between the parties is likely to be difficult and incomplete.
- *Frames are controllable, at least to some degree.* If negotiators understand what frame they are using and what frame the other party is using, they may be able to shift the conversation toward the frame they would like the other to adopt.
- *Conversations change and transform frames in ways negotiators may not be able to predict but may be able to control.* As parties discuss an issue, introduce arguments and evidence, and advocate a course of action, the conversation changes, and the frame may change as well. It is critical for negotiators to track this shift and understand where it might lead.
- *Certain frames are more likely than others to lead to certain types of processes and outcomes.* For example, parties who are competitive are likely to have positive identity frames of themselves, negative characterization frames of each other, and a preference for more win-lose processes of resolving their dispute. Recognizing these tendencies may empower the parties to be able to reframe their views of themselves, the other, or the dispute resolution mechanism to pursue a process that will resolve the conflict more productively.

■ Cognitive Biases in Negotiation

So far we have examined how information is perceived, filtered, distorted, and framed. In this section, we examine how negotiators use information to make decisions during the negotiation. Rather than being perfect processors of information, it is quite clear that negotiators have a tendency to make systematic errors when they process information.[22] These errors, collectively labelled cognitive biases, tend to impede negotiator performance; they include (1) the irrational escalation of commitment, (2) the mythical belief that the issues under negotiation are all fixed-pie, (3) the process of anchoring and adjustment in decision making, (4) issue and problem framing, (5) the availability of information, (6) the winner's curse, (7) negotiator overconfidence, (8) the law of small numbers, (9) self-serving biases, (10) the endowment effect, (11) the tendency to ignore others' cognitions, and (12) the process of reactive devaluation. Next, we will discuss each of these in more detail.

1. Irrational Escalation of Commitment

Negotiators sometimes maintain commitment to a course of action even when that commitment constitutes irrational behaviour on their part. This is an example of a broader psychological phenomenon known as "escalation of commitment," which is the tendency for an individual to make decisions that stick with a failing course of action.[23] Classic examples include a country that continues to pour military resources into an unwinnable armed conflict, or an investor who continues to put more money into a declining stock in hopes its fortunes will turn ("throwing good money after bad," as escalation of commitment is sometimes colloquially described). Escalation of commitment is due in part to biases in individual perception and judgment. Once a course of action is decided, negotiators often seek supportive (confirming) evidence for that choice, while ignoring or failing to seek disconfirming evidence. Initial commitments become set in stone (see the section on anchoring and adjustment, below), and a desire for consistency prevents negotiators from changing them. This desire for consistency is often exacerbated by a desire to save face and to maintain an impression of expertise or control in front of others. No one likes to admit error or failure, especially when the other party may perceive doing so as a weakness. One way to combat these tendencies is to have an advisor serve as a reality checkpoint—someone who is not consumed by the "heat of the moment" and who can warn negotiators when they inadvertently begin to behave irrationally.

2. Mythical Fixed-Pie Beliefs

Many negotiators assume that all negotiations involve a fixed pie.[24] Negotiators often approach integrative negotiation opportunities as zero-sum situations or win-lose exchanges. Those who believe in the mythical fixed pie assume there is no possibility for integrative settlements and mutually beneficial trade-offs, and they suppress efforts to search for them.[25] In a salary negotiation, the job applicant who assumes that salary is the only issue may insist on $45,000 when the employer is offering $42,000. Only when the two parties discuss the possibilities further do they discover that moving expenses and starting date can also be negotiated, which may facilitate resolution of the salary issue.

The tendency to see negotiation in fixed-pie terms varies depending on how people view the nature of a given conflict situation.[26] Negotiators focusing on personal interests are most likely to come under the influence of fixed-pie beliefs and approach the situation competitively. Negotiators focusing on values are less likely to see the problem in fixed-pie terms and more inclined to approach the situation co-operatively.

3. Anchoring and Adjustment

We first introduced the concept of the anchoring effect in Chapter 2 because it has such a powerful impact on outcomes in distributive situations. Cognitive biases in anchoring and adjustment are related to the effect of the standard (or anchor) against which subsequent adjustments are made during negotiation. The choice of an anchor (e.g., an initial offer or an intended goal) might well be based on faulty or incomplete information and thus be misleading in and of itself. However, once the anchor is defined, parties tend to treat it as a real, valid benchmark by which to adjust other judgments, such as the size of one side's opening offer.[27] For example, research shows that real estate agents' house appraisals are strongly affected by its asking price.[28] The asking price serves as a convenient anchor to use in appraising the value of the house. Goals in negotiation—whether set realistically or carelessly—can also serve as anchors. These anchors may be visible or invisible to the other party (a published market price versus an uncommunicated expectation), and, similarly, the person who holds them may do so consciously or unconsciously (a specific expectation versus an unexamined, unquestioned expectation or norm). Thorough preparation, along with the use of a devil's advocate or reality check, can help prevent errors of anchoring and adjustment.

4. Issue Framing and Risk

As we discussed earlier in this chapter, a frame is a perspective or point of view that people use when they gather information and solve problems. Frames can lead people to seek, avoid, or be neutral about risk in negotiation. The way a negotiation is framed can make negotiators more or less risk averse or risk seeking. For instance, people respond quite differently when they are negotiating to "gain" something rather than to "not lose" something.[29]

This positive/negative framing process is important because the same offer can elicit dramatically different courses of action depending on how it is framed in gain-loss terms. Negotiations in which the outcomes are negatively framed tend to produce fewer concessions and reach fewer agreements, and negotiators perceive outcomes as less fair than negotiations in which the outcomes are positively framed.[30] Remedies for the potentially pernicious effects of framing are similar to those we have mentioned for other cognitive biases (e.g., sufficient information, thorough analysis, and reality checks) but can be difficult to achieve because frames are often tied to deeply held values and beliefs or to other anchors that are hard to detect.

5. Availability of Information

Negotiators must also be concerned with the potential bias caused by the availability of information or how easy information is to retrieve—that is, how easily it can be recalled and used to inform or evaluate a process or a decision. In negotiation, the availability bias operates when information that is presented in vivid, colourful, or attention-getting ways becomes easy to recall, and thus also becomes central and critical in evaluating events and options. Information presented through a particularly clear chart, diagram, or formula (even one that is oversimplified) will likely be believed more readily than information presented in a confusing or detailed format—regardless of the accuracy of each. The availability of information also affects negotiation through the use of established search patterns. If negotiators have a favourite way of collecting information or looking for key signals, they will use these patterns repeatedly and may overvalue the information that comes from them.

6. The Winner's Curse

The winner's curse refers to the tendency of negotiators, particularly in an auction setting, to settle quickly on an item and then subsequently feel discomfort about a negotiation win that comes too easily.[31] If the other party capitulates too quickly, the negotiator is often left wondering, "Could I have gotten this for less?" or asking, "What's wrong with the item/product/option?" The negotiator may suspect that the other party knows too much or has insight into an unseen advantage; thus, either "I could have done better" or "This must be a bad deal."

For example, in an antique store several years ago one of the authors of this book saw a clock that he and his wife fell in love with. After spending the afternoon in the neighbourhood deciding on a negotiation strategy (opening offer, bottom line, timing, feigned disinterest, the good guy/bad guy tactic), the author and his wife returned to the store to enact their strategy. The store owner accepted their first offer. Upon arriving home, suffering from the winner's curse, they left the clock in the garage, where it remains collecting dust.

The best remedy for the winner's curse is to prevent it from occurring. Thorough investigation and preparation can provide negotiators with independent verification of appropriate settlement values. Negotiators can also try to secure performance or quality guarantees from the other party to make sure the outcome is not faulty or defective.

7. Overconfidence

Overconfidence is the tendency of negotiators to believe that their ability to be correct or accurate is greater than is actually true. Overconfidence has a double-edged effect: (1) it can solidify the degree to which negotiators support positions or options that are incorrect or inappropriate, and (2) it can lead negotiators to discount the worth or validity of the judgments of others, in effect shutting down other parties as sources of information, interests, and options necessary for a successful integrative negotiation. One study found that negotiators who were not trained to be aware of the overconfidence heuristic tended to overestimate their probability of being successful, and they were significantly less likely to compromise or reach agreements than trained negotiators.[32] In another study, overconfident individuals were more persistent and were more concerned about their own outcomes than were the realistically confident negotiators.[33] This does not mean, however, that negotiators should always seek to suppress confidence or optimism. Research on distributive bargaining found that negotiators biased toward optimism achieved more profitable settlements compared to negotiators with accurate perceptions or a bias toward pessimism. Clearly, more research is needed on the interplay of optimism, overconfidence, and negotiation outcomes.[34]

8. The Law of Small Numbers

In decision theory, the law of small numbers refers to the tendency of people to draw conclusions from small sample sizes. In negotiation, the law of small numbers applies to the way negotiators learn and extrapolate from their own experience.

If that experience is limited in time or in scope (e.g., if all of one's prior negotiations have been hard-fought and distributive), the tendency is to extrapolate prior experience onto future negotiations (e.g., all negotiations are distributive). This tendency will often lead to a self-fulfilling prophecy, as follows: People who expect to be treated in a distributive manner will (1) be more likely to perceive the other party's behaviour as distributive, and (2) treat the other party in a more distributive manner. The other party will then likely interpret the negotiator's behaviour as evidence of a distributive tendency, and will therefore respond in kind. The smaller the prior sample (i.e., the more limited the negotiation experience), the greater the possibility that past lessons will be erroneously used to infer what will happen in the future. Styles and strategies that worked in the past may not work in the future, and they certainly will not work if future negotiations differ significantly from past experiences.

9. Self-Serving Biases

People often explain another person's behaviour by making attributions, either to the person (i.e., the behaviours were caused by internal factors such as ability, mood, or effort) or to the situation (i.e., the behaviours were caused by external factors such as the task, other people, or fate).[35] In "explaining" another person's behaviour, the tendency is to overestimate the causal role of personal or internal factors and underestimate the causal role of situational or external factors. For example, consider the student who arrives late for a morning class. Perhaps she is lazy (an internal, dispositional explanation), or perhaps she had a flat tire driving to campus (an external, situational explanation). Absent other information, the professor tends to be biased toward the internal explanation (she's lazy). Perceptual biases are often exacerbated by the *actor–observer effect*, in which people tend to attribute their own behaviour to situational factors, but attribute others' behaviours to personal factors, saying in effect, "If I mess up, it's bad luck (the situation, someone else's fault, etc.); if you mess up, it's your fault!"[36]

Research has documented the effects of self-serving biases on the negotiation process. For instance, one study found that negotiators in different school districts chose comparison school districts in a self-serving way; that is, the districts they chose as comparison standards for their own district's activities were those that made their districts look most favourable.[37] Another study found that negotiators believed that they used more constructive tactics than their counterparts and that the strength of this self-serving bias increased with the strength of the conflict between the parties.[38]

Perceptual error may also be expressed in the form of biases or distortions in the evaluation of data. For instance, the *false-consensus effect* is a tendency to overestimate the degree of support and consensus that exists for one's own position, opinions, or behaviours.[39] This can seriously damage a negotiation effort—negotiators subject to it would make faulty judgments regarding tactics or outcome probabilities.

10. Endowment Effect

The endowment effect is the tendency to overvalue something you own or believe you possess. The existence of the endowment effect was shown rather dramatically in a series of experiments involving coffee mugs.[40] In one experiment, some participants were asked whether they would prefer a sum of money or the mug at various possible dollar levels. Based on their responses, it could be determined that they assigned an average value of just over $3.00 to the mug. Other participants were asked to value the mug as a potential buyer; the average value they assigned to the mug was just under $3.00. Members of a third group were actually given the mug and then asked if they would sell the mug for various amounts. Their answers indicated that they placed a value of more than $7.00 on the mug!

In negotiation, the endowment effect can lead to inflated estimations of value that interfere with reaching a good deal. Discussing endowment effects in the context of negotiations over environmental issues, Max Bazerman and his colleagues argued that the status quo serves as a "potentially dysfunctional anchor point, making mutually beneficial trades more difficult."[41]

11. Ignoring Others' Cognitions

Negotiators often don't ask about the other party's perceptions and thoughts, which leaves them to work with incomplete information, and thus produces faulty results. Failure to consider others' cognitions allows negotiators to simplify their thinking about otherwise complex processes; this usually leads to a more distributive strategy and causes a failure to recognize the contingent nature of both sides' behaviours and responses. Although this "failure to consider" might be attributed to some basic, underlying bias against the other party, research suggests that it is more often a way to make the complex task of decision making under conditions of risk and uncertainty more manageable.[42] Research also suggests that training and awareness of this trap reduces its effects only modestly.[43] The drive to ignore others' cognitions is very deep-seated, and it can be avoided only if negotiators explicitly focus on putting in the effort needed to form an accurate understanding of the other party's interests, goals, and perspectives.

Although we will never know for sure, it is likely the Ontario government failed in its negotiation with the Dionne sisters partly because it misunderstood what was motivating the sisters. As part of the government's apology, they did admit to mishandling the negotiation because they did not understand the main issue was about justice and restitution, and not about government handouts.

12. Reactive Devaluation

Reactive devaluation is the process of devaluing the other party's concessions simply because the other party made them.[44] Such devaluation may be based in emotionality ("I just don't like him") or on distrust fostered by past experience. Reactive devaluation leads negotiators to minimize the magnitude of a concession made by a disliked other, to reduce their willingness to respond with a concession of equal size, or to seek even more from the other party once a concession has been made.[45] Reactive devaluation may be minimized by maintaining an objective view of the process, by assigning a colleague to do this task, by clarifying each side's preferences on options and concessions before any are made,[46] or by using a third party to mediate or filter concession-making processes.

■ Managing Misperceptions and Cognitive Biases in Negotiation

Misperceptions and cognitive biases typically arise as negotiators gather and process information. The question of how best to manage perceptual and cognitive bias is a difficult one. Certainly the first level of managing such distortions is to be aware that they can occur. We encourage you to build awareness of these biases into the process of preparing for a negotiation; that is, each time you negotiate, ask yourself to what degree you might be susceptible to each of them. If you happen to dislike your negotiation counterpart, is it likely you will dismiss their honest efforts to share information (reactive devaluation)? Or, if you are selling something that you own, is it possible that you inflate your expectations of its market value simply because you own it (an endowment effect)?

Sometimes, awareness by itself may not be enough; research evidence shows that simply telling people about misconceptions and cognitive biases does little to counteract their effects.[47] For example, Foreman and Murnighan (1996) tried to teach students to avoid the winner's curse in a series of auction simulations. They told students about the results of 128 auctions over a four-week period but found that the training had little impact on reducing the winner's curse. Other research suggests that both problem definition and problem evaluation are important components of reducing fixed-pie bias. Careful discussion of the issues and preferences by both negotiators may reduce the effects of perceptual biases.[48] So, the best advice that negotiators can follow is simply to be aware of the negative aspects of these effects and to discuss them in a structured manner within their team and with their counterparts.

Reframing

It is likely that negotiators will apply several different frames to the same negotiation. When different negotiators apply different, or mismatched, frames, they will find the bargaining process ambiguous and frustrating. In such situations it may become necessary to reframe the negotiation systematically, to assist the other party in reframing the negotiation, or to establish a common frame or set of frames within which the negotiation may be conducted more productively. Reframing might involve any of a number of approaches. For instance, rather than perceiving a particular outcome as a loss, the negotiator might reframe it as an opportunity to gain, that is, as a bright-side alternative to approaching a given situation.[49]

Negotiators can also reframe by trying to perceive or understand the situation in a different way or from a different perspective. For instance, they can constructively reframe a problem by defining it in terms that are broader or narrower, bigger or smaller, riskier or less risky, or subject to a longer or shorter time constraint. Because reframing requires negotiators to be flexible during the negotiation itself, they should anticipate—during planning—that multiple contingencies may arise during negotiations. The ebb and flow of the framing and issue development processes mean that negotiators cannot completely plan the sequence of a negotiation at the outset but rather need to be prepared for shifts in the discussion.

◼ Mood, Emotion, and Negotiation

Research on negotiation has been dominated by views that have favoured rational, cognitive, economic analyses of the negotiation process. These approaches have tended to analyze the rationality of negotiation, examine how negotiators make judgment errors that deviate from rationality, or assess how negotiators can optimize their outcomes. Negotiators are portrayed as rational beings who seem calculating, calm, and in control. But, this overlooks the role played by emotion in negotiation.

moods
states of feeling that are mild in intensity, last for an extended period of time, and are not directed at anything

emotions
intense feelings that often last for a short duration and are clearly directed as someone or something

The role of mood and emotion in negotiation has been the subject of an increasing body of theory and research during the last decade.[50] **Moods** are states of feeling that are mild in intensity, last for an extended period of time, and are not directed at anything. **Emotions**, on the other hand, are intense feelings that often last for a short duration and are clearly directed as someone or something.[51] The distinction between mood and emotion is based on three characteristics: specificity, intensity, and duration. Mood states are more diffuse, less intense, and more enduring than emotion states, which tend to be more intense and directed at more specific targets.[52] Emotions play important roles at various stages of negotiation interaction. There are many new and exciting developments in the study of mood, emotion, and negotiation, and we can present only a limited overview here. The following are some selected findings.

Negotiations Create Both Positive and Negative Emotions Positive emotions can result from being attracted to the other party, feeling good about the development of the negotiation process and the progress that the parties are making, or liking the results that the negotiations have produced.[53] Conversely, negative emotions can result from being turned off by the other party, feeling bad about the development of the negotiation process and the progress being made, or disliking the results. Positive emotions tend to be classified under the single term *happiness*, but we tend to discriminate more precisely among negative emotions.[54] Some negative emotions may tend to be based in dejection while others are based in agitation. Dejection-related emotions result from feeling disappointed, frustrated, or dissatisfied, while agitation-related emotions result from feeling anxious, fearful, or threatened.[55] Dejection-related emotions may lead negotiators to act aggressively, while agitation-related emotions may lead negotiators to try to retaliate or to get out of the situation.[56]

Positive Emotions Generally Have Positive Consequences for Negotiations Positive emotions can lead to these consequences:

- *Positive feelings are more likely to lead the parties toward more integrative processes.* Researchers have shown that negotiators who feel positive emotions toward each other are more likely to strive for integrative agreements and more likely to be flexible in how they arrive at a solution to a problem.[57]

- *Positive feelings also create a positive attitude toward the other side.* When negotiators like the other party, they tend to be more flexible in the negotiations. Having a positive attitude toward the other increases concession making, lessens hostile behaviours, and builds trust among the parties.[58]

- *Positive feelings promote persistence.* If negotiators feel positively attracted, they are more likely to feel confident and, as a result, to persist in trying to get their concerns and issues addressed in the negotiation and to achieve better outcomes.[59]

Aspects of the Negotiation Process Can Lead to Positive Emotions Researchers have begun to explore the emotional consequences of negotiation. Here are two findings regarding how the negotiation process shapes emotion-related outcomes:

- *Positive feelings result from fair procedures during negotiation.* Researchers have explored how emotional responses are related to the experience of fairness during the negotiation process. Findings indicate that negotiators who see the process as fair experience more positive feelings and are less inclined to express negative emotions following the encounter.[60]

- *Positive feelings result from favourable social comparisons.* Evidence shows that individual satisfaction after a negotiation is higher when the individual negotiator's outcomes compare favourably with others in similar situations.[61] Interestingly, however, this finding for so-called external social comparisons (comparing your outcome to others outside the negotiation that just took place) do not hold for "internal" social comparisons (comparing your outcome to the counterpart with whom you just negotiated). This may occur because comparisons with an opponent—even favourable ones—focus the negotiator's attention on forgone chances to claim additional value.

Negative Emotions Generally Have Negative Consequences for Negotiations As we noted above, negative feelings may be based either in dejection or in agitation, one or both parties may feel the emotions, and the behaviour of one may prompt the emotional reaction in the other. Some specific results from studies are as follows:

- *Negative emotions may lead parties to define the situation as competitive or distributive.* A negative mood increases the likelihood that the actor will increase belligerent behaviour toward the other.[62] In a negotiation situation, this negative behaviour is most likely to take the shape of a more distributive posture on the issues.

- *Negative emotions may undermine a negotiator's ability to analyze the situation accurately, which adversely affects individual outcomes.* Research indicates that angry negotiators are less accurate at judging the other party's interests and at recalling their own interests, compared to negotiators with neutral emotion.[63] It is noteworthy that the experimental manipulation of anger in this study was unrelated to the negotiation itself—anger was aroused during what subjects believed was a separate experiment preceding the negotiation experiment. This carryover effect of anger highlights the power of negative emotion to divert one's attention and focus from the negotiation problem at hand.

- *Negative emotions may lead parties to escalate the conflict.* When the mood is negative—more specifically, when both parties are dejected, frustrated, and blame the other—conflict is likely to become personal, the number of issues in the conflict may expand, and other parties may become drawn into the dispute.[64]

- *Negative emotions may lead parties to retaliate and may thwart integrative outcomes*. When the parties are angry with each other, and when their previous interaction has already led one party to seek to punish the other, the other may choose to retaliate.[65] Negative emotions may also lead to less effective outcomes. The more a negotiator holds the other responsible for destructive behaviour in a previous interaction, the more anger and less compassion he or she feels for the other party. This in turn leads to less concern for the other's interests and a lower likelihood of discovering mutually beneficial negotiated solutions.[66]

Aspects of the Negotiation Process Can Lead to Negative Emotions As with positive emotion, research exploring the negative emotional consequences of negotiation is recent and limited. Here are two findings:

- *Negative emotions may result from a competitive mindset*. Negotiators with a fixed-pie perception of the situation tend to be less satisfied with negotiated outcomes than those with an integrative orientation. This may stem from the perception that when a negotiation is viewed as zero-sum, the other party's gains mean an equivalent loss for self.[67]
- *Negative emotions may result from impasse*. When a negotiation ends in impasse, negotiators are more likely to experience negative emotions such as anger and frustration compared to negotiators who successfully reach agreement.[68] However, people with more confidence in their negotiating ability may be less likely to experience negative emotion in the wake of impasse. This is important because impasse is not always a bad thing—the goal is achieving a good outcome, not merely reaching an agreement.

The Effects of Positive and Negative Emotion in Negotiation It is possible for positive emotion to generate negative outcomes, and for negative feelings to elicit beneficial outcomes, as we explain here:

- *Positive feelings may have negative consequences*. First, negotiators in a positive mood may be less likely to examine closely the other party's arguments. As a result, they may be more susceptible to a competitive opponent's deceptive tactics.[69] In addition, because negotiators with positive feelings are less focused on the arguments of the other party, they may achieve less-than-optimal outcomes.[70] Finally, if positive feelings create strong positive expectations, parties who are not able to find an integrative agreement are likely to experience the defeat more strongly and perhaps treat the other party more harshly.[71]
- *Negative feelings may create positive outcomes*. Just as positive emotions can create negative outcomes, it is clear that negative emotions can create positive consequences for negotiation. First, negative emotion has information value. It alerts the parties that the situation is problematic and needs attention, which may motivate them to either leave the situation or resolve the problem.[72] An expression of anger may alert the other party that there is a problem in the relationship and lead both parties to work on fixing the problem. Anger can thus serve as a danger signal that motivates both parties to confront the problem directly and search for a resolution.[73]

Emotions Can Be Used Strategically as Negotiation Gambits Finally, we have been discussing emotions as though they were genuine. Given the power that emotions may have in swaying the other side toward one's own point of view, emotions may also be used strategically and manipulatively as influence tactics within negotiation. For example, negotiators may intentionally manipulate emotion to get the other side to adopt certain beliefs or take certain actions.[74] In one study, negotiators who were coached to implement a positive emotional tone were more likely to reach agreements that incorporated a future business relationship between the parties compared to those implementing a negative or neutral emotional strategy. Negotiators exhibiting positive emotionality were more likely to induce compliance with ultimatum offers.[75]

Did emotions play a role in the government and Dionne sister negotiation? Most certainly. There is little evidence regarding the emotional states of the negotiating parties; however, it was clear that the story created strong emotional reactions among the general population. Support for the Dionnes was overwhelming, and played a major role in driving the government to the negotiation table.

Beyond the strategic expression of one's own (genuine or fabricated) emotions, negotiators may also engage in the regulation or management of the emotions of the other party. Effective negotiators are able to adjust their messages to adapt to what they perceive as the other party's emotional state.[76] Some psychologists regard the ability to perceive and regulate emotions as a stable individual difference that has come to be known as emotional intelligence.[77]

In this chapter we have taken a multifaceted look at the role of perception, cognition, and emotion in negotiation. The first portion of the chapter presented a brief overview of the perceptual process and discussed four types of perceptual distortions: stereotyping, halo effects, selective perception, and projection. We then turned to a discussion of how framing influences perceptions in negotiation and how reframing and issue development both change negotiator perceptions during negotiations. We ended with a discussion of common cognitive biases and the effects of mood and emotion in negotiation.

We conclude with a few observations of some of the key points covered in the chapter:

1. Be on the lookout for your own tendency to be influenced by perceptual distortions and cognitive biases. However, it is just as important to watch out for these tendencies from your counterparts. These factors often help to explain why negotiators perceive their counterparts to be acting irrationally. Perhaps their behaviour appears to be risk-seeking. Could it be caused by framing effects? Or perhaps they are selling something and can't possibly imagine that someone else might value the thing they are selling less then they value it. Could this be caused by the endowment effect?

2. Watch for the effects of emotions and moods on your own and your counterpart's behaviour. For the most part, positive emotions produce positive results, while negative emotions create tension and frustration. Do what you can to create the right mood because it can influence your likelihood of success.

Key Terms

Emotions, p. 106
Frame, p. 93
Halo effects, p. 92
Moods, p. 106
Perception, p. 91

Projection, p. 93
Reference point, p. 95
Selective perception, p. 93
Stereotyping, p. 92

CHAPTER 6

Communication Process and Outcomes

LEARNING OBJECTIVES

After reading this chapter you should be able to:

1. Positively communicate, using verbal and non-verbal techniques,

2. Ask questions in a way that increases the likelihood that your counterpart will respond in an honest and co-operative manner, and

3. Build trust, repair trust, and enhance perceptions of your reputation and fairness.

Consider the following question: Does the manner in which we speak influence our success? Research does, in fact, provide substantial support for the link between speech styles and subsequent status attainment. When we say speech styles, we mean things like hesitation (e.g., "well," "um"), hedges (e.g., "kinda," "sort of"), disclaimers (e.g., "This may be a bad idea, but ..."), and formal addresses (e.g., "no sir"). People who speak assertively, by avoiding these tentative speech styles, are judged by observers as more likely to be promoted and supported by superiors. These effects also work in negotiation—people who use assertive speech are judged to be more competent and co-operative by negotiation counterparts.[1]

Because they have such a powerful effect on negotiation processes and outcomes, we now turn our attention to the communication patterns used by negotiators and the effects these patterns have on things like trust, reputation, and perceptions of justice and fairness. Specifically, we explain what is communicated during negotiations, how people communicate using language and non-verbal techniques, and provide advice on how to improve communication using question, listening, and role-reversal.

What Is Communicated during Negotiation?

One of the fundamental questions that researchers in communication and negotiation have examined is: What is communicated during negotiation? This work has taken several different forms but generally involves audiotaping or videotaping negotiation role-plays and analyzing the patterns of communication that occur in them. In one study, researchers videotaped executives who participated in a

60-minute, three-person negotiation involving two oil companies.[2] The researchers found that over 70 percent of the verbal tactics that buyers and sellers used during the negotiation were integrative. In addition, buyers and sellers tended to behave reciprocally—when one party used an integrative tactic, the other tended to respond with an integrative tactic. This behaviour is consistent with the phenomenon known as the *norm of reciprocity*, which we describe in more detail in the next chapter.

Most of the communication during negotiation is not about negotiator preferences.[3] Although the blend of integrative versus distributive content varies as a function of the issues being discussed, it is also clear that the content of communication is only partly responsible for negotiation outcomes.[4] For example, one party may choose not to communicate certain things (e.g., the reason she chose a different supplier), so her counterpart (e.g., the supplier not chosen) may be unaware why some outcomes occur. In the following sections, we discuss five different categories of communication that take place during negotiations and then consider the question of whether more communication is always better than less communication.

1. Offers, Counteroffers, and Motives

Among the most important communications in negotiation are those that convey offers and counteroffers.[5] Bargainers have definite preferences and exhibit rational behaviour by acting in accordance with those preferences. A negotiator's preferences reflect in good measure his or her underlying motivations, which are also communicated during a negotiation, and they can have a powerful influence on the actions of the other party and on negotiation outcomes. A communicative framework for negotiation is based on the assumptions that (1) the communication of offers is a dynamic process (the offers change or shift over time); (2) the offer process is interactive (bargainers influence each other); and (3) various internal and external factors (e.g., time limitations, reciprocity norms, alternatives, constituency pressures) drive the interaction and "motivate a bargainer to change his or her offer."[6] In other words, the offer–counteroffer process is dynamic and interactive, and subject to situational and environmental constraints. This process constantly revises the parameters of the negotiation, eventually narrowing the bargaining range and guiding the discussion toward a settlement point.

2. Information about Alternatives

Another important aspect that has been studied is how sharing information with the other party influences the negotiation process. For instance, is simply having a good BATNA sufficient to give a negotiator an advantage over the other party? Should one's BATNA be communicated to the other person? Research suggests that the existence of a good BATNA changes several things in a negotiation: (1) compared to negotiators without attractive BATNAs, negotiators with attractive BATNAs set higher reservation prices for themselves than their counterparts, (2) negotiators whose counterparts had attractive BATNAs set lower reservation points for themselves, and (3) when both parties were aware of the attractive BATNA that one of the negotiators had, that negotiator received a more positive negotiation outcome.[7] The results of this research suggest that negotiators with an attractive BATNA should tell the other party about it if they expect to receive its full benefits. We hasten to add that the style and tone used to convey information about an attractive BATNA matters. Politely (even subtly) making the other party aware of one's good alternative can provide leverage without alienating the other party. On the other hand, waving a good BATNA in the other party's face in an imposing or condescending manner may be construed as aggressive and threatening. See Negotiation Point 6.1 for more on information about alternatives.

3. Information about Outcomes

Researcher Leigh Thompson and her colleagues examined the effects of sharing different types of information on negotiators' evaluations of success.[8] The study focused on how winners and losers evaluated their negotiation outcomes (winners were defined as negotiators who received more points in the negotiation simulation). Thompson and her colleagues found that winners and losers evaluated their own outcomes equally when they did not know how well the other party had done, but if they found out that the other negotiator had done better, or was simply pleased with his or her outcome, then negotiators felt less positive about their own outcome. Another study suggests that even when negotiators learn that the other party did relatively poorly, they are less satisfied with the outcome than when they have no comparison information.[9] Taken together, these findings suggest that negotiators should be cautious about sharing their outcomes or even their positive reactions to outcomes with the other party, especially if they are going to negotiate with that party again in the future.

4. Social Accounts

Another type of communication that occurs during negotiation consists of the "social accounts" that negotiators use to explain things to the other party, especially when negotiators need to justify bad news.[10] Three types of explanations are important: (1) explanations of mitigating circumstances, where negotiators suggest that they had no choice in taking the positions they did; (2) explanations of exonerating circumstances, where negotiators explain their positions from a broader perspective, suggesting that while their current position may appear negative, it derives from positive motives (e.g., an honest mistake); and (3) reframing explanations, where

---

6.1

A Naval Stand-Off

Sometimes, awareness of a counterpart's alternatives can have a dramatic effect on a negotiation or dispute. The following story tells of an encounter between Canadian and American naval personnel off the coast of Newfoundland. An American naval ship was sailing in foggy waters when it detected it was on a collision course with Canadian naval personnel. In an attempt to avoid this collision, the American naval ship contacted the Canadians via radio and asked them to change their course. The Canadians refused their request and instead asked the Americans to change their course. Both parties continued to deny the other's request until the Americans threatened to take whatever measures necessary to ensure the safety of its ship. In response to this threat, the Canadians simply stated that they were unable to alter their course because they were a lighthouse.

Although this is an urban legend and cannot be verified, it is a good example of how sharing information about one's alternatives can alter the course of a negotiation!

outcomes can be explained by changing the context (e.g., short-term pain for long-term gain).[11] Negotiators who use multiple explanations are more likely to have better outcomes, and the negative effects of poor outcomes can be alleviated by communicating explanations for them.[12]

5. Communication about Process

Lastly, some communication is about the negotiation process itself—how well it is going or what procedures might be adopted to improve the situation. For example, some communication strategies in negotiation are used to halt conflict spirals that might otherwise lead to impasse or less-than-ideal outcomes.[13] One such strategy involves calling attention to the other party's contentious actions and explicitly labelling the process as counterproductive. Research examining conflict spirals suggests that negotiators seeking to break out of a conflict spiral should resist the natural urge to reciprocate contentious communication from the other party.[14]

■ How People Communicate in Negotiation

Research in negotiation shows that *how* negotiators communicate is as important as *what* they have to say. In this section we address three aspects related to the "how" of communication: the characteristics of language that communicators use, the use of nonverbal communication in negotiation, and the selection of a communication channel for sending and receiving messages.

Use of Language

In negotiation, language operates at two levels: the *logical* level (for proposals or offers) and the *pragmatic* level (semantics, syntax, and style). The meaning conveyed by a proposition or statement is a combination of one logical surface message and several pragmatic (i.e., hinted or inferred) messages. In other words, it is not only what is said and how it is said that matters but also what additional, veiled, or subsurface information is intended, conveyed, or perceived in reception. By way of illustration, consider threats. We often react not only to the substance of a threatening statement but also (and frequently more strongly) to its unspoken messages. Threats can be made more credible and more compelling by varying the intensity or immediacy of the language used to convey the threat.[15]

Whether the intent is to command and compel, sell, persuade, or gain commitment, how parties communicate in negotiation would seem to depend on the ability of the speaker to encode thoughts properly, as well as on the ability of the listener to understand and decode the intended message(s). In addition, negotiators' use of idioms or colloquialisms is often problematic, especially in cross-cultural negotiations. The meaning conveyed might be clear to the speaker but confusing to the listener. Even if the meaning is clear, the choice of a word or metaphor may convey a lack of sensitivity or create a sense of exclusion, as is often done when men relate strategic business concerns by using sports metaphors ("Well, it's fourth down and goal to go; this is no time to drop the ball"). Because people generally aren't aware of the potential for such miscommunication with someone of similar background, they are less well prepared to deal with such miscommunication than they would be if the person were from a different background or culture.

Finally, a negotiator's choice of words may not only signal a position but also shape and predict it. Researcher Tony Simons examined the linguistic patterns of communication in negotiation and found that parties whose statements communicated interests in both the substance of the negotiation (things) and the relationship with the other party (people) achieved better, more integrative solutions than parties whose statements were concerned solely with either substance or relationship.[16]

Use of Nonverbal Communication

Much of what people communicate to one another is transmitted with nonverbal communication. Examples include facial expressions, body language, head movements, and tone of voice, to name just a few. Some nonverbal acts, called *attending behaviours*, are particularly important in connecting with another person during a coordinated interaction like negotiation. They let the other know that you are listening and prepare the other party to receive your message. We will discuss three important attending behaviours: eye contact, body position, and encouraging.

Make Eye Contact Dishonest people and cowards are not supposed to be able to look people in the eye. Poets claim that the eye is the lens that permits us to look into a person's soul. These and other bits of conventional wisdom illustrate how important people believe eye contact to be. In general, making eye contact is one way to show others you are paying attention and listening and that you consider them important. Of course, it is possible to listen very well even when not looking at the other person. In fact, it may be easier to look away because you can focus on the spoken words and not be confused by visual information. But the point is that by not making eye contact, you are not providing the other person with an important cue that you are listening.

When persuading someone, it is important to make eye contact when delivering the most important part of the message.[17] Having the verbal and nonverbal systems in parallel at this point emphasizes the importance of the message that is being sent. Also, one should maintain eye contact not only when speaking but when receiving communication as well.[18] It is important to recognize, however, that these patterns are characteristic of Western society. In other parts of the world, different patterns prevail. In some Asian societies, for example, keeping one's eyes down while the other is speaking is a sign of respect.[19]

Adjust Body Position Parents frequently advise their children about how to stand and sit, particularly when they are in formal settings such as school or dinner parties. The command "Sit up!" is often accompanied by "And pay attention!" Here the parent is teaching the child another widely held belief—one's body position indicates whether or not one is paying attention to the other party. To ensure that others know you are attentive to them, hold your body erect, lean slightly forward, and face the other person directly.[20] If you accept and endorse the others' message, care needs to be taken not to show disrespect with body position by slouching, turning away, or placing feet on the table.[21] In contrast, crossing arms, bowing the head, furrowing the brow, and squeezing eyebrows together all can signal strong rejection or disapproval of the message.[22]

Nonverbally Encourage or Discourage What the Other Says One can indicate attention and interest in what another is saying through a variety of simple behaviours. A head nod, a simple hand gesture to go on, or a murmured "unh hunh" to indicate understanding all tell the other person to continue, that you are listening. In fact, one can encourage someone to continue to speak about many subjects by simply nodding your head as he or she is speaking. Brief eye contact or a smile and a nod of the head will both provide encouraging cues. Similarly, a frown, a scowl, a shake of the head, or a grab of one's chest in mock pain will signal disapproval of the other's message.

Nonverbal communication—done well—may help negotiators achieve better outcomes through mutual coordination. One study compared the development of rapport between negotiators who did or did not have visual access to each other while negotiating. The researchers defined rapport as "a state of mutual positivity and interest that arises through the convergence of nonverbal expressive behaviour in an interaction."[23] They found that face-to-face interaction stimulated rapport through nonverbal communication, which in turn enhanced coordination and led to higher joint gains. Of course, these benefits will presumably arise only to the extent that parties are able to interpret nonverbal communication accurately.

Selection of a Communication Channel

Communication is experienced differently when it occurs through different channels. We may think of negotiation as typically occurring face-to-face—an assumption reinforced by the common metaphor of the "negotiation table." But the reality is that people negotiate through a variety of communication media: over the telephone, in writing, and increasingly through electronic channels such as e-mail, instant messaging, and teleconferencing systems. The use of network-mediated information technologies in negotiation is sometimes referred to as **virtual negotiations**. The use of a particular channel shapes both perceptions of the communication task at hand and norms regarding appropriate behaviour; accordingly, channel variations have potentially important effects on negotiation processes and outcomes.[24]

The key variation that distinguishes one communication channel from another is **social presence**—the ability of a channel to carry and convey subtle social cues from sender to receiver that go beyond the literal text of the message itself.[25] For example, as an alternative to face-to-face interaction, the telephone preserves one's ability to transmit social cues through inflection or tone of voice, but forfeits the ability to communicate through facial expressions or physical gestures. In written communication, there are only the words and symbols on paper, although one's choice of words and the way they are arranged can certainly convey tone, (in)formality, and emotion.

E-mail, as an increasingly ubiquitous mode of personal and organizational communication, can be viewed as simply another form of written communication that happens to involve electronic transmission. There are, however, important distinctions between e-mail and other forms of written communication. Many people, treating e-mail as a highly informal medium, are comfortable sending messages that are stylistically or grammatically unpolished in situations (such as on the job) where they would never send a carelessly written communication on paper. Some people incorporate text-based *emoticons* to convey emotional social cues in their messages (the notorious smiley face [:-)] is the best known emoticon). Some research on interpersonal

virtual negotiation
negotiations conducted using network-mediated information technology

social presence
variability across communication channels regarding the ability to convey subtle social cues

and small-group communication through computers indicates that the lack of social cues lowers communicator inhibition and leads to more aggressive communication behaviour.[26] See Negotiation Point 6.2 for a story about how one of the authors discovered this. However, much of the research into computer-mediated communication has focused on anonymous interaction. It is not clear that reduced social cues have the same effect in a communication context, such as negotiation, where the parties are known to each other, and in fact may know each other quite well.[27]

Researchers have been examining the effects of channels in general, and e-mail in particular, on negotiation processes and outcomes during much of the past decade. Unfortunately, there are few consistent findings that point to clear effects. We do know that interacting parties can more easily develop personal rapport in face-to-face communication compared to other channels,[28] and that face-to-face negotiators are more inclined to disclose information truthfully, increasing their ability to attain mutual gain.[29] There is evidence that negotiation through written channels is more likely to end in impasse than negotiation that occurs face-to-face or by phone.[30] There is also evidence that e-mail negotiators reach agreements that are more equal (a balanced division of resources) than face-to-face negotiators.[31] By giving the individual a chance to ponder at length the other party's message, and to review and revise one's own communication, e-mail may indeed help less interpersonally skilled parties improve their performance, especially when the alternative is negotiating spontaneously (face-to-face or by phone) with a more accomplished other party.

6.2

Negotiating by E-mail—A Cautionary Tale

One of the authors had to purchase new appliances. As someone who does his homework, he spent hours going over consumer products reviews and assessing desired features. He then visited two appliance stores for the purpose of learning more about each of the appliances. At each store he thanked the salesperson for their time and asked if it would be possible to discuss the deal by e-mail. In both cases the salespeople were eager to do so.

After a few days, he sent an e-mail to the first store asking what type of discount might be possible considering that he would be purchasing five appliances. The retail price of all five appliances totalled approximately $9,500, and the salesperson responded quickly with a 10% discount. He then proceeded to e-mail the person at the second store informing them about the 10% reduction from the first store. This led to a reduction of an additional 8%. After a few

more days, and a few more e-mails, the author reached a deal with the first store for a price of $6,900 plus tax (and free delivery).

Unfortunately, when the appliances were delivered, the fridge was so large that it was difficult to get through the front door. When the author phoned the store about the fridge the store manager was so upset with the size of the discount given on the original deal that he was unwilling to even offer a discount on a second fridge.

This story illustrates a couple of things. One, when purchasing an everyday commodity like appliances, e-mail is a very powerful tool. It was easy for the author to push each salesperson to their limits because his BATNA was only a mouse click away and the perceived anonymity that e-mail creates allowed him to use stronger distributive tactics than he would in a face-to-face negotiation. Second, it is possible to get a deal that is *too good*. Although the discount on the original deal was quite substantial, the author claimed so much of the value that the store was unmotivated to help when a problem arose. It is important to remember that both sides need to feel they got something out of the deal.

A growing body of evidence points to the conclusion that negotiators using e-mail need to work harder at building personal rapport with the other party if they are to overcome limitations of the channel that would otherwise inhibit optimal agreements or fuel impasse. What e-mail negotiations lack is *schmoozing*—off-task or relationship-focused conversations that are often present in face-to-face negotiations.[32] Schmoozing is an important avenue for building rapport and establishing trust in the negotiation relationship. In one study, negotiators who schmoozed on the phone prior to e-mail negotiations reached more negotiated agreements, better outcomes, increased co-operation, and greater trust and optimism regarding future working relationships with the other party.[33] See Negotiation Point 6.3 for a list of additional ways to maximize effectiveness when negotiations occur in virtual environments.

Negotiation Point

6.3

Top Ten Rules for Virtual Negotiation

1. Take steps to create a face-to-face relationship before negotiation, or early on, so that there is a face or voice behind the e-mail.

2. Be explicit about the normative process to be followed during the negotiation.

3. If others are present in a virtual negotiation (on either your side or theirs) make sure everyone knows who is there and why.

4. Pick the channel (face-to-face, videophone, voice, fax, or e-mail, etc.) that is most effective at getting all the information and detail on the table so that it can be fully considered by both sides.

5. Avoid "flaming"; when you must express emotion, label the emotion explicitly so the other knows what it is and what's behind it.

6. Formal turn-taking is not strictly necessary, but try to synchronize offers and counter-offers. Speak up if it is not clear "whose turn it is."

7. Check out assumptions you are making about the other's interests, offers, proposals, or conduct. Less face-to-face contact means less information about the other party and a greater chance that inferences will get you in trouble, so ask questions.

8. In many virtual negotiations (e.g., e-mail) everything is communicated in writing, so be careful not to make unwise commitments that can be used against you. Neither should you take undue advantage of the other party in this way; discuss and clarify until all agree.

9. It may be easier to use unethical tactics in virtual negotiation because facts are harder to verify. But resist the temptation: The consequences are just as severe, and perhaps more so, given the incriminating evidence available when virtual negotiations are automatically archived.

10. Not all styles work equally well in all settings. Work to develop a personal negotiation style (collaboration, competition, etc.) that is a good fit with the communication channel you are using. One of the most difficult aspects of negotiation is the actual give-and-take that occurs at the table. Should I stick with this point, or is it time to fold? Should I open the bidding or wait for the other side to take the lead? It requires good judgment to make these choices.

Source: Adapted from R. J. Lewicki and B. R. Dineen, "Negotiating in Virtual Organizations," in R. Heneman and D. Greenberger (eds.), Human Resource Management in the Virtual Organization (New York: John Wiley and Sons, 2003).

◼ How to Improve Communication in Negotiation

Given the many ways that communication can be disrupted and distorted, we can only marvel at the extent to which negotiators can actually understand each other. Failures and distortions in perception, cognition, and communication are the paramount contributors to breakdowns and failures in negotiation. Research consistently demonstrates that even those parties whose goals are compatible or integrative may fail to reach agreement or may reach suboptimal agreements because of the misperceptions of the other party or because of breakdowns in the communication process.

Three main techniques are available for improving communication in negotiation: the use of questions, listening, and role reversal.

The Use of Questions

Questions are essential elements in negotiations for securing information; asking good questions enables negotiators to secure a great deal of information about the other party's position, supporting arguments, and needs. Questions can be divided into two basic categories: those that are manageable and those that are unmanageable and cause difficulty (see Table 6.1).[34] Manageable questions cause attention or prepare the other person's thinking for further questions ("May I ask you a question?"), get information ("How much will this cost?"), and generate thoughts ("Do you have any suggestions for improving this?"). Unmanageable questions cause difficulty, give information ("Didn't you know that we couldn't afford this?"), and bring the discussion to a false conclusion ("Don't you think we've talked about this enough?"). Unmanageable questions are more likely to produce defensiveness and anger in the other party. Although these questions may yield information, they are likely to make the other party feel uncomfortable and less willing to provide information in the future.

Negotiators can also use questions to manage difficult or stalled negotiations. Aside from their typical uses for collecting and diagnosing information or assisting the other party in addressing and expressing needs and interests, questions can also be used tactically to pry or lever a negotiation out of a breakdown or an apparent dead end. Table 6.2 identifies a number of such situations and suggests specific questions for dealing with them.[35] The value of such questions seems to be in their power to assist or force the other party to confront the effects or consequences of his or her behaviour, intended and anticipated or not.

Listening

"Active listening" and "reflecting" are terms commonly used in the helping professions such as counselling and therapy.[36] Counsellors recognize that communications are frequently loaded with multiple meanings and that the counsellor must try to identify these different meanings without making the communicator angry or defensive. There are three major forms of listening:

1. **Passive listening** involves receiving the message while providing no feedback to the sender about the accuracy or completeness of reception. Sometimes passive listening is itself enough to keep a communicator sending information. A negotiator whose counterpart is talkative may find that the best strategy is to sit and listen while the other party eventually works into, or out of, a position on his or her own.

TABLE 6.1 | Questions in Negotiation

Manageable Questions	Examples
Open-ended questions—ones that cannot be answered with a simple yes or no. *Who, what, when, where,* and *why* questions.	"Why do you take that position in these deliberations?"
Open questions—invite the other's thinking.	"What do you think of our proposal?"
Leading questions—point toward an answer.	"Don't you think our proposal is a fair and reasonable offer?"
Cool questions—low emotionality.	"What is the additional rate that we will have to pay if you make the improvements on the property?"
Planned questions—part of an overall logical sequence of questions developed in advance.	"After you make the improvements to the property, when can we expect to take occupancy?"
Treat questions—flatter the opponent at the same time as you ask for information.	"Can you provide us with some of your excellent insight on this problem?"
Window questions—aid in looking into the other person's mind.	"Can you tell us how you came to that conclusion?"
Directive questions—focus on a specific point.	"How much is the rental rate per square foot with these improvements?"
Gauging questions—ascertain how the other person feels.	"How do you feel about our proposal?"
Unmanageable Questions	**Examples**
Close-out questions—force the other party into seeing things your way.	"You wouldn't try to take advantage of us here, would you?"
Loaded questions—put the other party on the spot regardless of the answer.	"Do you mean to tell me that these are the only terms that you will accept?"
Heated questions—high emotionality, trigger emotional responses.	"Don't you think we've spent enough time discussing this ridiculous proposal of yours?"
Impulse questions—occur "on the spur of the moment," without planning, and tend to get conversation off the track.	"As long as we're discussing this, what do you think we ought to tell other groups who have made similar demands on us?"
Trick questions—appear to require a frank answer, but really are "loaded" in their meaning.	"What are you going to do—give in to our demands, or take this to arbitration?"
Reflective trick questions—reflects the other into agreeing with your point of view.	"Here's how I see the situation—don't you agree?"

Source: From Gerard Nierenberg, Fundamentals of Negotiating (New York: Hawthorn Books, 1973), pp. 125–26. Used with permission of the author.

2. **Acknowledgment** is the second form of listening, slightly more active than passive listening. When acknowledging, receivers occasionally nod their heads, maintain eye contact, or interject responses like "I see," "mm-hmm," "interesting," "really," "sure," "go on," and the like. These responses are sufficient to keep communicators sending messages, but a sender may misinterpret them as the receiver's agreement with his or her position, rather than as simple acknowledgments of receipt of the message.

TABLE 6.2 | Questions for Tough Situations

The Situation	Possible Questions
"Take it or leave it" ultimatums	"If we can come up with a more attractive alternative than that, would you still want me to 'take or leave' your offer?" "Do I have to decide now, or do I have some time to think about it?" "Are you feeling pressure to bring the negotiation to a close?"
Pressure to respond to an unreasonable deadline	"Why can't we negotiate about this deadline?" "If you're under pressure to meet this deadline, what can I do to help remove some of that pressure?" "What's magical about this afternoon? What about first thing in the morning?"
Highball or lowball tactics	"What's your reasoning behind this position?" "What would *you* think I see as a fair offer?" "What standards do you think the final resolution should meet?"
An impasse	"What else can either of us do to close the gap between our positions?" "Specifically what concession do you need from me to bring this to a close right now?" "If it were already six weeks from now and we were looking back at this negotiation, what might we wish we had brought to the table?"
Indecision between accepting and rejecting a proposal	"What's your best alternative to accepting my offer right now?" "If you reject this offer, what will take its place that's better than what you know you'll receive from me?" "How can you be sure that you will get a better deal elsewhere?"
A question about whether the offer you just made is the same as that offered to others	"What do you see as a fair offer, and given that, what do you think of my current offer to you?" "Do you believe that I think it's in my best interest to be unfair to you?" "Do you believe that people can be treated differently, but still all be treated fairly?"
Attempts to pressure, control, or manipulate	"Shouldn't we both walk away from this negotiation feeling satisfied?" "How would you feel if our roles were reversed, and you were feeling the pressure I'm feeling right now?" "Are you experiencing outside pressures to conclude these negotiations?"

Source: Adapted from S. Deep and L. Sussman, What to Ask When You Don't Know What to Say (Englewood Cliffs, NJ: Prentice Hall, 1993). Used by permission of the publisher, Prentice Hall/A Division of Simon & Schuster, Englewood Cliffs, NJ.

3. **Active listening** is the third form. When receivers are actively listening, they restate or paraphrase the sender's message in their own language. Here are a couple of examples of active listening:[37]

SENDER: I don't know how I am going to untangle this messy problem.

RECEIVER: Let me just make sure I understand you. You're really stumped on how to solve this one. Could you elaborate on that a bit?

NEGOTIATOR 1: As you know, we provide great service and charge rates that are comparable to others in the industry.

NEGOTIATOR 2: You just mentioned that your company provides great service and charges comparable rates. Is there anything else about those issues you think I should know?

Another option is to repeat back exactly what the other person said, and then pause. This often prompts your counterpart to expand upon their point and provide more detail. It also might prompt them to step back from a position that is initially aggressive or one-sided. People often expect a negotiation counterpart to rebut things they say, and are pleasantly surprised when someone shows they are actively listening to their side of the story.

In negotiation, it may appear initially that active listening is unsuitable because, unlike a counsellor, the receiver normally has a set position and may feel strongly about the issues. By recommending active listening we are not suggesting that receivers should automatically agree with the other party's position and abandon their own. Rather, we are suggesting that active listening is a skill that encourages people to speak more fully about their feelings, priorities, frames of reference, and, by extension, the positions they are taking. When the other party does so, negotiators will better understand his or her positions, the factors and information that support it, and the ways the position can be compromised, reconciled, or negotiated in accordance with their own preferences and priorities.

Role Reversal

Continually arguing for one particular position in debate leads to a "blindness of involvement," or a self-reinforcing cycle of argumentation that prohibits negotiators from recognizing the possible compatibility between their own position and that of the other party.[38] While discussing active listening above, we suggested that one objective was to gain an understanding of the other party's perspective or frame of reference. Active listening is, however, still a somewhat passive process. Role-reversal techniques allow negotiators to understand more completely the other party's positions by actively arguing these positions until the other party is convinced that he or she is understood. For example, someone can ask you how you would respond to the situation that he or she is in. In doing so, you can come to understand that person's position, perhaps accept its validity, and discover how to modify both of your positions to make them more compatible.

Research suggests that role reversal may be a useful tool for improving communication and the accurate understanding and appreciation of the other party's position in negotiation.[39] This may be most useful during the preparation stage of negotiation or during a team caucus when things are not going well. A close friend of one of the authors, who is a vice president at a large Canadian telecommunications company, reports that role reversal is a common part of the planning process among his colleagues. While a negotiation team is in the planning stage, they usually have one member of the team play the role of their counterpart. This person's explicit role is to act out simulated exchanges between the two sides, spot hidden assumptions, and help members of the negotiation team anticipate counter-arguments and formulate appropriate responses. These "simulated negotiations" can dramatically increase confidence and reduce anxiety.

■ Benefits Arising from Good Communication Patterns

Earlier we mentioned that negotiation outcomes are better when the parties manage to establish positive rapport. It should be no surprise, then, that good communication also leads to higher levels of trust. Given the importance of trust in virtually all negotiation situations, we now turn our attention to a more detailed examination of the concept. We conclude the chapter by discussing the issues of reputation and justice.

Trust

trust
an individual's belief in and willingness to act on the words, actions and decisions of another

Trust has been defined as "an individual's belief in and willingness to act on the words, actions and decisions of another."[40] There are three things that contribute to the level of trust one negotiator may have for another: the individual's chronic disposition toward trust (i.e., individual differences in personality that make some people more trusting than others); situation factors (e.g., the opportunity for the parties to communicate with each other adequately); and the history of the relationship between the parties.

Recent Research on Trust and Negotiation Many researchers have explored trust in negotiation.[41] As one might expect, higher levels of trust make negotiation easier, while lower levels of trust make negotiation more difficult. Similarly, integrative processes tend to increase trust, while more distributive processes are likely to decrease trust. Some of the more recent research on trust has revealed somewhat more complex relationships between trust and negotiation behaviour. Here is a summary of findings:

- Many people approach a new relationship with an unknown other party with remarkably high levels of trust. Thus, while people in new relationships might be expected to start their trust of the other at "zero," in fact, most of us assume that the other can be trusted and are remarkably willing to trust the other even with very little information or knowledge about the other.[42] Canadian researcher Mark Weber refers to these types of individuals as "consistent contributors" and his research has shown that this behaviour is much more common than is predicted by traditional economic models such as rational choice theory and game theory.[43]

- Trust tends to cue co-operative behaviour and vice-versa. Parties who trust each other approach each other with co-operative dispositions. Thus, trust tends to cue a more communal orientation to a relationship and more co-operative behaviour.[44]

- Individual motives also shape both trust and expectations of the other's behaviour. Parties who are more co-operatively motivated report higher initial trust of the other party and more positive initial impressions of the other than those who are individually motivated.[45]

- The nature of the negotiation task (distributive versus integrative) can shape how parties judge the trust. In a more distributive context, trustors tend to focus on the risks they face, while those who are in a position to receive and then reciprocate the others' trust focus on the benefits that the trustors have provided them. Given the framing biases just mentioned, however, neither party tends to consider the other's point of view prior to making a decision whether to reciprocate the other's trust. As a result, the possibilities for trust to break down or not be completed may increase because neither party truly understands the risks or rewards as perceived by the other. More reciprocity occurs among individuals who are better at taking the perspective of the other in a negotiation, and reciprocity can be increased by coaching a negotiator to consider the views of the other party in their decision making.[46]

- Greater expectations of trust between negotiators leads to greater information sharing with the other party; similarly, greater expectations of distrust lead to less information sharing.[47]

- Greater information sharing tends to enhance effectiveness in achieving a good negotiation outcome, and less information sharing tends to diminish effectiveness in achieving a good outcome, although this effectiveness may *not* necessarily be the result of greater trust.[48]

- Distributive processes lead negotiators to see the negotiation dialogue, and critical events in the dialogue, as largely about the nature of the negotiation task (i.e., how to divide the pie). Distributive processes also lead people to judge the other party with negative characterization frames (see our discussion of frames in Chapter 5). Both of these perspectives tend to reduce trust. In contrast, integrative processes lead negotiators to see the dialogue as largely about interests, relationships, and positive affect and to see the other with positive characterization frames; these perspectives tend to increase trust.[49]

- Trust increases the likelihood that negotiation will proceed on a favourable course over the life of a negotiation. Researchers have begun to examine turning points in negotiation, or key events, comments, or behaviours that turn the negotiation in a more positive (or more negative) direction. One study has generally shown that trust increases the likelihood of more facilitative turning points around interests and the relationship, and decreases the number of inhibitory turning points around discussion of a distributive task or negative characterization of the other party. These processes subsequently lead to higher levels of trust at the end of the negotiation and lower levels of mistrust.[50]

- Face-to-face negotiation encourages greater trust development than negotiation online. There is evidence that parties anticipating an online negotiation expect less trust before the negotiations begin, are less satisfied with their negotiation outcomes, are less confident in the quality of their performance during the negotiation, trust the other less after the negotiation, and have less desire for a future interaction with the other party.[51]

- Negotiators who are representing others' interests, rather than their own interests, tend to behave in a less trustworthy way, and tend to expect that the other will be trusting. As a result of being less trustworthy, negotiators engage in less give and take with the other party and expect the other to engage in less give and take.[52]

Trust Repair The preceding review of research clearly indicates that trust improves negotiation processes, leads to more integrative negotiations processes, and frequently produces better negotiation outcomes; and that *dis*trust hinders negotiation processes, leads to more distributive negotiations, and frequently diminishes strong negotiation outcomes. Since trust and positive negotiation processes and outcomes appear to be so critical, we should comment on ways that broken trust can be repaired to return negotiations to a more productive direction.

A number of studies have begun to investigate the ways that trust can be repaired.[53] One representative study has shown the following:

- The more severe the breach of trust (the greater the costs incurred by the other party), the more difficult it is to repair trust and reconcile the relationship.
- If the parties had a good past relationship, it was easier to repair trust than if the past relationship had been poor.
- The sooner an apology occurs after the breach of trust, the more effective the apology is likely to be.
- The more sincerely an apology is expressed, the more effective it was in repairing trust.
- Apologies where the actor took personal responsibility for having created the breach were more effective than those apologies where the actor tried to blame external causes for the breach. Apologies were even more effective when the actor took personal responsibility *and* the apology was viewed as sincere.
- Apologies were more effective when the trust breach appeared to be an isolated event rather than habitual and repetitive for the other party.[54]

Recent studies have also shown that following a period of untrustworthy behaviour, trust is more likely to be repaired if the trust violation was not accompanied by deception. Deception appears to harm trust far more than untrustworthy actions, and hence trust is much harder to repair if deception has occurred.[55]

Reputation

reputation
the impression other people have of a negotiator based on past experiences

Your reputation is how other people remember their past experience with you. Reputation is the legacy that negotiators leave behind after a negotiation encounter with another party. A **reputation** is a "perceptual identity, reflective of the combination of salient personal characteristics and accomplishments, demonstrated behaviour and intended images preserved over time, as observed directly and/or as reported from secondary sources."[56] Based on this definition, we can say several things about the importance of reputations:

- Reputations are perceptual and highly subjective in nature. It is not how we would like to be known by others, or how we think we are known—it is what they actually think of us, and their judgment is what counts.

- An individual can have a number of different, even conflicting, reputations because she may act quite differently in different situations. She may distributively bargain with the person who manages the vegetable stand down the road, but be quite integrative with the person who regularly services her computer. While individuals can elicit different reputations in different contexts, most commonly a reputation is a single and consistent image from many different constituent persons across many contexts—in most cases, there is generally shared agreement on who we are and how we are seen.

- Reputation is influenced by an individual's personal characteristics and accomplishments. These may include qualities such as age, race, and gender; education and past experience; and personality traits, skills, and behaviours. All of these work together over time to create a broad reputation—how other people remember us in general—as well as a specific reputation that comes from how we, or others, have experienced this particular other person in the past.

- Reputations develop over time and once developed, they are hard to change. Our early experiences with another—or what we have heard about them from other people—shape our views of them, which we bring to new situations in the form of expectations about the other. First impressions and early experiences with others are powerful in shaping others' expectations; once these expectations are shaped, they become hard to change. A negotiator who develops a reputation as a distributive "shark" early on will have a difficult time convincing the current other negotiator that he is honest and trustworthy and wants to work toward a mutually acceptable agreement.[57]

Research supports these statements. In one study, negotiators who knew that the other party had a strongly distributive reputation trusted the other party less, exchanged comparatively little critical information about key bargaining issues, and reaped poorer outcomes than those who were unaware of the other's reputation.[58] In contrast, knowing that the other party had a reputation for integrative negotiation (creating value) led negotiators to expect less deception from the other party, engage in a more candid discussion of specific needs, interests, and priorities, engage in significantly less non-negotiation small talk, and be more optimistic about their ability to reach a mutually beneficial agreement.[59] Thus, a "bad" (distributive, competitive) reputation can undermine your ability to be successful in a negotiation, not because of what you do, but because your reputation has negatively shaped the other's expectations of you. Similarly a "good" (integrative, co-operative) reputation can enhance your ability to be successful because your reputation has created positive expectations in the other party. Negotiation Point 6.4 discusses the real implications of reputations.

Finally, negative reputations are difficult to "repair." The more long-standing the negative reputation, the harder it is to change that reputation to a more positive one. Particularly when any event is likely to be seen by others in a negative light, we must work hard to defend and protect our reputation and to make sure that others do not remember the experience in a negative way. How we account for past behaviour, how we apologize and ask another person to overlook or discount the past, or how we use excuses or justifications to explain why we did something the other views unfavourably will have a major impact on how others remember us and their experience with us.

6.4

Can Riches Repair a Poor Reputation?

Since 2006, Canadian billionaire and co-founder of Research in Motion, Jim Balsillie, has failed in his attempts to purchase three National Hockey League (NHL) franchises, the Pittsburgh Penguins, the Nashville Predators, and, more recently, the Phoenix Coyotes. Among the reasons for these failures is that Balsillie has developed a poor reputation amongst other NHL franchise owners. Craig Leopold, owner of the Nashville Predators, spoke to Balsillie's reputation. "He's untrustworthy. He's deceiving. He's arrogant. He's a person who doesn't know how to be a partner in our business … This is a person I could never support as an owner." After Balsillie's failed attempt to purchase the Phoenix Coyotes, the NHL commented, "There is something sad about Mr. Balsillie's inability to grasp the plain fact that it is his conduct, insensitivity, perceived lack of trustworthiness and unwillingness to accept responsibility for his own actions over several years that has caused the NHL Board of Governors to wish to not be associated with him in the business of hockey."

Source: C. Gillis, "Why Balsillie went ballistic," Macleans.ca, September 30, 2009; "NHL nixes Balsillie application to buy Phoenix Coyotes," Reuters.com, July 29, 2009; "Court decision could end Balsillie's NHL dream or lead to more battles," The Canadian Press, Sept. 1, 2009.

Justice

We conclude the chapter by turning to the question of what is fair or just when negotiators attempt to evaluate their processes and outcomes. Again, justice has been a major issue in the organizational sciences. Individuals in organizations often debate whether their pay is fair, whether they are being fairly treated, or whether the organization might be treating some group of people (e.g., women, minorities, people from other cultures) in an unfair manner.

Justice can take several forms:[60]

distributive justice
the perceived fairness of outcomes

- **Distributive justice** is about the distribution of outcomes. Parties may be concerned that one party is receiving more than he or she deserves, that outcomes should be distributed equally, or that outcomes should be distributed based on needs.[61] One study showed that outcome fairness is often determined in a distributive negotiation as the point midway between the opening position of the two parties (what is often known as a "split-the-difference" settlement). The presence of such an obvious settlement point appears to increase both concession making and the likelihood of settlement.[62]

procedural justice
the perceived fairness of processes used to determine outcomes

- **Procedural justice** is about the process of determining outcomes. Parties may be concerned that they were not treated fairly during the negotiation, that they were not given a chance to offer their point of view or side of the story, or that they were not treated with respect. For example, people who do not feel that their recent performance appraisals gave them credit for several new workplace innovations are likely to have strong complaints about the procedure.[63]

interactional justice
the perceived fairness of the interpersonal treatment patterns between parties

- **Interactional justice** is about how parties treat each other in one-to-one relationships. Research has shown that people have strong expectations about the ways another party should treat them; when those standards are violated, parties feel unfairly treated. When the other party practices deception, is not candid and forthcoming, acts rudely, asks improper questions, makes prejudicial and discriminatory statements, or makes decisions or takes precipitous actions without justification, negotiators feel that fairness standards have been violated.[64]

systemic justice
the perceived fairness patterns among and between groups

- Finally, **systemic justice** is about how organizations appear to treat groups of individuals and the norms that develop for how they should be treated. When some groups are discriminated against, disfranchised, or systematically given poorer salaries or working conditions, the parties may be less concerned about specific procedural elements and more concerned that the overall system may be biased or discriminatory in its treatment of certain groups and their concerns.

The issue of fairness is beginning to receive some systematic investigation in negotiation dynamics. The following conclusions can be drawn:

- Involvement in the process of helping to shape a negotiation strategy increases commitment to that strategy and willingness to pursue it. This is the familiar procedural justice effect, in that parties involved in the process of shaping a decision are more committed to that decision. Negotiators who helped develop a group negotiation strategy were more committed to it and to the group's negotiation goals.[65]

- Negotiators (buyers in a market transaction) who are encouraged ("primed") to think about fairness are more co-operative in distributive negotiations. They make greater concessions, act more fairly and reach agreement faster, and have stronger positive attitudes toward the other party. They also demand fair treatment from the other in return. However, when the other party did not reciprocate the negotiator's co-operative behaviour, the negotiator actively retaliated and punished the other's competitive behaviour. Thus, stating one's own intention to be fair and encouraging the other to be fair may be an excellent way to support fair exchanges; but watch out for the negotiator whose fairness gestures are double-crossed.[66]

- Similarly, parties who receive offers they perceive as unfair may reject them out of hand, even though the amount offered may be better than the alternative settlement, which is to receive nothing at all. Here we see the role of intangibles entering into a negotiation. Economists would predict than any deal better than zero should be accepted (if the only alternative is zero), but research has shown that negotiators will often reject these small offers.[67] Clearly, a less-than-fair small offer creates feelings of anger and wounded pride, and negotiators will often act spitefully to sink the entire deal rather than accept a token settlement.

- Establishment of some objective standard of fairness has a positive impact on negotiations and satisfaction with the outcome. We discussed the role of setting an objective standard for fairness in Chapter 3.[68] Among students who participated in a simulation of a corporate takeover, buyers who knew what a fair selling price would be for the company were more satisfied with those offered selling prices, more willing to buy the company, and more willing to do business with the other party in the future.

- Judgments about fairness are subject to the type of cognitive biases described earlier. For example, most negotiators have an egocentric bias, which is the tendency to regard a larger share for oneself as fair, even if the obvious fairness rule is an equal split. This egocentric bias can be diminished by strong interactional justice. That is, recognizing the need to treat the other person fairly, and actually treating the other fairly, lead to a smaller egocentric bias, a more even split of the resources, quicker settlements, and fewer stalemates.[69]

These egocentric biases vary across cultures. At least one study has shown that egocentric biases are stronger in cultures that are individualistic, where the self is served by focusing on one's positive attributes in order to stand out and be better than others, compared to more collectivist cultures where the self is served by focusing on one's negative characteristics, so as to blend in with others.[70]

Each of the concepts we discussed in this chapter—communication, trust, reputation, and justice—interact with each other in shaping expectations of the other's behaviour. For example, when one party feels the other has acted fairly in the past or will act fairly in the future, he or she is more likely to trust the other.[71] We would also predict that acting fairly leads to being trusted and also enhances a positive reputation. Conversely, when parties are unfairly treated, they often become angry and retaliate against either the injustice itself or those who are seen as having caused it. Unfair treatment is likely to lead to distrust and a bad reputation.[72]

Communication patterns influence, and are influenced by, each of the other three concepts. For example, one of the most powerful means you can use to build trust with another party is to share information. Giving the other side honest and accurate information about your priorities and preferences has been shown to positively influence trust perceptions. Similarly, a person who generally communicates in a co-operative manner is likely to develop a reputation for honesty and integrity, and therefore be in a good position to advocate their perspective as fair.

Key Terms

Distributive justice, p. 127

Interactional justice, p. 127

Procedural justice, p. 127

Reputation, p. 125

Social presence, p. 116

Systemic justice, p. 128

Trust, p. 123

Virtual negotiation, p. 116

CHAPTER 7

Negotiation Power and Persuasion

LEARNING OBJECTIVES

After reading this chapter you should be able to:

1. Understand the different sources of power in negotiations and explain the uses and limits of power,

2. Become more comfortable in dealing with others who have more power,

3. Explain the two different "routes" to persuasion, and

4. Consider the various influence tools and techniques that are available through each of the two routes.

Most negotiators believe that power is important because it gives one negotiator an advantage over the other party. Why? Negotiators who have this advantage usually want to use it to secure a greater share of the outcomes or achieve their preferred solution. In general, negotiators who don't care about their power or who have matched power—equally high or low—will find that their deliberations proceed with greater ease and simplicity toward a mutually satisfying and acceptable outcome. In contrast, negotiators who do care about their power and seek to match or exceed the other's power are probably seeking a solution in which they either do not lose the negotiation (a defensive posture) or dominate the negotiation (an offensive posture).

An extraordinary example of the limits of power can be seen in Canadian billionaire Jim Balsillie's recent attempts to purchase the Phoenix Coyotes, a bankrupt hockey team. Initially Balsillie, the co-founder of Research in Motion, offered US$212.5 million to the owner of the Coyotes in an effort to buy and relocate the team to Canada.[1] However, although the owner of the Coyotes was receptive to the offer, which was significantly higher than other offers, the governors of the National Hockey League (who have authority over who can join the League) rejected Balsillie's application to become a NHL member by a 26-0 vote.[2] Balsillie sought the support of Canadians by creating a Web site called www.makeitseven.ca, referring to the possibility of a seventh NHL team in Canada. Over 200,000 hockey fans supported Balsillie's bid online. And even though Balsillie repeatedly increased the offer, including up to US$242.5 million, the NHL adamantly refused to allow him to join the League. Later, when Balsillie pursued the sale in bankruptcy court, the NHL asked the bankruptcy judge to throw out the BlackBerry tycoon's bid to buy the Coyotes based on the League's overwhelming rejection of Balsillie. The NHL defended its position not to accept Balsillie by telling the judge that no court could force the League to admit Balsillie into their club. Although court documents stated that all of the parties "at the negotiation table are sophisticated and have extensive experience with the purchase and sale of major league sports teams," Balsillie's numerous offers were unsuccessful. Ultimately, the judge agreed with the League that it had the right to approve its own membership (we discussed the role of Balsillie's reputation as perceived by team owners in the previous chapter).[3]

As we can see from this scenario, being one of the richest and most powerful men in the world does not guarantee success in every situation. Power is situational, fluid, and comes from many sources. Power can be created in many different ways in many different contexts, and as a source of leverage can shift from one category to another. Expert negotiators know how to diagnose their sources of power, even when it appears they have little power, and use that power effectively. They also appreciate the power of persuasion. That is, they know how to use persuasive techniques to induce attitudinal and behavioural change in their opponents. Therefore, the focus of this chapter is to illustrate the sources of power, ways to increase your perceived power, and introduce techniques that can be used to persuade your counterparts.

Sources of Power—How People Acquire Power

In this section we will take a broad perspective on power as it relates to negotiation and aggregate the major sources of power into several different groupings (see Table 7.1):

- informational sources of power,
- power based on position in an organization,
- network or relationship-based sources of power, and
- contextual sources of power.

Informational Sources of Power

There is more than a grain of truth to the phrase "information is power." Within the context of negotiation, information is perhaps the most common and influential source of power. Information power is derived from the negotiator's ability to assemble and organize facts and data to support his or her position, arguments, or desired outcomes. Negotiators may also use information as a tool to challenge the other party's position or desired outcomes or to undermine the effectiveness of the other's negotiating arguments. Even in the simplest negotiation, the parties take a position and then present arguments and facts to support that position.

In Chapter 2 we briefly discussed how access to information has shifted power in favour of consumers of new automobiles. Consumers who know the dealer cost to obtain a car from the manufacturer are much more likely to pay less than a consumer who only knows the list price of the car. Because information provides such a distinct advantage in negotiation, it is worth reiterating the advice we provided in Chapter 4 about doing your homework prior to negotiating.

TABLE 7.1 | Major Sources of Power

Source of Power	Description
Informational	• Information: the accumulation and presentation of data intended to change the other person's point of view or position on an issue.
	• Expertise: an acknowledged accumulation of information, or mastery of a body of information, on a particular problem or issue.
	Expertise power can be positive (we believe the other because of their acknowledged expertise) or negative (we so distrust the other that their claimed expertise leads us to pursue a course of action opposite to the one they advocate.)
Position-based power	Power derived from being located in a particular position in an organizational or communication structure; leads to several different kinds of leverage:
	• Legitimate power, or formal authority, derived from occupying a key position in a hierarchical organization. However, legitimate power can also influence social norms, such as
	• Reciprocity, or the expected exchange of favours
	• Equity, or the expected return when one has gone out of one's way for the other
	• Dependence, or the expected obligation one owes to others who cannot help themselves
	• Resource control, or the accumulation of money, raw material, labour, time, and equipment that can be used as incentives to encourage compliance or as punishments for noncompliance. Resource control is manifested in
	• Reward power, the use of tangible rewards or personal approval to gain the other's compliance
	• Punishment power, the use of tangible punishments or withholding of personal approval to gain the other's compliance
Relationship-based power	• Goal interdependence—how the parties view their goals.
	Referent power—based on an appeal to the other based on common experiences, group membership, status, etc. Referent power can also be positive (we believe the other because we respect them) or negative (we so disrespect the other that we pursue a course of action opposite to the one they advocate).
	• Access to or control over information, resources supply flows, or access, derived from location within flows in a network.
Contextual power	• Power derived from the context in which negotiations take place.
	Common sources of contextual power include
	• Availability of BATNAs
	• Organizational and national culture
	• Availability of agents, constituencies, and audiences who can directly or indirectly affect the outcomes of the negotiation

Power derived from expertise is a special form of information power. The power that comes from information is available to anyone who assembles facts and figures to support arguments, but expert power is accorded to those who are seen as having achieved some level of command and mastery of a body of information. Experts are accorded respect, deference, and credibility based on their experience, study, or accomplishments. One or both parties in a negotiation will give experts' arguments more credibility than those of non-experts—but only to the extent that the expertise is seen as functionally relevant to the persuasion situation.[4] For example, someone knowledgeable about cars may not be an expert on motorcycles. Thus, a negotiator who would like to take advantage of his or her expertise will often need to demonstrate that this expertise (1) actually exists, and (2) is relevant to the issues under discussion.

Power Based on Position in an Organization

We discuss two major sources of power based on position in an organization: (1) legitimate power, which is grounded in the title, duties, and responsibilities of a job description and "level" within an organization hierarchy; and (2) power based on the control of resources (budget, funding, etc.) associated with that position.

Legitimate Power   Legitimate power is derived from occupying a particular job, office, or position in an organizational hierarchy. In this case, the power resides in the title, duties, and responsibilities of the position itself, and the "legitimacy" of the officeholder comes from the title and duties of the job description within that organization context. Thus, a newly promoted vice president acquires some legitimate power merely from being a vice president.

There are times when people respond to directions from another, even directions they do not like, because they feel it is proper (legitimate) for the other to direct them and proper (obligatory) for them to obey. This is the effect of legitimate power.

Legitimate power is at the foundation of our social structure. When individuals and groups organize into any social system—a small business, a combat unit, a union, a political action organization, a sports team, a task force—they almost immediately create some form of structure and hierarchy. They elect or appoint a leader and may be willing to give up their right to participate in every decision by vesting authority in that leader who can act on their behalf. By creating a group structure that gives one person a power base, group members generate a willingness within themselves to obey that person's directives.

People can acquire legitimate power in several ways. First, it may be acquired at birth. Elizabeth II has the title of Queen of England and all the stature the title commands. She also controls a great deal of the personal wealth of the monarchy. However, she has little actual power in terms of her ability to run the day-to-day affairs of Britain, and even less so in Canada. Second, legitimate power may be acquired by election to a designated office: the Prime Minister of Canada has substantial legitimate power derived from that elected position. Third, legitimate power is derived simply by appointment or promotion to some organizational position. Thus, holding the title of director or general manager entitles a person to all the rights, responsibilities, and privileges that go with that position. Finally, some legitimate authority comes to an individual who occupies a position for which other people simply show respect, such as a priest. Usually, such respect is derived from the intrinsic social good or important social values of that person's position or organization.

The effectiveness of formal authority is derived from the willingness of followers to acknowledge the legitimacy of the organizational structure and the system of rules and regulations that empowers its leaders.[5] In short, legitimate power cannot function without obedience or the consent of the governed. If enough British citizens question the legitimacy of the queen and her authority—even given the hundreds of years of tradition and law on which the monarchy is founded—her continued rule will be in serious jeopardy. Because legitimate power can be undermined if followers choose to no longer recognize the power holder's authority, it is not uncommon for power holders to accumulate other power sources (such as resource control or information) to fortify their power base.

Although we have been talking about organizational structures and positions as conferring "legitimacy," it is also possible to apply the notion of legitimacy to certain social norms or conventions that exert strong control over people.[6] Examples include the following:

1. The legitimate power of reciprocity, a very strong social norm that suggests that if one person does something positive or favourable for the other, the gesture or favour is expected to be returned ("One good turn deserves another").

2. The legitimate power of equity, another strong social norm, taps into the concept of fairness, where one agent perceives the right to expect a benefit or opportunity from another because it is the just thing ("First in line first served").

3. The legitimate power of responsibility or dependence, a third strong social norm that says we have an obligation to help others who cannot help themselves and are dependent on us ("Everyone needs a helping hand").

Resource Control People who control resources have the capacity to give them to someone who will do what they want or deny or rescind them (or take them away) from someone who doesn't do what they want. Resources can be many things. Particular resources are more useful as instruments of power to the extent that they are highly valued by participants in the negotiation. In an organizational context, some of the most important resources are the following:

1. Money, in its various forms: cash, salary, budget allocations, grants, bonus money, expense accounts, and discretionary funds.

2. Supplies: raw materials, components, pieces, and parts.

3. Human capital: available labour supply, staff that can be allocated to a problem or task, temporary help.

4. Time: free time, the ability to meet deadlines, the ability to control a deadline. If time pressure is operating on one or both parties, the ability to help someone meet or move a deadline can be extremely powerful.

5. Equipment: machines, tools, technology, computer hardware and software, vehicles.

6. Critical services: repair, maintenance, upkeep, installation and delivery, technical support, transportation.

7. Interpersonal support: verbal praise and encouragement for good performance or criticism for bad performance. This is an interesting resource because it is available to almost anyone, does not require significant effort to acquire, and is quite powerful on its own.

To use resources as a basis for power, negotiators must develop or maintain control over some desirable reward that the other party wants—such as physical space, jobs, budget authorizations, or raw materials—or control over some punishment the other seeks to avoid. As noted, these rewards and punishments could be tangible or intangible, such as liking, approval, respect, and so on. Successful control over resources also requires that the other party must deal directly with the power holder. Finally, the power holder must be willing to allocate resources depending on the other's compliance or co-operation with the power holder's requests. The increasing scarcity of resources of all kinds has led to the new golden rule of organizations: "Whoever has the gold makes the rules."

Power Based on Networks

Power also comes from location in an organizational structure, but not necessarily a hierarchical structure. In this case, power is derived from whatever flows through that particular location in the structure (usually information and resources, such as money). The person occupying a certain position may not have a formal title or office; his or her leverage comes from the ability to control and manage what "flows" through that position. For example, before China modernized in the 1980s, automobile chauffeurs held enormous power even though their title was not prestigious. If a chauffeur did not like a passenger or did not feel like driving to a certain location, he could make life very difficult and impose consequences in several areas (e.g., departure time, duration of trip, lunch time, and location).

This example shows that even without a lofty position or title, individuals can become powerful because of the way that their actions and responsibilities are embedded in the flows of information, goods and services, or contacts. For example, individuals who have access to a large amount of information, or who are responsible for collecting, managing, and allocating vital resources (money, raw materials, permissions and authorizations), may become very powerful.[7] The job may not have a fancy title, a large staff, or a large corner office, but it can confer a significant amount of power by virtue of the amount of information and resources that pass through it. Expert negotiators know that power comes not just from who you control, but also from whom you are connected to.

Contextual Sources of Power

Finally, while power can be located within individuals and their relationships, power is also based in the context, situation, or environment in which negotiations take place. While these forms of power often go unrecognized in the short term (because of our tendency to see power as an individual quality rather than embedded in the structure or context of a conflict), these sources are just as critical.

BATNA In earlier chapters we discussed the role of a best alternative to a negotiated agreement—that is, an alternative deal that a negotiator might pursue if she or he does not come to agreement with the current other party. Although we are discussing BATNA near the end of our discussion of sources of power—don't be mistaken—having a great BATNA is one of the strongest sources of power there is. With a great BATNA you have a choice between accepting the other party's proposal or an attractive alternative deal. Because BATNA is such an important source of power, it is worth reiterating that you should do everything possible to improve your BATNA before negotiating. You never know, with additional information you may find that the deal you are considering is actually worse than your best alternative.

Culture　Culture determines the "meaning system" of a social environment. Culture often shapes what kinds of power are seen as legitimate and illegitimate or how people use influence and react to influence. For example, in one organization known to the authors of this book, the CEO introduced ideas for major changes in business strategy in management team meetings. Senior managers made very few critical comments about these ideas in the meeting, but they then actively expressed their disagreement with the idea in one-to-one conversations with each other or the CEO. This public lack of openness and honesty—a cultural value in this organization—contributed to many decisions that were apparently made by consensus, but then consistently undermined in private by those who made the decision. Cultures will often contain many implicit "rules" about use of power and whether "power over" or "power with" processes are seen as more or less appropriate.[8]

National cultures also differ in the degree to which these "power over" or "power with" orientations are supported or encouraged. We explore this approach in greater depth in our treatment of international negotiation in Chapter 11.

Finally, culture—both organizational and national—often translates into deeply embedded structural inequalities in a society. The degree to which women, religious or ethnic groups, certain social classes, or other minority interests are treated unjustly in a society reflects long-standing historical evolution of power inequalities in social structures and institutions. Many significant social problems and negotiations about how to change them can be traced to the historical evolution of these dispositions within a culture, and they require significant effort and attention over many years to introduce meaningful change.

Agents, Constituencies, and External Audiences　Most negotiations that we describe in this book take place one-to-one—just you and the other negotiator. But negotiations become significantly more complex when negotiators are representing others' views (e.g. acting as an agent representing their organization or being represented by another person) and when there are multiple parties, the public media, and/or audiences present to observe, critique, and evaluate the negotiations. When all of these other parties are present in a negotiation, they can become actively involved to formally or informally pressure others as part of the negotiation process.

■ Dealing with Others Who Have More Power

Thus far we have been focusing on the numerous ways that negotiators can assemble and use power to their advantage in a negotiation. However, negotiators are often on the receiving end of that power. Very little research has focused on how parties can deal with others who have significantly more power (from one or more of the sources we have mentioned in this chapter). We end this section with some advice to negotiators who are in a low-power position. Michael Watkins specifically addresses the problem of "dancing with elephants" (striking a deal with an opponent much bigger than you) and highlights ways that lower power parties can deal with the big players in business deals and partnerships. Here is some of his advice:[9]

1. **Never do an all-or-nothing deal.** Relying on a single party and creating a make-or-break deal with them leaves the low-power party highly vulnerable. For example, a small business that accepts a contract agreeing that Zellers will be its sole customer runs the risk of being completely controlled by Zellers. Low-power parties should attempt to diversify their risk by entering into deals with several other partners so that no single high-power player could wipe the low-power partner out.

2. **Make the other party smaller.** In dealing with a high-power party, particularly if it is a group or organization, one should attempt to establish multiple relationships and engage in multiple negotiations. By dealing with a variety of different individuals and departments in the high-power party, one diversifies the relationships and the multiple interests that may be served in working with these different subgroups.

3. **Make yourself bigger.** Similarly, low-power players should attempt to build coalitions with other low-power players so as to increase their collective bargaining power.

4. **Build momentum through doing deals in sequence.** Early deals can be done to build a relationship, strengthen the relationship with the high-power party, and perhaps acquire resources (information, technology, seed capital, etc.).

5. **Use the power of competition to leverage power.** This is a variation on the power of a BATNA. If you have something to offer, make sure you offer it to more than one high-power party. If you can get them competing against each other for what you want, some may actually do a deal with you simply to keep you from doing a deal with one of their competitors.

6. **Constrain yourself.** Tie your hands by limiting the ways that you can do business or who you can do business with. However, while these constraints might drive away your competition, they also have the liability of constraining you as well.

7. **Good information is always a source of power.** Seek out information that strengthens your negotiating position and case. Anticipate the information that would be most compelling or persuasive to the other side; organize it so that you can draw on it quickly and assemble it to be maximally persuasive.

8. **Do what you can to manage the process.** If the high-power party controls the negotiation process (the agenda, the cadence, the timing, and the location), they will do it in a way to assure outcomes they want. If the low-power party controls the process, they are more likely to be able to steer the deal in an advantageous direction.[10]

See Negotiation Point 7.1 for information on the relationship between power and emotions.

7.1

Can Anger Be Used as a Source of Power?

Conventional wisdom suggests that the use of anger in negotiations can help negotiators get more of what they want, but can anger help you get more of what you want from a more powerful counterpart? Researchers Gerben van Kleef of the University of Amsterdam and Stephane Cote of the University of Toronto found, in a simulated negotiation, that negotiators with lower power, or fewer available alternatives in lieu of a negotiated settlement, claimed less value from an angry counterpart.

However, the way negotiators with higher power dealt with angry counterparts depended on the extent to which they believed their counterpart's anger toward them was justified. Specifically, negotiators with higher power demanded more value from counterparts who they believed had no reason to be angry with them than from counterparts who they believed had a justifiable reason to be angry with them. The researchers explain that these greater demands are likely in retaliation against what higher power negotiators believe to be inappropriate displays of anger by their counterpart. These findings suggest that negotiators would not benefit from displaying anger toward a more powerful counterpart.

Source: G. A. van Kleef, & S. Cote, "Expressing anger in conflict: When it helps and when it hurts," Journal of Applied Psychology, 92, 6, (2007) 1557–69.

Summary of Power

In closing our discussion of power we wish to stress two key points. First, while we have presented many vehicles for attaining power in this chapter, it must be remembered that power can be highly elusive and fleeting in negotiation. Almost anything can be a source of power if it gives the negotiator a temporary advantage over the other party (e.g., a BATNA or a piece of critical information). Second, power is only the capacity to influence; using that power and skilfully exerting influence on the other requires a great deal of sophistication and experience. We now turn our attention to power's complement—persuasion.

Persuasion

During negotiations, actors frequently need to convince the other party that they have offered something of value, their offer is reasonable, and they cannot offer more. If you have power, this can generally be done in an easier and quicker fashion than when you have little power. However, it is important to keep in mind that you do not need power to be persuasive. There are numerous techniques negotiators can use to change their counterparts attitude and behaviour. Our focus in the rest of this chapter is on helping you understand these techniques, how to use them, and how to respond when they are used against you.

■ Two Routes to Persuasion

central route
a type of persuasion using direct behaviours and statements

Researchers who study persuasion and influence have found that there are two general ways that people can be persuaded. The first route, known at the **central route**, refers to those direct behaviours and statements that quite literally convince the other side that your arguments are valid and worthy of consideration. An example of this type of persuasion would be to present a potential buyer of a property with data supporting the market value of your property and comparable properties in the area.

peripheral route
a type of persuasion relying on indirect behaviours and manipulation of subtle cues

The second type of persuasion, known as the **peripheral route**, is less direct, and is characterized by manipulation of subtle cues that lead the other party to change their behaviour or attitude almost subconsciously. An example of this type of persuasion would be someone at a conference changing their mind about a topic based on the impressive credentials of the speaker rather than the arguments presented by the speaker. As these brief examples show, the two routes to persuasion are quite different. The central route tends to be rational, cognitive, and based on information. In contrast, the peripheral route tends to be grounded in emotional and motivational changes. Because the two types are so different, we discuss them separately, beginning with the central route.

The Central Route: Framing and Delivering a Message

Facts and ideas are clearly important in changing another person's opinions and perceptions, but the effectiveness of a persuasion effort depends on how the facts and ideas are selected, organized, and presented. There are three major issues to consider when constructing a message: the *content* of the message (the facts and topics that should be covered), the *structure* of the message (how the topics and facts should be arranged and organized), and the *delivery style* (how the message should be presented).

1. Make the Offer Attractive to the Other Party In structuring the message, negotiators should emphasize the advantage the other party gains from accepting the proposal.[11] Although this may seem obvious, it is surprising how many negotiators spend more time explaining what aspects of their offer are attractive to themselves rather than identifying what aspects are likely to be attractive to the other party. Experienced negotiators ensure that the other party understands what he or she will gain by accepting an offer. To do this well, negotiators need to understand the other party's needs.

2. Frame the Message So the Other Party Will Say "Yes" Advertisers discovered long ago that people who agree with one statement or proposal, even though it may be minor, are likely to agree with a second, more significant statement or proposal from the same person or on the same topic.[12] If you can get the other party to agree to something—almost anything—then you have laid the foundation for subsequent agreement. The task is to find something that the other party can agree with that puts him or her in the mind-set of saying yes. A real estate salesperson who gets potential buyers to agree that the house they are visiting is in a nice neighbourhood or has a nice yard for their children has made the first step toward getting them to say yes to buying the house (even if it is not the ideal size, layout, or price).

3. Make the Message Normative It is easy to assume that people are driven by simple and direct self-interest. There is plenty of evidence, however, to indicate that people are motivated to behave consistently with their values, that is, their religious, social, or ethical standards. These standards become part of people's self-image, a concept in their mind of what they are really like. People will go to considerable lengths to act or say things consistent with their self-image. At times, people act politely when in fact they are feeling quite hostile. People can act generously when they are actually financially strained and feel like being greedy.[13]

A powerful argument in negotiation is to show the other person that by following a course of action (your proposal), she will be acting in accordance both with her values and with some higher (more noble, moral, or ethical) code of conduct. At times, the simple statement "This is the right thing to do" may carry considerable weight. People work hard to take responsibility for actions that lead to positive outcomes.[14]

4. Suggest an "Agreement in Principle" There are times when getting the other party to accept an "agreement in principle" may be a valuable step in a negotiation. For example, when there is bitter conflict between two parties who cannot seem to agree on anything, getting agreement on a general principle, such as a cease-fire, may be the first "yes" statement to which both parties can ascribe. In the negotiations between Israel and Egypt over the Sinai, no details were settled about the fate of the Palestinians, but an agreement on the principle of Palestinian self-rule was reached. Although an agreement in principle is desirable when other options are blocked, it still takes a great deal of work to turn such an agreement into one that contains actionable details. Principles sound good, and most people may agree with what they advocate, but there is usually great uncertainty about how a principle applies to a specific situation.

5. One- and Two-Sided Messages When negotiators try to persuade the other party it is because they believe that the other holds an opinion different from theirs. Many people deal with this problem by ignoring arguments and opinions that might support the other party's position—a *one-sided* approach. Many politicians not only do not mention their opponent's point of view but may never even mention their opponent's name. An alternate approach to ignoring the competition is to mention and describe the opposing point of view, and then show how and why it is less desirable than the presenter's point of view—a *two-sided* approach. In general, two-sided messages are considered to be more effective than one-sided messages.[15]

6. Message Components Big ideas or large propositions are hard to grasp and accept, especially when they are significantly different from your own. Negotiators can help the other party understand and accept their arguments by breaking them into smaller, more understandable pieces.[16] It is even better if they can show that the component parts contain statements that the other party has already accepted or agreed with. For example, a company that is having trouble getting the union to accept significant revisions to the collective agreement could break its presentation down into separate discussions of specific components: shift transfers, changes in work classifications, and so on. Breaking down complex arguments into smaller parts also helps the parties see the possibilities to logroll, bundle, and trade off across issues because the issues will be seen in sharper focus.

7. Use Vivid Language and Metaphors The vividness and intensity of the language negotiators use have a major effect on their persuasiveness. Saying "This is certainly the best price you will get" is more compelling than saying "This is quite a good price." The intensity of language can also be increased through the use of colourful metaphors, swear words, or a change in intonation—from quiet to loud or loud to quiet.

You might think that the most intense language would also be the most persuasive. On the contrary, language of relatively low intensity is at times more effective.[17] Evidence indicates that people react negatively to persuasive attempts using language they perceive as too intense.[18] People under stress seem to be particularly receptive to messages using low-intensity language and more inclined to reject those using high-intensity language.[19] However, the effect of intense language depends in part on who uses it. Sources with high credibility can use more intense language than those who are not seen as credible.[20]

Metaphors and analogies are a particularly useful way to elevate the vividness of a message in the service of persuasion.[21] An auto salesperson can give a potential customer details about a car's carburetor, the miles per gallon of gasoline used at different speeds, and rates of acceleration, but can make these points just as well by saying, "This car flies like the wind and doesn't guzzle gas." The same salesperson could show a car's fine finish, point out the body undercoating, and draw attention to the immaculate condition of the engine, or he could say, "This car is as sleek as a cat." Using metaphors to excess may lead the other party to believe that you're filled with hot air (itself a metaphor for not having the facts to support arguments), but using them to summarize some facts or to establish clear visual impressions can be valuable in persuasion.

Section Summary

In summary, negotiators need to take care when they construct a message to persuade another party to their point of view. Aspects of the message content, message structure, and delivery style can all influence the extent to which a message is persuasive. In other words, how one says something can be as important as what one has to say, and if the other party is not persuaded by the arguments, then perhaps the negotiator did not construct the message effectively. When messages are well crafted and influence does successfully occur through the "central route," the change in the target's attitudes is more likely to be long lasting and resistant to counterinfluence.

Peripheral Routes to Persuasion

In the peripheral route to persuasion the receiver attends less to the substance of the arguments and is instead susceptible to more "automatic" influence through subtle cues. This usually occurs when the target of influence is either *unmotivated* or *unable* to focus carefully on the substance contained within a persuasive message. Persuasion that occurs through the peripheral route is less likely to bring about real attitude change, more likely to last a shorter time, and more vulnerable to counterinfluence.

In our discussion of peripheral routes to influence we draw in part on the work of psychologist Robert Cialdini, who argues that this type of persuasion can work almost automatically, like an eye blink or a startle response.[22] Cialdini spent many years investigating why people comply with requests that, upon further reflection, they would rather not have agreed to. His research represents a skilful blend of laboratory investigation and observation of "compliance experts" such as salespeople, fund-raisers, and marketing and advertising experts. The insights that emerge are useful not only for achieving successful influence in negotiation and other contexts, but also for avoiding being a "victim" of these persuasive traps.

Our discussion of peripheral routes to influence will consider three sets of strategies: message aspects, attributes of the persuader, and elements of the influence context.

Aspects of Messages That Foster Peripheral Influence When targets of influence are unmotivated or unable to pay close attention to the influence seeker's message, they are susceptible to being influenced by message elements that exist apart from the actual arguments involved. We discuss two such elements here: the way in which the influence seeker chooses to order those arguments, and the use of distraction to interfere with the target's ability to think effortfully about the arguments in play.

1. **Message Order** In preparing a persuasive argument, negotiators usually have one major point, piece of information, or illustration that is particularly important or compelling. Where should it be placed in the message? At the beginning? In the middle? At the end? Research tells us one thing clearly—do not place the important point in the middle of the message.[23] Should it be at the beginning or at the end? When the topics are familiar, interesting, or controversial to the receiver, the important points should be made early, exposing the receiver to the **primacy effect**: The first item in a long list of items is the one most likely to be remembered. In contrast, when the topic is uninteresting, unfamiliar, or not very important to the receiver, the most critical point should be placed at the end of the message to take advantage of the **recency effect**: the tendency for the last item presented to be the best remembered.[24]

   primacy effect
   the tendency for the first item in a list to be most easily remembered

   recency effect
   the tendency for the last item in a list to be more easily remembered

2. **Distractions** Persuasion is complex because people start to defend themselves against being influenced as soon as they suspect that someone is trying to persuade them. As they listen, part of their attention is devoted to what is being said, but a large portion is also devoted to developing counterarguments.[25] Persuasion efforts are more effective if they can reduce the other party's efforts to develop defensive counterarguments. One way to do this is to have a distraction occur at the same time the message is sent. When receivers are distracted, they are less able to engage in issue-relevant thinking, and hence they may be more susceptible to processing peripheral cues that may push them toward a particular choice.[26] For example, during an oral presentation of the economic advantages of an offer, negotiators could lay out papers with charts and graphs, hand them to the other party, and help that person turn from one chart to another as the oral presentation continues. Presumably, the charts and graphs absorb that part of the other party's attention that might normally go into formulating counterarguments. Distractions seem to inhibit the receiver's subvocalization (what people say to themselves as they hear a message).

Source Characteristics That Foster Peripheral Influence When the recipients of a persuasive message are unmotivated or unable to attend closely to the substance of the persuasive appeal, they become vulnerable to source effects. In other words, someone who is not paying close attention to the message may be unduly influenced by the characteristics of the person or organization delivering the message. A wide variety of source effects can potentially have an effect on the recipient of a persuasive message. We group them here into three broad categories: credibility, attractiveness, and authority.

1. **Source Credibility** During a negotiation, both parties exchange information, opinions, and interpretations. What, and how much, should be believed? As a negotiator, you cannot check every fact and statement. The more information one is willing to accept from the other party without independent verification, the easier that person's job will be. The reverse is also true—the more credible you are to the other party, the more persuasive you will be. Source credibility depends mostly on three things: the qualifications of the source, the perceived trustworthiness of the source, and self-presentation.

   First, *qualifications*: When people are determining how much to believe another person, they often ask, "Is this person in a position to possess the information he or she claims to have? That is, is he or she competent and qualified?" The stronger the person's perceived qualifications and expertise, the higher the credibility.[27] Second, *trustworthiness*: "Is this person reporting accurately what he or she knows? That is, is he or she personally believable or reliable?" Third, *self-presentation*: People appear more or less credible because of the way they present themselves to others. Three components of behaviour are instrumental in creating a favourable presence: composure, sociability, and extroversion.[28] A person who seems hesitant, confused, or uncertain when giving information is not as convincing as a person who appears calm, confident, and comfortable. A friendly, open person is easier to talk to (and therefore to believe) than someone who is distant, abrasive, or haughty. A person with a dynamic vocal style and a strong delivery is often more persuasive than one without these attributes.

2. **Personal Attractiveness** People will treat others better when they like them than when they don't. They are less likely to feel that attractive negotiators will be dishonest or attempt to coerce them. They are more likely to accept their influence, to believe them, and to trust them.[29] Being nice and pleasant is a logical step to being more persuasive. It is not clear why personal attractiveness increases persuasiveness. People may have a tendency to let their guard down and trust attractive people more readily. The following tactics are some of the many ways that an individual can enhance his or her personal attractiveness to a target of influence or a negotiating opponent.

   - *Friendliness* A critically important attribute that a negotiator can have is the ability to be friendly and outgoing and to establish personal relationships with others—particularly the other parties in the negotiation. Warmth, empathy, and simple direct, personal interest in others all help to soften the harder edges of some of the other power sources. Friendliness also involves an emotional component, appealing to the other party's moods and feelings as well as to his or her intellect. Rather than immediately getting down to business, successful negotiators use friendliness to make the other party feel comfortable and at ease, to get to know the other negotiator, and to discover things that they may have in common.

- *Ingratiation* Ingratiation involves enhancing the other's self-image or reputation through statements or actions, and thus enhancing one's own image in the same way.[30] Flattering another person by giving compliments is perhaps the most obvious form of ingratiation. Because it is obvious, ingratiation is used often; but if used poorly, it can backfire. When people are complimented for attributes they do not have or actions they know they did not perform well, or when the praise seems excessive, they are likely to become wary, wondering about the ingratiator's hidden agenda or ulterior motives.

- *Likability* The liking principle is quite straightforward: People you like have more influence over you. If you like the sender, you are more likely to be persuaded by him or her and less likely to contest a weak or counter-attitudinal argument.[31] However, research has shown that likability is less important than other credibility factors, such as expertise.[32] The effects of the liking principle are insidious. Liking can occur through many different approaches, and defending against them all would be impossible; it would be useless to try to prevent yourself from liking others.[33] Rather, you should let the liking occur and then explore why you like the other person. Separating liking the other party from an evaluation of the deal should be enough to moderate the influence of the liking principle in your negotiations.

- *Perceived Similarity* When meeting for the first time, people often try to find something they have in common. Perhaps they attended the same school, grew up in the same neighbourhood, or have friends in common. The more similarities they find, the more bonds they establish, the better both parties feel, and more important, the more receptive they will be to each other's messages and efforts at persuasion.[34] A useful negotiating tactic, therefore, is to identify and discuss experiences, characteristics, and opinions you hold in common with the other party. But if it is to your advantage to find and explore commonalities in experience, attitude, and background with the other party, it is also to your disadvantage to highlight those areas where you differ.

- *Emotion* We discussed emotion earlier in this chapter in connection with the use of language to construct a message, but emotion can also be a source factor. Emotion combined with persistence leads to assertiveness and determination. Used effectively, emotion may enhance a message source's attractiveness by instilling in listeners the belief that the speaker holds appealing deep-seated values (this may also enhance the speaker's credibility). Emotion can be powerful because it offers a stark contrast to the expectation that negotiation is a cool, calm, rational exchange of information, driven by logical analysis of outcome maximization and economic valuation of alternatives.

3. **Authority** The principle of authority is quite simple: People with authority have more influence than those without authority. Researchers have long been interested in the effects of authority figures on human behaviour. Stanley Milgram's classic studies of obedience to authority suggest that people will go to great lengths when their behaviour is legitimized by an authority figure.[35] Most people will obey the orders of a person wearing a uniform, even if there is apparent emergency. This, too, is an effect of the principle of authority.

In negotiation, the principle of authority can be used in many ways. The use of a title, such as *doctor* or *professor*, gives the user more authority and thus more influence.[36] A friend of one of the authors uses the title *doctor* whenever ordering airline tickets. He found out early in his career that airlines would telephone doctors when there was a flight delay but would ignore the other passengers. This simple illustration shows the esteem with which some titles (or positions) are held in society.

Cialdini offers the following advice for dealing with authority figures who may have influence over you. Ask two questions: "Is this authority truly an expert?" and "How truthful can you expect this expert to be?"[37] The first question forces you to verify that the person really does have expertise in the situation and not just the appearance (title, attire) of expertise. The second question brings into focus the motive of the alleged authority.

Aspects of Context That Foster Peripheral Influence Finally, we explore aspects of the situation beyond the message itself and the sender of the message that create opportunities to pursue the peripheral route to influence. Five strategies are discussed: reciprocity, commitment, social proof, scarcity, and reward and punishment.

norm of reciprocity
a social norm that suggests you should return something in the future when you receive something

1. **Reciprocity** The **norm of reciprocity** has been studied for years by philosophers, anthropologists, sociologists, and other social scientists. This norm suggests that when you receive something from another person, you should respond in the future with a favour in return. This norm is thought to be pan-cultural in that groups around the world appear to respect it.[38]

The norm of reciprocity plays an important role in negotiations. Negotiators give concessions and expect concessions in return. For instance, negotiator A does a small favour for negotiator B and later asks for a larger favour from B in return. The net advantage goes to A. Although one may think that the norm of reciprocity should apply only to favours of comparable degree, this does not appear to be the case. In fact, many sales pitches rely on giving the consumer a small gift early in an exchange and then asking for a large concession from the consumer later, such as an exercise towel for enrolling into a long term gym contract.

Similar opportunities exist in other negotiation situations. A compliment, such as a reference to the other party's positive behaviour in a prior discussion, will make that person feel good and set the scene for him or her to act positively. Giving a quick concession on an issue that the other party wants will both please that party and create the implicit obligation for him or her to do the same.

Given the apparent powerfulness of the norm of reciprocity, how can the negotiator counter its effects? One possibility is to refuse all favours in a negotiation setting, but this would probably cause more problems than it resolves. For instance, refusing a cup of coffee from your host may remove the effects of the norm of reciprocity but at the same time may insult the host, especially if five minutes later you go out to get a cup of coffee yourself. Perhaps the other person was simply being polite. Perhaps he or she was setting a positive tone for the meeting. Or perhaps he or she was trying to use the norm of reciprocity to create a small sense of indebtedness.[39] Cialdini suggests that you should respond politely to a favour and accept what is offered if it is something you want. If it becomes apparent that the favour was an attempt at manipulation, however, then you should redefine the event as a trick rather than a favour. This will remove the obligation of the rule of reciprocity because the "rule says that favours are to be met with favours; it does not require that tricks be met with favors."[40]

commitment to a position
personal and interpersonal pressure to remain consistent once we have taken a stance on something

2. **Commitment** Researchers have long recognized that once people have decided something, they can be remarkably persistent in their beliefs. This process has been labelled **commitment to a position**, and it relies heavily on the common need that people have to appear consistent, both to themselves and to others. Most people are familiar with the bait-and-switch sales technique. Unscrupulous organizations advertise merchandise for sale at an incredibly low price but "run out" of stock by the time you arrive at the store. They then try to sell you alternate merchandise at a higher price. Why does this technique work? One reason is that once you have made the decision to purchase a product (a commitment), you almost automatically follow through with the commitment (even at a higher price).

Commitment strategies are very powerful devices for making people comply. One way to increase commitment is to write things down. Some encyclopaedia companies that have customers complete their own order forms have a far lower cancellation rate than those companies that have salespeople write out the form. Many consumer-product companies have people write testimonials about their products to enter a drawing for a prize. Why? Apparently, writing testimonials increases the commitment to buy the product.[41] Research has shown that even signing a petition can increase your compliance with a request to do something more intrusive several days later.[42]

How can commitment work in a negotiation? Usually, it is incremental. Agreement to innocuous statements early in the negotiation may be used as a foundation for further and further concessions. Such strategies are difficult to combat. Frequently, one will have already been influenced and agreed to something before even realizing that manipulation has taken place. To some extent, being forewarned about these techniques is being forearmed. Watch for your body's warning signals when these techniques are in use.[43] Either you will feel uncomfortable when subtle commitments are being made, or something in the deal will just not seem quite right. If you encounter these thoughts or feelings when negotiating, look out for use of a commitment strategy by the other party. At the very least, be aware of all the agreements you strike during a negotiation, even those small, innocuous ones. They may be the setup for the next move.

social proof
judging the appropriateness of our response based on the extent to which others are doing or thinking the same thing

3. **Social Proof** The principle of **social proof** suggests that people look to others to determine the correct response in many situations. This principle suggests that people often behave in certain ways because everyone else is doing so. This is the principle that makes laugh tracks effective on television comedies.[44] It also explains why marketers like to proclaim previously satisfied customers; if other people used the product and liked it, then it must be good. Celebrities are hired to endorse products for similar reasons.

   In negotiation situations, the principle of social proof can act as a powerful influence strategy. Salespeople will show lists of happy customers, knowing that few people will take the time to verify the list. Sweepstakes advertisements feature celebrities as spokesperson and highlight previous winners. Negotiators will talk about how popular their new product is and how sales have really increased this year. Real estate agents will be sure that you are aware that many other people are interested in the house that you are considering buying.

   The principle of social proof works because questionable information ("everyone thinks this product is good") is given weight in decisions. One way to dilute its effectiveness is to identify the false information and give it the weight it deserves.[45] In negotiations, this means careful preparation and being aware of "facts" about the others' advocated views that do not seem to match your preparation. When the other party offers "evidence" about the popularity of an item, do not automatically trust that the other party is being completely honest; rather, ask the other to substantiate the claims.

principle of scarcity
when opportunities seem more valuable because they are less available

4. **Scarcity** The **principle of scarcity** suggests that when things are less available, they will have more influence. Frequently, salespeople will tell customers that they are not sure if the product the customers would like to purchase is currently in stock.[46] Before making the trip to the stockroom they ask if they should grab one before another salesperson gets it. Typically shoppers will say yes and will feel relieved (or lucky) when the salesperson returns with the "last one" in the store. This is the scarcity principle at work; people are easier to influence when they feel that they are obtaining a scarce resource.

   In negotiation situations, the scarcity influence strategy may be operating whenever there appears to be a great demand for a product. Some organizations deliberately keep their products in short supply to give the appearance that they are very widely sought (e.g., popular Christmas toys). Any time negotiators talk about "exclusive opportunities" and "time-limited offers," they are using the scarcity principle. Auctions also rely on the principle of scarcity by selling unique (one-of-a-kind) pieces to the highest bidder—the more scarce the item, the higher the bids. The scarcity principle is difficult to combat when used effectively. It creates in the victim an activity trap focused on obtaining the item and effectively suspends cognitive evaluation of the broader situation.[47]

5. **Use of Reward and Punishment** Earlier we indicated that control over resources was a strong source of power. These resources can be used in at least two major ways. First, negotiators can use *exchange*—the process of offering resources or favours (promises and assistance) to secure the other's compliance and co-operation. Exchange relies on resources as the power base, particularly resources that can be translated into rewards for the

other—favours, benefits, incentives, treats, perks, and the like. Thus, exchange frequently invokes the use of promises and commitments as persuasive tools—obligations that you are willing to make in exchange for the other's co-operation, compliance, or commitment to give you what you want.

A second way that negotiators attempt to use this power is through *pressure*—that is, by the threat of punishment. An influencer can make demands, suggest consequences if the demands are not met, carry out surveillance to determine status, issue frequent reminders about what is expected, and eventually enforce the punishment if the demand is not met. A sales manager may cut a salesperson's pay for repeatedly failing to achieve sales target projections. A supplier may issue a late charge on an overdue bill to a customer. Like rewards and the use of praise, coercion or punishment can be as effective in the verbal form as in the withdrawal or denial of tangible resources. If the sales manager berates a salesperson for failing to make target sales quotas (rather than firing), the impact may be just as great.

Pressure tactics produce, at best, short-term compliance with requests, but they also are likely to elicit resistance from the other party. Frequent use of pressure tactics alienates the other party and leads to very high resistance, in which the severity of consequences and the willingness to invoke them must escalate. Pressure tactics should be used selectively and sparingly because their use is likely to corrode the relationship between the parties, and frequent use is likely to destroy it. One is better off with praise and rewards if the goal is to maintain the target's good will; criticism and sanctions are more appropriate when changing behaviour is more important than maintaining good will.[48]

■ The Role of Receivers—Targets of Influence

We now examine factors related to the person who is the target of influence. At first glance, one might think there is not much receivers can do to exert leverage. Not true! Just as negotiators-as-message-senders can work to increase their credibility and attractiveness, receivers can signal the sender about the general acceptability and favourableness of the message being sent, and senders can monitor the receiver's receptiveness and adapt the message accordingly. Receivers need to be conscious about the signals they send; senders need to monitor the other's receptiveness. Let us review a few key factors.

Exploring or Ignoring the Other's Position

Negotiators frequently give very little attention to the other party's opinions and point of view. This is unfortunate, because as previously noted information is power and so it is very much to your advantage to understand what the other party really wants, how things look to them, and how they developed their position. One can explore the other party's perspective with questions designed to reveal his or her needs and interests. Exploring the other person's outlook not only provides more information, potentially highlighting common ground, but further increases the other party's feeling of being listened to and enhances their receptiveness to meeting your needs. However, questions are often used as a weapon of attack. Questions such as "How in the world can you say that?" or "What possible justification can you have for that position?" are likely to make the other party feel defensive and combative and may make the tone of the negotiations quite negative.

Actively Listen & Selectively Paraphrase Active listening requires listeners to pay full attention to the speaker and turn off the instinct to formulate counter-arguments in their head while the speaker is speaking. Then, paraphrasing what was said ensures that both parties have understood each other accurately. It is important to restate your understanding of what was said and to repeat again if corrected. Repeat the message in your own words, starting with "Let me see if I understand the point you just made." Vocalizing the other person's ideas helps you remember them better than simply hearing them. When people have an important message to get across, they will talk vigorously and at length, often emphasizing the same point over and over. Once your paraphrasing indicates that the other person has been understood, he or she will usually move on; hence, paraphrasing can be very helpful in moving a discussion forward.

You can also ask the other party to restate or paraphrase what you have said. You might say, "What I have said is very important to me, so I would appreciate it if you could tell me what you understood." This asks the other party to listen closely, gives you the opportunity to check out the accuracy of his or her understanding, and emphasizes the most important points of your presentation.

Reinforce Points You Like in the Other Party's Proposals Negotiators are frequently ineffective because they respond only to what they dislike in the other party's statement or proposal and ignore the things they like. Responding in this way ignores a powerful means of shaping and guiding what the other party is saying.

The simplest way to reward people for what they say during a negotiation is to acknowledge and support a point they have made: "That is an interesting point," "I had not heard that before." Give a simple "Yes, I see" or a nod of the head. Statements and actions like these separate a key statement from other points the speaker has made. Second, compliment speakers when they make points you want emphasized, and express appreciation to them for considering your interests and needs. A third approach is to separate particular parts of a statement that you like from those parts you don't like and to encourage the other party to develop the favourable points.

Resisting the Other's Influence

In addition to the variety of things a negotiator can do to encourage, support, or direct the other's communication, there are at least three major things that listeners can do to resist the other's influence efforts: have good alternatives to a negotiated agreement, make a public commitment (or get the other party to make one), and inoculate yourself against the other's persuasive message.

Have a BATNA, and Know How to Use It Earlier we emphasized BATNA as a source of power.[49] There is no question that having a good BATNA enables a negotiator to walk away from a given negotiation, since it means they can get their needs met and interests addressed somewhere else. Of course, having a BATNA is a source of leverage at the negotiation table only if the other party is aware of it. To use a BATNA effectively, a negotiator must assess the other party's awareness that it exists and, if necessary, share that fact. This often must be done deftly—conveying the existence of a BATNA could be interpreted by the other party as an imminent threat to walk away. Keep in mind also that a BATNA can always be improved. Good negotiators will work to improve their BATNA before and even during an ongoing negotiation as a way to enhance their leverage.

Make a Public Commitment One of the most effective ways to get someone to stand firm on a position is to have them make a public commitment to that position. Union leaders have said to their rank and file such things as, "I will resign if we can't get an agreement with management." After making that statement, the union leader faces several pressures. One is the potential loss of face with union members that would come with backing away from that position—the leader may be unceremoniously thrown out of office if he or she does not actually resign. A second pressure is that the leader's credibility with management will be sharply reduced in the future if there is no follow-through on the commitment. Finally, the leader may have his or her own cognitive inconsistency to deal with because failing to resign will be inconsistent with the earlier commitment.

Sometimes negotiators want the other party to make a public commitment. If you can get the other party to make a public statement that supports something you want, that party will be hard-pressed not to stand by the statement. Sometimes negotiators simply make a statement such as "I'm committed to finding an agreement that we can both benefit from," and then invite the other party to make a similar statement. Even better than eliciting statements of commitment is enticing the other party to make a behavioural commitment. For example, retail merchants use down payments and layaway plans to get a behavioural commitment from customers when it is not possible to complete the total sale at that time. See another example in Negotiation Point 7.2.

Negotiation Point

7.2

Persuasion, Patriotism, and Public Commitment

In 2004, Canadian Prime Minister Paul Martin and Newfoundland and Labrador Premier Danny Williams engaged in negotiations over the distribution of revenue generated from the province's natural resources. Negotiations ceased after Williams claimed Martin was not honouring an election campaign promise that would allow Newfoundland and Labrador to keep 100% of its offshore oil and natural gas revenues. Following this breakdown in negotiations, Williams ordered the removal of the Canadian flag from all provincial government buildings. Amidst the controversy created by this move, Martin publicly stated his commitment to his election promise and his desire to resume negotiations once all Canadian flags were restored. Williams explained the rationale for his decision by stating, "History has proven that the only way to get the attention of the federal government in Newfoundland and Labrador is to get the attention of Canadians. This is exactly what we achieved when we removed the flags. Not everyone may have agreed with our decision, but we were able to focus the attention of the country on our issue."

Source: Hutton, Fred. *"Canadian flag flying over Newfoundland."* CTV.ca, 11 January 2005; *"In Depth: Danny Williams,"* Oct. 17, 2006, CBC News; *"Danny Williams: It's not just about Newfoundland, Mr. Harper,"* National Post, Feb. 7, 2009.

On the other hand, at times negotiators will want to prevent the other party from making public commitments to positions that might interfere with reaching an agreement. The other party may later need to back off the commitment to complete a deal. Although it might be tempting to taunt or scold the other party for making a commitment that cannot be kept, a savvy negotiator will realize that it may be in his or her interest to help the other party escape an ill-advised commitment in a face-saving way.

Inoculate Yourself against the Other Party's Arguments One of the likely outcomes of listening carefully to the other party and exploring and understanding his or her point of view is that negotiators may change some of their own positions. At times they may not want to change their position, and therefore they may want to "inoculate" themselves against the other party's arguments.[50] For instance, managers who must support organizational policies with which they disagree may want to inoculate themselves against subordinates' arguments by preparing and rehearsing counterarguments that can be used to refute the key points the other is likely to make. Research reveals that the best way to inoculate against being influenced is to develop arguments *both for your original position* and *against your position*, and then develop counterarguments to refute both.

This chapter discussed the distinct, but related, concepts of power and persuasion. As the story of Jim Balsillie's effort to buy the Phoenix Coyotes illustrates, having substantial power does not guarantee success. In that situation, relationships between Balsillie and the League and its owners were so strained that the League preferred its BATNA (taking over the team) to Balsillie's lucrative financial offer. Clearly, power can be fleeting and influential in different ways in different contexts. Expert negotiators are aware of their sources of power and the limits of the power they do wield. In the next chapter we further explore power and its role in dispute situations.

Persuasion is one way negotiators with low power can increase their success in negotiation. Each of the techniques presented in the chapter can help, but only in situations where they are appropriate. Familiarity with each technique, and attention to our suggestions regarding when to use them, can go a long way towards improving your outcomes. We close this chapter with the optimistic observation that even negotiators who appear to have low power can advance their interests.

Key Terms

Central route, p. 140

Commitment to a
  position, p. 147

Norm of reciprocity, p. 146

Peripheral route, p. 140

Primacy effect, p. 143

Principle of scarcity, p. 148

Recency effect, p. 143

Social proof, p. 148

Disputes and Third-Party Help

LEARNING OBJECTIVES

The main purpose of this chapter is to provide an overview of dispute situations and introduce a framework for resolving disputes. We also introduce various roles third-parties can play when negotiations break down and the parties are stuck in their positions. After reading the chapter you should be able to:

1. Recognize dispute situations,

2. Appreciate the different approaches available for handling a dispute,

3. Understand the difference between arbitration and mediation, and

4. Consider the approaches that managers can take in dealing with disputes between subordinates or peers.

In the introductory chapter we observed that a frequent consequence of interdependent relationships is conflict. Conflict has many sources; it can result from the strongly divergent needs of the two parties or from misperceptions and misunderstandings. Conflict can occur when the two parties are working toward the same goal and generally want the same outcome or when both parties want very different outcomes. Consider the example of Harrison and Wallace McCain.

In the early 1990s the McCain brothers, Harrison and Wallace, then co-CEOs of the McCain Foods Limited frozen food empire, had a public feud over control of the company. The brothers, each owning one-third of the stock, had initially planned to retire together at the age of 75 and slowly allow their sons and nephews to take over major operations. However, their plans soured when younger brother Wallace unilaterally appointed his son as head of the McCain operations in the United States. In response, Harrison was able to persuade the majority of shareholders to demote his younger brother from his position as co-CEO. The family feud became so disruptive that it had a negative impact on customers and suppliers. The battle between brothers only worsened when it turned into a legal battle and continued in a New Brunswick courtroom. In 1995, the court upheld the decision of Harrison and directors to remove Wallace as co-CEO. After being ousted from the company, Wallace ended up in Toronto, taking over Maple Leaf Foods with two of his sons. Although Wallace and his family still have about a third of the shares in the privately-held firm, the brothers apparently never reconciled before Harrison passed away in 2004.[1]

The story of the McCain brothers is just one of the many examples we could have chosen to illustrate the frequency of conflict in business and personal relationships. Every day we hear of similar stories, whether in business, politics, or family relationships. Pause for a second and ask yourself how you handle yourself in conflict situations. What do you say? What do you feel? Does your answer depend on the situation?

Sometimes, we are able to recognize that it is possible to handle the conflict ourselves, and sometimes the situation escalates so far out of control that efforts on our part only make things worse. It is important to be able to diagnose whether or not we can handle problems ourselves, and if we cannot, to know who to turn to for help. It is also important to realize that many of the negotiation skills we have been discussing so far can be useful in handling conflict and disputes.

■ What Are Disputes?

dispute
when one party makes a claim or demand on another party and that claim is rejected

When one person or party makes a claim or demand on another person or party, and that claim is rejected, we can say a **dispute** has emerged. To resolve a dispute the parties must turn their opposing positions into a single outcome. This can happen in several ways: they can work out a solution by themselves, they can have their problem resolved by an outside party, such as an arbitrator, the more powerful party can impose an outcome, or the party making the claim can decide do drop it.

For example, Rogers Communications Inc., Canada's largest telecommunications business, for years described itself as "Canada's most reliable network" in its advertising. A rival firm, Telus Corp., launched a new high-speed wireless network in 2009 and requested that Rogers drop the claims of running the fastest and most reliable network. Rogers refused the request, and so Telus filed suit with the Supreme Court of British Columbia. The court ruled that "the technological advantage that allowed Rogers to represent that it has Canada's most reliable network has disappeared" and that it would be misleading to continue doing so. In response, Rogers released the following public statement: "We are perplexed by the decision. We continue to believe that our network reliability claim is valid. Today we have filed an appeal with the B.C. Court of Appeal. Further steps will be taken shortly."[2] The process continues.

To explain dispute resolution approaches, we introduce a framework developed by Ury, Brett, and Goldberg that compares three different strategic approaches to disputes: interests, rights, and power.[3] Negotiators focus on *interests* when they strive to learn about the other party's interests and priorities as a way to work toward a mutually satisfying agreement that creates value. Negotiators focus on *rights* when they seek to resolve a dispute by drawing upon rules or standards grounded in principles of law, fairness, or perhaps an existing contract. Negotiators focus on *power* when they use threats, exert demands, or other means to try to coerce the other party into making concessions.

A Framework for Resolving Disputes: Interests, Rights, and Power

Parties have a choice about how they approach a negotiation in terms of interests, rights, and power; the same negotiation can be framed in different ways and will likely lead to different consequences. For example, consider the situation of a student who has a dispute with a local car repair shop near campus over the cost of fixing an automobile. The student thinks she was dramatically overcharged for the work—the garage did more work than requested, used the most expensive replacement parts, and didn't give her the chance to review the bill before the work was done. How might this situation play out from each of the three dispute resolution perspectives?

Interests People are often concerned about what they need, desire, or want. People talk about their "positions," but often what is at stake is their underlying interests. Parties who focus on interests in a dispute are often able to find ways to resolve that dispute.

If adopting an interest-based perspective, the student might consider the other's interest and conclude, "Well, small businesses have a right to charge a fair price for good quality work. I will go in and try to understand the shop owner's system for pricing repair work; we will talk about what is a fair price for the work and I will pay it, and I will probably go back to the shop again."

Rights People may also be concerned about who is "right"—that is, who has legitimacy, who is correct, or what is fair. Disputes about rights are often resolved by helping the parties find a fair way to determine who is "right," or that they can both be "right." This resolution often requires the use of some standard or rule such as "taking turns," "split it down the middle," or "first come first served" to settle the dispute. Disputes over rights are often referred to formal or informal arbitrators to decide whose standards or rights are more appropriate.

The student in our example worked in a garage herself one summer and knows that car repairs are priced on what standard manuals state it will generally cost for the labour (hours of work × payment per hour), plus the cost of the parts. If adopting a rights-based perspective, the student might consider, "I will ask to see the manual and the invoice for the parts. I will also go to the garage where I worked myself and ask the owner of that garage if he thinks this bill is inflated. I'll propose to pay for the parts at cost and the labour based on the mechanic's hourly pay rate."

Power People may wish to resolve a negotiation on the basis of power. Negotiations resolved by power are sometimes based on who is physically stronger or is able to coerce the other, but more often, it is about imposing other types of costs—economic pressures, expertise, authority, and so on. Disputes settled by power usually create clear winners and losers, with all the consequences that come from polarizing the dispute and resolving it in this manner.

If adopting a power-based approach, our student might say things like this: "I'll go in and start yelling at the owner about gouging, and I'll also threaten to tell all my friends not to use this garage. I'll write letters to the student newspaper about how bad this repair shop is. My dad is a lawyer and I'll have him call the owner. I'll teach them a thing or two!"

Note that the different approaches are likely to lead to very different discussions between the student and the garage owner. Moreover, the way the student approaches the problem with the garage owner will probably influence how the garage owner responds. The more the student uses power, the more likely the garage owner is to respond with power of his own (e.g., keep the car until the student pays and not reduce the price at all, and call his own lawyer); the confrontation could become angry and lead the parties into small claims court. In contrast, the more the student uses interests, the more the garage owner may in turn be likely to consider the student's interests. The parties will have a discussion about what is fair given the services rendered; while the student may wind up paying more (than if she "won" the power argument), the tone of the discussion is likely to be far different, and the student may be in a much better position to get discounts or consideration in the future.

This framework assumes that all three approaches can potentially exist in a single situation; negotiators make choices about where to place their focus. But do negotiators really use all three? Should they? These questions were addressed in a study by Anne Lytle, Jeanne Brett, and Debra Shapiro.[4]

Lytle and her colleagues found that most negotiators cycled through all three strategies—interests, rights, and power—during the same encounter. They also found that negotiators tended to reciprocate these strategies. A coercive power strategy, for example, may be met with a power strategy in return, which can lead to a negative conflict spiral and a poor (or no) agreement.

They developed some important implications for the use of power in negotiation:

- Starting a negotiation by conveying your own power to coerce the other party could bring a quick settlement if your threat is real and credible. If the other party calls your bluff, however, you are left to either carry out your threat or lose face, both of which may be undesirable.

- Power tactics (and rights tactics) may be most useful when the other party refuses to negotiate or when negotiations have broken down and need to be restarted. In these situations, not much is risked by making threats based on rights or power, but the threat itself may help the other party appreciate the severity of the situation.

- The success of power tactics (and rights tactics) depends to a great extent on how they are implemented. To be effective, threats must be specific and credible, targeting the other party's high-priority interests. Otherwise, the other party has little incentive to comply. Make sure that you leave an avenue for the other party to "turn off" the threat, save face, and reopen the negotiations around interests.

Which Approach Should You Use?

According to Ury, Brett, and Goldberg, you should evaluate four criteria when deciding whether to focus your energy on an interest, rights, or power approach. First, you should analyse *transaction costs*. This involves an assessment of the likely costs associated with each approach. On this issue we offer one important bit of advice: people involved in disputes tend to underestimate the costs associated with exercising a rights and/or power-based approach. An example involved a legal dispute in which a former employee filed a discrimination case against a social service agency. The case was filed at a provincial Human Rights Commission, and when it went to mediation the CEO of the agency walked away from a settlement that would have paid the former employee approximately one year's wages. In the end, the agency lost the case and publicly available documents revealed they had spent up to half a million dollars in legal fees. Clearly, this is an example of a situation where transaction costs were underestimated. Transaction costs can be both tangible and intangible, such as the high financial expenses incurred in litigation by the agency and the cost incurred with the loss of reputation by the agency.

A second factor to consider is *satisfaction with outcomes*. How will the parties feel about possible settlements under each type of approach? Satisfaction tends to be influenced by the outcome, of course, but also by the perceived fairness of the dispute resolution process. In general, people are more satisfied with outcomes that use an interest-based approach than a rights or power approach.

A third factor is the *effect on the relationship*. What is the impact or the effect each approach will have on how the parties feel about each other afterwards? Once again, this is affected by both the outcomes and the processes used to settle or resolve the dispute.

Finally, you should consider the *likelihood of recurrence*. Will resolution of the dispute be more or less likely to occur again under one of the three approaches?

As a general rule, resolving disputes based on interests will be "less costly" than using rights or power. In addition, resolving disputes based on rights is "less costly" than using power. When we say costly we mean the extent to which the approach is measured against the four criteria above, not just dollars and cents.

Other Considerations

Although we generally advocate the use of an interest-based approach for resolving disputes, we also must highlight the fact that in many situations this is not possible or desirable. When interests are diametrically opposed, such as the situation between loggers and environmental groups, lawsuits or attempts at disruption might be the only recourse. A rights-based approach is often required in matters of public importance.

At first glance, it would appear that a powerful party should avoid using an interest-based approach when dealing with a party having less power. However, even though power might win in the end, the costs associated with imposing one's will on another party can be high. Anyone who has been subjected to a threat by a more powerful counterpart can likely appreciate the possible costs of the threat; these costs include things like decreased co-operation, anger, resentment, and even a need for revenge.

There is an interesting irony associated with the use of power. The use of power comes at a cost, and sometimes when you use power to win, you also lose. If you find yourself in an ongoing relationship and use power to resolve a dispute, chances are high that you will also lose the relationship. Winning with power can lead to hollow victories, especially when the parties must continue working together.

To conclude our discussion of disputes, we offer the following advice and observations regarding rights and power:

- It is difficult for parties in a dispute to agree on the standards to apply when attempting to use a rights-based approach. Each party is likely to suggest, or advocate, a standard that most benefits themselves. As such, it's helpful to have neutral evaluators available to the parties.

- When trying to decide what rights-based standard to present, try to anticipate what the other side will consider fair.

- Using both rights and power to resolve disputes generally results in winners and losers. This can have long term negative consequences for existing relationships.

threat
an "if/then" statement that warns of the cost of noncompliance

- Threats are a precursor to the use of power. Only use a **threat** (defined as an "if/then" statement that warns about the cost of noncompliance) when you are willing to carry out the action you are warning about. When doing so, make sure the other party knows exactly what they need to do, and when, to prevent you from using your power.

- When in a dispute the parties' BATNAs are usually linked. If one party decides to do nothing, the claim will rarely just go away. When wise negotiators find themselves in a dispute they usually think about their worst alternative to a negotiated agreement. Consider what the other party can do to you if no agreement is reached.

■ Third-Party Help

third party
someone who isn't directly involved in the dispute or negotiation, but who can help in resolving it

There are times when negotiations break down and negotiators are unable to reach an agreement on their own. When this happens, it is a good idea to ask a **third party** to step in. A third party is someone who isn't directly involved in the dispute or negotiation, but who can help in resolving it. There are several types of third party intervention, but in general they differ on the degree to which the parties give up control of one or both of the following aspects: control over *process* and control over *outcome*. The two most common forms of third party intervention, mediation and arbitration, differ on these two dimensions. When using mediation, the mediator has control over the process. For example, they determine the agenda, who speaks and when, whether or not to separate the parties into different rooms, how much information is shared, and so on. The mediator does not, however, determine the outcome. This is determined by the parties themselves with the assistance of the mediator. In contrast, an arbitrator takes control of shaping and determining the outcome while giving control over the process to the parties themselves. An arbitrator imposes a decision based on the submissions and options put forth by the parties. In the rest of this section we elaborate on these third-party approaches and provide advice regarding when to bring in a third party.

Reasons to Use a Third Party

According to Christopher Moore,[5] there are many signs indicating that a third party might be appropriate. You should look out for these factors:

- the emotional level between the parties is high, with lots of anger and frustration,
- communication between the parties is poor or has completely broken down, or the parties appear to be talking "past" each other,
- behaviour is negative (such as name calling),
- the parties strongly disagree about what information is necessary, available, or required,
- differences in interests appear to be irreconcilable, or
- negotiations have broken down and there is an impasse.

alternative dispute resolution (ADR)
third-party approaches to resolving disputes

The term alternative dispute resolution (ADR) is commonly used to refer to third-party approaches to resolving disputes. Over the last few decades there has been a strong emphasis on taking disputes of all kinds out of the court system and referring them to third parties. In Canada, ADR is often a prerequisite before full litigation in various areas of law and jurisdictions. For example:

- The Sports Dispute Resolution Centre of Canada was created in 2003 to serve as an independent organization whose mission is to provide the sports community with a national alternative dispute resolution service for addressing sports disputes. Applicants must first attempt to resolve their disputes at the local organizational level prior to applying to the Centre for ADR assistance.

- In Saskatchewan, the *Farm Land Security Act* introduced a formal mediation process to resolve disputes between farmers and lenders in 1985. In 1988 mediation became mandatory for facilitating settlements in agricultural disputes.

- Section 29 of British Columbia's *Homeowner Protection Act* requires that if one party to any provincial Supreme Court action involving residential construction elects to invoke mediation then all parties must attend a minimum of one mediation session.

- All provinces have entered into an Agreement on Internal Trade, which aims to reduce barriers to the movement of persons, goods, services, and investments within Canada. The Agreement provides a formal dispute resolution mechanism that requires parties to engage in and exhaust all applicable dispute avoidance and resolution processes prior to proceeding with litigation.

- In some industries, such as construction, contracts are drafted to include dispute resolution clauses, which require parties to participate in mediation and resort to litigation only when other attempts to reach a solution have failed.

The Ministry of the Attorney General of Ontario indicates that over 90 percent of all lawsuits settle before trial stage.[6] Ontario has a Mandatory Mediation Program for certain types of civil lawsuits, such as estates, trust, substitute decision-making cases, etc. These cases are referred to a mediation session early in the litigation process to give parties an opportunity to discuss and potentially settle the issues in dispute. The mediation is conducted by a private-sector mediator whom the parties select from the Program's roster of mediators. If the parties cannot agree on a mediator, one will be appointed for them by the Local Mediation Coordinator, who is responsible for administering the Program. All parties must attend the mediation session. If a party is represented by a lawyer, the lawyer must also attend. A lawyer may not attend in the place of a party. All parties share the cost of the mediation session.

Other provinces have a similar mandatory mediation programs. For example, in Saskatchewan 80 percent of all civil cases (non-family) filed with the Court of Queen's Bench are processed through mandatory mediation.[7] British Columbia has three forms of mediation: voluntary, quasi-mandatory (a hybrid model), and mandatory. British Columbia's quasi-mandatory mediation process is commenced when one party to the litigation issues a Notice to Mediate, which requires other parties to the lawsuit to attend a single mediation session. The Attorney General of British Columbia notes that quasi-mandatory mediation is now used in more than 4000 motor vehicle personal injury cases annually.[8] While it requires compulsory attendance at the mediation and does not require a settlement, such cases usually do settle. Settlement rates at mediation have held steady over 10 years at approximately 75 percent.

You might be wondering who performs ADR and third-party services. There are many people who perform these services, including formal arbitrators, professional mediators, ombudspersons, social workers, managers, or even friends of the disputing parties. Many universities now offer graduate degrees in ADR, which is part of an overall trend towards legitimizing ADR as a distinct profession. See Negotiation Point 8.1 for a discussion of how ADR has moved to online formats. Next, we describe the two most common forms of third-party intervention: arbitration and mediation.

Arbitration

arbitrator
a third party who takes control of shaping and determining an outcome

An **arbitrator** is a third party who takes control of shaping and determining an outcome. The disputants or negotiators themselves retain control over the process. Each party is allowed to present its position about the dispute to the arbitrator and request an outcome. The arbitrator then makes a decision about the dispute. Arbitrator rulings can be

Negotiation Point

8.1

Online Dispute Resolution at EBay

EBay is a well-known online auction site that makes it possible for sellers and buyers located anywhere in the world to deal with one another. EBay itself is not a party to any transaction and, in general, does not assume responsibility for problems that arise between buyers and sellers. Have you ever wondered what happens when problems arise between buyers and sellers? EBay decided in 1999 that having a dispute resolution process might improve trust between buyers and sellers. At that time, eBay selected a new Internet start-up, named Square-Trade, to be its dispute resolution provider. SquareTrade usually follows a two-step process. They generally begin with a technology supported negotiation process in which parties try to resolve the dispute themselves. If this process fails to resolve the dispute, they provide a human mediator for a modest fee. The conversation between the buyer and seller is facilitated

by the mediator using a Web interface. Because the parties are using the Web they do not need to participate at the same time.

Most people who file complaints with SquareTrade have already tried to negotiate using e-mail and have reached an impasse. Negotiating via the Web appears to be more successful than e-mail and the parties also appear more willing to communicate. One reason for this is that the SquareTrade Web site provides more structure than traditional e-mail. SquareTrade discovered early on that eBay disputes tended to fall into about eight different categories, which allowed them to create forms that clarify and highlight areas of disagreement and possible solutions. The parties still have an opportunity to describe concerns in their own words. However, the forms and the form summaries reduce the amount of free text complaining and demanding, thereby lowering the degree of anger and hostility between the parties. This experience again reinforces the idea that the third party's control over the process and structuring of the communication can help facilitate resolutions.

voluntary or binding, depending on the situation, legal context, and previous commitments of the parties. In formal proceedings, like many of the examples discussed above, there is usually a very clear set of policies and practices about the scope and nature of the arbitrator's decision and how it will be made and enforced.

In traditional arbitration, each side submits a proposed resolution to the arbitrator who then comes up with a settlement that both sides must agree to. The arbitrator can decide to choose settlement terms advocated by one party, or they can also develop a solution that falls somewhere in the middle. In this type of arbitration each side has a clear incentive to shape the arbitrator's judgment by presenting offers that are self-serving. When each side presumes that the arbitrator will develop a solution that falls in the middle they are more likely to advocate extreme positions. This behaviour is known as the **chilling effect**.

A second type of arbitration, known as **final offer arbitration**, was developed to try and encourage parties to formulate less extreme positions. The key difference between traditional arbitration and final offer arbitration is that in final offer arbitration the arbitrator must choose one of the proposals put forth by a disputant. The arbitrator is not permitted to formulate a settlement that falls in the middle or create the arbitrator's own terms for a desired outcome.

The major advantages of arbitration are:

1. the negotiation or dispute ends with a final solution,

2. the solution is usually binding, meaning that parties usually cannot choose whether to follow the solution or not,

3. the solution is often seen as credible because arbitrators tend to be perceived as wise, fair, and impartial, and

4. the costs of prolonging the dispute are avoided.

There are also some disadvantages to arbitration, including:

1. by placing control over the outcome in another person's hands, each party takes a risk that the solution is one that they cannot live with,

2. parties may not like the outcome and issues may remain outstanding,

3. in comparison to mediation, which we discuss next, there is less commitment to an arbitrator decision. When parties feel less committed to a decision, they will be less likely to implement it or be more resentful and so the resolution may not be permanent.

Mediation

A **mediator** is a third party who works toward helping disputing parties create a solution themselves by facilitating communication and dispute resolution techniques among the parties. Why would the parties to a dispute get help from a third party who does not have the power to resolve the dispute? For the most part, mediated settlements are viewed to be much fairer than settlements in which a solution has been imposed. Mediators may also help resolve the root causes of an ongoing conflict rather than simply solving the dispute, an almost impossible outcome for arbitration to achieve. Finally, mediation can help reduce or remove barriers to settlements, adding value to the negotiation process because it tends to produce or enhance much of what parties desire and value in negotiation itself.

chilling effect
the tendency for parties to advocate extreme positions on the belief that an arbitrator will develop a solution near the middle

final offer arbitration
a type of arbitration where the arbitrator must choose between one of the last offers put forth by the parties

mediator
a third party who works toward helping disputing parties create a solution themselves by facilitating communication and dispute resolution techniques among the parties

Source: Pearls Before Swine © UFS. Reprinted with permission.

Source: Pearls Before Swine © UFS. Reprinted with permission.

The Mediation Process What can you expect if you find yourself in the middle of a dispute that has gone to mediation? Usually, the mediator begins with an opening statement. In their opening statement, they often explain the following issues: (1) an explanation of the mediator's role, (2) an explanation of the parties' role, which is to work with the mediator to develop an acceptable settlement, (3) some expectations about process, such as whether or not the parties will remain in the same room, and (4) some expectations about ground rules, including things like interruptions and whether the settlement is binding.

After the opening statement, the process varies considerably depending on the style of the mediator and the nature of the dispute. For example some mediators prefer to keep the parties around the same table as much as possible, whereas others prefer to keep them separate. Regardless of whether the parties are separate or together the mediator tries to identify and understand the issues. The mediator looks for underlying interests, priorities, and concerns, and finds areas for potential collaboration or compromise. A mediator can invent proposals or recommend possible solutions, but none of these can be imposed on parties.

Factors Necessary for Success in Mediation The most important characteristic determining mediator success is that they be seen by the parties as impartial and unbiased. The mediator's actions will not be trusted if one side perceives that the mediator favours the other party.

Although the mediator plays a prominent role in determining how the process unfolds, how the process ends up depends on the parties themselves. If the parties do not agree that they need help, or are so hostile to each other that they cannot communicate constructively, then the likelihood of successful mediation declines. The parties also must be willing to make concessions and find a compromise solution.

Mediation is more often successful under the following circumstances:

- the level of conflict is moderate and not excessively high,
- the positions of the parties are understood by both parties,
- both parties are motivated to settle,
- the issues do not involve a basic conflict of values, and
- the level of power is relatively equal between the parties or the power differential is appreciated by both parties.

Hybrid Approaches

Med-Arb In response to the strengths and weaknesses of mediation and arbitration, some scholars and practitioners advocate a merging of the two approaches. Mediation-arbitration (or Med-Arb) consists of two phases. In the first phase the parties use traditional mediation. If they fail to reach an agreement, they move to the second phase, which is arbitration. The same person acts as both mediator and arbitrator, and arbitration is only engaged if mediation fails.

In a laboratory study of arbitration and negotiation, Grigsby and Bigoness[9] found that anticipated mediation reduced the chilling effect in negotiators expecting final-offer arbitration, but negotiators expecting conventional or no arbitration were more subject to the chilling effect when they were anticipating mediation as an intervening step. Med-Arb tends to work best in cases where the parties are expecting final-offer arbitration because they realize that mediation is their best opportunity for compromise.

Arb-Med Arbitration-mediation (or Arb-Med) is a three phase process. The third party begins by holding an arbitration hearing and making a decision, which is placed in a sealed envelope and is not revealed to the parties. In phase two the parties participate in a mediation. If mediation fails to produce a voluntary agreement by an agreed-upon deadline, the parties enter the final phase, known as the ruling phase. The third party then removes the ruling from the envelope and reveals the binding ruling to the disputants. Perhaps the greatest benefit of Arb-Med is that it encourages parties to settle their differences themselves. In a study that compared Arb-Med to Med-Arb, Conlon, Moon, and Ng found that Arb-Med led to higher resolution rates and higher joint outcomes than Med-Arb.[10]

Managerial Interventions

Managers are frequently involved in the handling of disputes between subordinates and colleagues. How are these situations usually handled? In a classic study designed to answer this question, Sheppard asked practicing managers to describe the last time they intervened in a dispute between their subordinates and then coded their responses according to the amount of process and decision control the manager used. He concluded that managers use one of the three dominant styles when they intervene in a subordinate conflict (see Figure 8.1):

1. **Inquisitorial intervention.** This was the most common style. A manager using an inquisitorial intervention exerts high control over both the process and the decision. Both sides are told to present their cases, several questions are

asked to probe each side's position, and there is a high degree of control over how frequently they are allowed to speak and what topics they may discuss. The manager then invents a solution they think will resolve the dispute and imposes that solution on both parties.

2. **Adversarial intervention.** Managers who use adversarial intervention exert high control over the decision but not the process. The manager does not ask questions, try to get the whole story, or control the destructive aspects of the conflict between the parties. Instead, the manager passively listens to what each side chooses to reveal and then tells the parties how to solve the conflict based on their presentations.

3. **Providing impetus.** Managers who provide impetus typically do not exert control over the decision, and they exert only a small amount of control over the process. The manager typically tries to make a quick diagnosis of what the conflict is about and then tells the parties that if they don't find a solution one will be imposed on them. In short, the manager first asks, "what is going on here?" Then, the manager replies with, "you'd better solve this problem, or else I'll solve it for you, and neither of you will like the solution!"

Which Approach Is More Effective? Sheppard's research indicates that managers spontaneously act like an inquisitorial judge or an arbitrator, or they threaten to settle the dispute for the parties in an undesirable way if they can't settle it themselves. Note that the remaining cell in Figure 8.1, which we have labelled "mediational intervention," is the same as formal mediation, but is not a style commonly observed among managers. While subsequent research examining how managers behave has shown that they claim to prefer mediation as a third-party style, it is not clear that managers actually use mediation unless they are specifically trained in the process.[11] When managing conflict, managers seem to assume that because the parties cannot resolve the dispute on their own, the manager must primarily deal with deciding the outcome. Managers appear to think they mediate, but when observed in actual situations they typically exert far more control over the outcome than mediators. Their actual behaviour is more like an inquisitor than a mediator.

Sheppard's work has generated a growing body of research on informal managerial disputes intervention. A. R. Elangovan, from the University of Victoria, has

FIGURE 8.1 | Managerial Third-Party Intervention Styles

Degree of Managerial Outcome Control

	High	Low
High	Inquisitorial Intervention	Mediational Intervention
Low	Adversarial Intervention	Providing Impetus

Degree of Managerial Process Control

Source: Adapted from B. H. Sheppard, "Managers as Inquisitors: Some Lessons from the Law," in M. Bazerman and R. J. Lewicki, eds., Negotiating in Organizations (Beverly Hills, CA: Sage Publications, 1983).

developed a well-known prescriptive model to guide managers in choosing intervention strategies (see Figure 8.2). The model provides a decision tree in which potential
third parties ask a series of diagnostic questions about the dispute (see the questions
at the top of Figure 8.2). Based on whether the dispute is judged to be high or low
on each of these questions, the potential third party arrives at an endpoint on the
decision tree that suggests a particular style. These styles, described as means control, ends control, full control, part control, and low control, are similar to the styles
described in Figure 8.1, except Elangovan explicitly chooses not to use the more
common terms mediation and arbitration to describe these styles (see Table 8.1 for
his description of the styles). Elangovan prefers to describe the degree of outcome
and process control, which provides more precision about what the third party
should do, while avoiding value laden terms like mediation and arbitration, which
may be confusing because of their numerous variations and forms.

TABLE 8.1 | Managerial Dispute Intervention Strategies

Mediator–parties relationship
Improve acceptance of mediation by the parties.
Increase parties' trust in the mediator.

Relationship between the parties
Control communication between the parties.
Have separate meetings with the parties to influence them.

The issues
Uncover the underlying interests and concerns.
Set agendas.
Package, sequence, and prioritize agenda items.
Interpret and shape proposals.
Make suggestions for possible settlements.

The parties
Help parties save face when making concessions.
Help parties resolve internal disagreements.
Help parties deal with constituents.
Apply positive incentives for agreement or concession making.

*Source: Adapted from P. J. D. Carnevale and Dean G. Pruitt, "Negotiation and Mediation," Annual Review of
Psychology 43 (1992), pp. 531–42.*

It is clear that managers and others in authority usually have the right to intervene in disputes. Not only are they interested in workplace disputes and their resolutions, but they usually have the power to involve themselves. Research by Conlon,
Carnevale, and Murnighan[12] found that managers as third parties chose to impose
outcomes about two thirds of time, and even more often when they perceived the
disputants as being uncooperative.

There is also good evidence that mediation should be used more often as an
informal third-party intervention style. Researcher Rekha Karambayya, now at York
University, studied classroom simulations and found that managers assume different
roles depending on how they diagnose the situation.[13] The results showed general
support for Sheppard's model and reported that mediation in particular leads to
fairer outcomes than other forms of dispute resolution. Mediation was also perceived
to be a fair process by disputants, lending support to the advice that managers

FIGURE 8.2 | A Prescriptive Model for Managerial Dispute Intervention

DI   How important is this dispute to the effective functioning of the organization?

TP   How important is it to resolve the dispute as quickly as possible?

ND   Does the dispute concern the interpretation of existing rules, procedures, and arrangements or the changing of existing rules, procedures, and arrangements?

NR   What is the expected frequency of future work-related interactions between the disputants?

CP   If you were to impose a settlement on your subordinates (disputants), what is the probability that they would be committed to it?

DO   What is the orientation of the disputants? That is, if you were to let your subordinates (disputants) settle the dispute, what is the probability that they would come to an organizationally compatible settlement?

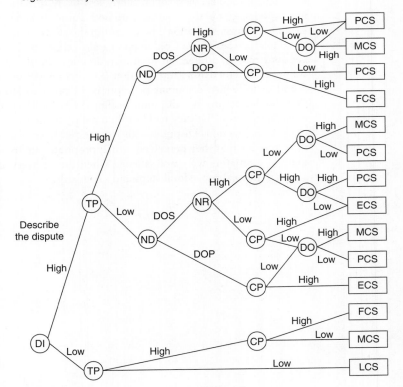

Legend:

MCS = Means-control strategy

ECS = Ends-control strategy

LCS = Low control strategy

FCS = Full control strategy

PCS = Part control strategy

Source: Reprinted with permission of Academy of Management P. O. Box 3020, Briarcliff Manor, NY 10510-8020. From A. R. Elangovan, "Managerial Third-Party Dispute Intervention: A Prescriptive Model of Strategy Selection," Academy of Management Review 20, no. 4 (1995), p. 820. Reproduced by permission of the publisher via Copyright Clearance Center.

should act as mediators when addressing workplace conflict amongst subordinates or co-workers. In a later study, Karambayya and her colleagues found that managers were more likely to intervene in autocratic or mediational styles, but that relative authority and experience had distinct effects.[14] Experience aside, third parties in authority over the disputants were more likely to be autocratic than those who were not in authority, and peer interveners were no more likely to act like mediators. Autocratic interventions tended to produce one-sided outcomes and impasses, whereas mediational interventions tended to produce compromises. Managers likely fail to use mediation more extensively due to beliefs about the managerial role, in that managers have a tendency to frame conflicts as hands-on opportunities, which may cause them to decide not to mediate. Interveners with greater managerial experience, though, were significantly less likely to be autocratic than those with less experience, and third parties with both authority and more experience tended to exhibit the most mediational behaviour in the study.

Finally, research by Conlon and Fasalo[15] suggests that while mediational interventions may be preferable to autocratic ones, timing appears to be critical. The timing of the mediators intervention (i.e., earlier versus later in the dispute) was found to influence disputant perceptions of procedural fairness. Quick interventions tended to produce disputant feelings of lack of control and loss of voice; that is, the negotiators felt they had lost their ability to have a say in presenting their case to their satisfaction. Disputants also expressed lower satisfaction with third-party interventions that they perceived or inappropriate due to violations of due process; that is, negotiators were not satisfied when they perceived that they were denied access to normal procedural steps and safeguards.

In this chapter we examined the basic structure of dispute situations and introduced the interests, rights, and power framework for handling disputes. We also noted that when negotiations break down and the parties are unable to reach an agreement, a third-party intervention might help.

When you find yourself in a dispute situation, there are a number of things you should keep in mind. We conclude the chapter by summarizing some of the most important.

1. If possible, begin using an interest-based approach,

2. Remember that in disputes the BATNAs of the parties are usually linked. This is much less common in other negotiation situations.

3. There is a time and a place for using either a rights-based or power-based approach. However, we suggest that you carefully consider the possible costs, in a broad sense, before proceeding.

4. When deciding whether or not to involve a third-party, consider how their role is likely to affect the process and the outcome.

Key Terms

Alternative dispute resolution (ADR), p. 160
Arbitrator, p. 161
Chilling effect, p. 162
Dispute, p. 155

Final offer arbitration, p. 162
Mediator, p. 162
Third party, p. 159
Threat, p. 159

Ethics in Negotiation

In this chapter, we explore the question of whether there are, or should be, accepted ethical standards for behaviour in negotiations. This topic has received increased attention from researchers in recent years. It is our view that fundamental questions of ethical conduct arise in every negotiation. The effective negotiator must recognize when the questions are relevant and what factors must be considered to answer them. We will identify the major ethical dimensions raised in negotiations, describe how people tend to think about these ethical choices, and provide a framework for making informed ethical decisions.

LEARNING OBJECTIVES

These situations are hypothetical; however, the problems they present are real ones for negotiators. People in and out of organizations are routinely confronted with important decisions about the strategies they will use to achieve important objectives, particularly when a variety of influence tactics are open to them. These decisions frequently carry ethical implications. In this chapter, we will address the major ethical questions that arise in negotiation through consideration of these questions:

1. What are ethics and why do they apply to negotiation?

2. What questions of ethical conduct are likely to arise in negotiation?

3. What motivates unethical behaviour, and what are the consequences?

4. How can negotiators deal with the other party's use of deception?

Source: ©Scott Adams/Dist. by United Feature Syndicate, Inc.

A Sampling of Ethical Quandaries

Consider the following situations:

1. You are trying to sell your home theatre system to raise money for an upcoming trip overseas. The system works great, and an audiophile friend tells you that if he were in the market for the equipment (which he isn't), he'd give you $500 for it. A few days later the first potential buyer comes to see the system. The buyer looks it over and asks a few questions about how it works. You assure the buyer that it works well. When asked how much, you tell the buyer that you have already had an offer for $500. The buyer buys the system for $550.

   Is it ethical to have said what you said about having another offer?

2. You are an entrepreneur interested in acquiring a business that is currently owned by a competitor. The competitor, however, has not shown any interest in either selling his business or merging with your company. To gain inside knowledge of his firm, you hired a consultant you know to call contacts in your competitor's business and ask if the company is having any serious problems that might threaten its viability. If there are such problems, you might be able to use the information to either hire away the company's employees or get the competitor to sell.

   Is this an ethical course of action? Would you be likely to do it if you were the entrepreneur?

3. You are a vice president of human resources, negotiating with a union representative for a new labour contract. The union refuses to sign a new contract unless the company agrees to raise the number of paid holidays from six to seven. Management estimates it will cost approximately $220,000 for each paid holiday, and argues that the company cannot afford to meet the demand. However, you know that, in reality, money is not the issue—the company simply doesn't think the union's demand is justified. To convince the union leaders that they should withdraw their demand, you have been considering these alternatives: (a) tell the union that the company simply can't afford it, without further explanation; (b) prepare erroneous financial statements that show it will cost about $300,000 per paid holiday, which you simply can't afford; and (c) offer union leaders an all-expenses-paid "working" trip to a Mexican resort if they will simply drop the demand.

   Do any of the strategies raise ethical concerns? Which ones? Why?

4. You are about to graduate from the MBA program of a leading university. You specialized in management information systems (MIS) and will start a job with a company that commercially develops Web pages. You own a personal computer that is a couple of years old. You have decided to sell it and buy new equipment later after you see what kinds of projects your employer has you working on, so you post a flyer on campus bulletin boards about the computer for sale. You have decided not to tell prospective buyers that your hard drive acts like it is about to fail and that the computer occasionally crashes without warning.

   Is this ethical? Would you be likely to do this if you were this particular student?

5. You buy a new pair of shoes on sale. The printed receipt states very clearly that the shoes are not returnable. After you get them home, you wear the shoes around the house for a day and decide that they just don't fit you correctly. So you take the shoes back to the store. The clerk points to the message on the receipt; but you don't let that deter you. You start to yell angrily about the store's poor quality service, so that people in the store start to stare. The clerk calls the store manager; after some discussion, the manager agrees to give you your money back.

   Is this ethical? Would you be likely to do this if you were this customer?

What Do We Mean by "Ethics" and Why Do They Matter in Negotiation?

Ethics Defined

ethics
broadly applied social standards for what is right or wrong in a particular situation, or a process for setting those standards

Ethics are broadly applied social standards for what is right or wrong in a particular situation, or a process for setting those standards. They differ from morals, which are individual and personal beliefs about what is right and wrong. Ethics grow out of particular philosophies, which purport to (1) define the nature of the world in which we live, and (2) prescribe rules for living together. Different philosophies adopt distinct perspectives on these questions, which means in practice that they may lead to different judgments about what is right and wrong in a given situation. The "hard work" of ethics in practice is figuring out how ethical philosophies differ from one another, deciding which approaches are personally preferable, and applying them to real-world situations at hand.

ethical dilemma
when possible actions or strategies put the potential economic benefits of doing a deal in conflict with one's social obligations to other involved parties or one's broader community

Our goal is to distinguish among different criteria, or standards, for judging and evaluating a negotiator's actions, particularly when questions of ethics might be involved. Although negotiation is our focus, the criteria involved are really no different than what might be used to evaluate ethics in business generally. An **ethical dilemma** exists for a negotiator when possible actions or strategies put the potential economic benefits of doing a deal in conflict with one's social obligations to other involved parties or one's broader community.

Many writers on business ethics have proposed frameworks that capture competing ethical standards (and as we shall see later, these typically map onto classical theories of ethical philosophy that have been around a long time). Drawing on some of these writers, here are four standards for evaluating strategies and tactics in business and negotiation:[1]

- choose a course of action on the basis of results I expect to achieve (e.g., greatest return on investment)
- choose a course of action on the basis of my duty to uphold appropriate rules and principles (e.g., the law)
- choose a course of action on the basis of the norms, values, and strategy of my organization or community (e.g. the cultural values and norms)
- choose a course of action on the basis of my personal convictions (e.g., what my conscience tells me to do)

Each of these approaches reflects a fundamentally different approach to ethical reasoning. The first may be called *end-result ethics*, in that the rightness of an action is determined by evaluating the pros and cons of its consequences. The second is an example of what may be called *duty ethics*, in that the rightness of an action is determined by one's obligation to adhere to consistent principles, laws, and social standards that define what is right and wrong and where the line is. The third represents a form of *social contract ethics*, in that the rightness of an action is based on the customs and norms of a particular community. Finally, the fourth may be called *personalistic ethics*, in that the rightness of the action is based on one's own conscience and moral standards. See Table 9.1 for an overview of these four approaches.

Applying Ethical Reasoning to Negotiation

Each of these approaches could be used to analyze the five hypothetical situations at the beginning of the chapter. For instance, in the first situation involving selling a home theatre and the statement to a prospective buyer about the existence of another potential buyer:

- If you believed in *end-result* ethics, then you might do whatever was necessary to get the best possible outcome (including lie about an alternative buyer).
- If you believed in *duty* ethics, you might perceive an obligation never to engage in subterfuge, and might therefore reject a tactic that involves an outright lie.

- If you believed in *social contract* ethics, you would base your tactical choices on your view of appropriate conduct for behaviour in your community; if others would use deception in a situation like this, you lie.
- If you believed in *personalistic* ethics, you would consult your conscience and decide whether your need for cash for your upcoming trip justified using deceptive or dishonest tactics.

What this example shows is that the approach to ethical reasoning you favour affects the kind of ethical judgment you make, and the consequent behaviour you choose.

Ethics versus Prudence versus Practicality versus Legality

Discussions of business ethics frequently confuse what is *ethical* (appropriate as determined by some standard of moral conduct) versus what is *prudent* (wise, based on trying to understand the efficacy of the tactic and the consequences it might have on the relationship with the other) versus what is *practical* (what a negotiator can actually make happen in a given situation) versus what is *legal* (what the law defines as acceptable practice).[2] In earlier chapters, we evaluated negotiation strategies and tactics by the prudence and practicality criteria; in this chapter, the focus is on evaluating negotiation strategies and tactics by ethical criteria.

Figure 9.1 presents a helpful way to think about what it means to comprehend and analyze an ethical dilemma. The figure shows a model of the process of analyzing a moral problem developed by Larue Hosmer, a writer on business ethics.[3] According to Hosmer, before one can ponder solutions, the first step is developing a complete understanding of the moral problem at hand. As shown on the left side of Figure 9.1, this means grasping the various subjective standards (norms, beliefs, values, etc.) in play among involved parties and recognizing the mix of potential harms, benefits, and rights that are involved in the situation. With the problem fully defined, the path to a convincing solution travels through the three modes of analysis shown on the right side of the figure: (1) a determination of economic outcomes of potential courses of action, (2) a consideration of legal requirements that bear on the situation, and (3) an assessment of the ethical obligations to other involved parties regarding what is "'right' and 'just' and 'fair'".[4] This last element—ethical reasoning—refers to the basic ethical frameworks mentioned earlier (see again Table 9.1).

FIGURE 9.1 | Analytical Process for the Resolution of Moral Problems

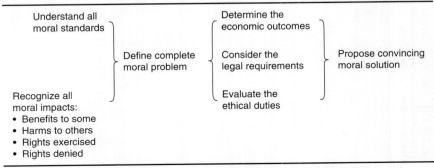

Understand all moral standards

Recognize all moral impacts:
- Benefits to some
- Harms to others
- Rights exercised
- Rights denied

Define complete moral problem

Determine the economic outcomes

Consider the legal requirements

Evaluate the ethical duties

Propose convincing moral solution

Source: L. T. Hosmer, The Ethics of Management (4th ed.) (New York: McGraw-Hill/Irwin, 2003).

TABLE 9.1 | Four Approaches to Ethical Reasoning

Ethical System	Definition	Major Proponent	Central Tenets	Major Concerns
End-result ethics	Rightness of an action is determined by considering consequences	Jeremy Bentham (1748–1832) John Stuart Mill (1806–1873)	• One must consider all likely consequences.	• How does one define happiness, pleasure, or utility?
			• Actions are more right if they promote more happiness, more wrong as they produce unhappiness.	• How does one measure happiness, pleasure, or utility?
			• Happiness is defined as presence of pleasure and absence of pain.	• How does one trade off between short-term vs. long-term happiness?
			• Promotion of happiness is generally the ultimate aim.	• If actions create happiness for 90% of the world and misery for the other 10%, are they still ethical?
			• Collective happiness of all concerned is the goal.	
Duty ethics	Rightness of an action is determined by considering obligations to apply universal standards and principles.	Immanuel Kant (1724–1804)	• Human conduct should be guided by primary moral principles, or "oughts."	• By what authority do we accept particular rules or the "goodness" of those rules?
			• Individuals should stand on their principles and restrain themselves by rules.	• What rule do we follow when rules conflict?
			• The ultimate good is a life of virtue (acting on principles) rather than pleasure.	• How do we adapt general rules to fit specific situations?
			• We should not adjust moral law to fit our actions, but adjust our actions to fit moral law.	• How do rules change as circumstances change?
				• What happens when good rules produce bad consequences?
				• Are there rules without any exceptions?
Social contract ethics	Rightness of an action is determined by the customs and norms of a community.	Jean-Jacques Rousseau (1712–1778)	• People must function in a social, community context to survive.	• How do we determine the general will?

TABLE 9.1 | *(Concluded)*

Ethical System	Definition	Major Proponent	Central Tenets	Major Concerns
			• Communities become "moral bodies" for determining ground rules.	• What is meant by the "common good"?
			• Duty and obligation bind the community and the individual to each other.	• What do we do with independent thinkers who challenge the morality of the existing social order (e.g., Jefferson, Gandhi, Martin Luther King)?
			• What is best for the common good determines the ultimate standard.	• Can a state be corrupt and its people still be "moral" (e.g., Nazi Germany)?
			• Laws are important, but morality determines the laws and standards for right and wrong.	
Personalistic ethics	Rightness of an action is determined by one's conscience.	Martin Buber (1878–1965)	• Locus of truth is found in human existence.	• How could we justify ethics other than by saying, "It felt like the right thing to do"?
			• Conscience within each person calls them to fulfill their humanness and to decide between right and wrong.	• How could we achieve a collective definition of what is ethical if individuals disagreed?
			• Personal decision rules are the ultimate standards.	• How could we achieve cohesiveness and consensus in a team that only fosters personal perspectives?
			• Pursuing a noble goal by ignoble means leads to an ignoble end.	• How could an organization assure some uniformity in ethics?
			• There are no absolute formulas for living.	
			• One should follow one's group but also stick up for what one individually believes.	

Source: Derived from W. Hitt, Ethics and Leadership: Putting Theory into Practice (Columbus, OH: Battelle Press, 1990).

What Questions of Ethical Conduct Arise in Negotiation?

Why do some negotiators choose to use tactics that may be unethical? The first answer that occurs to many people is that such negotiators are corrupt, degenerate, or immoral. However, that answer is much too simplistic. As we discussed in Chapter 5, people tend to regard *other people's* unsavoury behaviour as caused by disposition or personality, while attributing the causes of their *own* behaviour to factors in the social environment.[5] Thus, a negotiator might consider an adversary who uses an ethically questionable tactic unprincipled, profit-driven, or willing to use any tactic to get what he or she wanted. In contrast, when attempting to explain why you as the negotiator might use the same tactic, you would tend to say that you are highly principled but had very good reasons for deviating from those principles just this one time.

In this section we will discuss negotiation tactics that bring issues of ethicality into play. We will first discuss what we mean by tactics that are "ethically ambiguous," and we will link negotiator ethics to the fundamental issue of truth telling. We will then describe research that has sought to identify and classify such tactics and analyze people's attitudes toward their use. We will also distinguish between active and passive forms of deception—lies of omission versus commission. The section concludes with a model that portrays the negotiator's decision-making process with respect to the possible use of such tactics.

Ethically Ambiguous Tactics: It's (Mostly) All about the Truth

Here we will discuss what kinds of tactics are ethically ambiguous and how they can work to afford a temporary strategic advantage. Our use of the phrase *ethically ambiguous* reflects a carefully considered choice of words. One dictionary defines "ambiguous" as "open to more than one interpretation . . . doubtful or uncertain." We are interested in tactics that may or may not be improper, depending on an individual's ethical reasoning and circumstances.

Most of the ethics issues in negotiation are concerned with standards of truth telling—how honest, candid, and disclosing a negotiator should be. The attention here is more on what negotiators *say* (communicate about) or what they say they will do (and how they say it) than on what they actually do (although negotiators may act unethically as well). Some negotiators may cheat (violate formal and informal rules—e.g., claiming that rules about deadlines or procedures don't apply to them) or steal (e.g., break into the other party's or competitor's database or headquarters to secure confidential documents or briefing memoranda), but most of the attention in negotiator ethics has been on lying behaviour.

Most negotiators would probably place a high value on a reputation for being truthful. Yet what does being truthful mean? Questions about truth telling are straightforward, but the answers are not so clear. First, how does one define *truth?* Do you follow a clear set of rules, determine what the social contract is for truth in your group or organization, or follow your conscience? Second, how does one define and classify deviations from the truth? Are all deviations lies, no matter how small and minor they are? Finally, one can add a relativistic dimension to these questions: Should a person tell the truth all the time, or are there times when not telling the truth is an acceptable (or even necessary) form of conduct? These are questions of major concern to negotiators (and philosophers since time immemorial!) who are trying to decide what they can and cannot say and still remain ethical.

A number of articles in business journals have addressed the ethical issues surrounding truth telling. For example, a businessman named Carr argued almost 40 years ago in a controversial *Harvard Business Review* article titled "Is Business Bluffing Ethical?" that strategy in business is analogous to strategy in a game of poker.[6] He advocated that, short of outright cheating (the equivalent of marking cards or hiding an ace up your sleeve), businesspeople ought to play the game as poker players do. Just as good poker playing often involves concealing information and bluffing (convincing others that you have the cards when you really don't), so do many business transactions. From time to time, most executives find themselves compelled, for their own interests or the interests of their companies, to practice some form of deception in their dealings with customers, suppliers, labour unions, government officials, or even other key executives. Through conscious misstatements, concealment of pertinent facts, or exaggeration—in short, bluffing—they seek to persuade others to agree with them. Carr argues that if an executive refuses to bluff periodically—if he or she feels obligated to tell the truth, the whole truth, and nothing but the truth all the time—he or she is probably ignoring opportunities permitted under the rules of business and is probably at a heavy disadvantage in business dealings.[7]

Bluffing, exaggeration, and concealment or manipulation of information, he maintained, are legitimate ways for both individuals and corporations to maximize their self-interest. Such strategies may be either advantageous or disadvantageous. An executive might plead poverty in a contract negotiation with a key employee and thereby save a significant amount of money for the company. However, a similar cost-cutting focus might lead the same executive to fail to make safety or quality improvements on one of the company's products, which could have severe long-term business consequences. As you can well imagine, Carr's position sparked lively debate among *Harvard Business Review* readers. A number of critics argued that individual businesspeople and corporations should be held to higher standards of ethical conduct, and they took Carr to task for his position.[8]

Questions and debate regarding the ethical standards for truth telling in negotiation are ongoing. As we pointed out when we discussed interdependence (Chapter 1), negotiation is based on information dependence—the exchange of information regarding the true preferences and priorities of the other negotiator.[9] Arriving at a clear, precise, effective negotiated agreement depends on the willingness of the parties to share accurate information about their own preferences, priorities, and interests. At the same time, because negotiators may also be interested in maximizing their self-interest, they may want to disclose as little as possible about their positions—particularly if they think they can do better by manipulating the information they disclose to the other party. This results in fundamental negotiation dilemmas involving trust and honesty. The *dilemma of trust* is that a negotiator who believes everything the other says can be manipulated by dishonesty. The *dilemma of honesty* is that a negotiator who tells the other party all of his exact requirements and limits will, inevitably, never do better than his walk-away point. Sustaining the bargaining relationship, means choosing a middle course between complete openness and complete deception.[10]

As a final point on the subject of truth telling, there is, beyond ethics, the matter of *legal* obligations to be truthful. Deception in negotiation can rise to the level of legally actionable fraud. The law on this subject (like on most subjects!) is complex and often hard to pin down. See Negotiation Point 9.1 for a guide to the (il)legality of lying in negotiation.[11]

Negotiation Point

9.1

When Is It Legal to Lie?

Although a major focus in the ethics of negotiation is on the morality of using deception in negotiation, it also behooves the effective negotiator to be familiar with the *legality* of doing so. Richard Shell, a lawyer and professor who writes about and teaches negotiation, offered an interpretation of U.S. law in his article "When Is It Legal to Lie in Negotiation?" Although Shell focuses specifically on American law, Canadian negotiators should be aware that his analysis applies in Canada as well.

Shell starts with a basic "common law" definition of fraud: "a *knowing misrepresentation* of a *material fact* on which the victim reasonably *relies* and which *causes* damage" (p. 94; emphasis not in original).

A closer look at the meaning of the key (italicized) words in this definition brings legal issues involving lying in negotiation into focus.

- A *misrepresentation*: An affirmative misstatement of something.

- A *knowing* misrepresentation: Shell says a misrepresentation is "knowing" when you know that what you say is false when you say it. Does this mean you can skirt liability by avoiding coming into contact with the knowledge involved? Shell says no—courts would regard that as reckless disregard for the truth.

- A *fact*: To be illegal, in theory, the thing being misrepresented generally has to be an objective fact. But in practice, Shell

points out that misstating an opinion or an intention can get you into trouble if it builds on factual misrepresentation or is particularly egregious—especially if you know the falsity at the time you make the statement or promise.

- A *material* fact: Not all "facts" are objective or material. Shell says that by the standards of legal practice, demands and reservation points are not regarded as "material" to the deal, so it is not actionable fraud to bluff about them. He cautions, however, that lying about alternatives or other offers or other buyers can get you into trouble. It's not clear that these are always material, but this kind of thing may be left up to a jury to decide if a claim of fraud went to trial.

- *Reliance/causation*: For a deceptive statement to be legally fraudulent, the receiver must prove that he or she relied on the information and that doing so caused harm.

Does this mean that illegal deception always involves affirmative statements that are false? Will silence protect you from legal liability? Shell says no: There are conditions under which you are legally bound to share truthful information. For instance, you are obligated to disclose in these situations:

- If you make a partial disclosure that would be misleading.

- If the parties stand in fiduciary relationship to one another.

- If the nondisclosing party has "superior information" that is "vital."

- In cases involving certain specialized transactions, such as insurance contracts.

Source: Adapted from G. Richard Shell, "When Is It Legal to Lie in Negotiations?" Sloan Management Review 32, no. 3 (1991), pp. 93–101.

Identifying Ethically Ambiguous Tactics and Attitudes toward Their Use

What Ethically Ambiguous Tactics Are There? Deception and subterfuge may take several forms in negotiation. Researchers have been working to identify the nature of these tactics, and their underlying structure, for almost 20 years.[12] They have extensively explored the nature and conceptual organization of ethically ambiguous negotiating tactics. The general approach has been to ask students and executives to rate a list of tactics on several dimensions: the appropriateness of the tactic, the rater's likelihood of using the tactic, and/or the perceived efficacy of using the tactic. Analyzing these questionnaire results, researchers learned that six clear categories of tactics emerged and have been confirmed by additional data collection and analysis.[13] These categories are listed in Table 9.2. It is interesting to note that of the six categories, two—emotional manipulation and the use of "traditional competitive bargaining" tactics—are viewed as generally appropriate and likely to be used. These tactics, therefore, while mildly inappropriate, are nevertheless seen as appropriate and effective in successful distributive bargaining. The other four categories of tactics—misrepresentation, bluffing, misrepresentation to opponent's network, and inappropriate information collection—are generally seen as inappropriate and unethical in negotiation.

TABLE 9.2 | Categories of Marginally Ethical Negotiating Tactics

Category	Example
Traditional competitive bargaining	Not disclosing your walkaway; making an inflated opening offer
Emotional manipulation	Faking anger, fear, disappointment; faking elation, satisfaction
Misrepresentation	Distorting information or negotiation events in describing them to others
Misrepresentation to opponent's networks	Corrupting your opponent's reputation with his peers
Inappropriate information gathering	Bribery, infiltration, spying, etc.
Bluffing	Insincere threats or promises

Source: Adapted from R. Robinson, R. J. Lewicki, and E. Donahue, "Extending and Testing a Five Factor Model of Ethical and Unethical Bargaining Tactics: The SINS Scale," Journal of Organizational Behavior 21 (2000), pp. 649–664; and B. Barry, I. S. Fulmer, and A. Long, Ethically Marginal Bargaining Tactics: Sanction, Efficacy, and Performance. Presented at the annual meeting of the Academy of Management, Toronto, August, 2000.

Is It All Right to Use Ethically Ambiguous Tactics? Research suggests that there are tacitly agreed-on rules of the game in negotiation. In these rules, some minor forms of untruths—misrepresentation of one's true position to the other party, bluffs, and emotional manipulations—may be seen as ethically acceptable and within the rules. In contrast, outright deception and falsification are generally seen as outside the rules. However, we must place some strong cautionary notes on these conclusions. First, these statements are based on ratings by large groups of people (mostly business students); in no way do they, or should they, predict how any one individual negotiator will perceive and use the tactics or how any one target who experiences them will rate them. (We will discuss reactions from the "victim's" perspective later in this chapter.) Second, these observations are based primarily on what people said they would do, rather than what they actually did. Perceptions and reactions may well be different when the parties are making decisions in an actual negotiation, rather than rating the tactics on a questionnaire removed from any direct experience with another person in a meaningful social context. Third, by engaging in research on ethically ambiguous tactics (as the authors of this book have) and reporting these results, we do not mean to endorse the use of any marginally ethical tactic. Instead, our objective is to focus debate among negotiators on exactly when these tactics might be appropriate or should be used. Finally, we acknowledge that this is a Western view, in which individuals determine what is ethically acceptable; in some other cultures (e.g., Asia), a group or organization would decide on ethics, while in other cultures (e.g., some nations with emerging free markets), ethical constraints on negotiated transactions may be minimal or hard to determine clearly, and "let the buyer beware" at all times!

Deception by Omission versus Commission

The use of deceptive tactics can be active or passive. To illustrate, consider a study that examined the tendency for negotiators to misrepresent their interests on a common-value issue—an issue for which both parties are seeking the same outcome.[14] A negotiator using this tactic deceives the other party about what she wants on the common-value issue and then (grudgingly) agrees to accept the other party's preference, which in reality matches her own. By making it look as though she has made a concession, she can seek a concession from the other party in return. Overall, 28 percent of subjects in the study misrepresented the common-value issue in an effort to obtain a concession from the other party. The researchers discovered that negotiators used two forms of deception in misrepresenting the common-value issue: misrepresentation by *omission* (failing to disclose information that would benefit the other) and misrepresentation by *commission* (actually lying about the common-value issue).

In another set of studies, students took part in a role-play involving the sale of a car with a defective transmission.[15] Students could lie by omission—by simply failing to mention the defective transmission—or by commission—by denying that the transmission was defective even when asked by the other party. Far more students were willing to lie by omission (not revealing the whole truth) than by commission (falsely answering a question when asked). This finding clearly reinforces the norm of caveat emptor (let the buyer beware), suggesting that it is up to the buyer to ask the right questions and be appropriately sceptical when accepting the other's sales pitch.

■ Why Use Deceptive Tactics? Motives and Consequences

In the preceding pages we discussed at length the nature of ethics and the kinds of tactics in negotiation that might be regarded as ethically ambiguous. Now we turn to a discussion of why such tactics are tempting and what the consequences are of succumbing to that temptation. We begin with motives, and motives inevitably begin with power.

The Power Motive

The purpose of using ethically ambiguous negotiating tactics is to increase the negotiator's power in the bargaining environment. As we discussed in Chapter 7, information is a major source of leverage in negotiation. Information has power because negotiation is intended to be a rational activity involving the exchange of information and the persuasive use of that information. One view of negotiation is that it is primarily an exchange of facts, arguments, and logic between two wholly rational information-processing entities. Often, whoever has better information, or uses it more persuasively, stands to "win" the negotiation.

Such a view assumes that the information is accurate and truthful. To assume otherwise—that it is not truthful—is to question the very assumptions on which daily social communication is based and the honesty and integrity of the presenter of that information. Of course, raising such questions openly might insult the others and reduce the implied trust we placed in them. Moreover, investigating someone else's truthfulness and honesty is time and energy consuming. So any inaccurate and untruthful statements (i.e., lies) introduced into this social exchange manipulate information in favour of the introducer. Through the tactics we described earlier—bluffing, falsification, misrepresentation, deception, and selective disclosure—the liar gains advantage. In fact, it has been demonstrated that individuals are more willing to use deceptive tactics when the other party is perceived to be uninformed or unknowledgeable about the situation under negotiation, particularly when the stakes are high.[16]

Other Motives to Behave Unethically

The motivation of a negotiator can clearly affect his or her tendency to use deceptive tactics. A person's "motivational orientation"—whether negotiators are motivated to act co-operatively, competitively, or individualistically toward each other—can affect the strategies and tactics they pursue. In one study, researchers manipulated the negotiators' motivational orientation to the situation, predisposing parties to either an "individualistic" or a "co-operative" orientation toward the other.[17] Individualistic negotiators—those looking to maximize their own outcome, regardless of the consequences for the other—were more likely to use misrepresentation as a strategy. Cultural differences may also map onto motivational influences: There is evidence that individuals in a highly individualistic culture are more likely to use deception for personal gain than those in a more collectivist culture.[18]

But the impact of motives may be more complex. In one early study on tactics, negotiators were asked about their predisposition to use ethically ambiguous tactics.[19] Different versions of the questionnaire explicitly told respondents to assume either a competitive or a co-operative motivational orientation toward the other party and to assume that the other party would be taking either a competitive or a co-operative motivational orientation. The researchers predicted that competitive motivations would elicit the strongest endorsement of ethically ambiguous tactics. The results revealed that differences in the negotiators' *own* motivational orientation—co-operative versus competitive—did *not* cause differences in their view of the appropriateness of using the tactics, but the negotiators' perception of the *other's* expected motivation did! In other words, negotiators were significantly more likely to see the ethically ambiguous tactics as appropriate if they anticipated that the other would be competitive versus co-operative. These (preliminary) findings suggest that negotiators may rationalize the use of marginally ethical tactics in anticipation of the other's expected conduct rather than take personal responsibility for using these tactics in the service of their own competitive orientation.

The Consequences of Unethical Conduct

A negotiator who employs an unethical tactic will experience consequences that may be positive or negative, based on three aspects of the situation: (1) whether the tactic is effective; (2) how the other person, his or her constituencies, and audiences evaluate the tactic; and (3) how the negotiator evaluates the tactic. We discuss each in turn.

Effectiveness Let us first consider the consequences that occur based on whether the tactic is successful or not. Clearly, a tactic's effectiveness will have some impact on whether it is more or less likely to be used in the future (essentially, a simple learning and reinforcement process). If using the tactic allows a negotiator to attain rewarding outcomes that would be unavailable if he had behaved ethically, and if the unethical conduct is not punished by others, the frequency of unethical conduct is likely to increase because the negotiator believes he can get away with it. Thus, real consequences—rewards and punishments that arise from using a tactic or not using it—should not only motivate a negotiator's present behaviour but also affect his or her predisposition to use similar strategies in similar circumstances in the future. (For the moment, we will ignore the consequences of these tactics on the negotiator's reputation and trustworthiness, an impact that most deceptive negotiators unfortunately ignore in the short term.)

These propositions have not been tested in negotiating situations, but they have been tested extensively in other research studies on ethical decision making. For example, when research participants expected to be rewarded for making an unethical decision by participating in a laboratory-simulated kickback scheme, they not only participated but also were willing to participate again when a second opportunity arose.[20] Moreover, when there were also strong pressures on the research subjects to compete with others—for example, announcing how well each person had done on the task and giving a prize to the one with the highest score—the frequency of unethical conduct increased even further.

Reactions of Others A second set of consequences may arise from judgments and evaluations by the person who was the "target" of the tactic, by constituencies, or by audiences that can observe the tactic. Depending on whether these parties recognize the tactic and whether they evaluate it as proper or improper to use, the negotiator may receive a great deal of feedback. If the target person is unaware that a deceptive tactic was used, he or she may show no reaction other than disappointment at having lost the negotiation. However, if the target discovers that deception has occurred, he or she is likely to react strongly. People who discover that they have been deceived or exploited are typically angry. In addition to perhaps having "lost" the negotiation, they feel foolish for having allowed themselves to be manipulated or deceived by a clever ploy. The victim is unlikely to trust the unethical negotiator again, may seek revenge from the negotiator in future dealings, and may also generalize this experience to negotiations with others.

These negative consequences were apparent in research showing that victims had strong emotional reactions to deception when they had an intimate relationship with the subject, when the information at stake was very important, and when they saw lying as an unacceptable type of behaviour for that relationship (i.e., when strong expectations of truth telling were clearly violated).[21] In a majority of cases the discovery of the lie was instrumental in an eventual termination of the relationship with the other person, and in most cases the termination was initiated by the victim. The more the deception was serious, personal, and highly consequential for trust between the parties, the more destructive it was to the relationship. In a similar vein, there is also evidence that individuals who are deceptive are regarded as less truthful and less desirable for future interactions.[22] In sum, although the use of unethical tactics may create short-term success for the negotiator, it may also create an adversary who is bent on revenge and retribution.

Reactions of Self Under some conditions—such as when the other party has truly suffered—a negotiator may feel some discomfort, stress, guilt, or remorse. Of course, the actor who sees no problem in using the tactic may be likely to use it again and may even begin to ponder how to use it more effectively. On the one hand, while the use of these tactics may have strong consequences for the negotiator's reputation and trustworthiness, parties seldom appear to take these outcomes into consideration in the short term. On the other hand, and particularly if the tactic has worked, the negotiator may be able to rationalize and justify the use of the tactic. We explore these rationalizations and justifications next.

Explanations and Justifications

When a negotiator has used an ethically ambiguous tactic that may elicit a reaction—as we described above—the negotiator must prepare to defend the tactic's use to himself (e.g., "I see myself as a person of integrity, and yet I have decided to do something that might be viewed as unethical"), to the victim, or to constituencies and audiences who may express their concerns. The primary purpose of these explanations and justifications is to rationalize, explain, or excuse the behaviour—to verbalize some good, legitimate reason why this tactic was necessary. There is an increasing stream of research on those who employ unethical tactics and the explanations and justifications they use to rationalize them. Some examples include:[23]

- *The tactic was unavoidable.* Negotiators frequently justify their actions by claiming that the situation made it necessary for them to act the way they did. The negotiator may feel that she was not in full control of her actions or had no other option; hence she should not be held responsible. Perhaps the negotiator had no intent to hurt anyone but was pressured to use the tactic by someone else.

- *The tactic was harmless.* The negotiator may say that what he did was really trivial and not very significant. People tell white lies all the time. For example, you may greet your neighbour with a cheery "Good morning, nice to see you" when, in fact, it may not be a good morning, you are in a bad mood, and you wish you hadn't run into your neighbour because you are angry about his dog barking all night. Exaggerations, bluffs, or peeking at the other party's private notes during negotiations can all be easily explained away as harmless actions. Note, however, that this particular justification interprets the harm from the actor's point of view; the victim may not agree and may have experienced significant harm or costs as a result.

- *The tactic will help to avoid negative consequences.* When using this justification, negotiators are arguing that the ends justify the means. In this case, the justification is that the tactic helped to avoid greater harm. It is OK to lie to an armed robber about where you have hidden your money to avoid being robbed. Similarly, negotiators may see lying (or any other means–ends tactic) as justifiable if it protects them against even more undesirable consequences should the truth be known.

- *The tactic will produce good consequences, or the tactic is altruistically motivated.* Again, the end justifies the means, but in a positive sense. A negotiator who judges a tactic on the basis of its consequences is acting in accord with the tenets of utilitarianism—that the quality of any given action is judged by its consequences. Utilitarians will argue that certain kinds of lies or means–ends tactics are appropriate because they may provide for the larger good—for example, Robin Hood tactics in which someone robs from the rich to make the poor better off. In reality, most negotiators use deceptive tactics for their own advantage, not for the general good.

- *"They had it coming," or "They deserve it," or "I'm just getting my due."* These are all variations on the theme of using lying and deception either against an individual who may have taken advantage of you in the past or against some generalized source of authority (i.e., "the system"). Polls have noted an erosion of honesty in North America—people increasingly think it appropriate to take advantage of the system in various ways, including tax evasion, petty theft, shoplifting, improper declaration of bankruptcy, journalistic excesses, and distortion in advertising.[24]

- *"They were going to do it anyway, so I will do it first."* Sometimes a negotiator legitimizes the use of a tactic because he or she anticipates that the other intends to use similar tactics. One study found that people were most willing to use deception when negotiating with a partner who had a reputation for being unethical.[25] Another study linked one's own inclination to deceive and judgments of the other party's integrity: The more an individual was tempted to engage in misrepresentation, the more he or she believed that the other would also misrepresent information.[26] Thus, one's own temptation to misrepresent creates a self-fulfilling logic in which one believes one needs to misrepresent because the other is likely to do it as well. At the same time, subjects in this study consistently rated themselves as more ethical than the other party, which suggests that people experience some combination of positive illusions about themselves and their own behaviour, and negative illusions about the other and the other's likely behaviour.

- *"He started it."* This is a variation on the last point. In this case, the rationale is that others have *already* violated the rules, therefore legitimizing the negotiator's right to violate them as well. In such cases, unethical tactics are employed in a tit-for-tat manner, to restore balance, or to give others their due.

- *The tactic is fair or appropriate to the situation.* This approach uses a kind of moral (situational) relativism as a rationale or justification. Most social situations, including negotiations, are governed by a set of generally well-understood rules of proper conduct and behaviour. For example, recall the earlier arguments of Carr, that business is a game and that the game has a special ethos to it that legitimizes normally unethical actions.[27] Others have countered these arguments, contending that deceit in business is just as immoral as it is in other areas of life and that the game analogy of business no more legitimizes unethical conduct than other analogies.[28] As a general matter, ethical relativism—the idea that moral standards shift with changing circumstances—frequently comes under fire as an unacceptable take on morality. As one writer put it, "If all ethical systems are equally valid, then no firm moral judgments can be made about individual behaviour, and we are all on our own to do as we like to others, within economic limits and legal constraints."[29] We leave it to the reader to decide if this is a good thing or a bad thing.

As self-serving rationalizations for one's own conduct, explanations allow the negotiator to convince others—particularly the victim—that conduct that would ordinarily be wrong in a given situation is acceptable. Explanations and justifications help people rationalize the behaviour to themselves as well. But there is a risk: We surmise that the more frequently negotiators engage in this self-serving process, the more their judgments about ethical standards and values will become biased, diminishing their ability to see the truth for what it is. The tactics involved may have been used initially to gain power in a negotiation, but negotiators who use them frequently may experience a loss of power over time. These negotiators will be seen as having low credibility or integrity, and they will be treated accordingly as people who will act exploitatively if the opportunity arises. Good reputations are easier to maintain than to restore once damaged.

How Can Negotiators Deal with the Other Party's Use of Deception?

A chapter such as this would not be complete without briefly noting some of the things that you as a negotiator can do when you believe the other party is using deceptive tactics. If you think the other party may be using deceptive tactics (see Table 9.3), here are some options:

Ask Probing Questions

Research shows that most buyers fail to ask questions, and that asking questions can reveal a great deal of information, some of which the negotiator may intentionally leave undisclosed.[30] In an experimental simulation of a negotiation over the sale of a computer, buyers were either strongly prompted to ask questions of the seller about the condition of the computer, or not prompted to ask questions.[31] Findings indicate that across the board, asking questions about the condition of the computer reduced the number of the seller's deceptive comments (lies of commission). However, under some conditions, asking questions also increased the seller's use of lies of omission about other aspects of the computer. Thus, while asking questions can help a negotiator determine whether another negotiator is being deceptive, such cross-examination may actually increase the seller's tendency to be deceptive in areas where questions are not being asked. (Refer back to Chapter 6 for a more extensive examination of asking good questions.)

TABLE 9.3 | Detecting Deception

Researchers have identified a number of verbal tactics that you can use to determine whether the other party is acting deceptively.

Tactic	Explanation and Examples
Intimidation	Force the other to admit he is using deception by intimidating him into telling the truth. Make a no-nonsense accusation of the other. Criticize the other. Hammer the other with challenging questions. Feign indifference to what he has to say ("I'm not interested in anything you have to say on the matter").
Futility portrayal	Emphasize the futility and impending danger associated with continued deceit: "The truth will come out someday," "Don't dig the hole deeper by trying to cover it up," "If you try to cover it up, it will only be worse in the future," "You are all alone in your deception."
Discomfort and relief	State the maxim, "Confession is good for the soul." Help the other reduce the tension and stress associated with being a known deceiver.
Bluffing	Lie to the other to make her believe you have uncovered her deception: "Your sins are about to be uncovered." Indicate that you know what she knows but will not discuss it.
Gentle prods	Encourage the other to keep talking so that he gives you information that may help you separate true facts from deceptions. Ask him to elaborate on the topic being discussed. Ask questions but indicate that you are asking because "other people want to know." Play devil's advocate and ask playful questions. Praise the other so as to give him confidence and support that may lead to information sharing.
Minimization	Play down the significance of any deceptive act. Help the other find excuses for why she was deceptive; minimize the consequences of the action; indicate that others have done worse; shift the blame to someone else.
Contradiction	Get the other to tell his story fully to discover more information that will allow you to discover inconsistencies and contradictions in his comments or reports. Point out and ask for explanations about apparent contradictions. Ask the speaker the same question several times and look for inconsistencies in his response. Present contradictions back and ask the speaker to explain. Put pressure on the speaker and get him to slip up or say things he doesn't want to say.
Altered information	Alter information and hopefully trick the other into revealing deception. Exaggerate what you believe is the deception, hoping that the other will jump in to "correct" the statement. Ask the suspected deceiver a question containing incorrect information and hope she corrects you.
A chink in the defence	Try to get the other to admit a small or partial lie about some information, and use this to push for admission of a larger lie: "If you lied about this one little thing, how do I know you have not lied about other things?"
Self-disclosure	Reveal a number of things about yourself, including, perhaps, dishonesty on your own part, hoping the other will begin to trust you and reciprocate with disclosures of dishonesty.
Point of deception cues	Point out behaviours you detect in the other that might be an indication he is lying: sweating, nervousness, change of voice, inability to make eye contact, and so on.
Concern	Indicate your true concern for the other's welfare: "You are important to me," "I care deeply about you," "I feel your pain."

TABLE 9.3 | *(Concluded)*

Tactic	Explanation and Examples
Keeping the status quo	Admonish the other to be truthful to maintain her good name. "What will people think?" Appeal to her pride and desire to maintain a good reputation.
Direct approach	"Simply tell me the truth." "Let's be honest here." "Surely you have no objection to telling me everything you know."
Silence	Create a "verbal vacuum" that makes the other uncomfortable and gets him to talk and disclose information. When he tells a lie, simply maintain direct eye contact but remain silent.

Source: Adapted from Pamela J. Kalbfleisch, "The Language of Detecting Deceit," Journal of Language and Social Psychology 13, no. 4 (1994), pp. 469–96.

Use Contingency Contracts

Have you ever been involved in a negotiation where you were skeptical of your counterpart's ability to meet the terms and conditions of your agreement? One way to satisfy your skepticism is by using a contingency contract, an agreement that satisfies negotiator interests by taking into account negotiator differences concerning future events.[32] For example, a homeowner who is skeptical of a contractor's ability to complete a home renovation on, or before, a certain date may create an agreement that specifies a financial penalty to the contractor if renovations are completed past the expected completion date and/or offers a financial incentive to the contractor if renovations are completed prior to the expected completion date. Advantages of contingency contracts include building trust and goodwill between the parties, protecting less informed parties from deception, reducing the risk of non-compliance, and allowing parties to claim greater value in negotiations. For contingency contracts to be effective you must ensure that they are enforceable by creating terms and conditions are clearly stated and provide for measureable outcomes. You must also ensure that you set reasonable incentives that do not compromise your outcome. Revisiting the above example, the homeowner would be wise not to set an unrealistic completion date, or create too large of a penalty and/or incentive that would jeopardize the quality of the home renovation.

Force the Other Party to Lie or Back Off

If you suspect the other party is being cagey or deceptive about an issue but is not making a clear statement in plain language, pose a question that forces him or her to tell a direct lie (if the assertion is false) or else abandon or qualify the assertion. For instance, if the seller of a piece of property alludes to other interested buyers and implies there are other offers, ask a question about other offers in a clear way that calls for a yes or no answer. This can be a useful strategy because, as we noted earlier, research shows people are more inclined to lie by omission than by commission. Some people are comfortable being cagey or misleading, but they will run headlong into their conscience if forced to flatly lie while looking someone in the eye. Conscience aside, this kind of question may also make the other party nervous about liability for fraudulent negotiator behaviour. Hence the timely use of a sharp, direct question will induce some adversaries to back off rather than fib to your face. (Granted, the pathological liar may well rise to the challenge.)

"Call" the Tactic

Indicate to the other side that you know he is bluffing or lying. Do so tactfully but firmly, and indicate your displeasure. (Note, however, that spotting lies is not always easy—see Negotiation Point 9.2.)

Discuss What You See and Offer to Help the Other Party Change to More Honest Behaviours

This is a variation on calling the tactic, but it tries to assure the other party that telling the truth is, in the long term, more likely to get him what he wants than any form of bluffing or deception will.

Respond in Kind

If the other party bluffs, you bluff more. If she misrepresents, you misrepresent. We do not recommend this course of action at all, because it simply escalates the destructive behaviour and drags you into the mud with the other party, but if she recognizes that you are lying too, she may also realize that the tactic is unlikely to work.

Ignore the Tactic

If you are aware that the other party is bluffing or lying, simply ignore it. Table 9.3 has additional suggestions for dealing with situations where you suspect that the other party is engaged in deception.

Negotiation Point

9.2

Is There Such a Thing as an "Honest Face"?

Though people in general are not particularly good at spotting lies, some people continue to believe that they can tell by looking into someone's face if that person is inclined to be dishonest or truthful on a regular basis. But how accurate are such assessments?

A study asked participants to view photographs of the same people as children, adolescents, and adults and to rate their attractiveness and honesty based on an assessment of their faces. These results were compared to self-reports of honest behaviour provided by the people in the photographs. The results demonstrated that

structural qualities of the face, such as attractiveness, "babyfaceness," eye size, and symmetry each individually contributed to perceptions of greater honesty in observers. The self-reports revealed that men who looked more honest early in life actually were more honest as they grew older. On the other hand, women whose behaviour was less honest when they were young grew to appear more honest as they aged, even though their behaviour did not change significantly. Study participants were able to correctly identify the most honest men in the group as they aged, but their assessment of women was largely inaccurate. The researchers concluded that men's faces accurately reflected their tendency toward honesty, but women's faces were not particularly valid indicators of their truthfulness.

Source: Adapted from L. A. Zebrowitz, L. Voinescu, and M. A. Collins, "Wide-Eyed and Crooked-Faced: Determinants of Perceived and Real Honesty across the Life Span," Personality and Social Psychology Bulletin 22 (1996), pp. 1258–69.

In this chapter, we have discussed factors that negotiators consider when they decide whether particular tactics are deceptive and unethical. We approached the study of ethically ambiguous tactics from a decision-making framework, examining the ethical overtones of the choices that negotiators make.

We began by drawing on a set of hypothetical scenarios to discuss how ethical questions are inherent in the process of negotiation, and then presented four fundamental approaches to ethical reasoning that might be used to make decisions about what is ethically appropriate. We proposed that a negotiator's decision to use ethically ambiguous (or flatly unethical) tactics typically grows out of a desire to increase one's negotiating power by manipulating the landscape of (presumably accurate) information in the negotiation. We discussed the different forms that ethically ambiguous tactics take, and we analyzed the motives for and consequences of engaging in unethical negotiation behaviour. Finally, we addressed how negotiators can respond to another party that may be using tactics of deception or subterfuge.

In closing, we suggest that negotiators who are considering the use of deceptive tactics ask themselves the following questions:

- Will they really enhance my power and help me achieve my objective?
- How will the use of these tactics affect the quality of my relationship with the other party in the future?
- How will the use of these tactics affect my reputation as a negotiator?

Negotiators frequently overlook the fact that, although unethical or expedient tactics may get them what they want in the short run, these same tactics typically lead to tarnished reputations and diminished effectiveness in the long run.

Key Terms

Ethical dilemma, p. 172

Ethics, p. 171

Multiparty and Team Negotiations

LEARNING OBJECTIVES

In this chapter we focus on how these extra layers of complexity affect negotiations. Specifically, the purpose of this chapter is to understand how the negotiation process changes when there are more than two parties at the table simultaneously and when groups of people are negotiating in teams. We will note the factors that make multiparty negotiations more difficult to manage than one-on-one negotiations. We will also comment on some of the key stages and phases of multiparty deliberations, and for each phase consider a variety of strategies that can be used to manage multiparty negotiations effectively. We conclude the chapter by considering the case where teams are negotiating, paying specific attention to the preparation and coordination challenges presented in team negotiation situations. After reading this chapter you should be able to:

1. Appreciate the factors that make multiparty negotiations more complex than one-on-one negotiations,

2. Effectively manage, or participate in, a multiparty negotiation, and

3. Understand how to plan for, and conduct, a team negotiation.

In earlier chapters we implicitly assumed that the negotiation situations we were discussing occurred in a "one-on-one" fashion. That is, each side was negotiating against the other side without having to worry about multiple parties with different agendas or multiple parties working together on the same side.

Now consider the negotiation of the North American Free Trade Agreement (NAFTA), which came into force on 1 January 1994. This negotiation produced a trilateral agreement that allows for the reduction and/or elimination of tariffs on goods and services exchanged between Canada, the United States, and Mexico, and formed one of the largest trading blocs in the world. Not only did the negotiation of this agreement involve multiple parties, each negotiating party consisted of multiple negotiators and negotiating teams. For example, Canada's negotiating team consisted of a trade representative, a chief negotiator, a deputy chief negotiator, 5 assistant chief negotiators, 15 assistant negotiators in charge of working groups, and a chief legal counsel.[1]

Also consider the example of the British Columbia Treaty Process (BCTP). The BCTP facilitates the negotiation of issues pertaining to British Columbia's First Nations such as land ownership, governance, and wildlife and environmental management. The British Columbia Treaty Commission is an independent body that currently oversees 45 negotiations between the British Columbia provincial government, the Canadian federal government, and 116 First Nations.[2]

■ The Nature of Multiparty Negotiations

We define a multiparty negotiation as one where more than two parties are working together to achieve a collective objective. To illustrate the nature of a multiparty negotiation, take the following simple example. A group of four students are selling a stereo system, including a CD/DVD player, receiver, and five speakers. They put up notices in the dorm and dining areas. A year ago, each put in $200 to buy the system; now they have different preferences for what they should do with it. Aaron (A) wants to sell it and simply split up the money because he wants to buy a new bike for himself; Bill (B) wants to sell it and buy a newer but inexpensive stereo system; Chuck (C) wants to sell it and buy a super-high-quality system that will require each of them to chip in a lot more money; and Dan (D) doesn't want to sell it at all and thinks the whole thing is a dumb idea. Each party has his own preferences and priorities, and the roommates must collectively decide what to do as a group if and when the system is sold. They might agree to make a single collective decision about what to do next, or they might agree to align together in subgroups to pool their money, or each might go his separate way. When the parties agree to hold a meeting to discuss the options and make a collective decision, this is a multiparty negotiation that involves unique dynamics in a collective decision-making process.

The general model for a multiparty negotiation is represented in Figure 10.1. Each of the parties (A, B, C, and D) is representing his or her own interests. In a different situation (e.g., they might be representatives of different corporate departments meeting together as a task force), they could be representing the interests of others (see Figure 10.2). Most of the complexities described in this section will increase linearly, if not exponentially, as more parties, constituencies, and audiences are added.

FIGURE 10.1 | A Multiparty Negotiation

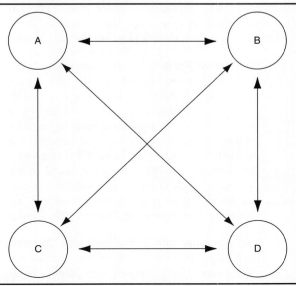

FIGURE 10.2 | A Multiparty Negotiation with Constituents

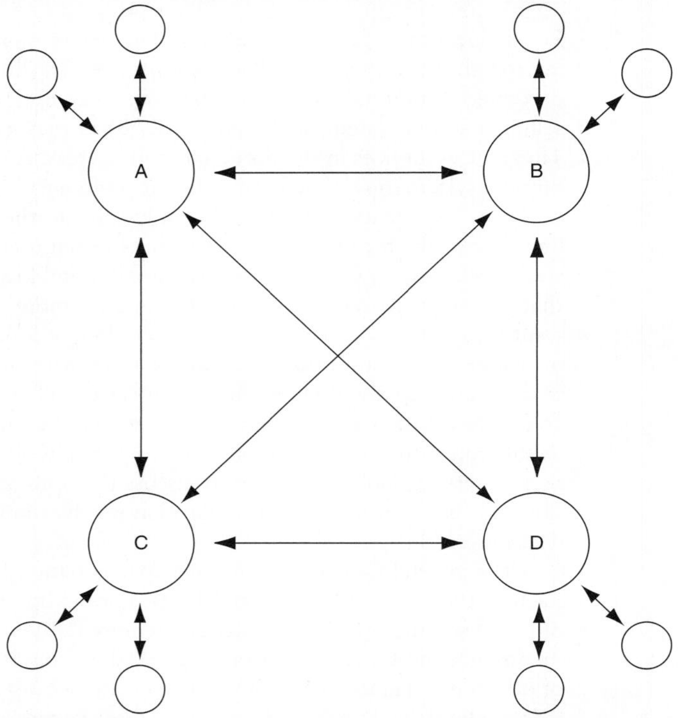

Differences between Two-Party Negotiations and Multiparty Negotiations

Multiparty negotiations differ from two-party deliberations in several important ways. In every case, the differences are what make multiparty negotiations more complex, challenging, and difficult to manage.

Number of Parties The first difference is the most obvious one: multiparty negotiations have more negotiators at the table. Thus, negotiations simply become bigger. This creates challenges for managing several different perspectives and ensuring that each party has adequate time to speak and be heard. Each party may be acting as a principal—that is, representing his or her own interests (Figure 10.1)—or an agent—representing the interests of at least one other party (the constituency) (Figure 10.2). In addition, parties may have different social roles outside the negotiation (e.g., president, vice president, director, board chairman) that may lead to either equal or unequal levels of power and status in the negotiation (see Chapter 7). If the parties are all equals (e.g., all vice presidents), the exchange within the negotiation should be more open than if one party has higher status or power than the others.

Informational and Computational Complexity A second difference in multiparty negotiations is that more issues, more perspectives on issues, and more total information (facts, figures, viewpoints, arguments, documentary support) are introduced: "One of the most fundamental consequences of increasing the number of parties is that the negotiation situation tends to become less lucid, more complex, and therefore, in some respects, more demanding. As size increases, there will be more values, interests, and perceptions to be integrated or accommodated."[3] Keeping track of all this information, the perspectives of each side, and the parameters into which a solution must fit becomes a major challenge for the negotiators.

Social Complexity A third difference is that as the number of parties increases, the social environment changes from a one-on-one dialogue to a small-group discussion. As a result, all the dynamics of small groups begin to affect the way the negotiators behave. Research shows that how the process evolves may depend on the motivational orientation of the parties toward each other. Parties with a co-operative (versus an individualistic) motivational orientation are much more likely to achieve a higher-quality outcome in their deliberations. Co-operatively motivated parties are also more trusting and engage in less argumentation than individualistic ones, which affects the way parties discuss issues (see below).[4] Social pressures may also develop for the group to act cohesively, yet the members may be in conflict with each other and cannot be cohesive unless they can find an acceptable solution. As group size increases, members tend to compare themselves to one another, evaluate themselves against one another, and use a variety of influence tactics to persuade one another toward their point of view. Strong pressures for conformity develop as members pressure other members to adopt a common perspective or definition of the problem or to endorse a particular solution.

Procedural Complexity A fourth way in which multiparty negotiations are more complex than two-party ones is that the process they have to follow is more complicated. In one-on-one negotiations, the parties simply take turns in either presenting their issues and perspectives, challenging the other's perspectives, or moving the negotiation along from its early stages to the later ones. When more parties are involved, the procedural rules become far less clear. Whose turn is it to do what? How do the parties coordinate where they are in the negotiations (e.g., opening statements, presentation of viewpoints, moving toward agreement)? There are several consequences of this procedural complexity. First, negotiations will take longer,[5] so more time must be allowed. Second, the greater the number of parties, the more out of control the process can become—particularly if some parties choose to adopt a strategy of tough positional bargaining and dominate the process in an effort to railroad through their particular viewpoints.[6] Third, as a result of the first two elements, negotiators will probably have to devote explicit discussion time to how they will manage the process to arrive at the type of solution or agreement they want. Finally, the parties must decide how they want to approach multiple issues on the table. Parties who discuss multiple issues simultaneously—considering all the issues at once and looking for ways to trade one off against another—achieved higher quality agreements and increased the likelihood of achieving agreement compared to groups that approached the issues sequentially (one at a time, in a fixed or negotiated sequence).[7]

Strategic Complexity Finally, multiparty negotiations are more strategically complex than two-party ones. In one-on-one negotiations, the negotiator need only attend to the behaviour of the other negotiator; strategy is therefore driven by the negotiator's objectives, the other party's actions, and the tactics they each use. In a group negotiation, complexity increases significantly. The negotiator must consider the strategies of all the other parties at the table and decide whether to deal with each of them separately or as a group. The actual process of dealing with each of them usually evolves into a series of one-on-one negotiations, but conducted within the view of all the other group members. Viewed in this manner, this series of one-on-one negotiations can have several consequences.

First, these exchanges are subject to surveillance by the audience. Negotiators will be sensitive to being observed and may feel the need to be tough to show their firmness and resolve (both to the other party and to bystanders or audiences). As a result, negotiators may adopt distributive strategies and tactics—even if they did not intend to do so—simply to show their toughness and resolve to others. The short-term result is that negotiators in the group may become strongly positional unless specific actions are taken to manage the group beyond this competitive escalation. A related dynamic is that once the parties have become strongly positional, negotiators will have to find satisfactory ways to explain modification of their positions—concession making or movement toward compromises and consensus—to their constituencies without the face-threatening dynamics discussed earlier. Even without constituencies, negotiators will not want to lose face with the other negotiators present.

Second, negotiators who have some way to control the number of parties at the table (or even in the room) may begin to act strategically, using this control to serve their objectives. The tactic used will be determined by the strategic interests to be served by adding other parties. Additional parties may be invited to add support or credence to the negotiator's position, to provide "independent" testimony or support to a point of view, or simply to present a show of force. For example, when communities are in dispute about whether to build a new shopping centre or school, change a zoning law, or present a new tax package, it is not uncommon for the agents who will publicly speak to the issue to pack the audience with a large number of supporters who will occasionally show their enthusiasm and support (or opposition) for a position. Thus, negotiators can strategically add parties to the negotiation, either to enhance their perceived power through sheer numbers or to present some credible threat about the consequences that will occur if the negotiators do not get their way.

Third, negotiators can explicitly engage in coalition building as a way to marshal support. Parties may explicitly or implicitly agree to support each other's positions to add collective weight to their combined view, and then use this coalition to either dominate the negotiation process or shape the desired settlement. Coalitions may be explicitly formed prior to negotiations or during negotiation recesses and breaks, or they may emerge as the discussion proceeds. Members of coalitions can exert their strength in multiparty negotiations in a number of ways: by expressing solidarity with each other, by agreeing to help each other achieve their common or individual objectives, by dominating discussion time, and by agreeing to support each other as particular solutions and negotiated agreements emerge. One author has suggested that the emergence of consensus in decision-making groups proceeds as a "snowballing coalition." Coalitions are built one party at a time. Thus, in a group discussion, as parties share information and then deliberate possible solutions, a few people will emerge with a common perspective and then tacitly or explicitly agree to support each other's views. Other individuals then negotiate with the emerging coalition to incorporate their own views. Those who may be unwilling to negotiate or modify their views are eventually rejected and left out of the group decision.[8]

The risk for those on the outside of an influential coalition is that they will not be an active participant in the discussions, some of which may occur in caucuses away from the main negotiating table. Negotiators who are excluded from part of a multiparty negotiation often receive a lesser share of the outcome than those who are present for the duration. This is particularly damaging to the excluded party when he or she misses the second half of the discussion. The lesson seems to be that simply being present when key discussions occur is important, especially in the later stages as the parties hone in on a final settlement.[9]

Finally, relationships are the most significant force in shaping which parties will enter coalitions with each other in a multiparty negotiation. When a relationship is in place, parties extensively incorporate the element of time into their deliberations and side negotiations with each other. Thus, what the parties have done for each other in the past, and/or what they think they can do for each other in the future, have a strong impact on the current discussions.[10] Relationships may lead the parties to have similar preferences, to have strong concern for the others and a desire to help the others achieve their outcomes, and to create and sustain strong trust among group members.

Summary There are five ways in which the complexity increases as three or more parties simultaneously engage in negotiation. First, there are simply more parties involved in the negotiation, which increases the number of speakers, increases the demand for discussion time, and increases the number of different roles the parties may play. Second, more parties bring more issues and positions to the table, and thus more perspectives must be presented and discussed. Third, negotiations become socially more complex—social norms emerge that affect member participation, and there may be stronger pressures to conform and suppress disagreement. Fourth, negotiations become procedurally more complex, and the parties may have to negotiate a new process that allows them to coordinate their actions more effectively. Finally, negotiations become more strategically complex because the parties must monitor the moves and actions of several other parties in determining what each will do next. In addition, the possibility of coalitions increases the likelihood that decisions will not be made by a comprehensive negotiated consensus, but by some subgroup that can dominate the discussion and decision-making processes.

■ Managing Multiparty Negotiations

Given the additional complexity that occurs in a multiparty negotiation, what is the most effective way to cope? There are three key stages that characterize multilateral negotiations: pre-negotiation, actual negotiation, and managing the agreement. In addressing these three stages, we will also identify what a single negotiator can do when:

- The individual is simply one of the parties in a multiparty negotiation and wants to ensure that his or her own issues and interests are clearly incorporated into the final agreement.

- The individual wants to ensure that the group reaches the highest quality and best possible final agreement.
- The individual is responsible for managing a multiparty negotiation process to ensure that many of the strategic and procedural complexities are effectively managed.[11]

The Pre-negotiation Stage

This stage is characterized by lots of informal contact among the parties. They tend to work on the following issues:

Participants The parties must agree on who is going to be invited to the talks. If the group is already an intact one, this is an easy question. However, many complex international negotiations give a great deal of time to the question of who will be recognized and who can speak for others. Issues about participants can be decided on the basis of the following:

- Who must be included if a deal is to be reached (key coalition members)?
- Who could spoil the deal if they were excluded (veto players)?
- Whose presence is likely to help other parties achieve their objectives (desirable coalition members)?
- Whose presence is likely to keep other parties from achieving their objectives (key coalition blockers)?
- Whose status will be enhanced simply by being at the table?

Coalitions It is not uncommon for coalitions to exist before negotiations begin or for coalitions to organize in anticipation of the meeting of all the parties. Naturally, coalitions will form to either promote or block a particular agenda.

Understanding the Costs and Consequences of No Agreement Negotiators need to understand the costs and consequences that will ensue if the group fails to agree and everyone falls back on their BATNA. For example, suppose a group of vice presidents in a computer company is trying to decide which models of a new line of personal computers should be built next year and the quantities of each. To make this decision effectively, they must include in their decision options a consideration of what will happen if they fail to agree on what to do. Will someone else (i.e., the president) step in and decide for them? How will the president feel about the group if the members can't agree? Are the costs of impasse the same for every negotiator? Usually this is not the case—different agents have different costs associated with no agreement. For example, if the vice presidents cannot agree, the president may mandate the model line and quantities, which may have greater costs for the engineering and manufacturing departments (which would have to change over) than for the marketing and sales departments (which would have to design a new marketing and ad campaign regardless of what was done). The group members with the better impasse alternatives are likely to have more power in the negotiation because they care less about whether the group reaches a particular solution relative to no agreement.[12] Finally, do group members perceive their agreement and no-agreement options accurately? There is much evidence that negotiators are prone to perceptual biases that lead them to believe they are better than others, their options are better than others' options, they are more likely to achieve their outcomes than others, and they have more control over shaping an outcome than others.[13] In multiparty negotiations, these biases are likely to affect negotiators by inflating their sense of power and ability to win—leading them to believe that the no-agreement alternative is much better than it really is. Reality checking with others is important in keeping these biases under control.

Learning the Issues and Constructing an Agenda   Finally, parties spend a great deal of time familiarizing themselves with the issues, absorbing information, and trying to understand one another's interests. They will also spend time constructing an agenda. There are many reasons why an agenda can be an effective decision aid:

- It establishes the issues that will be discussed.
- Depending on how the issues are worded, it can also define how each issue is discussed (refer back to our discussion of framing in Chapter 5).
- It can define the order in which issues are discussed.
- It can be used to introduce process issues (decision rules, discussion norms, member roles, discussion dynamics), as well as substantive issues, simply by including them.
- It can assign time limits to various items, thereby indicating the importance of the different issues.

The Formal Negotiation Stage—Managing the Group Process and Outcome

Much of the multiparty negotiation process is a combination of the group discussion, bilateral negotiation, and coalition-building activities described earlier in this chapter. It also incorporates a great deal of what we know about how to structure a group discussion to achieve an effective and endorsed result. The following approaches are likely to ensure a high-quality group decision.

Appoint an Appropriate Chair   Multiparty negotiations will proceed more smoothly when it is clear to everyone involved who is chairing or facilitating the process. Often this role will be played by one of the interested parties, but multiparty negotiations can be greatly facilitated by the presence of a neutral chairperson who can implement many of the tactics described below. When feasible, the parties should seriously consider designating a chair who has little stake in the specific outcome but a strong commitment to an open and fair process. In this case, the chairperson functions as a third party who has no stake in any particular outcome but does have a strong interest in ensuring that the group works toward achieving the best possible outcome. Such a chairperson would be adopting similar roles as those adopted by mediators, which we discussed in Chapter 8.

As a practical matter, it is frequently the case that the chair will be drawn from within the circle of interested parties. Keep in mind that if a chairperson is also advocating a particular position or preferred outcome, it will be most difficult for that individual to act or be seen as neutral, because the solution the person wants to obtain on the issues is likely to compromise (or be perceived to compromise) his or her neutrality or objectivity with respect to facilitating the process. See Negotiation Point 10.1 for an inventory of constructive approaches to acting as a chair in multiparty negotiations.

Negotiation Point

10.1

Chairing a Multiparty Negotiation

Chairpersons of multiparty negotiations must be sensitive to keeping tight control over the group process while not directly affecting the group's outcome. When a group wants to achieve a consensus or unanimous decision, the responsibility of the chair is to be constantly attentive to the group process. Some pointers for how to chair a multiparty negotiation effectively include:

- Explicitly describe the role you will take as chair. Be clear that you are there only to manage process and that the group will determine the outcome.

- Introduce the agenda or build one based on the group's issues, concerns, and priorities. Make sure the group has an opportunity to discuss, modify, or challenge the agenda before you begin.

- Make logistical arrangements that will help the negotiation process. Does the physical setup of the room offer the best possible configuration for constructive discussion? Arrange for a flip chart, blackboard, or overhead projector to write down issues and interests. Many negotiators find they benefit from common visual access to issues, proposals, and other information during the discussion.

- Introduce necessary ground rules or let the parties suggest them. How long will the group meet? What is the expected output or final product? Will minutes be taken? Will the group take breaks? Where will negotiations take place? How and when can group members consult with their constituents?

- Create or review decision standards and rules. Find standards for what parties believe will be a fair or reasonable settlement. What criteria will be used to assess whether a particular solution is fair, reasonable, and effective? How will the group ultimately decide to adopt an agreement?

- Assure individual members that they will have an opportunity to make opening statements or other ways of placing their individual concerns and issues on the table. Be clear that once parties are familiar with the issues, simultaneous discussion of several issues can take place. This will permit trade-offs among issues rather than forcing a compromise on each individual issue.

- Be an active gatekeeper. Make sure that people have a chance to speak and that the more vocal people do not dominate so that the less vocal people become silent and drop out. Ask the more vocal people to hold back and explicitly invite the more silent people to make comments and input. Often, as a group moves toward some form of agreement or consensus, some people participate less. Make sure that they have chosen not to participate, rather than simply dropped out because they don't think their views are worthwhile or important.

- Listen for interests and commonalities. Encourage people to express interests, mirror them back, and encourage people to identify not only what they want, but also why they want it. Listen for priorities and concerns. Once the issues and interests have been identified, explicitly set aside a time for inventing options. Use brainstorming and other group decision-making techniques to generate options and evaluate them.

- Introduce external information (studies, reports, statistics, facts, testimony from experts) that will help illuminate the issues and interests. Ask for hard data to support assertions (but be careful to refrain from engaging in aggressive "cross-examination" that will compromise your neutrality).

- Summarize frequently, particularly when conversation becomes stalled, confused, or tense. State where you think the group is, what has been accomplished, and what needs to be done. Paraphrasing and summarizing bring the group back to reality and back on task.

Use and Restructure the Agenda A critical way to control the flow and direction of negotiation is through an agenda. Either the chair or the parties to the negotiation may introduce and coordinate the agenda. An agenda adds a high degree of structure, organization, and coordination to a discussion. Agendas provide low-power or disadvantaged groups a vehicle for getting their issues heard and addressed, assuming that they can get them on the agenda. However, the manner in which an agenda is built (by collective consensus at the beginning of a meeting versus by one person prior to the meeting) and who builds it will have a great deal of impact on the flow of the negotiation. Unless group members feel comfortable challenging the person who introduces a pre-emptive agenda, the agenda will go unquestioned and hence the implicit discussion structure and format it suggests will prevail. Negotiators entering a multiparty negotiation for which an (unacceptable) agenda has been created in advance should consider letting other parties know ahead of time that they view the agenda itself as open to discussion or change. In other words, make sure that possible modifications to the agenda are part of the agenda.

Although an agenda may add needed structure to a complex negotiation, a drawback is that it may artificially partition related issues; as a result, issues may be discussed separately rather than coupled or traded off to exploit integrative potential. The parties using an agenda must be sensitive to the implicit structure it imposes, and they must be willing to challenge and reconfigure it if doing so will facilitate the emergence of an integrative, consensus-based agreement.

Ensure a Diversity of Information and Perspectives A third way to facilitate the negotiation is to ensure that the group receives a wide variety of different perspectives about the task and different sources of information. Because the nature of the information changes depending on the group's task—for example, designing and implementing a change, finding the best possible solution to a problem, or simply finding a solution that is politically acceptable to several constituencies—it is difficult to prescribe what information is critical and how to ensure that the group is exposed to it. This can simply be a matter of making sure that the voices of all participants are heard.

If there is a chair, he or she can ensure that the group receives input from each group member; that various constituencies and stakeholders have an opportunity to provide input (through written comments or opportunities for open testimony before the group); and that relevant reports, documents, or statistical analyses are circulated and discussed. There are five key process steps that a chair can implement to assure having an effective, amicable disagreement on a team:

1. **Collect your thoughts and composure before speaking.** Avoid the temptation to "shoot from the hip" with emotion rather than reasoned arguments.

2. **Try to understand the other person's position.** Rely on techniques such as listening skills, mirroring, and role reversal to understand the other.

3. **Try to think of ways whereby you both can win.**

4. **Consider how important this issue is to you.** Is this your most important issue in the negotiation? Can you afford to sacrifice all or part of your position on this issue for gains elsewhere?

5. **Remember that you will probably have to work together with these people in the future.** Even out of anger and frustration, don't use tactics that will make you regret the conversation tomorrow.[14]

Ensure Consideration of All the Available Information One way to ensure that the group discusses all available information is to monitor discussion norms, that is, the way the group engages in sharing and evaluating the information introduced.[15]

Although it would be highly desirable to do so, groups seldom consider in advance what discussion norms they are going to follow. Several group norms can undermine an effective discussion:

- *Unwillingness to tolerate conflicting points of view and perspectives.* One or more members dislike conflict, are afraid that conflict will be uncontrollable, or see conflict as destructive to group cohesiveness. But as we noted elsewhere in the book, the absence of conflict can also lead to disastrous decisions.

- *No means for defusing an emotionally charged discussion.* Unless there is a way to release it, anger, frustration, or resentment can become mixed in with the substantive issues and hamper the group's efforts. Although a great deal of negotiation literature suggests that parties should simply be calm and rational at all times, doing so is simply not humanly possible. The more the parties care about a particular issue and are invested in it, the more likely it is that emotions will creep in. Vehicles must exist to allow the parties to vent their emotions productively.

- *Coming to a meeting unprepared.* Unfortunately, preparation for a meeting often consists of either no preparation at all or simply preparing one's own position. Attention to the others' positions or to assessing underlying interests and priorities requires thorough preparation.

Several strategies may be used to manage each of these three potentially destructive discussion norms. The parties must generate and exchange ideas in a manner that permits full exploration and allows everyone to have some input, yet avoids some of the destructive conflict and emotions that can occur. There are several group decision-making and brainstorming techniques that are frequently used to achieve this objective:

The Delphi Technique A moderator structures an initial questionnaire and sends it out to all parties, asking for input. Parties provide their input and send it back to the moderator. The moderator summarizes the input and sends it back to the parties. Parties then evaluate the report, make further input, and return it to the moderator. Over a number of rounds, through the questions and inquiries shaped by the moderator, the parties can exchange a great deal of information and share different perspectives.

Brainstorming In brainstorming, the parties are instructed to define a problem and then to generate as many solutions as possible without criticizing any of them. Many of the suggestions may be unrealistic or impractical, but the purpose is to suggest a large number of potential solutions and to be as creative as possible in suggesting them. Brainstorming tends to generate a wider variety of solution options than might normally occur, particularly because it invites everyone to participate rather than just a small, vocal minority. Negotiation Point 10.2 offers a list of critical rules to be used in brainstorming.

Nominal Group Technique The nominal group technique typically follows brainstorming. Once the brainstormed list of solution options is created, group members can rank, rate, or evaluate the alternatives in terms of the degree to which each

Negotiation Point

10.2

Rules for Brainstorming

- **No criticism is allowed.** No other member can say whether an idea is good or bad.

- **Questions can be asked only for clarification of an idea.**

- **Free-wheeling is a plus.** Wild and crazy ideas are welcome, and in fact they may help trigger other ideas from team members. Don't worry about whether the idea you voice is good, bad, silly, or realistic; just say it.

- **Go for quantity.** The more ideas you get from team members, the better this team effort will be.

- **Combine and improve ideas.** It is certainly fine to build on someone else's idea.

Source: C. C. Manz, Christopher P. Neck, James Mancuso, and K. P. Manz, For Team Members Only (New York: AMACOM, 1997), p. 135. Used by permission of Vivian Scott Hixson.

alternative solves the problem. The leader collects, posts, and records these ratings so that all group members have an opportunity to formally evaluate the options and to vote on the ones they consider to be most effective.[16]

Manage Conflict Effectively As implied by many of the suggestions offered throughout this section, groups must generate many ideas and approaches to a problem—which usually creates conflict—while not allowing that conflict to either disrupt the information flow or create personal animosity. When done well, conflict is a natural part of group life that improves members' ability to complete tasks, work together, and sustain these relationships. When done poorly, conflict actively disrupts all of these processes. One study examined the development and management of conflict over time in high-performance task groups. The authors examined three kinds of conflict typical to work groups: relationship conflict (interpersonal incompatibilities, dislike among group members, and feelings of tension, friction, annoyance, frustration, and dislike); task conflicts (awareness of difference in viewpoints about the group's task); and process conflict (awareness of controversies about how task accomplishment will proceed—who will do what, how much one should get from a result, etc.). High-performing teams were characterized by low, but increasing, levels of process conflict, low levels of relationship conflict with a rise near the deadline, and moderate levels of task conflict at the midpoint of the interaction. Those teams that were able to create this ideal conflict profile had similar pre-established work-related value systems among the group members, high levels of trust and respect, and open discussion norms around conflict during the middle stages of the interaction.[17]

Review and Manage the Decision Rules In addition to monitoring the discussion norms and managing the conflict processes effectively, the parties also need to manage the decision rules—that is, the way the group will decide what to do. In decision-making groups, the dominant view is to assume that the majority rules and, at some point, take a vote of all members, assuming that any settlement option that receives more than 50 percent of the votes will be the one adopted. Obviously, this is not the only option. Groups can make decisions by dictatorship (one person decides); oligarchy (a dominant minority coalition decides); simple majority (one more person than half the group decides); two-thirds majority; quasi-consensus (most of the group agrees, and those who dissent agree not to protest or raise objections); and true unanimity, or consensus (everyone agrees). Determining the group's decision rule before deliberations begin will also significantly affect the group process. For example, if a simple majority will make the decision in a five-person group, then only three people need to agree. Thus, any three people can get together and form a coalition during or even prior to the meeting. In contrast, if the decision rule will be consensus, or unanimity, then the group must meet and work hard enough to ensure that all parties' interests are raised, discussed, and incorporated into the group decision. Whether a coalition-building strategy or a complete sharing of positions and interests and problem solving will be necessary requires significantly different approaches.[18]

Strive for a First Agreement Finally, if the objective is consensus or the best quality solution, negotiators should not strive to achieve it all at once. Rather, they should strive for a *first agreement* that can be revised, upgraded, and improved. As we have discussed, the additional complexity of multiparty negotiations increases the complexity of the events, the likelihood of communication breakdown, and the likelihood that the parties will negotiate more positionally (either because of the competitive dynamics or the consequences of audience or constituency dynamics). Given these conditions, achieving true consensus among the parties becomes much more difficult, even if a true consensus solution exists. As a result, it is often better to set a more modest objective for these negotiations: to reach a preliminary agreement or a tentative consensus that can then be systematically improved through "renegotiation," using the first agreement as a plateau that can be modified, reshaped, and improved upon in a follow-up negotiation effort.

The drawback, of course, is that many group members may be satisfied with the first solution—either because it already incorporates their views or because the difficulty of achieving it may sap their enthusiasm for exerting any time and energy to improve it. First agreements typically reflect the position of a group's majority or the views of a small number of powerful group members. These parties may not be open to dissenting views that would otherwise stimulate consideration of a wider set of possible alternative outcomes.[19]

This resistance to further deliberations by parties who are happy with the first agreement may be overcome by taking a break after the first agreement is reached, encouraging the group to critique and evaluate the first agreement, and explicitly planning to come back with a commitment to try second-agreement negotiations (renegotiations). In addition, if the group has been through a great deal of divisive and unproductive conflict to reach the first agreement, then the renegotiations must specifically attend to changing and managing the conflict process.[20]

The Agreement Phase

The third and final stage in managing multiparty negotiations is the agreement stage. During the agreement stage, the parties must select among the alternatives on the table. They are also likely to encounter some last-minute problems and issues, such as deadline pressures, the discovery of new issues that were not previously addressed, the need for more information on certain problems or concerns, and the tendency for some parties to threaten veto power while they lobby to get their specific pet idea or project included in the final group agreement. Four key problem-solving steps need to occur during this phase:

- **Select the best solution.** Earlier in this chapter, we reviewed a number of strategies for making a decision. The group must weigh the alternatives they have considered and either select a single alternative or combine alternatives into a package that will satisfy as many members as possible.

- **Develop an action plan.** This increases the likelihood that the solution will be implemented completely, effectively, and on time. For example, a good action plan might include a list of key steps, the objectives to be achieved at each step, when the step should be started and completed, what resources are needed to complete the step, and who has responsibility for completing the step. Working on this plan with the group also has the advantage of surfacing points that may be neglected, ambiguous, or incomplete in the group solution. If these ambiguities or omissions can be surfaced and discussed at this point, it could prevent greater conflict down the road when implementation has begun and the parties recognize that key points were undefined or unclear.

- **Implement the action plan.** This is likely to take place after the group disbands or outside the scope of the group, but it needs to follow the guidelines established by the group. Without an effective action plan, the problems that might have been recognized at this point are sure to occur.

- **Evaluate the just-completed process.** This is a very important step in the life of the group, but it is often underutilized. It takes extra time to do this, it may surface wounds and differences that were left unresolved and incomplete, and it can be politically unpopular. Even more problematically, if the group thinks it has done everything right, yet has achieved a superficial or incomplete agreement, group members may also believe that they have not made any mistakes, and hence that any kind of post-mortem is unnecessary. However, particularly for teams that are just learning to work together and expect to have ongoing working relationships in the future, conducting an evaluation of the process and the outcome can be critical for surfacing data about the group's working effectiveness. This evaluation need not occur at the same time or place as the decision meeting, but it should not be deferred or omitted. If team members are unwilling to raise criticisms publicly, anonymous questionnaires can be completed, summarized, and sent back to the group by the leader or a neutral facilitator, who can then use the data to highlight specific concerns about faulty process or incomplete outcomes. For example, in hostage negotiations, police hostage teams specifically debrief after every incident to determine what they can learn and how to perform more effectively in the future.[21]

What the Chair Can Do to Help In addition to the list of chair responsibilities outlined in Negotiation Point 10.1 here are some things a group facilitator can do to keep the group moving toward a successful completion:

- *Move the group toward selecting one or more of the options.* Use the process rules we discussed earlier, as well as the wide variety of techniques for achieving an integrative agreement presented in Chapter 3. Listen for the emergence of the "snowballing coalition" among key members. Permit and encourage packaging and trade-offs among multiple issues or modification of the first agreement or tentative agreement reached earlier. If the decision is particularly laden with conflict, pursue a first agreement with the understanding that the group will take a break and come back to renegotiate the agreement at a later date.

- *Shape and draft the tentative agreement.* Write it down. Work on language. Write the wording on a board, flip chart, or overhead projection that can be displayed to the entire group, so that all can see it and edit it freely. Test to make sure all parties understand the agreement and its implications and consequences. Remember that the person who does the writing often has more power than others because he or she gets to write the agreement in his or her own language and may bias or selectively remember some points and omit others.

- *Discuss whatever implementation and follow-up or next steps need to occur.* Make sure that individuals who have a role in this process understand what they need to do. Make assignments to individuals to ensure that key action steps are designed and executed. Schedule a follow-up meeting. Plan for another meeting in the future to evaluate how the agreement is working.

- *Thank the group for their participation, their hard work, and their efforts.* If the discussion has been particularly difficult or required a large time commitment, a small group celebration and formal thank-you notes or gifts may be in order. Have dinner or a party together to celebrate all the hard work.

- *Organize and facilitate the post-mortem.* Have group members discuss the process and the outcome, and evaluate what they might do better or differently the next time. This will ensure learning for both the group members and the chair.

■ Team Negotiation

Team negotiation occurs when more than one person joins together to jointly represent one of the parties at the negotiation table. Although it is often possible for just one person to do the negotiation, there is usually a benefit to a group working together. Do teams actually provide benefits in comparison to individuals acting alone? Research comparing the effects of teams versus individuals has shown that when at least one of the parties at the negotiation table is a team, more value tends to be created. One of the reasons this happens is teams tend to share more information than individuals acting alone. Thus, teams often facilitate the integrative dimension of negotiations. However, teams are not necessarily better at claiming value. Although they may not be better in distributive situations, it should also be pointed out that teams are not necessarily worse.

Preparing to Negotiate as a Team

Recall that in Chapter 4 we discussed how to plan for a negotiation. For the most part, this advice applies whether or not you find yourself negotiating solo or in a team. You should also be aware, however, that teams add a level of complexity to the planning process that individuals do not need to consider. In this section we cover some of the factors teams should consider as they prepare for an upcoming negotiation.

Putting the Team Together A negotiation team should have a balance of expertise and skills. Three types of expertise are usually helpful. The first type of expertise is *negotiation expertise*. Having at least one member who understands negotiation dynamics, such as distributive and integrative bargaining, is tremendously helpful. A second type of expertise to look for is *technical expertise*, which refers to expertise that relates to the domain of the negotiation. Finally, having team members with strong *interpersonal skills* can reduce the likelihood that the team will fail to communicate and establish rapport with the other side. See Negotiation Point 10.3 for additional details on putting the team together.

Prepare as a Team Preparation is just as important for teams as it is for individuals, and perhaps even more so. Experienced negotiators often mention that team preparation is more effective when each team member has a chance to prepare by themselves before meeting as a team. Each team member should develop a tentative list of the key issues as discussed in Chapter 4. For example, each negotiator should identify the main issues, consider the team's BATNA, and give some thought to the team's worst-case and best-case scenario. It is a good idea for each team member to individually work through the Negotiation Planning Guide found in Chapter 4. When this process is complete, the team should meet and begin planning.

   The team planning meeting should begin with a discussion of each individual's assessment of the important facts and information surrounding the upcoming negotiation. Having a discussion about things like reservation price and BATNA

Negotiation Point

10.3

Teams in Negotiation

When should teams be used in negotiation? Professor Elizabeth Mannix of the Johnson School of Management at Cornell University advises that the use of teams would be better suited in situations involving complex negotiations that require a broad array of knowledge, that have the potential for value creation through creativity, that have the involvement of multiple stakeholders, and that allow for enough time for coordination among team members. If you decide that your negotiation requires a team approach but have yet to select your negotiating team, Professor Lawrence Susskind of the Massachusetts Institute of Technology advises that team members should be selected to fill certain roles. Specifically, Susskind says that your negotiating team should have members that should fill the roles of team leader, stakeholder, bridge builder, and technical expert. He further adds that individuals occupying these roles should have specific knowledge, skills, and abilities. For example, team leaders should have the ability to facilitate joint problem-solving, stakeholders should have the ability to keep their constituents' interests in mind, bridge-builders should be people who have a good rapport with the other negotiating party, and technical experts should have strong knowledge of the specific aspects of the negotiation.

Source: Picking the right negotiating team. Negotiation. Harvard Law School; Nov. 2007, pp. 6–7.

is essential to minimize surprises during negotiation. When the team has reached agreement on the essential facts and information, it is time to move on to a discussion of strategy.

What are the major strategic considerations for a negotiating team? At a minimum, the team should consider the following questions:

- What should our opening offer be and how will we present it?
- What roles will each team member take during the negotiation? Be sure to clarify these roles in advance: (1) lead negotiator (the person who does most of the talking), (2) process manager (the person who is responsible for paying attention to learning about the other side and focusing on acquiring strategic information), (3) number cruncher (someone who has the role of attending to the numbers, and (4) the scribe (not just a note-taker, this person focuses on all the details).
- How will we know when it is time to take a break or plan a caucus session? Remember, though, not to spend too much time in private caucus. It tends to lead to an increase in suspicion and heightened anxiety for those on the other side.
- How can we use non-verbal communication to our advantage? Good teams anticipate the need to send signals to each other over the course of the negotiation without interrupting the flow of conversation. The closing of a laptop, a scratch of an arm, a quick glance; each of these behaviours can have strategic implications *if* the team has discussed them and planned for them in advance.

Challenges and Strategies in Team Negotiations

Once the team has prepared and is ready to begin negotiating, they should also be aware of the challenges teams face while trying to work together.

Information Processing Common sense dictates that two heads are better than one. After all, the reason negotiation teams are created is to capitalize on the diverse expertise that is shared among team members. Unfortunately, research has shown that groups often fail to capitalize on the benefits of distributed expertise. Groups have a strong tendency to discuss information that is shared between group members and spend less time discussing information that is held by only one or a few members. The problem, known as the *common knowledge effect*, can affect how negotiating groups process and discuss information over the course of a negotiation. For reasons that are not entirely clear, group members with unique information often fail to bring that unique information up when it is called for.

To counteract this tendency, we encourage negotiating groups to establish norms of information sharing at the outset. For example, when establishing roles in the planning phase, group members should acknowledge the fact that bringing relevant information to the table is *everyone's* responsibility, not just members with technical expertise. In addition, breaks and caucuses should be used as an opportunity to solicit input from everyone about what they know. A question like, "do you have any information that might help us here?" can go a long way towards opening up opportunities for creating value.

Stereotyping When negotiating with a counterpart, we often hold negative views about the other side based solely on affiliation. In a union–management negotiation the team on the management side might share a view that all union members are unsophisticated and lack the ability to see things from another perspective. The stereotype can be problematic because it leads to negotiation behaviours that are consistent with that impression. For example, the management side might use more distributive tactics because they assume this is the way the union side with act. Or, they might fail to use co-operative behaviours simply because they assume the union side lacks the knowledge to reciprocate those tactics. Unfortunately the management side is basing their strategy on untested assumptions that are based in stereotypes. Teams should be on the lookout for these tendencies and be ready to check for errors based on invalid assumptions.

Group Extremism Researchers have known for a long time that groups tend take more extreme positions and make more extreme choices than individuals acting alone. This effect, known as *group polarization*, is also likely to affect negotiation teams. Earlier we noted that teams are generally superior to individuals at creating value in negotiations. However, research on group polarization suggests that when things go bad in negotiations, they are likely to be worse in a team. Unless the team is fairly sophisticated with respect to conflict management strategies, conflict with the other side will often escalate to more extreme levels in teams. Something that can help when conflict escalates is to search for common identity between the disputing parties. Find areas of overlap and focus on discussing them. Also, be sure to ask plenty of questions. Research shows that a well-timed question can go a long way in terms of de-escalating a conflict situation.

Summary of Team Negotiation

Team negotiations share many of the characteristics of multiparty negotiations. They are complicated, tend to take a long time, and require thorough preparation. However, despite the challenges teams face, there are many reasons why negotiators use teams rather than acting alone. Practically speaking, the greatest strength of a team occurs before negotiations even begin. Teams composed of people with diverse backgrounds have the potential to dramatically improve the preparation process. Finally, be sure to capitalize on the diverse knowledge available, and use the team to role-play what the other side might do. In this way, the team will be thoroughly ready to take on any challenges they face at the negotiation table.

Most negotiation theory has been developed under the assumption that negotiation is a bilateral process—that there are only two focal negotiators opposing each other. Yet many negotiations are multilateral or group deliberations—more than two negotiators are involved, each with his or her own interests and positions, and the group must arrive at a collective agreement regarding a plan, decision, or course of action. One theme that runs through all forms of multiparty and team negotiation is the need to actively monitor and manage the negotiation process situations that are significantly more complex than two-party negotiations. We present here a brief set of questions that any participant in negotiations involving coalitions, multiple parties, or teams should keep in mind:

- What are the consequences of the parties failing to agree due to the increased complexities? What happens if there is no agreement?

- How will the parties involved actually make a decision? That is, what decision rules will be used? Why are these the best possible rules?

- How can the parties use iterations—multiple rounds of discussion—to achieve their objectives? (This may be particularly appropriate when the decision rule is consensus—or the best-quality agreement—because consensus may not be achievable in a single iteration.)

- Do we need a designated chair or facilitator? Should it be a neutral outsider, or can one of the parties fill this role? What tactics can a facilitator use to manage group process to ensure that the best decision is reached? (These tactics might include ensuring that the group is exposed to a variety of information sources, managing the process to make sure that the group considers and discusses all available information thoroughly, and structuring the group's agenda with care.)

If these issues are raised and thoughtfully considered, the parties involved are considerably more likely to feel better about the process and to arrive at an effective outcome than if these factors are left to chance.

CHAPTER 11

International and Cross-Cultural Negotiation

LEARNING OBJECTIVES

After reading this chapter you should have a deeper understanding of the following issues:

1. Factors that make international negotiation different, including both the environmental context and the immediate context,

2. How culture has been conceptualized, and the two approaches to culture used by academics and practitioners,

3. The influence of culture on negotiations, discussing this from managerial and research perspectives, and

4. Culturally responsive strategies available to the international negotiator.

Although there has been an interest in international negotiation for centuries,[1] the frequency of international negotiation has increased rapidly in the last 20 years. People today travel more frequently and farther, and business is more international in scope and extent than ever before. For many people and organizations, international negotiation has become the norm rather than an exotic activity that only occasionally occurs. Numerous books and articles, from both academic and practitioner perspectives, have been written about the complexities of negotiating across borders, be it with a person from a different country, culture, or region. Although the term *culture* has many possible definitions, we will use it to refer to the shared values and beliefs of a group of people. Countries can have more than one culture, and cultures can span national borders. As we discussed in earlier chapters, negotiating is a social process that is embedded in a much larger context. This context increases in complexity when more than one culture or country is involved, making international negotiation a highly complicated process.[2] For example, according to Foreign Affairs and International Trade Canada, since 1990, Canada has been, or currently is involved in, negotiations of economic partnership agreements with over 50 countries from around the world.[3]

It is important to recognize that this book has been written from a distinctly Western perspective—two authors are from American universities and two are from Canadian universities. This cultural filter has influenced how we think about negotiation, what we consider to be important aspects of negotiation, and our advice about how to become a better negotiator.[4] This chapter also reflects our own cultural filter, both in our choices about what we discuss and because we use Canadians and Americans as the base from which to make comparisons to other cultures.[5] That is not to say that all negotiators from the same country share the same culture.

In fact, there is evidence that people from countries as similar as the United States and Canada negotiate differently.[6] Within the United States and Canada, there are systematic regional and cultural differences (e.g., among English and French Canadians, and among Hispanics, African Americans, Southerners, New Yorkers, and other groups in many areas of the United States). See Negotiation Point 11.1 for a discussion of the differences between two different Canadian groups and their negotiation tendencies. At some level, however, Canadians do share (more or less) a common culture that is different from that of other countries. While recognizing the differences within Canada and the United States, we will use some common aspects of culture in our discussion of international and cross-cultural negotiation.

■ What Makes International Negotiation Different?

Phatak and Habib suggest that two overall contexts have an influence on international negotiations: the environmental context and the immediate context (see Figure 11.1).[7] The environmental context includes environmental forces that neither negotiator controls and which influence the negotiation. The *immediate context* includes factors over which negotiators appear to have some control. Understanding the role of factors in both the environmental and the immediate contexts is important to grasping the complexity of international negotiation processes and outcomes.

Environmental Context

Salacuse identified six factors in the environmental context that make international negotiations more challenging than domestic negotiations: political and legal pluralism, international economics, foreign governments and bureaucracies, instability,

Negotiation Point

11.1

Canadian Culture and Negotiations

Do cultural differences exist amongst negotiators within different regions of Canada? In a study published in the *Canadian Journal of Administrative Sciences*, Professor Nancy Adler of McGill University and Professor John Graham of the University of California, Irvine, compared the negotiating styles of French and English Canadian negotiators. The researchers found that Francophones were more likely than Anglophones to adopt more competitive approaches to negotiations through use communication strategies intended to influence the other party. Furthermore, Francophone negotiators tended to put greater value on honesty and on being imaginative than Anglophone negotiators. Also, Anglophone negotiators tended to put greater value on being helpful and forgiving than Francophone negotiators. The findings of this study suggest that negotiators cannot simply prepare for international negotiations on the basis of their counterpart's country of origin but must also consider their counterpart's cultural orientation.

Source: Adler, Nancy, J., & Graham, John L. (1987) Business negotiations: Canadians are not just like Americans. Canadian Journal of Administrative Sciences, 4, 3, 211–238.

FIGURE 11.1 | The Contexts of International Negotiations

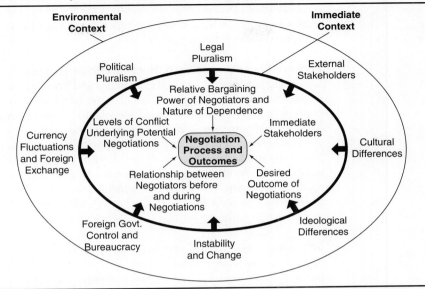

Source: Adapted from A. V. Phatak and M. H. Habib, "The Dynamics of International Business Negotiations," Business Horizons 39 (1996), pp. 30–38; and from J. W. Salacuse, "Making Deals in Strange Places: A Beginner's Guide to International Business Negotiations," Negotiation Journal 4 (1988), pp. 5–13.

ideology, and culture.[8] (Culture has received by far the most attention by those examining international negotiation, and it is discussed in a separate section later in this chapter.) Phatak and Habib have suggested an additional factor: external stakeholders.[9] These factors can act to limit or constrain organizations that operate internationally, and it is important that negotiators understand and appreciate their effects.

Political and Legal Pluralism Firms conducting business in different countries are working with different legal and political systems. There may be implications for taxes that an organization pays, labour codes or standards that must be met, and different codes of contract law and standards of enforcement (e.g., case law versus common law versus no functioning legal system). In addition, political considerations may enhance or detract from business negotiations in various countries at different times. For instance, the open business environment in the former Soviet republics in the 1990s is quite different than the closed environment of the 1960s, and conducting business in China today is quite different than even 10 years ago.

International Economics The exchange value of international currencies naturally fluctuates, and this factor must be considered when negotiating in different countries. In which currency will the agreement be made? The risk is typically greater for the party who must pay in the other country's currency.[10] The less stable the currency, the greater the risk for both parties. In addition, any change in the value of a currency (upward or downward) can significantly affect the value of the agreement for both parties, changing a mutually valuable deal into a windfall profit for one and a large loss for the other. Many countries also control the currency flowing across their borders. Frequently, purchases within these countries may be made only with hard currencies that are brought into the country by foreign parties, and domestic organizations are unable to purchase foreign products or negotiate outcomes that require payment in foreign currencies.

Foreign Governments and Bureaucracies Countries differ in the extent to which the government regulates industries and organizations. Generally, business negotiations in Canada and the United States occur without government approval, and the parties to a negotiation decide whether or not to engage in an agreement based on business reasons alone. In contrast, the governments of many developing and (former) communist countries closely supervise imports and joint ventures,[11] and frequently an agency of the government has a monopoly in dealing with foreign organizations.[12] In addition, political considerations, such as the effect of the negotiation on the government treasury and the general economy of the country, may influence the negotiations more heavily than what Western businesses would consider legitimate business reasons.

Instability Businesses negotiators within North America are accustomed to a degree of stability that is not present in many areas of the world. Instability may take many forms, including a lack of resources that North Americans commonly expect during business negotiations (paper, electricity, computers); shortages of other goods and services (food, reliable transportation, potable water); and political instability (coups, sudden shifts in government policy, major currency revaluations). The challenge for international negotiators is to anticipate changes accurately and with enough lead time to adjust for their consequences. Salacuse suggests that negotiators facing unstable circumstances should include clauses in their contracts that allow easy cancellation or neutral arbitration, and consider purchasing insurance policies to guarantee contract provisions.[13] This advice presumes that contracts will be honoured and that specific contract clauses will be culturally acceptable to the other party.

Ideology Canadians, and to a larger extent, Americans, tend to believe in individual rights, the superiority of private investment, and the importance of making a profit in business.[14] Negotiators from other countries do not always share this ideology. For example, negotiators from some countries (e.g., China, France) may instead stress group rights as more important than individual rights and public investment as a better allocation of resources than private investment; they may also have different prescriptions for earning and sharing profit. Ideological clashes increase the communication challenges in international negotiations in the broadest sense because the parties may disagree at the most fundamental levels about what is being negotiated.

Culture People from different cultures appear to negotiate differently.[15] In addition to behaving differently, people from different cultures may also interpret the fundamental processes of negotiations differently (such as what factors are negotiable and the purpose of the negotiations). According to Salacuse, people in some cultures approach negotiations deductively (they move from the general to the specific) whereas people from other cultures are more inductive (they settle on a series of specific issues that become the area of general agreement).[16] In some cultures, the parties negotiate the substantive issues while considering the relationship between the parties to be more or less incidental. In other cultures, the relationship between the parties is the main focus of the negotiation, and the substantive issues of the deal itself are more or less incidental. There is also evidence that preference for conflict resolution models varies across cultures.[17] See Negotiation Point 11.2 for more detail on this issue.

External Stakeholders Phatak and Habib defined external stakeholders as "the various people and organizations that have an interest or stake in the outcome of the negotiations."[18] These stakeholders include business associations, labour unions, embassies, and industry associations, among others.[19] For example, a labour union might oppose negotiations with foreign companies because of fears that domestic jobs will be lost. International negotiators can receive a great deal of promotion and guidance from their government via the trade section of their embassy, and from other business people via professional associations (e.g., a Chamber of Commerce in the country in which they are negotiating).

Immediate Context

At many points throughout this book we have discussed aspects of negotiation that relate to immediate context factors, but without considering their international implications. In this section, we will discuss the concepts from the Phatak and Habib model of international negotiation, highlighting that this context can have an important influence on negotiation.[20]

Relative Bargaining Power One aspect of international negotiations that has received considerable research attention is the relative bargaining power of the two parties involved. Joint ventures have been the subject of a great deal of research on international negotiation, and relative power has frequently been operationalized as the amount of equity (financial and other investment) that each side is willing to

---

Negotiation Point

11.2

Culture, Trust, and Tactics

Do negotiators really behave differently in cross-cultural negotiations? Researchers Mohammed Elahee, Susan Kirby, and Ercan Nasif investigated whether negotiators behaved differently in negotiations with someone from their own culture (i.e., intra-cultural negotiations) than in negotiations with someone from another culture (i.e., cross-cultural negotiations). In their sample of 248 Canadian, American, and Mexican business people they found that Mexican negotiators were more likely to engage in tactics such as bluffing, misrepresentation, and inappropriate information collection in cross-cultural negotiation than in intra-cultural negotiations. By contrast, Canadian and American negotiators did not behave differently in either intra-cultural or cross-cultural negotiation contexts. These findings underscore the importance of preparation when engaging in cross-cultural negotiations.

Source: M. Elahee, S. L. Kirby, & E. Nasif, "National culture, trust, and perceptions about ethical behavior in intra- and cross-cultural negotiations: An analysis of NAFTA countries," Thunderbird International Business Review, 44, 6, (2002), pp. 799–818.

invest in the new venture. The presumption is that the party who invests more equity has more power in the negotiation and therefore will have more influence on the negotiation process and outcome. Research by Yan and Gray questions this perspective, however, and suggests that relative power is not simply a function of equity, but appears to be due to management control of the project, which was found to be heavily influenced by negotiating.[21] In addition, several factors seem to be able to influence relative power, including special access to markets (e.g., in current or former communist countries); distribution systems (e.g., in Asia, where creating a new distribution system is so expensive that it may be a barrier to entering markets); or managing government relations (e.g., where the language and culture are quite different).

Levels of Conflict The level of conflict and type of interdependence between the parties to a cross-cultural negotiation will also influence the negotiation process and outcome. High-conflict situations—those based on ethnicity, identity, or geography—are more difficult to resolve.[22] There is historical evidence, however, that civil wars concluded through a comprehensive, institutionalized agreement that prohibits the use of coercive power and promotes the fair distributions of resources and political power lead to more stable settlements.[23] Also important is the extent to which negotiators frame the negotiation differently or conceptualize what the negotiation concerns, and this appears to vary across cultures, as do the ways in which negotiators respond to conflict.[24] For example, Fisher, Ury, and Patton discuss how conflicts in the Middle East were difficult to deal with for several years because the different parties had such different ways of conceptualizing what the dispute was about (e.g., security, sovereignty, historical rights).[25]

Relationship between Negotiators Phatak and Habib suggest that the relationships developed among the principal negotiating parties before the actual negotiations will also have an important impact on the negotiation process and outcome.[26] Negotiations are part of the larger relationship between two parties. The history of relations between the parties will influence the current negotiation (e.g., how the parties frame the negotiation), just as the current negotiation will become part of any future negotiations between the parties.

Desired Outcomes Tangible and intangible factors also play a large role in determining the outcomes of international negotiations. Countries often use international negotiations to achieve both domestic and international political goals. For instance, in recent ethnic conflicts around the world, numerous parties have threatened that unless they are recognized at the formal negotiations they will disrupt the successful resolution of the conflict (e.g., Northern Ireland). Ongoing tension can exist between one party's short-term objectives for the current negotiations and its influence on the parties' long-term relations. In trade negotiations between the United States and Japan, both sides often settle for less than their desired short-term outcomes because of the importance of the long-term relationship.[27]

Immediate Stakeholders The immediate stakeholders in the negotiation include the negotiators themselves as well as the people they directly represent, such as their managers, employers, and boards of directors.[28] Stakeholders can influence negotiators in many ways. The skills, abilities, and international experience of the negotiators themselves clearly can have a large impact on the process and outcome of international negotiations. In addition, the personal motivations of the principal negotiators and the other immediate stakeholders can have a large influence on the negotiation process and outcomes. People may be motivated by several intangible factors in the negotiation, including how the process or outcome will make them look in the eyes of both the other party and their own superiors, as well as other intangible factors like their personal career advancement.[29]

In summary, models such as Phatak and Habib's are very good devices for guiding our thinking about international negotiation.[30] It is always important to remember, however, that negotiation processes and outcomes are influenced by many factors, and that the influence of these factors can change in magnitude over time.[31] The challenge for every international negotiator is to understand the simultaneous, multiple influences of several factors on the negotiation process and outcome and to update this understanding regularly as circumstances change. This also means that planning for international negotiations is especially important, as is the need to adjust as new information is obtained through monitoring the environmental and immediate contexts.

■ Conceptualizing Culture and Negotiation

The most frequently studied aspect of international negotiation is culture, and the amount of research on the effects of culture on negotiation has increased substantially in the last 20 years.[32] There are many different meanings of the concept of culture, but all definitions share two important aspects.[33] First, culture is a group-level phenomenon. That means that a defined group of people share beliefs, values, and behavioural expectations. The second common element of culture is that these beliefs, values, and behavioural expectations are learned and passed on to new members of the group.

It is also important to remember that negotiation outcomes, both domestically and internationally, are determined by several different factors. While cultural differences are clearly important, negotiators must guard against assigning too much responsibility to cultural factors.[34] Dialdin, Kopelman, Adair, Brett, Okumura, and Lytle have labelled the tendency to overlook the importance of situational factors in favour of cultural explanations the *cultural attribution error*.[35] It is important to recognize that even though culture describes group-level characteristics, it doesn't mean that every member of a culture will share those characteristics equally.[36] In fact, there is likely to be as wide of a variety of behavioural differences *within* cultures as there is between cultures.[37] Although knowledge of the other party's culture may provide an initial clue about what to expect at the bargaining table, negotiators need to be open to adjusting their view very quickly as new information is gathered.[38]

The next section of the chapter examines two important ways that culture has been conceptualized: (1) culture as shared values and (2) culture as dialectic.[39]

Culture as Shared Values

One important approach to conceptualizing culture concentrates on understanding central values and norms and then building a model for how these norms and values influence negotiations within that culture.[40] Cross-cultural comparisons are made by finding the important norms and values that distinguish one culture from another and then understanding how these differences will influence international negotiation.

Geert Hofstede conducted an extensive program of research on cultural dimensions in international business.[41] Hofstede examined data on values that had been gathered from over 100,000 IBM employees from around the world, and over 50 cultures were included in the initial study. Statistical analysis of this data suggests that four dimensions could be used to describe the important differences among the cultures in the study: individualism/collectivism, power distance, career success-quality of life, and uncertainty avoidance.[42] Cultures ranking in the top 10 on each of these dimensions are listed in Table 11.1, and each dimension is discussed below.

TABLE 11.1 | Cultures Ranking in the Top 10 on the Cultural Dimensions Reported by Hofstede (1991)

Individualism	Power Distance	Career Success/ Quality of Life	Uncertainty Avoidance
1. United States	1. Malaysia	1. Sweden	1. Greece
2. Australia	2. Guatemala	2. Norway	2. Portugal
3. Great Britain	Panama	3. Netherlands	3. Guatemala
4. Canada	4. Philippines	4. Denmark	4. Uruguay
Netherlands	5. Mexico	5. Costa Rica	5. Belgium
6. New Zealand	Venezuela	Yugoslavia	Salvador
7. Italy	7. Arab countries	7. Finland	7. Japan
8. Belgium	8. Ecuador	8. Chile	8. Yugoslavia
9. Denmark	Indonesia	9. Portugal	9. Peru
10. France	10. India	10. Thailand	10. Argentina
Sweden	West Africa		Chile
			Costa Rica
			Panama
			Spain

Source: Based on G. Hofstede, Culture and Organizations: Software of the Mind (London, England: McGraw-Hill, 1991). Reproduced with permission of the McGraw-Hill Companies.

1. Individualism/Collectivism The individualism/collectivism dimension describes the extent to which a society is organized around individuals or the group. Individualistic societies encourage their young to be independent and to look after themselves. Collectivistic societies integrate individuals into cohesive groups that take responsibility for the welfare of each individual. Hofstede suggests that the focus on relationships in collectivist societies plays a critical role in negotiations—negotiations with the same party can continue for years, and changing a negotiator changes the relationship, which may take a long time to rebuild. Contrast this with individualistic societies, in which negotiators are considered interchangeable, and competency (rather than relationship) is an important consideration when choosing a negotiator. The implication is that negotiators from collectivist cultures will strongly depend on cultivating and sustaining a long-term relationship, whereas negotiators from individualistic cultures may be more likely to swap negotiators, using whatever short-term criteria seem appropriate.

2. Power Distance The power distance dimension describes "the extent to which the less powerful members of organizations and institutions (like the family) accept and expect that power is distributed unequally."[43] According to Hofstede, cultures with greater power distance will be more likely to concentrate decision making at the top, and all important decisions will have to be finalized by the leader. Cultures with low power distance are more likely to spread the decision making throughout the organization, and while leaders are respected, it is also possible to question their decisions. The consequences for international negotiations are that negotiators from comparatively high power distance cultures may need to seek approval from their supervisors more frequently, and for more issues, leading to a slower negotiation process.

3. Career Success/Quality of Life Hofstede found that cultures differed in the extent to which they held values that promoted career success or quality of life. Cultures promoting career success were characterized by "the acquisition of money and things, and not caring for others, the quality of life, or people."[44] Cultures promoting quality of life were characterized by concern for relationships and nurturing. According to Hofstede, this dimension influences negotiation by increasing the competitiveness when negotiators from career success cultures meet; negotiators from quality of life cultures are more likely to have empathy for the other party and to seek compromise.[45]

4. Uncertainty Avoidance Uncertainty avoidance "indicates to what extent a culture programs its members to feel either uncomfortable or comfortable in unstructured situations."[46] Unstructured situations are characterized by rapid change and novelty, whereas structured situations are stable and secure. Negotiators from high uncertainty avoidance cultures are less comfortable with ambiguous situations and are more likely to seek stable rules and procedures when they negotiate. Negotiators from low uncertainty avoidance cultures are likely to adapt to quickly changing situations and will be less uncomfortable when the rules of the negotiation are ambiguous or shifting.

Hofstede's work examines one model of understanding culture as shared values. The work of Shalom Schwartz and his colleagues provides another comprehensive example of the culture-as-values perspective (see Figure 11.2).[47] Schwartz concentrated on identifying the motivational goal underlying cultural values and found 10 fundamental values (see the values within the circle in Figure 11.2). These 10 values may conflict or be compatible with each other, and the values on the opposite side of the circle from a given value are most likely to be in conflict. Schwartz also proposed that the 10 values may be represented in two bipolar dimensions: openness to change/conservatism and self-transcendence/self-enhancement (see the outer wheel in Figure 11.2). Schwartz's cultural values and the two bipolar dimensions provide the most comprehensive exploration of cultural values to date, and they have been validated with extensive research. While this work has been slow to appear in the study of cross-cultural negotiation, references to it have recently started to appear.[48]

The culture-as-shared-value perspective provides explanations for why cross-cultural negotiations are difficult and have a tendency to break down. For example, a central value in the United States is individualism. Americans are expected to make individual decisions, defend their points of view, and take strong stands

FIGURE 11.2 | Schwartz's 10 Cultural Values

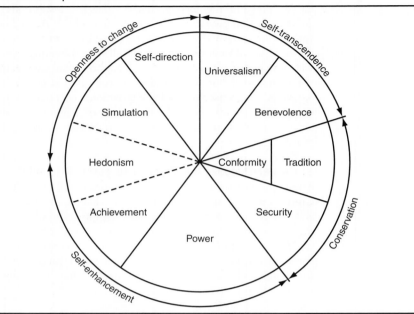

on issues that are important to them. On average, Canadians tend towards individualism, especially in comparison to countries such as China. A central value of the Chinese is collectivism. Chinese negotiators are expected to make group decisions, defend the group above the individual, and take strong stands on issues important to the group. When Western and Chinese negotiators meet, differences in the individualism/collectivism cultural value may influence negotiation in many ways. For instance, (1) the Chinese will likely take more time when negotiating because they have to gain the consensus of their group before they strike a deal; (2) Chinese use of multiple lines of authority will lead to mixed signals about the true needs of the group, and no single individual may understand all the requirements; and (3) because power is shared by many different people and offices, it may be difficult for foreigners to identify their appropriate counterpart in the Chinese bureaucracy.[49]

Culture as Dialectic

Another important approach to using culture to understand international negotiation recognizes that all cultures contain dimensions or tensions that are called *dialectics*. These tensions are nicely illustrated in parables from the Judeo-Christian tradition. Consider the following examples: "too many cooks spoil the broth" and "two heads are better than one." These adages offer conflicting guidance for those considering whether to work on a task alone or in a group. This reflects a dialectic, or tension, within the Judeo-Christian tradition regarding the values of independence and teamwork. Neither complete independence nor complete teamwork works all the time; each has advantages and disadvantages that vary as a function of the circumstances (e.g., the type of decision to be made or task to be addressed).

According to Janosik, the culture-as-dialectic approach has advantages over the culture-as-shared-values approach because it can explain variations within cultures (i.e., not every person in the same culture shares the same values to the same extent).[50] The culture-as-dialectic approach does not provide international negotiators with simple advice about how to behave in a given negotiation. Rather, it suggests that negotiators who want to have successful international negotiations need to appreciate the richness of the cultures in which they will be operating.

Recent theoretical work by Gelfand and McCusker provides a similar way to examine the effects of culture on negotiation, but through examining *cultural metaphors* rather than dialectics.[51] Gelfand and McCusker suggest that *negotiation metaphors* provide a very useful method for understanding cross-cultural negotiations. They define metaphors as "coherent, holistic meaning systems, which have been developed and cultivated in particular socio-cultural environments, [and] *function* to interpret, structure, and organize social action in negotiation."[52] Cultural negotiation metaphors help people understand things that happen in negotiation and "make sense" of them. Gelfand and McCusker suggest that *negotiation as sport* is the dominant metaphor for understanding negotiation in the United States, where negotiators concentrate on their own performance and winning, and negotiations are episodic. Contrast this with the dominant negotiation metaphor in Japan, *negotiation as ie* (traditional household). The fundamental challenge of *ie* is continuity and succession; negotiators concentrate on relationships and survival of the group, and negotiations are a continuous part of a larger whole. The greater the difference in cultural negotiation metaphors, the more likely it will be that negotiators will not understand each other and the challenge of having a positive negotiation outcome increases.

The Influence of Culture on Negotiation: Managerial Perspectives

Cultural differences have been suggested to influence negotiation in several different ways. Table 11.2 summarizes 10 different ways that culture can influence negotiations.[53] Each is discussed in turn below.

TABLE 11.2 | Ten Ways That Culture Can Influence Negotiation

Negotiation Factors	Range of Cultural Responses	
Definition of negotiation	contract	relationship
Negotiation opportunity	distributive	integrative
Selection of negotiators	experts	trusted associates
Protocol	informal	formal
Communication	direct	indirect
Time sensitivity	high	low
Risk propensity	high	low
Groups versus individuals	collectivism	individualism
Nature of agreements	specific	general
Emotionalism	high	low

Based on Foster (1992), Hendon and Hendon (1990), Moran and Stripp (1991), and Salacuse (1998).

Definition of Negotiation

The fundamental definition of negotiation, what is negotiable, and what occurs when we negotiate can differ greatly across cultures.[54] For instance, "Americans tend to view negotiating as a competitive process of offers and counteroffers, while the Japanese tend to view the negotiation as an opportunity for information-sharing."[55]

Negotiation Opportunity

Culture influences the way negotiators perceive an opportunity as distributive versus integrative. Negotiators in Western societies are predisposed to perceive negotiation as being fundamentally distributive.[56] This is not the case in many other regions, however, as there appears to be a great deal of variation across cultures in the extent to which negotiation situations are initially perceived as distributive or integrative.[57] Cross-cultural negotiations will be influenced by the extent that negotiators in different cultures have fundamental agreement or disagreement about whether or not the situation is distributive or integrative.

Selection of Negotiators

The criteria used to select who will participate in a negotiation is different across cultures. These criteria can include knowledge of the subject matter being negotiated, seniority, family connections, gender, age, experience, and status. Different cultures weigh these criteria differently, leading to varying expectations about what is appropriate in different types of negotiations.

Protocol

Cultures differ in the degree to which protocol, or the formality of the relations between the two negotiating parties, is important. Canadian and American culture are among the least formal cultures in the world. A familiar communication style is quite common; first names are used, for example, while titles are ignored. Contrast this with other cultures. Many European countries (e.g., France, Germany, England) are very formal, and not using the proper title when addressing someone (e.g., Mr., Dr., Professor, Lord) is considered insulting.[58] The formal calling cards or business cards used in many countries in the Pacific Rim (e.g., China, Japan) are essential for introductions there. Negotiators who forget to bring business cards or who write messages on them are frequently breaching protocol and insulting their counterpart.[59] Even the way that business cards are presented, hands are shaken, and dress codes are observed are subject to interpretation by negotiators and can be the foundation of attributions about a person's background and personality.

Communication

Cultures influence how people communicate, both verbally and nonverbally. There are also differences in body language across cultures; a behaviour that may be highly insulting in one culture may be completely innocuous in another.[60] To avoid offending the other party in negotiations, the international negotiator needs to observe cultural rules of communication carefully. For example, placing feet on a desk in Canada signals power or relaxation; in Thailand, it is considered very insulting (see Negotiation Point 11.3 for more examples). Clearly, there is a lot

11.3

Example of Communication Rules for International Negotiators

Never touch a Malay on the top of the head, for that is where the soul resides. Never show the sole of your shoe to an Arab, for it is dirty and represents the bottom of the body, and never use your left hand in Muslim culture, for it is reserved for physical hygiene. Touch the side of your nose in Italy and it is a sign of distrust. Always look directly and intently into your French associate's eye when making an important point. Direct eye contact in Southeast Asia, however, should be avoided until the relationship is firmly established. If your Japanese associate has just sucked air in deeply through his teeth, that's a sign you've got real problems.

Your Mexican associate will want to embrace you at the end of a long and successful negotiation; so will your Central and Eastern European associates, who may give you a bear hug and kiss you three times on alternating cheeks. Americans often stand farther apart than their Latin and Arab associates but closer than their Asian associates. In the United States people shake hands forcefully and enduringly; in Europe a handshake is usually quick and to the point; in Asia, it is often rather limp. Laughter and giggling in the West Indies indicates humour; in Asia, it more often indicates embarrassment and humility. Additionally, the public expression of deep emotion is considered ill-mannered in most countries of the Pacific Rim; there is an extreme separation between one's personal and public selves. Withholding emotion in Latin America, however, is often cause for mistrust.

Source: D. A. Foster, Bargaining across Borders: How to Negotiate Business Successfully Anywhere in the World (New York: McGraw-Hill, 1992), p. 281. Reproduced with the permission of The McGraw-Hill Companies.

of information about how to communicate that an international negotiator must remember to not insult, anger, or embarrass the other party during negotiations. Culture-specific books and articles can provide considerable advice to international negotiators about how to communicate in various cultures; seeking such advice is an essential aspect of planning for international negotiations.[61]

Time Sensitivity

Cultures largely determine what time means and how it affects negotiations.[62] In Canada, people tend to respect time by appearing for meetings at an appointed hour, being sensitive to not wasting the time of other people, and generally holding that "faster" is better than "slower" because it symbolizes high productivity. Other cultures have quite different views about time. In more traditional societies, especially in hot climates, the pace is slower than it is here. This tends to reduce the focus on time, at least in the short term. Canadians are perceived by other cultures as enslaved by their clocks because they watch time carefully and guard it as a valuable resource. In some cultures, such as China and Latin America, time per se is not important. The focus of negotiations is on the task, regardless of the amount of time it takes. The opportunity for misunderstandings because of different perceptions of time is great during cross-cultural negotiations. Canadians may be perceived as always being in a hurry and as flitting from one task to another, while Chinese or Latin American negotiators may appear to be doing nothing and wasting time.

Risk Propensity

Cultures vary in the extent to which they are willing to take risks. Some cultures tend to produce bureaucratic, conservative decision makers who want a great deal of information before making decisions. Other cultures produce negotiators who are more entrepreneurial and who are willing to act and take risks when they have incomplete information (e.g., "nothing ventured, nothing gained"). According to Foster, North Americans (especially those in the United States) fall on the risk-taking end of the continuum, as do some Asian cultures, while some European cultures are quite conservative (e.g., Greece).[63] The orientation of a culture toward risk will have a large effect on what is negotiated and the content of the negotiated outcome. Negotiators in risk-oriented cultures will be more willing to move early on a deal and will generally take more chances. Those in risk-avoiding cultures are more likely to seek further information and take a wait-and-see stance.

Groups versus Individuals

Cultures differ according to whether they emphasize the individual or the group. The United States is very much an individual-oriented culture, where being independent and assertive is valued and praised. Group-oriented cultures, in contrast, favour the superiority of the group and see individual needs as second to the group's needs. Group-oriented cultures value fitting in and reward loyal team players; those who dare to be different are socially ostracized—a large price to pay in a group-oriented society. This cultural difference can have a variety of effects on negotiation. Americans and Canadians are more likely to have one individual who is responsible for the final decision, whereas group-oriented cultures like the Japanese are more likely to have a group responsible for the decision. Decision making in group-oriented cultures involves consensus and may take considerably more time than Western negotiators are used to. In addition, because so many people can be involved in the negotiations in group-oriented cultures, and because their participation may be sequential rather than simultaneous, Western negotiators may be faced with a series of discussions over the same issues and materials with many different people. In a negotiation in China, one of the authors of this book met with more than six different people on successive days, going over the same ground with different negotiators and interpreters, until the negotiation was concluded.

Nature of Agreements

Culture also has an important effect both on concluding agreements and on what form the negotiated agreement takes. In Canada, agreements are typically based on logic (e.g., the low-cost producer gets the deal), are often formalized, and are enforced through the legal system if such standards are not honoured. In other cultures, however, obtaining the deal may be based on who you are (e.g., your family or political connections) rather than on what you can do. In addition, agreements do not mean the same thing in all cultures. Foster notes that the Chinese frequently use memorandums of agreement to formalize a relationship and to signal the start of negotiations (mutual favours and compromise).[64] Frequently, however, Canadians will interpret the same memorandum of agreement as the completion of the negotiations that is enforceable in a court of law. Again, cultural differences in how to close an agreement and what exactly that agreement means can lead to confusion and misunderstandings.

Emotionalism

Culture appears to influence the extent to which negotiators display emotions.[65] These emotions may be used as tactics, or they may be a natural response to positive and negative circumstances during the negotiation.[66] While personality likely also plays a role in the expression of emotions, there also appears to be considerable cross-cultural differences, and the rules that govern general emotional displays in a culture are likely to be present during negotiation.[67]

In summary, a great deal of practical advice has been written about the importance of culture in international negotiations. Although the word *culture* has been used to mean several different things, it is clearly a critical aspect of international negotiation that can have a broad influence on many aspects of the process and outcome of international negotiation. We now turn to examining research perspectives on how culture influences negotiation.

The Influence of Culture on Negotiation: Research Perspectives

A conceptual model of where culture may influence negotiation has been developed by Jeanne Brett (see Figure 11.3).[68] Brett's model identifies how the culture of both negotiators can influence the setting of priorities and strategies, the

FIGURE 11.3 | How Culture Affects Negotiation

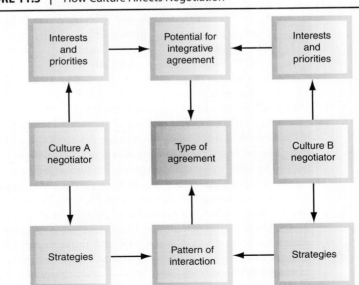

Source: J. M. Brett, Negotiating Globally (San Francisco: Jossey-Bass, 2001).

identification of the potential for integrative agreement, and the pattern of interaction between negotiators. Brett suggests that cultural values should have a strong effect on negotiation interests and priorities, while cultural norms will influence negotiation strategies and the pattern of interaction. Negotiation strategies and the pattern of interaction between negotiators will also be influenced by the psychological processes of negotiators, and culture has an influence on these processes.

Negotiation Outcomes

Researchers initially explored the fundamental question of how culture influences negotiation outcomes. Two approaches were taken to explore this question. In the first approach, researchers compared the outcomes of the same simulated negotiation with negotiators from several different cultures who only negotiated with other negotiators from their own culture. The goal of these *intracultural* studies was to see if negotiators from different cultures reached the same negotiation outcomes when presented with the same materials. The other approach to explore how culture influenced negotiation outcomes was to compare intracultural and *cross-cultural* negotiation outcomes to see if they were the same.Researchers investigated this by comparing negotiation outcomes when negotiators negotiated with people from the same culture with outcomes when they negotiated with people from other cultures. For example, did Japanese negotiators reach the same negotiation outcomes when negotiating with other Japanese negotiators as they did with American negotiators?

A series of research studies comparing intracultural negotiations in several different cultures was conducted by John Graham and his colleagues, using a very simple buyer/seller negotiation simulation in which negotiators have to decide on the prices of three products (televisions, typewriters, and air conditioners).[69] Graham and his colleagues found no differences in the profit levels obtained by negotiators in different cultures.[70]

More recent research by Jeanne Brett and her colleagues has used a richer negotiation simulation and also identified differences in negotiation outcomes in the simulation by negotiators in different cultures. For instance, Brett, Adair, Lempereur, Okumura, Shihkirev, Tinsley, and Lytle compared intracultural negotiators in six different cultures (France, Russia, Japan, Hong Kong, Brazil, United States) and found differences in joint gains achieved.[71] In addition, Dialdin, Kopelman, Adair, Brett, Okumura, and Lytle reported differences in individual gains for negotiators from five different cultures (United States, Hong Kong, Germany, Israel, Japan).[72] The Brett et al. and Dialdin et al. studies suggest that culture does have an effect on negotiation outcomes, but there were complex patterns across cultures.

The other approach to exploring cultural effects on negotiation outcomes compared the negotiation outcomes of intracultural and cross-cultural negotiations. Adler and Graham found that Japanese and English–Canadian negotiators received lower profit levels when they negotiated cross-culturally than when they negotiated intraculturally; American and French–Canadian negotiators negotiated the same average outcomes in cross-cultural and intracultural negotiations.[73] These results support Adler and Graham's hypothesis that cross-cultural negotiations will result in poorer outcomes compared to intracultural negotiations, at least some of the time.

In summary, research suggests that culture does have an effect on negotiation outcomes, although it may not be direct, and it likely has an influence through differences in the negotiation process in different cultures. In addition, there is some evidence that cross-cultural negotiations yield poorer outcomes than intracultural negotiations. Considerable research has been conducted recently to understand why, and this has been done by examining the intracultural negotiation process.

Negotiation Process

Graham and his colleagues found significant differences in the negotiation strategies and tactics in the cultures they studied.[74] Cai demonstrated how individualism/collectivism influenced negotiation planning: Negotiators from a more collectivist culture (Taiwan) spent more time planning for long-term goals, while negotiators from a more individualistic culture (the United States) spent more time planning for short-term goals.[75] Gelfand and Christakopoulou found that negotiators from a more individualistic culture (the United States) made more extreme offers during the negotiation than did negotiators from a more collectivist culture (Greece).[76]

Adair, Brett, Lempereur, Okumura, Shikhiriv, Tinsley, and Lytle found considerable difference in direct information sharing, with negotiators from the United States most likely to share information directly.[77] In addition, they found that while U.S. and Japanese negotiators both maximized their joint gains, they took different paths to do so. U.S. negotiators used *direct information exchange* about preferences and priorities and referred to similarities and differences between the parties to achieve joint gains. Japanese negotiators used *indirect information exchange* and inferred the preferences of the other negotiator by comparing several different offers and counteroffers, and they justified their trade-offs with persuasive arguments.

Adair, Kopelman, Gillespie, Brett, and Okumura examined the effect of information sharing on joint gains in negotiation in a cross-cultural context and found that negotiators from culturally similar countries (United States, Israel) were more likely to share information during negotiation than negotiators from less culturally similar countries (United States, Japan), and those differences in information led to higher joint gains for negotiators from the culturally similar countries.[78]

Adair, Okumura, and Brett examined negotiation outcomes and information sharing in both intracultural (within the United States and within Japan) and cross-cultural (United States–Japan) negotiations.[79] They found that both U.S. and Japanese intracultural negotiators reached higher joint gains than cross-cultural negotiators. The way that intracultural negotiators achieved these gains was different for the U.S. and Japanese negotiators, however. Intracultural U.S. negotiators were more likely to share information directly and less likely to share information indirectly than were intracultural Japanese negotiators. In cross-cultural negotiations, Japanese negotiators adapted to U.S. normative behaviours and Japanese cross-cultural negotiators were more likely to share information than Japanese intracultural negotiators. This increased direct information sharing by Japanese negotiators did not translate into higher joint gains in cross-cultural negotiations, however.

Wendi Adair, a professor at the University of Waterloo, has extended the research on the importance of culture on information sharing in negotiation by comparing integrative behaviour sequences in intracultural negotiations from several high- and low-context cultures and in cross-cultural negotiations from two mixed-context cultures.[80] Adair found that culture led to different communication patterns in intracultural negotiations, with negotiators from low-context cultures tending to use direct communication while negotiators from high-context cultures used more indirect communication.[81] In cross-cultural negotiations, direct integrative sequences of information exchange led to higher joint outcomes, which suggests that *both* negotiators need to exchange information integratively for cross-cultural negotiations to reach a successful conclusion.

Rosette, Brett, Barsness, and Lytle examined how culture influenced intra-cultural and cross-cultural e-mail negotiations with negotiators from high-context (Hong Kong) and low-context (U.S.) cultures.[82] They found that Hong Kong negotiators achieved higher joint gains in e-mail negotiations than in face-to-face negotiations, while there was no difference in the joint gains achieved for U.S. negotiators. The higher joint gains appear to be the result of the use of higher opening offers and more multiple-issue offers by Hong Kong negotiators when conducting e-mail negotiations. In the cross-cultural e-mail negotiation, Hong Kong negotiators achieved higher individual outcomes than U.S. negotiators, apparently as a function of more aggressive opening offers. There were no differences in the number of multiple-issue offers between Hong Kong and U.S. negotiators in the cross-cultural negotiation, likely due to negotiators reciprocating offers during the negotiation. The Rosette et al. study suggests that culture has an effect on the process of e-mail negotiations, which in turn appears to influence negotiation outcomes.

In summary, culture has been found to have significant effects on several aspects of the negotiation process, including how negotiators plan, the offers made during negotiation, the communication process, and how information is shared during negotiation.

Effects of Culture on Negotiator Cognition

Researchers have recently turned their attention to discovering how culture influences the psychological processes of negotiators,[83] and researchers are working to understand how culture influences the way that negotiators process information during negotiation and how this in turn influences negotiation processes and outcomes.

Gelfand and Realo found that accountability to a constituent influenced negotiators from individualistic and collectivistic cultures differently.[84] They found that accountability led to more competition among individualists but to higher levels of co-operation among collectivists. In addition, there were differences in negotiator cognitions: Individualists had more competitive behavioural intentions and thoughts before negotiating, acted less co-operatively during negotiations, and perceived the other party more negatively after the negotiation.

Gelfand, Nishii, Holcombe, Dyer, Ohbuchi, and Fukuno explored how people from a collectivist culture (Japan) and an individualist culture (the United States) perceived the same conflict.[85] They found that the Japanese were more likely to perceive the conflicts as involving compromise than were the Americans. Gelfand and associates also found that Japanese and Americans used different frames to make sense of some conflicts. For instance, the Japanese framed some conflicts as *giri violations* (breaches in social positions), while the Americans never used that frame. The Gelfand et al. study suggests that there are some universal ways of framing conflict (e.g., compromise-win) but there are also significant culturally specific ways (e.g., *giri* violations).

Another way to explore the influence of culture on negotiator cognition is to examine the extent to which well-known cognitive effects identified in Western cultures occur in other cultures. Gelfand and Christakopoulou found that negotiators from an individualistic culture (the United States) were more susceptible to fixed-pie errors (see Chapter 5) than were negotiators from a more collectivist culture (Greece).[86] In a series of creative studies examining the self-serving bias of fairness in other cultures, Gelfand, Higgins, Nishii, Raver, Dominguez, Murakami, Yamaguchi, and Toyama found that the self-serving bias was far stronger in an individualist culture (United States) than a collectivist culture (Japan).[87] Wade-Benzoni, Okumura, Brett, Moore, Tenbrunsel, and Bazerman reported a similar finding for cultural differences in how asymmetric social dilemmas are managed in the United States and Japan, with Americans providing less co-operative solutions and expecting others to be less co-operative than Japanese participants in the study.[88]

In summary, it appears that several aspects of negotiator cognition are significantly influenced by culture and that negotiators should not assume that findings on negotiator cognition from Western negotiators are universally applicable to other cultures.[89]

Effect of Culture on Negotiator Ethics and Tactics

Researchers have recently turned their attention to examining ethics and negotiation tactics in cross-cultural negotiations by exploring the broad question of whether negotiators in different cultures have the same ethical evaluation of negotiation tactics. For instance, Zarkada-Fraser and Fraser investigated perceptions of Lewicki and Robinson's negotiation tactics (see Chapter 9) with negotiators from six different cultures.[90] They found significant differences in the tolerance of different negotiation tactics in different cultures, with Japanese negotiators more intolerant of the use of misrepresentation tactics than negotiators from Australia, the United States, Britain, Russia, and Greece. Volkema and Fleury examined the responses of Brazilians and Americans to Lewicki and Robinson's ethics questionnaire and found similar evaluations of the level of acceptability of the tactics in Brazil and the United States, but American negotiators reported that they would be more likely to use the tactics, especially exaggerating their opening offers, than Brazilian negotiators.[91] Elahee, Kirby, and Nasif explored the influence of trust on the use of Lewicki and Robinson's tactics by American, Mexican, and Canadian negotiators.[92] They found that negotiators who trusted the other party were less likely to use questionable negotiation tactics. Elahee et al. also found that Mexican negotiators were least likely to trust foreign negotiators, and more likely to use tactics like bluffing and misrepresentation in cross-cultural than intracultural negotiations. Canadian and American negotiators reported no difference in the likelihood of using these tactics in cross-cultural and intracultural negotiations.

In summary, there has been considerable research on the effects of culture on negotiation in the last decade. Findings suggest that culture has important effects on several aspects of negotiation, including planning, the negotiation process, information exchange, negotiator cognition, and negotiator perceptions of ethical behaviour.

■ Culturally Responsive Negotiation Strategies

Although a great deal has been written about the challenge of international and cross-cultural negotiations, far less attention has been paid to what negotiators should do when faced with negotiating with someone from another culture.

The advice by many theorists in this area, either explicitly or implicitly, has been, "When in Rome, act as the Romans do."[93] In other words, negotiators are advised to be aware of the effects of cultural differences on negotiation and to take them into account when they negotiate. Many theorists appear to assume implicitly that the best way to manage cross-cultural negotiations is to be sensitive to the cultural norms of the other negotiator and to modify one's strategy to be consistent with behaviours that occur in that culture.

Several factors suggest that negotiators should *not* make large modifications to their approach when negotiating cross-culturally, however:

1. Negotiators may not be able to modify their approach effectively. It takes years to understand another culture deeply, and negotiators typically do not have the time necessary to gain this understanding before beginning a negotiation. Although a little understanding of another culture is clearly better than ignorance, it may not be enough to enable negotiators to make effective adjustments to their negotiation strategy. Attempting to match the strategies and tactics used by negotiators in another culture is a daunting task that requires fluency in their language as only one of many preconditions. Even simple words may be translated in several different ways with different nuances, making the challenge of communicating in different languages overwhelming.[94]

2. Even if negotiators can modify their approach effectively, it does not mean that this will translate automatically into a better negotiation outcome. It is quite possible that the other party will modify his or her approach too. The results in this situation can be disaster, with each side trying to act like the other "should" be acting, and both sides not really understanding what the other party is doing. Consider the following example contrasting typical Canadian and Japanese negotiation styles. Canadians are more likely to start negotiations with an extreme offer to leave room for concessions. Japanese are more likely to start negotiations with gathering information to understand with whom they are dealing and what the relationship will be. Assume that both parties understand their own and the other party's cultural tendencies (this is a large assumption that frequently is not met). Now assume that each party, acting out of respect for the other, decides to "act like the Romans do" and to adopt the approach of the other party. The possibilities for confusion are endless. When the Canadians gather information about the Japanese, are they truly interested or are they playing a role? It will be clear that they are not acting like Canadians, but the strategy that they are using may not be readily identified. How will they interpret the Japanese behaviour? The Canadians have prepared well for their negotiations and understand that the Japanese do not present extreme positions early in negotiations. When the Japanese do present an extreme position early in negotiations (to adapt to the Canadian negotiation style), how should the Canadians interpret this behaviour? They likely will think, "That must be what they really want, because they don't open with extreme offers." Adopting the other party's approach does not guarantee success, and in fact it may lead to more confusion than acting like yourself (where at least your behaviour is understood within your own cultural context).

3. Research suggests that negotiators may naturally negotiate differently when they are with people from their own culture than when they are with people from other cultures.[95] The implications of this research are that a deep understanding of how people in other cultures negotiate, such as Costa Ricans negotiating with each other, may not help a Canadian negotiating with a Costa Rican.[96]

4. Research by Francis suggests that moderate adaptation may be more effective than "acting as the Romans do."[97] In a simulation study of Americans' responses to negotiators from other countries, Francis found that negotiators from a familiar culture (Japan) who made moderate adaptations to American ways were perceived more positively than negotiators who made no changes or those who made large adaptations. These findings did not replicate for negotiators from a less familiar culture (Korea), however, and more research needs to be conducted to understand why. At the very least, the results of this study suggest that large adaptations by international negotiators will not always be effective.

Recent research findings have provided some specific advice about how to negotiate cross-culturally. Rubin and Sander suggests that during preparation, negotiators should concentrate on understanding three things: (1) their own biases, strengths, and weaknesses; (2) the other negotiator as an individual; and (3) the other negotiator's cultural context.[98] Brett and her colleagues suggest that cross-cultural negotiators should go further and ask themselves a series of questions about how culture may influence information sharing and the negotiation process (e.g., Does this culture share information directly or indirectly? Is it monochronic or polychronic?).[99] Learning about how another culture shares information and structures the negotiation process may help negotiators plan more strategically for the negotiation.[100] Finally, Adair, Okumura, and Brett suggest that both parties in a cross-cultural negotiation need to be prepared to communicate in the other party's culturally preferred method of direct or indirect communication to increase the chances of a successful negotiation outcome. Different strategies and options for improving cross-cultural negotiations are discussed next.[101]

Stephen Weiss, from York University, has proposed a useful way of thinking about the options we have when negotiating with someone from another culture.[102] Weiss observes that negotiators may choose from among up to eight different culturally responsive strategies. These strategies may be used individually or sequentially, and the strategies can be switched as the negotiation progresses. When choosing a strategy, negotiators should be aware of their own and the other party's culture in general, understand the specific factors in the current relationship, and predict or try to influence the other party's approach. Weiss's culturally responsive strategies may be arranged into three groups, based on the level of familiarity (low, moderate, high) that a negotiator has with the other party's culture. Within each group there are some strategies that the negotiator may use individually (unilateral strategies) and others that involve the participation of the other party (joint strategies).

Low Familiarity

Employ Agents or Advisers (Unilateral Strategy) One approach for negotiators who have very low familiarity with the other party's culture is to hire an agent or adviser who is familiar with the cultures of both parties. This relationship may range from having the other party conduct the negotiations under supervision (agent) to receiving regular or occasional advice during the negotiations (adviser). Although agents or advisers may create other challenges, they may be quite useful for negotiators who have little awareness of the other party's culture and little time to prepare.

Bring in a Mediator (Joint Strategy) Many types of mediators may be used in cross-cultural negotiations, ranging from someone who conducts introductions and then withdraws to someone who is present throughout the negotiation and takes responsibility for managing the negotiation process. Interpreters will often play this role, providing both parties with more information than the mere translation of words during negotiations. Mediators may encourage one side or the other to adopt one culture's approaches or a third cultural approach (the mediator's home culture).

Induce the Other Negotiator to Use Your Approach (Joint Strategy) Another option is to persuade the other party to use your approach. There are many ways to do this, ranging from making a polite request to asserting rudely that your way is best. More subtly, negotiators can continue to respond to the other party's requests in their own language because they "cannot express themselves well enough" in the other's language. Although this strategy has many advantages for the negotiator with low familiarity, there are also some disadvantages. For instance, the other party may become irritated or insulted by having to make the extra effort to deal with negotiators on their own cultural terms. In addition, the other negotiator may also have a strategic advantage because he or she may now attempt more extreme tactics and excuse their use on the basis of his or her "cultural ignorance" (after all, negotiators can't expect the other party to understand everything about how they negotiate).

Moderate Familiarity

Adapt to the Other Negotiator's Approach (Unilateral Strategy) This strategy involves negotiators making conscious changes to their approach so that it is more appealing to the other party. Rather than trying to act like the other party, negotiators using this strategy maintain a firm grasp on their own approach but make modifications to help relations with the other person. These modifications may include acting in a less extreme manner, eliminating some behaviours, and adopting some of the other party's behaviours. The challenge in using this strategy is to know which behaviours to modify, eliminate, or adopt. In addition, it is not clear that the other party will interpret modifications in the way that negotiators have intended.

Coordinate Adjustment (Joint Strategy) This strategy involves both parties making mutual adjustments to find a common process for negotiation. Although this can be done implicitly, it is more likely to occur explicitly ("How would you like to proceed?"), and it can be thought of as a special instance of negotiating the process of negotiation. This strategy requires a moderate amount of knowledge about the other party's culture and at least some facility with his or her language (comprehension, if not the ability to speak). Coordinate adjustment occurs on a daily basis in Montreal, the most bilingual city in North America (85 percent of Montrealers understand both English and French). It is standard practice for businesspeople in Montreal to negotiate the process of negotiation before the substantive discussion begins. The outcomes of this discussion are variations on the theme of whether the negotiations will occur in English or French, with a typical outcome being that either party may speak either language. Negotiations often occur in both languages, and frequently the person with the best second-language skills will switch languages to facilitate the discussion. Another outcome that occasionally occurs has both parties speaking in their second language (i.e., the French speaker will negotiate in English while the English speaker will negotiate in French) to demonstrate respect for the other party. Another type of coordinate adjustment occurs when the two negotiating parties adopt aspects of a third culture to facilitate their negotiations. For instance, during a trip to Latin America, one of the authors of this book conducted discussions in French with a Latin American colleague who spoke Spanish and French, but not English. On a subsequent trip to China, negotiations were conducted in French, English, and Mandarin since each of the six participants spoke two of the three languages.

High Familiarity

Embrace the Other Negotiator's Approach (Unilateral Strategy) This strategy involves adopting completely the approach of the other negotiator. To be used successfully, the negotiator needs to be completely bilingual and bicultural. In essence, the negotiator using this strategy doesn't act like a Roman; he or she is a Roman. This strategy is costly in preparation time and expense, and it places the negotiator using it under considerable stress because it is difficult to switch back and forth rapidly between cultures. However, there is much to gain by using this strategy because the other negotiator can be approached and understood completely on his or her own terms.

Improvise an Approach (Joint Strategy) This strategy involves crafting an approach that is specifically tailored to the negotiation situation, other negotiator, and circumstances. To use this approach, both parties to the negotiation need to have high familiarity with the other party's culture and a strong understanding of the individual characteristics of the other negotiator. The negotiation that emerges with this approach can be crafted by adopting aspects from both cultures when they will be useful. This approach is the most flexible of the eight strategies, which is both its strength and weakness. Flexibility is a strength because it allows the approach to be crafted to the circumstances at hand, but it is a weakness because there are few general prescriptive statements that can be made about how to use this strategy.

Effect Symphony (Joint Strategy) This strategy allows negotiators to create a new approach that may include aspects of either home culture or adopt practices from a third culture. Professional diplomats use such an approach when the customs, norms, and language they use transcend national borders and form their own culture (diplomacy). Use of this strategy is complex and involves a great deal of time and effort. It works best when the parties are familiar with each other and with both home cultures and have a common structure (like that of professional diplomats) for the negotiation. Risks of using this strategy include costs due to confusion, lost time, and the overall effort required to make it work.

In this chapter we examined various aspects of a growing field of negotiation that explores the complexities of international and cross-cultural negotiation. When you find yourself in a situation where you are negotiating in an international context, there are a number of things you should keep in mind. We conclude the chapter by summarizing some of the most important.

1. Do not assume that negotiation strategies that work in a North American context will also work in other cultural or national settings. Although English is increasingly seen as the global language of business, cultural differences in negotiation style are unlikely to be homogeneous any time soon.

2. Be ready to adapt your own style. For example, if you tend to be a co-operative negotiator and find yourself doing business in Israel, you might need to adopt a more confrontational approach.

3. Success in global negotiations requires that we set ethnocentric ideas aside. We also must understand that to succeed, we need to find ways to understand the other party. Asking questions about hidden assumptions is likely even more important in international negotiations than it is in domestic ones.

CHAPTER 12

Best Practices in Negotiations

Negotiation is an integral part of daily life and the opportunities to negotiate surround us. While some people may look like born negotiators, negotiation is fundamentally a skill involving analysis and communication that everyone can learn. The purpose of this book is to provide students of negotiation with an overview of the field of negotiation, perspective on the breadth and depth of the subprocesses of negotiation, and an appreciation for the art and science of negotiation. In this final chapter we reflect on negotiation at a broad level by providing 10 "best practices" for negotiators who wish to continue to improve their negotiation skills (see Table 12.1).

TABLE 12.1 | Ten Best Practices for Negotiators

1. Be prepared
2. Diagnose the fundamental structure of the negotiation
3. Identify and work the BATNA
4. Be willing to walk away
5. Master paradoxes
6. Remember the intangibles
7. Actively manage coalitions
8. Savour and protect your reputation
9. Remember that rationality and fairness are relative
10. Continue to learn from the experience

1. Be Prepared

We cannot overemphasize the importance of preparation, and we strongly encourage all negotiators to prepare properly for their negotiations (see Chapter 4). Negotiators who are better prepared have numerous advantages, including the ability to analyze the other party's offers more effectively and efficiently, to understand the nuances of the concession-making process, and to achieve their negotiation goals. Preparation should occur *before* the negotiation begins so that the time spent negotiating is more productive. Good preparation means understanding one's own goals and interests as well as possible and being able to articulate them to the other party skilfully. It also includes being ready to understand the other party's communication to find an agreement that meets the needs of both parties. Few negotiations are going to conclude successfully without both parties achieving at least some of their goals, and solid work up front to identify your needs and to understand the needs of the other party is a critical step to increasing the odds of success.

Good preparation also means setting aspirations for negotiation that are high but achievable. Negotiators who set their sights too low are virtually guaranteed to reach an agreement that is suboptimal, while those who set them too high are more likely to stalemate and end the negotiation in frustration. Negotiators also need to plan their opening statements and positions carefully so they are especially well prepared at the start of negotiations. It is important to avoid preplanning the complete negotiation sequence, however, because while negotiations do follow broad stages, they also ebb and flow at irregular rates. Over-planning the tactics for each negotiation stage in advance of the negotiation is not a good use of preparation time. It is far better that negotiators prepare by understanding their own strengths and weaknesses, their needs and interests, the situation, and the other party as well as possible so that they can adjust promptly and effectively as the negotiation proceeds.

2. Diagnose the Fundamental Structure of the Negotiation

Negotiators should make a conscious decision about whether they are facing a fundamentally distributive negotiation, an integrative negotiation, or a blend of the two, and choose their strategies and tactics accordingly. Using strategies and tactics that are mismatched will lead to suboptimal negotiation outcomes. For instance, using overly distributive tactics in a fundamentally integrative situation will almost certainly result in reaching agreements that leave integrative potential untapped because negotiators tend not to share readily the information needed to succeed in integrative negotiations in response to distributive tactics.

Similarly, using integrative tactics in a distributive situation may not lead to optimal outcomes either. Negotiators also need to remember that many negotiations will consist of a blend of integrative and distributive elements and that there will be distributive and integrative phases to these negotiations. It is especially important to be careful when transitioning between these phases within the broader negotiation because missteps in these transitions can confuse the other party and lead to impasse.

3. Identify and Work the BATNA

One of the most important sources of power in a negotiation is the alternatives available to a negotiator if an agreement is not reached. One alternative, the best alternative to a negotiated agreement (BATNA), is especially important because this is the option that likely will be chosen should an agreement not be reached.

Negotiators need to be vigilant about their BATNA. They need to know what their BATNA is relative to a possible agreement and consciously work to improve the BATNA so as to improve the deal. Negotiators without a strong BATNA may find it difficult to achieve a good agreement because the other party may try to push them aggressively, and hence they may be forced to accept a settlement that is later seen as unsatisfying.

For instance, purchasers who need to buy items from sole suppliers are acutely aware of how the lack of a positive BATNA makes it difficult to achieve positive negotiation outcomes. Even in this situation, however, negotiators can work to improve their BATNA in the long term. For instance, organizations in a sole supplier relationship have often vertically integrated their production and started to build comparable components inside the company, or they have redesigned their products so they are less vulnerable to the sole supplier. These are clearly long-term options and are not available in the current negotiation. However, it may be possible to refer to these plans when negotiating with a sole supplier to remind them that you will not be dependent forever.

Negotiators also need to be aware of the other negotiator's BATNA and to identify how it compares to what you are offering. Negotiators have more power in a negotiation when their potential terms of agreement are significantly better than what the other negotiator can obtain with his or her BATNA. On the other hand, when the difference between your terms and the other negotiator's BATNA is small, then negotiators have less room to manoeuvre. There are three things negotiators should do with respect to the other negotiator's BATNA: (1) monitor it carefully to understand and retain your competitive advantage over the other negotiator's alternatives; (2) remind the other negotiator of the advantages your offer has relative to her BATNA; and (3) in a subtle way, suggest that the other negotiator's BATNA may not be as strong as he or she thinks it is (this can be done in a positive way by stressing your strengths or in a negative way by highlighting competitors' weaknesses).

◼ 4. Be Willing to Walk Away

The goal of most negotiations is achieving a valued outcome, not reaching an agreement *per se*. Strong negotiators remember this and are willing to walk away from a negotiation when no agreement is better than a poor agreement. While this advice sounds easy enough to take in principle, in practice, negotiators can become so focused on reaching an agreement that they lose sight of the real goal, which is to reach a good outcome (and not necessarily an agreement). Negotiators can ensure that they don't take their eyes off the goal by making regular comparisons with the targets they set during the planning stage and by comparing their progress during their negotiation against their walkaway and BATNA. While negotiators are often optimistic about goal achievement at the outset, they may need to re-evaluate these goals during the negotiation. It is important to continue to compare progress in the current negotiation with the target, walkaway, and BATNA and to be willing to walk away from the current negotiation if their walkaway or BATNA becomes the truly better choice.

◾ 5. Master the Key Paradoxes of Negotiation

Excellent negotiators understand that negotiation embodies a set of paradoxes—seemingly contradictory elements that actually occur together. We will discuss five common paradoxes that negotiators face. The challenge for negotiators in handling these paradoxes is to strive for *balance* in these situations. There is a natural tension in choosing between one or the other alternative in the paradox, but the best way to manage paradox is to achieve a balance between the opposing forces.

Claiming Value versus Creating Value

All negotiations have a value *claiming* stage, where parties decide who gets how much of what, but many negotiations also have a value *creation* stage, where parties work together to expand the resources under negotiation. The skills and strategies appropriate to each stage are quite different; in general terms, distributive skills are called for in the value claiming stage and integrative skills are useful in value creation. Typically, the value creation stage will precede the value claiming stage, and a challenge for negotiators is to balance the emphasis on the two stages and the transition from creating to claiming value. One approach to manage this transition is to label it. For instance, negotiators could say something like "It looks like we have a good foundation of ideas and alternatives to work from. How can we move on to decide what is a fair distribution of the expected outcomes?" In addition, research shows that most negotiators are overly biased towards thinking that a negotiation is more about claiming value than about creating value, so managing this paradox will likely require an overemphasis on discussing the creating value dynamics.

Sticking by Your Principles versus Being Resilient

The pace and flow of negotiations can move from an intense haggle over financial issues to an intense debate over deeply held principles about what is right or fair or just. These transitions often create a second paradox for negotiators. On the one hand, effective negotiation requires flexible thinking and an understanding that an assessment of a situation may need to be adjusted as new information comes to light, that is, resiliency; achieving any deal will probably require both parties to make concessions. On the other hand, core principles are not something to back away from easily in the service of doing a deal. Effective negotiators are thoughtful about the distinction between issues of principle, where firmness is essential, and other issues where compromise or accommodation is the best route to a mutually acceptable outcome.

Sticking with the Strategy versus Opportunistic Pursuit of New Options

New information will frequently come to light during a negotiation, and negotiators need to manage the paradox of either sticking with their prepared strategy or pursuing a new opportunity that arises during the process. This is a challenging paradox for negotiators to manage because new "opportunities" may in fact be Trojan Horses harbouring unpleasant surprises. On the other hand, circumstances do change and legitimate "one-time," seize-the-moment deals do occur. The challenge for negotiators is to distinguish phantom opportunities from real ones.

Strong preparation is critical to being able to manage the "strategy versus opportunism" paradox. We also suggest that negotiators pay close attention to their intuition. If a deal doesn't feel right, if it "seems too good to be true," then it probably *is* too good to be true and is not a viable opportunity. If negotiators feel uneasy about the direction the negotiation is taking, then it is best to take a break and consult with others about the circumstances. Often explaining the "opportunity" to a colleague, friend, or constituent will help to distinguish real opportunities from Trojan Horses.

We are not suggesting that negotiators become overly cautious, however. There frequently are genuinely good opportunities that occur during a negotiation, legitimately caused by changes in business strategy, market opportunities, excess inventory, or a short-term cash flow challenge. Negotiators who have prepared well will be able to take full advantage of real opportunities when they arise and reduce the risk presented by Trojan Horses.

Honest and Open versus Closed and Opaque

Negotiators face the *dilemma of honesty:* how open and honest should I be with the other party? Negotiators who are completely open and tell the other party everything expose themselves to the risk that the other party will take advantage of them. In fact, research suggests that too much knowledge about the other party's needs can actually lead to suboptimal negotiation outcomes. On the other hand, being completely closed not only has a negative effect on your reputation (see below), but it is also an ineffective negotiation strategy because you don't disclose enough information to create the groundwork for agreement. The challenge of this paradox is deciding how much information to reveal and how much to conceal, both for pragmatic and ethical reasons.

We suggest that negotiators should remember that negotiation is an ongoing process. As the negotiators make positive progress, they should be building trust and hopefully feeling more comfortable about revealing more information to the other party. That said, there is some information that should probably not be revealed (e.g., the bottom line in a distributive negotiation) regardless of how well the negotiation is progressing.

Trust versus Distrust

As a mirror image of the dilemma of honesty, negotiators also face the *dilemma of trust:* how much to trust what the other party tells them. Negotiators who believe everything the other party tells them make themselves vulnerable to being taken advantage of by the other party. On the other hand, negotiators who do not believe anything the other party tells them will have a very difficult time reaching an agreement. As with the dilemma of honesty, we suggest that negotiators remember that negotiation is a process that evolves over time. First, as we noted, trust can be built by being honest and sharing information with the other side, which hopefully will lead to reciprocal trust and credible disclosure by the other side. There is no right or wrong approach to managing this dilemma. Strong negotiators are aware of this dilemma, however, and constantly monitor how they are managing this challenge.

■ 6. Remember the Intangibles

Intangibles frequently affect negotiation in a negative way, and they often operate out of the negotiator's awareness. As noted in Chapter 1, intangibles include winning, avoiding loss, looking tough or strong to others, not looking weak, being fair, and so on. For instance, if the other party is vying with his archrival at the next desk for a promotion, he may be especially difficult when negotiating with you in front of his boss to "look tough." The best way to identify the existence of intangible factors is to try to "see what is not there." In other words, if your careful preparation and analysis of the situation reveals no tangible explanation for the other negotiator's behaviour—adamant advocacy of a certain point, refusal to yield another one, or behaviour that just doesn't "make sense"—then it is time to start looking for the intangibles driving his behaviour.

For example, several years ago one of the authors of this book was helping a friend buy a new car, and the price offered from the dealer was $2,000 less than any other dealer in town. The only catch was that the car had to be sold that day. On the surface this looked like a trick (see "Strategy versus Opportunism" above) but there was no obvious tangible factor that explained this special price. The friend had never purchased from the dealer before, the car was new and fully covered by a good warranty, and the friend had visited several dealers and knew this price was substantially lower than at other dealers. As we continued to discuss the potential deal, the salesman became more and more agitated. Sweat was literally falling from his brow. The friend decided to purchase the car and as soon as he signed the salesman was simultaneously relieved and excited. He asked for a moment to telephone his wife to share with her some good news. It turned out that the salesman had just won a complicated incentive package offered by the dealer and the prize was a two-week, all-expenses-paid Caribbean vacation for his family of four.

Often negotiators do not learn what intangible factors are influencing the other negotiator unless the other chooses to disclose them. Negotiators can "see" their existence, however, by looking for changes in the other negotiator's behaviour from one negotiation to another, as well as by gathering information about the other party before negotiation begins. For instance, if you find out that the other party has a new boss that she doesn't like and she is subsequently more difficult to deal with in the negotiation, the intangible of the new boss may be to blame.

There are at least two more ways to discover intangibles that might be affecting the other. One way to surface the other party's intangibles is to ask questions. These questions should try to get the other party to reveal why he or she is sticking so strongly to a given point. It is important to remember that strong emotions and/or values are the root of many intangibles, so surfacing intangibles may result in the discussion of various fears and anxieties. The question-asking process should also be gentle and informal; if the questioning is aggressive, it may only make the other defensive, adding another intangible to the mix and stifling effective negotiations! A second way is to take an observer or listener with you to the negotiation. Listeners may be able to read the other's emotional tone or nonverbal behaviour, focus on road-block issues, or try to take the other's perspective and put themselves in the other's shoes (role reversal). A caucus with this listener may then help refocus the discussion so as to surface the intangibles and develop a new line of questions or offers.

Negotiators also need to remember that intangible factors influence their own behaviour (and that it is not uncommon for us to not recognize what is making us angry, defensive, or zealously committed to some idea). Are you being particularly difficult with the other party because he "does not respect you"? Are you "trying to teach a subordinate a lesson"? Or do you want to "win" this negotiation to "look better" than another manager? Without passing judgment on the legitimacy of these goals, we strongly urge negotiators to be aware of the effect of intangible factors on their own aspirations and behaviour. Often talking to another person—a sympathetic listener—can help the negotiator figure these out. Strong negotiators are aware of how both tangible and intangible factors influence negotiation, and they weigh both factors when evaluating a negotiation outcome.

■ 7. Actively Manage Coalitions

Negotiators should recognize three types of coalitions and their potential effects: (1) coalitions against you, (2) coalitions that support you, and (3) loose, undefined coalitions that may materialize either for or against you. Strong negotiators assess the presence and strength of coalitions and work to capture the strength of the coalition for their benefit. If this is not possible, negotiators need to work to prevent the other party from capturing a loose coalition for their purposes. When negotiators are part of a coalition, communicating with the coalition is critical to ensuring that the power of the coalition is aligned with their goals. Similarly, negotiators who are agents or representatives of a coalition must take special care to manage this process.

Successfully concluding negotiations when a coalition is aligned against a negotiator is an extremely challenging task. It is important to recognize when coalitions are aligned against you and to work consciously to counter their influence. Frequently this will involve a "divide and conquer" strategy where negotiators try to increase dissent within the coalition by searching for ways to breed instability within the coalition.

Coalitions occur in many formal negotiations, such as environmental assessments and reaching policy decisions in an industry association. Coalitions may also have a strong influence in less formal settings, such as work teams and families, where different subgroups of people may not have the same interests. Managing coalitions is especially important when negotiators need to rely on other people to implement an agreement. It may be possible for negotiators to forge an agreement when the majority of people influenced are not in favour, but implementing the outcomes of that agreement will be very challenging.

■ 8. Savour and Protect Your Reputation

Reputations are like eggs—fragile, important to build, easy to break, and very hard to rebuild once broken. Starting negotiations with a positive reputation is essential, and negotiators should be vigilant in protecting their reputations. Negotiators who have a reputation for breaking their word and not negotiating honestly will have a much more difficult time negotiating in the future than those who have a reputation for being honest and fair. Negotiators prepare differently for others with contrasting reputations. Negotiating with a tough but fair negotiator means preparing for potentially difficult negotiations while being aware that the other party will push hard for her perspective but will also be rational and fair in her behaviour. Negotiating with a tough but underhanded other party means that negotiators will need to verify what the other says, be vigilant for dirty tricks, and be more guarded about sharing information.

Rather than leaving reputation to chance, negotiators can work to shape and enhance their reputation by acting in a consistent and fair manner. Consistency provides the other party with a clear set of predictable expectations about how you will behave, which leads to a stable reputation. Fairness sends the message that you are principled and reasonable. Strong negotiators also periodically seek feedback from others about the way they are perceived and use that information to strengthen their credibility and trustworthiness in the marketplace.

9. Remember that Rationality and Fairness Are Relative

Research on negotiator perception and cognition is quite clear: People tend to view the world in a self-serving manner and define the "rational" thing to do or a "fair" outcome or process in a way that benefit themselves. First, negotiators need to be aware of this tendency in both themselves and the other party. Negotiators can do three things to manage these perceptions proactively. First, they can question their own perceptions of fairness and ground them in clear principles. Second, they can find external benchmarks and examples that suggest fair outcomes. Finally, negotiators can illuminate definitions of fairness held by the other party and engage in a dialogue to reach consensus on which standards of fairness apply in a given situation.

Moreover, negotiators are often in the position to collectively define what is right or fair as a part of the negotiation process. In most situations, neither side holds the keys to what is absolutely right, rational, or fair. Reasonable people can disagree, and often the most important outcome that negotiators can achieve is a common, agreed-upon perspective, definition of the facts, agreement on the right way to see a problem, or standard for determining what is a fair outcome or process. Be prepared to negotiate these principles as strongly as you prepare for a discussion of the issues.

10. Continue to Learn from Your Experience

Negotiation epitomizes lifelong learning. The best negotiators continue to learn from the experience—they know there are so many different variables and nuances when negotiating that no two negotiations are identical. These differences mean that for negotiators to remain sharp, they need to continue to practice the art and science of negotiation regularly. In addition, the best negotiators take a moment to analyze each negotiation after it has concluded, to review what happened and what they learned. We recommend a three-step process:

- Plan a personal reflection time after each negotiation.
- Periodically "take a lesson" from a trainer or coach.
- Keep a personal diary on strengths and weaknesses and develop a plan to work on weaknesses.

This analysis does not have to be extensive or time-consuming. It should happen after every important negotiation, however, and it should focus on *what* and *why* questions: What happened during this negotiation, why did it occur, and what can I learn? Negotiators who take the time to pause and reflect on their negotiations will find that they continue to refine their skills and that they remain sharp and focused for their future negotiations.

Moreover, even the best athletes—in almost any sport—have one or more coaches on their staff, and stop to "take a lesson." Negotiators have access to seminars to enhance their skills, books to read, and coaches who can help refine their skills. This book should be seen as one step along the way to sharpening and refining your negotiation skills, and we encourage you to continue to learn about the art and science of negotiation. We wish you the best of luck in all of your future negotiations!

Chapter 1

1. Thompson, Wang, and Gunia, 2010.
2. Lewicki, 1992; Rubin and Brown, 1975.
3. Deutsch, 1962, p. 176.
4. Fisher, Ury, and Patton, 1991.
5. Goffman, 1969; Pruitt and Rubin, 1986; Raven and Rubin, 1973; Ritov, 1996.
6. Alexander, Schul, and Babakus, 1991; Donohue and Roberto, 1996; Eyuboglu and Buja, 1993; Pinkley and Northcraft, 1994.
7. Gray, 1994; Kolb, 1985; Kolb and Putnam, 1997.
8. Pruitt, 1981.
9. Kelley, 1966.
10. Kimmel, Pruitt, Magenau, Konar-Goldband, and Carnevale, 1980; Putnam and Jones, 1982; Weingart, Thompson, Bazerman, and Carroll, 1990.
11. Raiffa, 1982; Selekman, Fuller, Kennedy, and Baitsel, 1964.
12. Lax and Sebenius, 1986.
13. Pruitt and Rubin, 1986, p. 4.
14. Hocker and Wilmot, 1985.
15. Deutsch, 1973.
16. As mentioned earlier, however, the goals may not actually be in opposition, and the parties need not compete. Perception is more determinant than reality.
17. Coser, 1956; Deutsch, 1973.

Chapter 2

1. Walton and McKersie, 1965.
2. See Lax and Sebenius, 1986. Integrative negotiation focuses on ways to create value but also includes a claiming stage where the value created is distributed. Integrative negotiation is discussed extensively in Chapter 3.
3. Thompson and Hrebec, 1996.
4. Raiffa, 1982.
5. Galinsky, Mussweiler, and Medvec, 2002.
6. Fisher, Ury, and Patton, 1991.
7. Fisher and Ertel, 1995.
8. We discuss power and leverage in bargaining in detail in Chapter 7.
9. Stein, 1996.
10. Refer to Walton and McKersie (1965, pp. 59–82) for a more extensive treatment of this subject.
11. See Schweitzer and Kerr, 2000.
12. Karrass, 1974.
13. Fassina and Whyte, (unpublished manuscript).
14. See Lim and Murnighan, 1994; Roth, Murnighan, and Schoumaker, 1988; and Walton and McKersie, 1965.
15. See de Dreu, 2003.

16. See Mosterd and Rutte, 2000.

17. Jacobs, 1951.

18. Cohen, 1980.

19. See Tutzauer, 1992.

20. See Brodt, 1994; Chertkoff and Conley, 1967; Cohen, 2003; Donohue, 1981; Hinton, Hamner, and Pohlan, 1974; Komorita and Brenner, 1968; Liebert, Smith, and Hill, 1968; Pruitt and Syna, 1985; Ritov, 1996; Van Pouke and Buelens, 2002; and Weingart, Thompson, Bazerman, and Carroll, 1990.

21. See Pruitt, 1981, and Tutzauer, 1991, for further discussion of these points.

22. Putnam and Jones, 1982; Yukl, 1974.

23. Weingart, Prietula, Heider, and Genovese, 1999.

24. Eyuboglu and Buja, 1993.

25. See Ghosh, 1996.

26. See Olekalns, Smith, and Walsh, 1996.

27. Galinsky, Seiden, Kim, and Medvec, 2002.

28. See Rapoport, Erev, and Zwick, 1995.

29. The term Boulwarism is named after the chief labour negotiator for the General Electric Company in the 1950s. Rather than let the union present its contract demands first, the company placed a single "fair" offer on the table and refused to negotiate further. The National Labor Relations Board eventually ruled against G.E. by stating that this practice was unfair because management did not engage in "good faith bargaining." See Northrup (1964) and Selekman, Selekman, and Fuller, (1958) for further discussion of this point.

30. See Baranowski and Summers, 1972; Crumbaugh and Evans, 1967; Deutsch, 1958; and Gruder and Duslak, 1973.

31. Rubin and Brown, 1975.

32. See Pruitt, 1981. Logrolling is discussed further in Chapter 3.

33. See Froman and Cohen, 1970; Neale and Bazerman, 1991; and Pruitt, 1981.

34. See Yukl, 1974.

35. Walton and McKersie, 1965.

36. See Cellich, 1997; Girard, 1989.

37. Girard, 1989.

38. For instance, see Aaronson, 1989; Brooks and Odiorne, 1984; Cohen, 1980; Levinson, Smith, and Wilson, 1999; and Schatzski, 1981.

39. Schneider, 2002.

40. Negotiation ethics are discussed in Chapter 8.

41. See Fisher, Ury, and Patton, 1991; Ury, 1991; and Adler, Rosen, and Silverstein, 1996, for an extended discussion of these points.

42. Fisher, Ury, and Patton, 1991; Ury, 1991; Weeks, 2001.

43. Brodt and Tuchinsky, 2000; Hilty and Carnevale, 1993.

44. Cohen, 1980.

45. Landon, 1997.

46. Cohen, 1980.

47. Hendon and Hendon, 1990.

Chapter 3

1. "No deal, no talks, no hockey: NHL players and owners reject each other's proposals, break off negotiations and dig in," *The Globe and Mail*, December 15, 2004.
2. "Here's how to end the NHL lockout." *The Globe and Mail*, October 28, 2004.
3. Cannella, S. and M. Bechtel "Ice breakers: The NHL and its union edge closer to ending their nine-month lockout," *Sports Illustrated*, June 20, 2005.
4. Walton and McKersie, 1965.
5. Butler, 1999; Pruitt, 1981; Thompson, 1991.
6. Butler, 1999; Kemp and Smith, 1994.
7. Kemp and Smith, 1994.
8. Olekalns, Smith, and Walsh, 1996.
9. Kelley, 1966.
10. Fisher, Ury, and Patton, 1991; Pruitt and Rubin, 1986.
11. Neale and Bazerman, 1991, p. 23.
12. Fisher, Ury, and Patton, 1991.
13. Fisher, Ury, and Patton, 1991, p. 40; originally told by Follett, 1940.
14. Lax and Sebenius, 1986.
15. See Chapter 5 of Sheppard, Lewicki, and Minton, 1992 for a more complete discussion of the role of "voice" in organizations.
16. Lax and Sebenius, 1986.
17. Clyman and Tripp, 2000.
18. Provis, 1996.
19. For example, see Neale and Bazerman, 1991; Pruitt, 1981, 1983; Pruitt and Carnevale, 1993; and, Pruitt and Lewis, 1975.
20. Olekalns, 2002.
21. Gillespie and Bazerman, 1997.
22. Tajima and Fraser, 2001.
23. Moran and Ritov, 2002.
24. Naquin, 2002. Note that negotiator satisfaction may be less when more issues are negotiated; however, this may be due to beliefs by negotiators that they "could have done better" on one or more issues. Negotiator cognition and satisfaction are discussed in more detail in Chapter 5.
25. Lax and Sebenius, 1986; Pruitt, 1981.
26. Mannix, Tinsley, and Bazerman, 1995.
27. Butler, 1996.
28. Pruitt and Carnevale, 1993; Pruitt and Rubin, 1986.
29. Fisher, Ury, and Patton, 1991; Pruitt, 1983.
30. For more detailed discussion of this step see Filley, 1975; Pruitt and Carnevale, 1993; Shea, 1983; and Walton and McKersie, 1965.
31. Fisher, Ury, and Patton, 1991.
32. Ibid.
33. Neale and Bazerman, 1991.
34. Lax and Sebenius, 2002.
35. Bazerman and Gillespie, 1999; Lax and Sebenius, 2002.
36. Lax and Sebenius, 2002.
37. Fisher, Ury, and Patton, 1991.

38. Gibb, 1961.
39. Butler, 1999; Tenbrunsel, 1999.
40. Kimmel, Pruitt, Magenau, Konar-Goldband, and Carnevale, 1980.
41. Fry, Firestone, and Williams, 1979; Kelley and Schenitzki, 1972.
42. Rubin and Brown, 1975.
43. Kelley and Schenitzki, 1972.
44. de Dreu, Giebels, and van de Vliert, 1998.
45. Gillespie and Bazerman, 1998.
46. Raiffa, 1982.
47. Neale and Bazerman, 1991.
48. Weingart, Hyder, and Prietula, 1996.
49. See Gentner, Loewenstein, and Thompson, 2003; Loewenstein and Thompson, 2000; Loewenstein, Thompson, and Gentner, 1999, 2003; Nadler, Thompson, and Van Boven, 2003; and Thompson, Gentner, and Loewenstein, 2000.

Chapter 4

1. Douglas, 1962; Greenhalgh, 2001; Morley and Stephenson, 1977.
2. Greenhalgh, 2001.
3. See Asherman and Asherman, 1990; Burnstein, 1995; Fisher and Ertel, 1995; Lewicki, Hiam, and Olander, 1996; Lewicki and Hiam, 1999; Greenhalgh, 2001; Richardson, 1977; and Watkins, 2002.
4. Watkins, 2002.
5. Rubin and Brown, 1975.
6. Raiffa, 1982.
7. Ury, 1991.
8. Rubin and Brown, 1975.
9. Watkins, 2002.
10. Calero and Oskam, 1983.
11. Karrass, 1974, p. 11.
12. Mintzberg and Quinn, 1991.
13. Quinn, 1991.
14. Pruitt and Rubin, 1986.
15. Savage, Blair, and Sorenson, 1989.
16. See also Johnston, 1982.
17. Cialdini, 2001; Homans, 1961.
18. Adapted from Johnston, 1982.
19. Lax and Sebenius, 1986.

Chapter 5

1. "Harris to give surviving Dionnes cash they rejected." *The Globe and Mail*, 28 February 1998.
2. Berton, 1977.
3. Babcock, Wang, and Loewenstein, 1996; de Dreu and van Lange, 1995; Thompson, 1995; Thompson and Hastie, 1990a.
4. de Dreu, 2003; Devine, 1989; Forgas and Fiedler, 1996.
5. Sherif, Harvey, White, Hood, and Sherif, 1988.

6. Cooper, 1981.

7. Bruner and Tagiuri, 1954.

8. Ibid.

9. Bateson, 1972; Goffman, 1974.

10. Thompson, 1998.

11. Roth and Sheppard, 1995, p. 94.

12. Follett, 1942, quoted in Putnam and Holmer, 1992.

13. Note that frames themselves cannot be "seen." They are abstractions, perceptions, and thoughts that people use to define a situation, organize information, determine what is important, what is not, and so on. We can infer other people's frames by asking them directly about their frames, by listening to their communication, and by watching their behaviour. Similarly, we can try to understand our own frames by thinking about what aspects of a situation we should pay attention to, emphasize, focus on, or ignore—and by observing our own words and actions. One cannot see or directly measure a frame, however.

14. Tversky and Kahneman, 1981.

15. Felstiner, Abel, and Sarat, 1980–81.

16. Jensen, 1995.

17. Putnam and Wilson, 1989; Putnam, Wilson, and Turner, 1990.

18. Ikle, 1964.

19. Lewicki, Weiss, and Lewin, 1992, p. 225.

20. Zartman, 1977; Zartman and Berman, 1982.

21. Putnam, 1994.

22. The foundations of this approach are in behavioural decision theory and the prospect theory of human judgment and decision making (e.g., Bazerman, 1998; Neale and Bazerman 1991; Tversky and Kahnemann, 1981). For reviews, see Bazerman and Carroll, 1987; Neale and Bazerman, 1992b; Thompson and Hastie, 1990b. Whether negotiators misperceive information or misprocess information remains a technical debate in the communication and negotiation literature that is beyond the scope of this book.

23. Brockner, 1992; Staw, 1981.

24. Thompson, 1990b.

25. Pinkley, Griffith, and Northcraft, 1995; Thompson and Hastie, 1990a, 1990b.

26. Harinck, de Dreu, and Van Vianen, 2000.

27. Diekmann, Tenbrunsel, Shah, Schroth, and Bazerman, 1996; Kristensen and Garling, 1997; Ritov, 1996.

28. Northcraft and Neale, 1987.

29. Bazerman, Magliozzi, and Neale, 1985; de Dreu, Carnevale, Emans, and van de Vliert, 1994; Neale, Huber, and Northcraft, 1987; Schurr, 1987. However, Bottom (1998) provides evidence that the influence of framing and risk propensity on negotiation outcomes varies with nature of the negotiation task.

30. Bazerman and Neale, 1992, p. 39.

31. Ball, Bazerman, and Carroll, 1991; Bazerman and Samuelson, 1983; Foreman and Murnighan, 1996.

32. Neale and Bazerman, 1983.

33. Lim, 1997.

34. Bottom and Paese, 1999.

35. Heider, 1958.

36. Jones and Nisbett, 1976.

37. Babcock, Wang, and Loewenstein, 1996.

38. de Dreu, Nauta, and van de Vliert, 1995.

39. Ross, Greene, and House, 1977.

40. Kahneman, Knetsch, and Thaler, 1990.

41. Bazerman, Moore, and Gillespie, 1999, p. 1288.

42. Carroll, Bazerman, and Maury, 1988.

43. Carroll, Delquie, Halpern, and Bazerman, 1990.

44. Stillenger, Epelbaum, Keltner, and Ross, 1990.

45. Neale and Bazerman, 1992b.

46. Stillenger et al., 1990.

47. Babcock and Loewenstein, 1997; Foreman and Murnighan, 1996; Thompson and Hastie, 1990a.

48. Arunachalam and Dilla, 1995.

49. Kahneman and Tversky, 1979.

50. For reviews of research literature on emotion in negotiation, see Allred, Mallozzi, Matsui, and Raia, 1997; Barry, Fulmer, and Van Kleef, 2004; Barry and Oliver, 1996; Kumar, 1997.

51. Morris, 1989.

52. Forgas, 1992; Parrott, 2001.

53. Carver and Scheir, 1990.

54. Kumar, 1997.

55. Higgins, 1987.

56. Berkowitz, 1989.

57. Carnevale and Isen, 1986; Isen and Baron, 1991.

58. Baron, 1990; Druckman and Broome, 1991; Pruitt and Carnevale, 1993.

59. Kramer, Pommerenke, and Newton, 1993.

60. Hegtvedt and Killian, 1999.

61. Novemsky and Schweitzer, 2004.

62. Veitch and Griffith, 1976.

63. Gonzalez, Lerner, Moore, and Babcock, 2004.

64. Kumar, 1997.

65. Allred, 1998; Bies and Tripp, 1998.

66. Allred, Mallozzi, Matsui, and Raia, 1997.

67. Thompson and DeHarpport, 1994.

68. O'Connor and Arnold, 2001.

69. Bless, Bohner, Schwaz, and Strack, 1988.

70. Kumar, 1997.

71. Parrott, 1994.

72. van de Vliert, 1985.

73. Daly, 1991.

74. Barry, 1999.

75. Kopelman, Rosette, and Thompson, 2004.

76. Thompson, Nadler, and Kim, 1999.

77. Mayer, Salovey, and Caruso, 2000.

Chapter 6

1. Fragale, 2006.
2. Alexander, Schul, and Babakus, 1991.
3. Carnevale, Pruitt, and Seilheimer, 1981.
4. Olekalns, Smith, and Walsh, 1996; Weingart, Hyder, and Prietula, 1996.
5. Tutzauer, 1992.
6. Tutzauer, 1992, p. 73.
7. Pinkley, 1995; Pinkley, Neale, and Bennett, 1994.
8. Thompson, Valley, and Kramer, 1995.
9. Novemsky and Schweitzer, 2004.
10. Bies and Shapiro, 1987; Shapiro, 1991.
11. Sitkin and Bies, 1993.
12. Ibid.
13. Brett, Shapiro, and Lytle, 1998.
14. Ibid.
15. Gibbons, Bradac, and Busch, 1992.
16. Simons, 1993.
17. Beebe, 1980; Burgoon, Coker, and Coker, 1986; Kleinke, 1986.
18. Kellerman, Lewis, and Laird, 1989.
19. Ivey and Simek-Downing, 1980.
20. Ibid.
21. Stacks and Burgoon, 1981.
22. Nierenberg and Calero, 1971.
23. Drolet and Morris, 2000, p. 27.
24. Bazerman, Curhan, Moore, and Valley, 2000; Lewicki and Dineen, 2003.
25. Short, Williams, and Christie, 1976.
26. Sproull and Kiesler, 1986.
27. Barry and Fulmer, 2004.
28. Drolet and Morris, 2000.
29. Valley, Moag, and Bazerman, 1998.
30. Ibid.
31. Croson, 1999.
32. Morris, Nadler, Kurtzberg, and Thompson, 2000.
33. Ibid.
34. Nierenberg, 1976.
35. Deep and Sussman, 1993.
36. Rogers, 1957, 1961.
37. These examples are from Gordon, 1977.
38. Rapoport, 1964.
39. Johnson, 1971; Walcott, Hopmann, and King, 1977.
40. McAllister, 1995, p. 25.
41. Butler, 1991; Kimmel, Pruitt, Magenau, Konar-Goldband, and Carnevale, 1980; Lindskold, Bentz, and Walters, 1986; Schlenkler, Helm, and Tedeschi, 1973; Zand, 1972, 1997.

42. Kramer, 1994; Myerson, Weick, and Kramer, 1996.
43. Weber and Murnighan, 2008.
44. Butler, 1995; 1999.
45. Olekalns, Lau, and Smith, 2002.
46. Malhotra, 2003.
47. Butler, 1999.
48. Butler, 1999; Olekalns and Smith, 2001.
49. Olekalns and Smith, 2001.
50. Ibid.
51. Naquin and Paulson, 2003.
52. Song, 2004.
53. See Bottom et al., (2002) Schweitzer et al., (2002).
54. Tomlinson, Lewicki, and Dineen, 2003.
55. Schweitzer, 2004.
56. Ferris, Blass, Douglas, Kolodinsky, and Treadway, 2005, p. 215.
57. Ferris, Blass, Douglas, Kolodinsky, and Treadway, 2005.
58. Tinsley, O'Connor, and Sullivan, 2002.
59. Tinsley and O'Connor, 2004.
60. See Sheppard, Lewicki, and Minton (1992) for one review of justice issues in organizations, and Albin (1993) for a commentary on the role of fairness in negotiation.
61. Benton and Druckman, 1974; Deutsch, 1985.
62. Joseph and Willis, 1963.
63. Greenberg, 1986.
64. Bies and Moag, 1986.
65. Jones and Worchel, 1992.
66. Maxwell, Nye, and Maxwell, 1999, 2003.
67. Pillutla and Murnighan, 1996.
68. Kristensen, 2000.
69. Leung, Tong, and Ho, 2004.
70. Gelfand et at., 2002.
71. Brockner and Siegel, 1996.
72. Sheppard, Lewicki, and Minton, 1992; Skarlicki and Folger, 1997.

Chapter 7

1. "Balsillie bids to buy bankrupt Pheonix Coyotes," *National Post*, 5 May 2009.
2. "Earn Bettman's wrath and he will hunt you down," *The Globe and Mail*, 13 May 2010.
3. "Judge shuts out Balsillie," *The Toronto Star*, June 16, 2009.
4. Cronkhite and Liska, 1976, 1980.
5. Barnard, 1938.
6. Raven, 1993; Raven, Schwartzwald, and Koslowski, 1998.
7. See Charan, 1991; Kaplan, 1984; Krackhardt and Hanson, 1993.
8. Schein, 1988.
9. Watkins, 2002.
10. Ibid.

11. Michener and Suchner, 1971.

12. Fern, Monroe, and Avila, 1986; Freedman and Fraser, 1966; Seligman, Bush, and Kirsch, 1976.

13. Reardon, 1981.

14. Schlenker and Riess, 1979.

15. Jackson and Allen, 1987.

16. Fisher, 1964; Ikle, 1964.

17. Bowers, 1964.

18. Burgoon and King, 1974.

19. Jones and Burgoon, 1975.

20. Burgoon and Stewart, 1975.

21. Conger, 1998.

22. Cialdini, 2001.

23. Bettinghaus, 1966.

24. Clark, 1984; Rosnow and Robinson, 1967.

25. Brock, 1963; Festinger and Maccoby, 1964.

26. Petty and Brock, 1981.

27. Ostermeier, 1967; Swenson, Nash, and Roos, 1984.

28. McCroskey, Jensen, and Valencia, 1973.

29. Chaiken, 1986; Eagly and Chaiken, 1975; Tedeschi, Schlenker, and Bonoma, 1973.

30. Jones, 1964.

31. Roskos-Ewoldsen, Bichsel, and Hoffman, 2002.

32. Eagly and Chaiken, 1975.

33. Cialdini, 2001.

34. O'Keefe, 1990; Oldmeadow, Platow, Foddy, and Anderson, 2003.

35. Milgram, 1974.

36. Cialdini, 2001.

37. Cialdini, 2001, p. 197.

38. Gouldner, 1960.

39. Note that many public-sector bargaining laws prohibit negotiators from even buying a cup of coffee for each other. Negotiators need to be aware of the laws and norms that may have implications for compliance strategies. In addition, there are cross-cultural differences in refusing a gift, and negotiators need to prepare carefully for such instances when they negotiate across borders.

40. Cialdini, 2001, p. 47.

41. Ibid.

42. Freedman and Fraser, 1966.

43. Cialdini, 2001.

44. Fuller and Sheehy-Skeffington, 1974.

45. Cialdini, 2001.

46. Ibid.

47. Ibid.

48. Kipnis, 1976.

49. Pinkley, Neale, and Bennett, 1994.

50. McGuire, 1964.

Chapter 8

1. See "McCain and able? (Harrison and Wallace McCain are bickering over who should succeed them as chief executive of their frozen-food and juice company)." *The Economist*, 17 September 1994; and "French fry tycoon Harrison McCain dead." CBCNews, 19 March 2004.

2. See "Judge blocks Rogers advertisement." *The Globe and Mail*, 24 November 2009.

3. Ury, Brett, and Goldberg, 1988.

4. Lytle, Brett, and Shapiro, 1999.

5. Moore, 1996.

6. Ministry of the Attorney General, "General Information—Ontario Mandatory Mediation Program," http://www.attorneygeneral.jus.gov.on.ca/english/courts/manmed/notice.asp.

7. "Mandatory Mediation," The Encyclopedia of Saskatchewan, http://esask.uregina.ca/entry/mandatory_mediation.html.

8. M. Jerry McHale, "Mediation in Civil and Family Cases in British Columbia," The Canadian Bar Association, http://www.cba.org/bc/bartalk_06_10/06_08/guest_mchale.aspx.

9. Grigsby and Bigoness, 1982.

10. Conlon, Moon, and Ng, 2002.

11. Lewicki and Sheppard, 1985.

12. Conlon, Carnevale, and Murnighan, 1994.

13. Karambayya and Brett, 1989.

14. Karambayya, Brett, and Lytle, 1992.

15. Conlon and Fasalo, 1990.

Chapter 9

1. Green, 1993; Hitt, 1990; Hosmer, 2003.

2. Missner, 1980.

3. Hosmer, 2003.

4. Hosmer, 2003, p. 87.

5. Miller and Ross, 1975.

6. Carr, 1968.

7. Ibid. p. 144.

8. Allhoff, 2003; Koehn, 1997.

9. Kelley and Thibaut, 1969.

10. Rubin and Brown, 1975.

11. Negotiation Point 9.1 on the legality of lying addresses U.S. law. Obviously, legal systems vary from country to country, and so too will legal doctrine regarding deception and fraud in negotiaion.

12. Lewicki, 1983; Lewicki and Robinson, 1998; Lewicki and Spencer, 1990; Lewicki and Stark, 1995.

13. Barry, Fulmer, and Long, 2000; Robinson, Lewicki, and Donahue 2000.

14. O'Connor and Carnevale, 1997.

15. Schweitzer, 1997; Schweitzer and Croson, 1998.

16. Boles, Croson, and Murnighan, 2000.

17. O'Connor and Carnevale, 1997.

18. Sims, 2002.
19. Lewicki and Spencer, 1991.
20. Hegarty and Sims, 1978.
21. McCornack and Levine, 1990.
22. Boles, Croson, and Murnighan, 2000.
23. Examples are drawn from Bok, 1978.
24. Patterson and Kim, 1991; Yankelovich, 1982.
25. Volkema and Fleury, 2002.
26. Tenbrunsel, 1998.
27. Carr, 1968.
28. Bowie, 1993; Koehn, 1997.
29. Hosmer, 2003, p. 89.
30. Schweitzer, 1997; Schweitzer and Croson, 1998.
31. Schweitzer and Croson, 2001.
32. Bazerman and Gillespie, 1999.

Chapter 10

1. Cameron and Tomlin, 2000.
2. British Columbia Provincial Government, Ministry of Aboriginal Relations and Reconciliation, "Frequently Asked Questions," 2010, http://www.gov.bc.ca/arr/treaty/faq.html#first.
3. Midgaard and Underal, 1977, p. 332.
4. Weingart, Bennett, and Brett, 1993.
5. Sebenius, 1983.
6. Bazerman, Mannix, and Thompson, 1988.
7. Weingart, Bennett, and Brett, 1993.
8. Murnighan, 1986.
9. Kim, 1997.
10. Polzer, Mannix, and Neale, 1995, 1998.
11. Touval, 1988.
12. Brett, 1991.
13. Taylor and Brown, 1988; Tyler and Hastie, 1991.
14. Manz, Neck, Mancuso, and Manz, 1997.
15. Brett, 1991.
16. Bazerman, Mannix, and Thompson, 1988.
17. Jehn and Mannix, 2004.
18. Brett, 1991.
19. Brett, 1991; Nemeth, 1986; 1989.
20. Brett, 1991.
21. Schwartz, 1994.

Chapter 11

1. See Hopmann, 1995.
2. Sebenius, 2002a.
3. Foreign Affairs and International Trade Canada, 2010. Posted at: http://www.international.gc.ca/trade-agreements-accords-commerciaux/agr-acc/index.aspx.

4. Brett and Gelfand, 2004.

5. Descriptions of the American negotiation style may be found in Druckman, 1996; Koh, 1996; LePoole, 1989; and McDonald, 1996.

6. See Adler and Graham, 1987; Adler, Graham, and Schwarz, 1987.

7. Phatak and Habib, 1996.

8. Salacuse, 1988.

9. Phatak and Habib, 1996.

10. Salacuse, 1988.

11. See Brouthers and Bamossy, 1997; Derong and Faure, 1995; Pfouts, 1994.

12. Salacuse, 1988.

13. Ibid.

14. Ibid.

15. Graham and Mintu-Wimsat, 1997.

16. Salacuse, 1988; also see Palich, Carini, and Livingstone, 2002; Xing, 1995.

17. Tinsley, 1997; 1998; 2001.

18. Phatak and Habib, 1996, p. 34.

19. Sebenius, 2002a.

20. Phatak and Habib, 1996; also see Lin and Miller, 2003.

21. Yan and Gray, 1994.

22. See Agha and Malley, 2002; Isajiw, 2000; Ross, 2000; Rubinstein, 2003; Stein, 1999; and Zartman, 1997.

23. Hartzell, 1999.

24. Abu-Nimer, 1996; Ohbuchi and Takahashi, 1994; Tinsley, 1998; see Weldon and Jehn, 1995, for a review.

25. Fisher, Ury, and Patton, 1991.

26. Phatak and Habib, 1996.

27. Ibid.

28. Ibid.

29. Ibid.

30. Ibid.

31. See Yan and Gray, 1994.

32. For reviews of this work see Brett, 2001, and Gelfand and Dyer, 2000.

33. See Avruch, 2000.

34. Rubin and Sander, 1991; Sebenius, 2002b; Weiss, 2003.

35. Dialdin, Kopelman, Adair, Brett, Okumura, and Lytle, 1999.

36. Avruch, 2000; Sebenius, 2002b.

37. Rubin and Sander, 1991.

38. Adler, 2002.

39. These are two of four ways that Janosik, 1987, identified that culture has been conceptualized in international negotiation. The other two are culture as learned behaviour and culture in context.

40. Faure, 1999; Sebenius, 2002a.

41. Hofstede, 1980a; 1980b; 1989; 1991.

42. Hofstede labelled career success–quality of life as masculine–feminine, but we have adopted gender-neutral labels for this dimension (see Adler, 2002). Subsequent research by Hofstede and Bond, 1988, suggested that a fifth dimension, labelled

Confucian Dynamism, be added. Confucian Dynamism contains three elements: work ethic, time, and commitment to traditional Confucian values. The dimension has received little attention in the negotiation literature; cf., Chan, 1998.

43. Hofstede, 1989, p. 195.

44. Hofstede, 1980a, p. 46.

45. Hofstede, 1989.

46. Ibid., p. 196.

47. See Schwartz, 1992, 1994; Schwartz and Bilsky, 1990; and Smith and Schwartz, 1997.

48. See Gelfand and Dyer, 2000; Kozan and Ergin, 1999.

49. See Faure, 1999; Pye, 1992.

50. Janosik, 1987.

51. Gelfand and McCusker, 2002.

52. Ibid.

53. Table 11.2 and the discussion that follows are based on the work of Foster, 1992; Hendon and Hendon, 1990; Moran and Stripp, 1991; Salacuse, 1998; and Weiss and Stripp, 1985.

54. See Ohanyan, 1999; Yook and Albert, 1998.

55. Foster, 1992, p. 272.

56. Thompson, 1990b.

57. Salacuse, 1998.

58. See Braganti and Devine, 1992.

59. Foster, 1992.

60. Axtell, 1990, 1991, 1993.

61. For example, see Binnendijk, 1987; Graham and Sano, 1989; Pye, 1992; and Tung, 1991.

62. See Mayfield, Mayfield, Martin, and Herbig, 1997.

63. Foster, 1992.

64. Ibid.

65. Salacuse, 1998.

66. See Kumar, 2004.

67. Salacuse, 1998.

68. Brett, 2001.

69. See Graham, 1993, for a review of these studies.

70. This included comparing the United States with Japan, Graham, 1983, 1984; China, Adler, Brahm, and Graham, 1992; Canada, Adler and Graham, 1987; Adler, Graham, and Schwarz, 1987; Brazil, Graham, 1983; and Mexico, Adler, Graham, and Schwarz, 1987.

71. Brett, Adair, Lempereur, Okumura, Shihkirev, Tinsley, and Lytle, 1998.

72. Dialdin, Kopelman, Adair, Brett, Okumura, and Lytle, 1999.

73. Adler and Graham, 1989.

74. Graham, 1983; Graham, Evenko, and Rajan, 1992; also see Adler, Brahm, and Graham, 1992; Adler, Graham, and Schwarz, 1987.

75. Cai, 1998.

76. Gelfand and Christakopoulou, 1999.

77. Adair, Brett, Lempereur, Okumura, Shikhiriv, Tinsley, and Lytle, 2004.

78. Adair, Kopelman, Gillespie, Brett, and Okumura, 1998.

79. Adair, Okumura, and Brett, 2001.

80. Adair, 2002, 2003; the low-context cultures included in the study were United States, Sweden, Germany and Israel; the high-context cultures were Japan, Hong Kong, Thailand, and Russia; and the mixed-context cultures were U.S.–Japan and U.S.–Hong Kong.

81. Adair, 2003.

82. Rosette, Brett, Barsness, and Lytle, 2004.

83. Gelfand and Dyer, 2000; Morris and Gelfand, 2004.

84. Gelfand and Realo, 1999.

85. Gelfand, Nishii, Holcombe, Dyer, Ohbuchi, and Fukuno, 2001.

86. Gelfand and Christakopoulou, 1999.

87. Gelfand, Higgins, Nishii, Raver, Dominguez, Murakami, Yamaguchi, and Toyama, 2002; note that negotiator definitions of fairness are influenced by what would benefit themselves (see Chapter 5).

88. Wade-Benzoni, Okumura, Brett, Moore, Tenbrunsel, and Bazerman, 2002.

89. Ibid.

90. Zarkada-Fraser and Fraser, 2001.

91. Volkema and Fleury, 2002.

92. Elahee, Kirby, and Nasif, 2002.

93. See Francis, 1991, and Weiss, 1994; for reviews of the over simplicity of this advice.

94. Adachi, 1998.

95. Adler and Graham, 1989; Natlandsmyr and Rognes, 1995.

96. See Drake, 1995; Weldon and Jehn, 1995.

97. Francis, 1991.

98. Rubin and Sander, 1991.

99. Brett, Adair, Lempereur, Okumura, Shihkirev, Tinsley, and Lytle, 1998.

100. Adair, Brett, Lempereur, Okumura, Shihkirev, Tinsley, and Lytle, 2004.

101. Adair, Okumura, and Brett, 2001.

102. Weiss, 1994.

Aaronson, K. (1989). *Selling on the fast track*. New York: Putnam.

Abu-Nimer, M. (1996). Conflict resolution approaches: Western and Middle Eastern lessons and possibilities. *American Journal of Economics and Sociology, 55*, 35–52.

Adachi, Y. (1998). The effects of semantic difference on cross-cultural business negotiation: A Japanese and American case study. *Journal of Language for International Business, 9*, 43–52.

Adair, W. (2002). *Reciprocal information sharing and negotiation outcomes in East/West negotiations*. Working paper. Dispute Resolution Research Center, Northwestern University, Evanston, IL.

Adair, W. (2003). Integrative sequences and outcome in same- and mixed-culture negotiations. *International Journal of Conflict Management* (14) (314), 273–296.

Adair, W., Brett, J., Lempereur, A., Okumura, T., Shihkirev, P., Tinsley, C., & Lytle, A. (2004). Culture and negotiation strategy. *Negotiation Journal, 20*, 87–110.

Adair, W., Kopelman, S., Gillespie, J., Brett, J. M., & Okumura, T. (1998). *Cultural compatibility in the U.S./Israeli negotiations: Implications for joint gains*. DRRC working paper. Evanston, IL: Northwestern University.

Adair, W. L., Okumura, T., & Brett, J. M. (2001). Negotiation behavior when cultures collide: The United States and Japan. *Journal of Applied Psychology, 86*, 371–85.

Adler, N. J. (2002). *International dimensions of organizational behavior* (4th ed.). Cincinnati, OH: South-Western.

Adler, N. J., Brahm, R., & Graham, J. L. (1992). Strategy implementation: A comparison of face-to-face negotiations in the People's Republic of China and the United States. *Strategic Management Journal, 13*, 449–66.

Adler, N. J. & Graham, J. L. (1987). Business negotiations: Canadians are not just like Americans. *Canadian Journal of Administrative Sciences, 4*, 211–38.

Adler, N. J. & Graham, J. L. (1989). Cross-cultural interaction: The international comparison fallacy? *Journal of International Business Studies, 20*, 515–37.

Adler, N. J., Graham, J. L., & Schwarz, T. (1987). Business negotiations in Canada, Mexico, and the United States. *Journal of Business Research, 15*, 411–29.

Adler, R., Rosen, B., & Silverstein, E. (1996) Thrust and parry: The art of tough negotiating. *Training and Development, 50*, 42–48.

Adorno, T. W., Frenkl-Brunswick, E., Levinson, D. J., & Sanford, R. N. (1950). *The authoritarian personality*, New York: HarperCollins.

Agha, H. & Malley, R. (2002). The last negotiation: How to end the Middle East peace process. *Foreign Affairs, 81*, 10–18.

Albin, C. (1993). The role of fairness in negotiation. *Negotiation Journal, 9*, 223–43.

Alexander, J. F., Schul, P. L., & Babakus, E. (1991). Analyzing interpersonal communications in industrial marketing negotiations. *Journal of the Academy of Marketing Science, 19*, 129–39.

Allhoff, F. (2003). Business bluffing reconsidered. *Journal of Business Ethics, 45*, 283–89.

Allred, K. G. (1999). Anger and retaliation: Toward an understanding of impassioned conflict in organizations. In R. J. Bies, R. J. Lewicki, & B. H. Sheppard (Eds.), *Research on negotiation in organizations* (Vol. 7), 27–58, Greenwich, CN: JAI Press.

Allred, K. G., Mallozzi, J. S., Matsui, F., & Raia, C. P. (1997). The influence of anger and compassion on negotiation performance. *Organizational Behavior and Human Decision Processes, 70*, 175–87.

Arunachalam, V. & Dilla, W. N. (1995). Judgment accuracy and outcomes in negotiation: A causal modeling analysis of decision-aiding effects. *Organizational Behavior and Human Decision Processes, 61*, 289–304.

Asherman, I. G. & Asherman, S. V. (1990). *The negotiation sourcebook*. Amherst, MA: Human Resource Development Press.

Avruch, K. (2000). Culture and negotiation pedagogy. *Negotiation Journal, 16*, 339–46.

Axtell, R. E. (1990). *Do's and taboos of hosting international visitors*. New York: John Wiley and Sons.

Axtell, R. E. (1991). Gestures: *The do's and taboos of body language around the world*. New York: John Wiley and Sons.

Axtell, R. E. (1993). *Do's and taboos around the world* (3rd ed.). New York: John Wiley and Sons.

Babcock, L. & Loewenstein, G. (1997). Explaining bargaining impasse: The role of self-serving biases. *Journal of Economic Perspectives, 11*(1) 109–26.

Babcock, L., Wang, X., & Loewenstein, G. (1996). Choosing the wrong pond: Social comparisons in negotiations that reflect a self-serving bias. *Quarterly Journal of Economics, 111*, 1–19.

Ball, S. B., Bazerman, M. H., & Carroll, J. S. (1991). An evaluation of learning in the bilateral winner's curse. *Organizational Behavior and Human Decision Processes, 48*, 1–22.

Baranowski, T. A. & Summers, D. A. (1972). Perceptions of response alternatives in a prisoner's dilemma game. *Journal of Personality and Social Psychology, 21*, 35–40.

Barnard, C. (1938). *The functions of the executive*. Cambridge, MA: Harvard University Press.

Baron, R. A. (1990). Environmentally induced positive affect: Its impact on self efficacy and task performance, negotiation and conflict. *Journal of Applied Social Psychology, 20*, 368–84.

Barry, B. (1999). The tactical use of emotion in negotiation. In R. Bies, R. J. Lewicki, & B. H. Sheppard (Eds.), *Research on negotiation in organizations* (Vol. 7, pp. 93–121), Stamford, CT: JAI Press.

Barry, B. & Fulmer, I. S. (2004). The medium and the message: The adaptive use of communication media in dyadic influence. *Academy of Management Review, 2*, 272–92.

Barry, B., Fulmer, I. S., & Long, A. (2000). Ethically marginal bargaining tactics: Sanction, efficacy, and performance. Presented at the annual meeting of the Academy of Management, Toronto.

Barry, B., Fulmer, I. S., & Van Kleef, G. A. (2004). I laughed, I cried, I settled: The role of emotion in negotiation. In M. Gelfand and J. Brett (Eds.), *Culture and negotiation: Integrative approaches to theory and research*. Palo Alto, CA: Stanford University Press.

Barry, B. & Oliver, R. L. (1996). Affect in dyadic negotiation: A model and propositions. *Organizational Behavior and Human Decision Processes, 67*, 127–43.

Bateson, G. (1972). *Steps to an ecology of mind*. New York: Ballantine Books.

Bazerman, M. (1998). *Judgment in managerial decision making* (4th ed.). New York: John Wiley and Sons.

Bazerman, M. H. & Carroll, J. S. (1987). Negotiator cognition. In B. M. Staw & L. L. Cummings. *Research in organizational behavior* (Vol. 9, pp. 247–88), Greenwich, CT: JAI Press.

Bazerman, M. H., Curhan, J. R., Moore, D. A., & Valley, K. L. (2000). Negotiation. *Annual Review of Psychology, 51*, 279–314.

Bazerman, M. H. & Gillespie, J. J. (1999). Betting on the future: The virtues of contingent contracts. *Harvard Business Review*, Sept–Oct, 155–60.

Bazerman, M. H., Magliozzi, T., & Neale, M. A. (1985). Integrative bargaining in a competitive market. *Organizational Behavior and Human Decision Processes, 35*, 294–313.

Bazerman, M. H., Mannix, E. A., & Thompson, L. L. (1988). Groups as mixed motive negotiations. In E. J. Lawler & B. Markovsky (Eds.), *Advances in group processes* (Vol. 5, pp. 195–216). Greenwich, CT: JAI Press.

Bazerman, M. H., Moore, D. A., & Gillespie, J. J. (1999). The human mind as a barrier to wiser environmental agreements. *American Behavioral Scientist, 42*, 1277–1300.

Bazerman, M. H. & Neale, M. A. (1992). *Negotiating rationally.* New York: Free Press.

Bazerman, M. H. & Samuelson, W. F. (1983). I won the auction but don't want the prize. *Journal of Conflict Resolution, 27*, 618–34.

Beebe, S. A. (1980). Effects of eye contact, posture, and vocal inflection upon credibility and comprehension. *Australian SCAN: Journal of Human Communication, 7–8*, 57–70.

Benton, A. A. & Druckman, D. (1974). Constituent's bargaining orientation and intergroup negotiations. *Journal of Applied Social Psychology, 4*, 141–50.

Berkowitz, L. (1989). The frustration–aggression hypothesis: An examination and reformulation. *Psychological Bulletin, 106*, 59–73.

Berton, P. (1977). *The Dionne Years: A Thirties Melodrama.* Toronto: McLelland & Stewart.

Bettinghaus, E. P. (1966). *Message preparation: The nature of proof.* Indianapolis: Bobbs-Merrill.

Bies, R. & Moag, J. (1986). Interactional justice: Communication criteria of fairness. In R. J. Lewicki, B. H. Sheppard, and M. H. Bazerman (Eds.), *Research on negotiation in organizations* (Vol. 1, pp. 43–55). Greenwich, CT: JAI Press.

Bies, R. & Shapiro, D. (1987). Interactional fairness judgments: The influence of causal accounts. *Social Justice Research, 1*, 199–218.

Bies, R. & Tripp, T. (1998). Revenge in organizations: The good, the bad and the ugly. In R. W. Griffin, A. O'Leary-Kelly, & J. Collins (Eds.), *Dysfunctional behavior in organizations*, Vol. 1: *Violent behavior in organizations*, 49–68, Greenwich, CT: JAI Press.

Binnendijk, H. (1987). *National negotiating styles.* Washington, DC: Foreign Service Institute, Department of State.

Bless, H., Bohner, G., Schwarz, N., & Strack, F. (1988). Happy and mindless: Moods and the processing of persuasive communication. Unpublished manuscript, Mannheim, GR.

Bok, S. (1978). *Lying: Moral choice in public and private life.* New York: Pantheon.

Boles, T. L., Croson, R. T. A., & Murnighan, J. K. (2000). Deception and retribution in repeated ultimatum bargaining. *Organizational Behavior and Human Decision Processes, 83*, 235–59.

Bottom, W. P. (1998). Negotiator risk: Sources of uncertainty and the impact of reference points on negotiated agreements. *Organizational Behavior And Human Decision Processes, 76*, 89–112.

Bottom, W. P. & Paese, P. W. (1999). Judgment accuracy and the asymmetric cost of errors in distributive bargaining. *Group Decision and Negotiation, 8*, 349–64.

Bottom, W. P., Gibson, K., Daniels, S., & Murnighan, J. K. (2002) When talk is not cheap: Substantive penance and expressions of intent in the reestablishment of cooperation. *Organization Science, 13*, 497–513.

Bowers, J. W. (1964). Some correlates of language intensity. *Quarterly Journal of Speech, 50*, 415–20.

Bowie, N. (1993). Does it pay to bluff in business? In T. L. Beauchamp & N. E. Bowie (Eds.), *Ethical theory and business* (pp. 449–54). Englewood Cliffs, NJ: Prentice Hall.

Braganti, N. L. & Devine, E. (1992). *European customs and manners: How to make friends and do business in Europe* (rev. ed.). New York: Meadowbrook Press.

Brett, J. (1991). Negotiating group decisions. *Negotiation Journal, 7*, 291–310.

Brett, J., Adair, W., Lempereur, A., Okumura, T., Shihkirev, P., Tinsley, C., & Lytle, A. (1998). Culture and joint gains in negotiation. *Negotiation Journal, 14* (1), 61–86.

Brett, J. & Gelfand, M. (2004). *A cultural analysis of the underlying assumptions of negotiation theory.* Unpublished paper. Dispute Resolution Research Center, Northwestern University, Evanston, IL.

Brett, J. M. (2001). *Negotiating globally.* San Francisco: Jossey-Bass.

Brett, J. M., Shapiro, D. L., & Lytle, A. L. (1998). Breaking the bonds of reciprocity in negotiation. *Academy of Management Journal, 41,* 410–24.

Brock, T. C. (1963). Effects of prior dishonesty on post-decision dissonance. *Journal of Abnormal and Social Psychology, 66,* 325–31.

Brockner, J. (1992). The escalation of commitment to a failing course of action: Toward theoretical progress. *Academy of Management Review, 17,* 39–61.

Brockner, J. & Siegel, P. (1996). Understanding the interaction between procedural and distributive justice: The role of trust. In R. Kramer & T. Tyler (Eds.), *Trust in organizations* (pp. 390–413). Thousand Oaks, CA: Sage.

Brodt, S. E. (1994). "Inside information" and negotiator decision behavior. *Organizational Behavior and Human Decision Processes, 58,* 172–202.

Brodt, S. E. & Tuchinsky, M. (2000). Working together but in opposition: An examination of the "Good-Cop/Bad-Cop" negotiating team tactic. *Organizational Behavior and Human Decision Processes, 81* (2), 155–77.

Brooks, E. & Odiorne, G. S. (1984). *Managing by negotiations.* New York: Van Nostrand.

Brouthers, K. D. & Bamossy, G. J. (1997). The role of key stakeholders in international joint venture negotiations: Case studies from Eastern Europe. *Journal of International Business Studies, 28,* 285–308.

Bruner, J. S. & Tagiuri, R. (1954). The perception of people. In G. Lindzey (Ed.), *The handbook of social psychology* (Vol. 2, pp. 634–54). Reading, MA: Addison-Wesley.

Burgoon, J. K., Coker, D. A., & Coker, R. A. (1986). Communication of gaze behavior: A test of two contrasting explanations. *Human Communication Research, 12,* 495–524.

Burgoon, M. & King, L. B. (1974). The mediation of resistance to persuasion strategies by language variables and active-passive participation. *Human Communication Research, 1,* 30–41.

Burgoon, M. & Stewart, D. (1975). Empirical investigations of language: The effects of sex of source, receiver, and language intensity on attitude change. *Human Communication Research, 1,* 244–48.

Burnstein, D. (1995). *Negotiator pro.* Beacon Expert Systems, 35 Gardner Road, Brookline, MA.

Butler, J. (1995). Behaviors, trust and goal achievement in a win-win negotiation role play. *Group & Organization Management, 20,* 486–501.

Butler, J. (1999) Trust, expectations, information sharing, climate of trust and negotiation effectiveness and efficiency. *Group & Organization Management, 24*(2), 217–38.

Butler, J. K. (1991). Toward understanding and measuring conditions of trust: Evolution of a conditions of trust inventory. *Journal of Management, 17,* 643–63.

Butler, J. K., Jr. (1996). Two integrative win-win negotiating strategies. *Simulation and Gaming, 27,* 387–92.

Cacioppo, J. T. & Petty, R. E. (1985). Central and peripheral routes to persuasion: The role of message repetition. In L. F. Alwitt & A. A. Mitchell (Eds.), *Psychological processes and advertising effects: Theory, research, and application* (pp. 91–111). Hillsdale, NJ: Lawrence Erlbaum.

Cai, D. A. (1998). Culture, plans, and the pursuit of negotiation goals. *Journal of Asian Pacific Communication, 8,* 103–23.

Cameron, M. A. & Tomlin, B. W. (2000). The making of NAFTA: How the deal was done. Cornell University Press: Ithaca, NY.

Carnevale, P. J. & Isen, A. M. (1986). The influence of positive affect and visual access on the discovery of integrative solutions in bilateral negotiation. *Organizational Behavior and Human Decision Processes, 37,* 1–13.

Carnevale, P. J. D. & Pruitt, D. G. (1992). Negotiation and mediation. In M. Rosenberg & L. Porter (Eds.), *Annual review of psychology* (Vol. 43, pp. 531–82). Palo Alto, CA: Annual Reviews, Inc.

Carnevale, P. J. D. Pruitt, D. G., & Seilheimer, S. D. (1981). Looking and competing: Accountability and visual access in integrative bargaining. *Journal of Personality and Social Psychology, 40,* 111–20.

Carr, A. Z. (1968, January–February). Is business bluffing ethical? *Harvard Business Review, 46,* 143–53.

Carroll, J., Bazerman, M., & Maury, R. (1988). Negotiator cognitions: A descriptive approach to negotiators' understanding of their opponents. *Organizational Behavior and Human Decision Processes, 41,* 352–70.

Carroll, J., Delquie, P., Halpern, J., & Bazerman, M. (1990). *Improving negotiators' cognitive processes.* Working paper. Massachusetts Institute of Technology, Cambridge, MA.

Carver, C. S. & Scheir, M. E. (1990). Origins and foundations of positive and negative affect: A control process view. *Psychological Review, 97,* 19–35.

Cellich, C. (1997). Closing your business negotiations. *International Trade Forum, 1,* 14–17.

Chaiken, S. (1986). Physical appearance and social influence. In C. P. Herman, M. P. Zanna, & E. T. Higgins (Eds.), *Physical appearance, stigma, and social behavior: The Ontario symposium* (Vol. 3, pp. 143–77). Hillsdale, NJ: Lawrence Erlbaum.

Chaiken, S. (1987). The heuristic model of persuasion. In M. Zanna, J. Olson & C. Herman (Eds.), *Social influence: The Ontario symposium* (Vol. 5, pp. 3–39). Hillsdale, NJ: Lawrence Erlbaum.

Chan, C. W. (1998). Transfer pricing negotiation outcomes and the impact of negotiator mixed-motives and culture: Empirical evidence from the U.S. and Australia. *Management Accounting Research, 9,* 139–61.

Charan, R. (1991). How networks reshape organizations—for results. *Harvard Business Review, 69* (5), 104–15.

Chertkoff, J. M. & Conley, M. (1967). Opening offer and frequency of concessions as bargaining strategies. *Journal of Personality and Social Psychology, 7,* 181–85.

Cialdini, R. B. & Goldstein, N. J. (2004). Social influence: Compliance and conformity. *Annual Review of Psychology, 55,* 591–621.

Cialdini, R. B. (2001). *Influence: Science and practice* (4th ed.). Boston: Allyn and Bacon.

Clark, R. A. (1984). *Persuasive messages.* New York: Harper & Row.

Clyman, D. R. & Tripp, T. M. (2000). Discrepant values and measures of negotiator performance. *Group Decision and Negotiation, 9,* 251–74.

Cohen, H. (1980). *You can negotiate anything.* Secaucus, NJ: Lyle Stuart.

Cohen, W. H. (2003). The importance of expectations on negotiation results. *European Business Review, 15* (2), 87–93.

Coleman, P. (1997). Refining ripeness: A social-psychological perspective. *Peace and Conflict: Journal of Peace Psychology, 3,* 81–103.

Coleman, P. (2000) Power and Conflict. In M. Deutsch & P. Coleman (Eds.), *Handbook of conflict resolution.* San Francisco: Jossey-Bass.

Conger, J. A. (1998). The necessary art of persuasion. *Harvard Business Review, 76* (3), 84–95.

Conlon, D. E., Carnevale, P. J. D., & Murnighan, K. (1994). Intravention: Third-party intervention with clout. *Organizational Behavior and Human Decision Processes, 57,* 387–410.

Conlon, D. E. & Fasolo, P. M. (1990). Influence of speed of third-party intervention and outcome on negotiator and constituent fairness judgments. *Academy of Management Journal, 33,* 833–846.

Conlon, D. E., Moon, H., & Ng, K. Y. (2002). Putting the cart before the horse: The benefits of arbitrating before mediating. *Journal of Applied Psychology, 87,* 978–984.

Cooper, W. (1981). Ubiquitous halo. *Psychological Bulletin, 90,* 218–44.

Coser, L. (1956). *The functions of social conflict.* New York: Free Press.

Cronkhite, G. & Liska, J. (1976). A critique of factor analytic approaches to the study of credibility. *Communication Monographs, 32,* 91–107.

Cronkhite, G. & Liska, J. (1980). The judgment of communicant acceptability. In M. E. Roloff & G. R. Miller (Eds.), *Persuasion: New directions in theory and research* (pp. 101–39). Beverly Hills, CA: Sage.

Croson, R. T. A. (1999). Look at me when you say that: An electronic negotiation simulation. *Simulation & Gaming, 30,* 23–37.

Crumbaugh, C. M. & Evans, G. W. (1967). Presentation format, other persons' strategies and cooperative behavior in the prisoner's dilemma. *Psychological Reports, 20,* 895–902.

Daly, J. (1991). The effects of anger on negotiations over mergers and acquisitions. *Negotiation Journal, 7,* 31–39.

de Dreu, C. K. W. (2003). Time pressure and closing of the mind in negotiation. *Organizational Behavior and Human Decision Processes, 91,* 280–95.

de Dreu, C. K. W., Carnevale, P. J. D., Emans, B. J. M., & van de Vliert, E. (1994). Effects of gain-loss frames in negotiation: Loss aversion, mismatching, and frame adoption. *Organizational Behavior and Human Decision Processes, 60,* 90–107.

de Dreu, C. K. W., Giebels, E., & van de Vliert, E. (1998). Social motives and trust in integrative negotiation: The disruptive effects of punitive capability. *Journal of Applied Psychology, 83,* 408–22.

de Dreu, C. K. W., Nauta, A., & van de Vliert, E. (1995). Self-serving evaluations of conflict behavior and escalation of the dispute. *Journal of Applied Social Psychology, 25,* 2049–66.

de Dreu, C. K. W. & van Lange, P. A. M. (1995). The impact of social value orientation on negotiator cognition and behavior. *Personality and Social Psychology Bulletin, 21,* 1178–88.

Deep, S. & Sussman, L. (1993). *What to ask when you don't know what to say: 555 powerful questions to use for getting your way at work.* Englewood Cliffs, NJ: Prentice Hall.

Derong, C. & Faure, G. O. (1995). When Chinese companies negotiate with their government. *Organization Studies, 16,* 27–54.

Deutsch, M. (1958). Trust and suspicion. *Journal of Conflict Resolution, 2,* 265–79.

Deutsch, M. (1962). Cooperation and trust: Some theoretical notes. In M. R. Jones (Ed.), *Nebraska symposium on motivation* (pp. 275–318). Lincoln, NE: University of Nebraska Press.

Deutsch, M. (1973). *The resolution of conflict.* New Haven, CT: Yale University Press.

Deutsch, M. (1985). *Distributive justice: A social-psychological perspective.* New Haven, CT: Yale University Press.

Deutsch, M. & Coleman, P. (2000). *The handbook of conflict resolution.* San Francisco: Jossey-Bass.

Devine, P. G. (1989). Stereotypes and prejudice: Their automatic and controlled components. *Journal of Personality and Social Psychology, 56,* 5–18.

Dialdin, D., Kopelman, S., Adair, W., Brett, J. M., Okumura, T., & Lytle, A. (1999). *The distributive outcomes of cross-cultural negotiations.* DRRC working paper. Evanston, IL: Northwestern University.

Diekmann, K. A., Tenbrunsel, A. E., Shah, P. P., Schroth, H. A., & Bazerman, M. H. (1996). The descriptive and prescriptive use of previous purchase price in negotiations. *Organizational Behavior and Human Decision Processes, 66,* 179–91.

Donohue, W. A. (1981). Analyzing negotiation tactics: Development of a negotiation interact system. *Human Communication Research, 7*, 273–87.

Donohue, W. A. & Roberto, A. J. (1996). An empirical examination of three models of integrative and distributive bargaining. *International Journal of Conflict Management, 7*, 209–99.

Douglas, A. (1962). *Industrial peacemaking.* New York: Columbia University Press.

Drake, L. E. (1995). Negotiation styles in intercultural communication. *International Journal of Conflict Management, 6*, 72–90.

Drolet, A. L. & Morris, M. W. (2000). Rapport in conflict resolution: Accounting for how face-to-face contact fosters mutual cooperation in mixed-motive conflicts. *Journal of Experimental Social Psychology, 36*, 26–50.

Druckman, D. (1996). Is there a U.S. negotiating style? *International Negotiation, 1*, 327–34.

Druckman, D. & Broome, B. (1991). Value difference and conflict resolution: Familiarity or liking? *Journal of Conflict Resolution, 35* (4), 571–93.

Eagly, A. H. & Chaiken, S. (1975). An attribution analysis of the effect of communicator characteristics on opinion change: The case of communicator attractiveness. *Journal of Personality and Social Psychology, 32*, 136–44.

Elahee, M. N., Kirby, S. L., & Nasif, E. (2002). National culture, trust, and perceptions about ethical behavior in intra- and cross-cultural negotiations: An analysis of NAFTA countries. *Thunderbird International Business Review, 44*, 799–818.

Eyuboglu, N. & Buja, A. (1993). Dynamics of channel negotiations: Contention and reciprocity. *Psychology & Marketing, 10*, 47–65.

Fassina, N. E. & Whyte, G. (unpublished manuscript). "Quite frankly this is an insult": The effects of strategic demurral in negotiations.

Faure, G. O. (1999). The cultural dimension of negotiation: The Chinese case. *Group Decision and Negotiation, 8*, 187–215.

Felstiner, W. L. F., Abel, R. L., & Sarat, A. (1980–81). The emergence and transformation of disputes: Naming, blaming, and claiming. *Law and Society Review, 15*, 631–54.

Fern, E. F., Monroe, K. B., & Avila, R. A. (1986). Effectiveness of multiple request strategies: A synthesis of research results. *Journal of Marketing Research, 23*, 144–52.

Ferris, G. R., Blas, F. R., Douglas, C., Kolodinsky, R. W., & Treadway, D. C. (2005) Personal reputation in organizations. In J. Greenberg (Ed.), *Organizational behavior: The state of the science.* Mahwah, NJ: Lawrence Erlbaum.

Festinger, L. A. & Maccoby, N. (1964). On resistance to persuasive communication. *Journal of Abnormal and Social Psychology, 68*, 359–66.

Filley, A. C. (1975). *Interpersonal conflict resolution.* Glenview, IL: Scott Foresman.

Fisher, R. (1964). Fractionating conflict. In R. Fisher (Ed.), *International conflict and behavioral science: The Craigville papers.* New York: Basic Books.

Fisher, R. & Ertel, D. (1995). *Getting ready to negotiate: The getting to yes workbook.* New York: Penguin.

Fisher, R., Ury, W., & Patton, B. (1991). *Getting to yes: Negotiating agreement without giving in* (2nd ed.). New York: Penguin.

Follett, M. P. (1940). *Dynamic administration: The collected papers of Mary Parker Follett.* H. C. Metcalf & L. Urwick (Eds.). New York: Harper & Brothers.

Follett, M. P. (1942). Constructive conflict. In H. C. Metcalf & L. Urwick (Eds.), *Dynamic administration: The collected papers of Mary Parker Follett* (pp. 30–49). New York: Harper & Brothers.

Foreman, P. & Murnighan, J. K. (1996). Learning to avoid the winner's curse. *Organizational Behavior and Human Decision Processes, 67,* 170–80.

Forgas, J. P. (1992). Affect in social judgments and decisions: A multiprocess model. *Advances in Experimental Social Psychology, 25,* 227–75.

Forgas, J. P. & Fiedler, K. (1996). Us and them: Mood effects on intergroup discrimination. *Journal of Personality and Social Psychology, 70,* 28–40.

Foster, D. A. (1992). *Bargaining across borders: How to negotiate business successfully anywhere in the world.* New York: McGraw-Hill.

Fragale, A.R. (2006). The power of powerless speech: The effects of speech style and task interdependence on status conferral. *Organizational Behavior and Human Decision Processes,* 101, 243–61.

Francis, J. N. P. (1991). When in Rome? The effects of cultural adaptation on intercultural business negotiations. *Journal of International Business Studies, 22,* 403–28.

Freedman, J. L. & Fraser, S. C. (1966). Compliance without pressure: The foot in the door technique. *Journal of Personality and Social Psychology, 4,* 195–202.

French, J. R. P. & Raven, B. (1959). The bases of social power. In D. Cartwright (Ed.), *Studies in social power.* Ann Arbor, MI: Institute for Social Research.

Froman, L. A. & Cohen, M. D. (1970). Compromise and logrolling: Comparing the efficiency of two bargaining processes. *Behavioral Sciences, 15,* 180–83.

Frost, P. (1987). Power, politics and influence. In F. M. Jablin, *Handbook of organizational communication,* (pp. 403–548). Newbury Park, CA: Sage.

Fry, W. R., Firestone, I. J., & Williams, D. (1979, April). Bargaining process in mixed-singles dyads: Loving and losing. Paper presented at the annual meeting of the Eastern Psychological Association, Philadelphia, PA.

Fuller, R. G. C. & Sheehy-Skeffington, A. (1974). Effects of group laughter on responses to humorous materials: A replication and extension. *Psychological Reports, 35,* 531–34.

Galinsky, A. D. & Mussweiler, T. (2001). First offers as anchors: The role of perspective-taking and negotiator focus. *Journal of Personality and Social Psychology, 81* (4), 657–69.

Galinsky, A. D., Mussweiler, T., & Medvec, V. H. (2002). Disconnecting outcomes and evaluations: The role of negotiator focus. *Journal of Personality and Social Psychology, 83* (5), 1131–40.

Galinsky, A. D., Seiden, V. L., Kim, P. H., & Medvec, V. H. (2002). The dissatisfaction of having your first offer accepted: The role of counterfactual thinking in negotiations. *Personality and Social Psychology Bulletin, 28* (2), 271–83.

Gelfand, M. & McCusker, C. (2002). Metaphor and the cultural construction of negotiation: A paradigm for theory and practice. In M. Gannon & K. L. Newman (Eds.), *Handbook of cross-cultural management.* New York: Blackwell.

Gelfand, M., Higgins, M., Nishii, L. H., Raver, J. L., Dominguez, A., Murakami, F., Yamaguchi, S., & Toyama, M. (2002). Culture and egocentric perceptions of fairness in conflict and negotiation. *Journal of Applied Psychology, 87* (5), 833–45.

Gelfand, M. J., Nishii, L. H., Holcombe, K. M., Dyer, N., Ohbuchi, K., & Fukuno, M. (2001). Cultural influences on cognitive representations of conflict: Interpretations of conflict episodes in the United States and Japan. *Journal of Applied Psychology, 86,* 1059–74.

Gelfand, M. J. & Christakopoulou, S. (1999). Culture and negotiator cognition: Judgment accuracy and negotiation processes in individualistic and collectivistic cultures. *Organizational Behavior and Human Decision Processes, 79,* 248–69.

Gelfand, M. J. & Dyer, N. (2000). A cultural perspective on negotiation: Progress, pitfalls, and prospects. *Applied Psychology: An International Review, 49,* 62–99.

Gelfand, M. J. & Realo, A. (1999). Individualism—collectivism and accountability in intergroup negotiations. *Journal of Applied Psychology, 84*, 721–36.

Gentner, J., Loewenstein, J., & Thompson, L. (2003). Learning and transfer: A general role for analogical encoding. *Journal of Educational Psychology, 95*, 393–408.

Ghosh, D. (1996). Nonstrategic delay in bargaining: An experimental investigation. *Organizational Behavior and Human Decision Processes, 67*, 312–25.

Gibb, J. (1961). Defensive communication. *Journal of Communication, 3*, 141–48.

Gibbons, P., Bradac, J. J., & Busch, J. D. (1992). The role of language in negotiations: Threats and promises. In L. Putnam & M. Roloff (Eds.), *Communication and negotiation* (pp. 156–75). Newbury Park, CA: Sage.

Gillespie, J. J. & Bazerman, M. H. (1998, April). Pre-settlement settlement (PreSS): A simple technique for initiating complex negotiations. *Negotiation Journal, 14*, 149–59.

Gillespie, J. J. & Bazerman, M. H. (1997). Parasitic integration: Win-win agreements containing losers. *Negotiation Journal, 13*, 271–82.

Girard, J. (1989). *How to close every sale.* New York: Warner Books.

Goffman, E. (1969). *Strategic interaction.* Philadelphia, PA: University of Philadelphia Press.

Goffman, E. (1974). *Frame analysis.* New York: Harper & Row.

Gonzalez, R. M., Lerner, J. S., Moore, D. A., & Babcock, L. C. (2004). *Mad, mean, and mistaken: The effects of anger on strategic social perception and behavior.* Paper presented at the annual meeting of the International Association for Conflict Management, Pittsburgh.

Gordon, T. (1977). *Leader effectiveness training.* New York: Wyden Books.

Gouldner, A. W. (1960). The norm of reciprocity: A preliminary statement. *American Sociological Review, 25*, 161–78.

Graham, J. L. (1983). Brazilian, Japanese, and American business negotiations. *Journal of International Business Studies, 14*, 47–61.

Graham, J. L. (1984). A comparison of Japanese and American business negotiations. *International Journal of Research in Marketing, 1*, 50–68.

Graham, J. L. (1993). The Japanese negotiation style: Characteristics of a distinct approach. *Negotiation Journal, 9*, 123–40.

Graham, J. L., Evenko, L. L., & Rajan, M. N. (1992). An empirical comparison of Soviet and American business negotiations. *Journal of International Business Studies, 23*, 387–418.

Graham, J. L. & Mintu-Wimsat, A. (1997). Culture's influence on business negotiations in four countries. *Group Decision and Negotiation, 6*, 483–502.

Graham, J. L. & Sano, Y. (1989). *Smart bargaining.* New York: Harper Business.

Gray, B. (1994). The gender-based foundation of negotiation theory. In B. H. Sheppard, R. J. Lewicki, & R. J. Bies (Eds.), *Research in negotiation in organizations* (Vol. 4, pp. 3–36). Greenwich, CT: JAI Press.

Green, R. M. (1993). *The ethical manager.* New York: Macmillan.

Greenberg, J. (1986). Organizational performance appraisal procedures: What makes them fair? In R. J. Lewicki, B. H. Sheppard, & M. H. Bazerman (Eds.), *Research on negotiation in organizations* (Vol. 1, pp. 25–42). Greenwich, CT: JAI Press.

Greenhalgh, L. (1986). Managing conflict. *Sloan Management Review, 27*, 45–51.

Greenhalgh, L. (2001). *Managing strategic relationships:* The key to business success. New York: Free Press.

Greenhalgh, L. & Chapman, D. (1996). Relationships between disputants: Analysis of their characteristics and impact. In S. Gleason (Ed.), *Frontiers in dispute resolution and human resources* (pp. 203–28). East Lansing, MI: Michigan State University Press.

Greenhalgh, L. & Gilkey, R. W. (1993). The effect of relationship orientation on negotiators cognitions and tactics. *Group Decision and Negotiation, 2*, 167–86.

Greenhalgh, L. & Kramer, R. M. (1990). Strategic choice in conflicts: The importance of relationships. In K. Zald (Ed.), *Organizations and nation states: New perspectives on conflict and cooperation* (pp. 181–220). San Francisco: Jossey-Bass.

Grigsby, D. W. & Bigoness, W. J. (1982). Effects of mediation and alternative forms of arbitration on bargaining behavior: A laboratory study. *Journal of Applied Psychology, 67,* 549–554.

Gruder, C. L. & Duslak, R. J. (1973). Elicitation of cooperation by retaliatory and nonretaliatory strategies in a mixed motive game. *Journal of Conflict Resolution, 17,* 162–174.

Harinck, F., de Dreu, C. K. W., & Van Vianen, A. E. M. (2000). The impact of conflict issues on fixed-pie perceptions, problem solving, and integrative outcomes in negotiation. *Organizational Behavior and Human Decision Processes, 81,* 329–58.

Hartzell, C. A. (1999). Explaining the stability of negotiated settlements to intrastate wars. *Journal of Conflict Resolution, 43,* 3–22.

Hegarty, W. & Sims, H. P. (1978). Some determinants of unethical decision behavior: An experiment. *Journal of Applied Psychology, 63,* 451–57.

Hegtved, K. A. & Killian, C. (1999). Fairness and emotions: Reactions to the process and outcomes of negotiations. *Social Forces, 78,* 269–303.

Heider, F. (1958). *The psychology of interpersonal relations.* New York: John Wiley and Sons.

Hendon, D. W. & Hendon, R. A. (1990). *World-class negotiating: Dealmaking in the global marketplace.* New York: John Wiley and Sons.

Hendon, D. W., Roy, M. H., & Ahmed, Z. U. (2003) Negotiation concession patters: A multicountry, multiperiod study. *American Business Review, 21,* 75–83.

Higgins, E. T. (1987). Self discrepancy theory: A theory relating self and affect. *Psychological Review, 94,* 319–40.

Hilty, J. A. & Carnevale, P. J. (1993). Black-hat/white-hat strategy in bilateral negotiation. *Organizational Behavior and Human Decision Processes, 55,* 444–69.

Hinton, B. L., Hamner, W. C., & Pohlan, N. F. (1974). Influence and award of magnitude, opening bid and concession rate on profit earned in a managerial negotiating game. *Behavioral Science, 19,* 197–203.

Hitt, W. (1990). *Ethics and leadership: Putting theory into practice.* Columbus, OH: Battelle Press.

Hocker, J. L. & Wilmot, W. W. (1985). *Interpersonal conflict* (2nd ed.). Dubuque, IA: Wm. C. Brown.

Hofstede, G. (1980a). Motivation, leadership, and organization: Do American theories apply abroad? *Organizational Dynamics, 9,* 42–63.

Hofstede, G. (1980b). *Culture's consequences: International differences in work related values.* Beverly Hills, CA: Sage.

Hofstede, G. (1989). Cultural predictors of national negotiation styles. In. F. Mautner-Markhof (Ed.), *Processes of international negotiations* (pp. 193–201). Boulder, CO: Westview Press.

Hofstede, G. (1991). *Culture and organizations: Software of the mind.* London, UK: McGraw-Hill.

Hofstede, G. & Bond, M. H. (1988). Confucius and economic growth: New trends in culture's consequences. *Organizational Dynamics, 16,* 4–21.

Homans, G. C. (1961). *Social behavior: Its elementary forms.* New York: Harcourt, Brace & World Co.

Hopmann, P. T. (1995). Two paradigms of negotiation: Bargaining and problem solving. *Annals of the American Academy, 542,* 24–47.

Ibarra, H. & Andrews, S. (1993) Power, social influence and sense making: Effects of network centrality and proximity on employee perceptions. *Administrative Science Quarterly, 38,* 277–303.

Ikle, F. C. (1964). *How nations negotiate.* New York: Harper & Row.

Isajiw, W. W. (2000). Approaches to ethnic conflict resolution: paradigms and principles. *International Journal of Intercultural Relations, 24,* 105–24.

Isen, A. M. & Baron, R. A. (1991). Positive affect as a factor in organizational behavior. In B. M. Staw & L. L. Cummings (Eds.), *Research in organizational behavior* (Vol. 13, pp. 1–53). Greenwich, CT: JAI Press.

Ivey, A. E. & Simek-Downing, L. (1980). *Counseling and psychotherapy.* Englewood Cliffs, NJ: Prentice Hall.

Jackson, S. & Allen, M. (1987). Meta-analysis of the effectiveness of one-sided and two-sided argumentation. Paper presented at the annual meeting of the International Communication Association, Montreal, Quebec, Canada.

Jacobs, A. T. (1951). Some significant factors influencing the range of indeterminateness in collective bargaining negotiations. Unpublished doctoral dissertation. University of Michigan, Ann Arbor, MI.

Janosik, R. J. (1987). Rethinking the culture-negotiation link. *Negotiation Journal, 3,* 385–95.

Jehn, K. & Mannix, E. (2001). The dynamic nature of conflict: A longitudinal study of intragroup conflict and group performance, *Academy of Management Journal, 44,* (2), 238–251.

Jensen, L. (1995). Issue flexibility in negotiating internal war. *Annals of the American Academy of Political and Social Science, 542,* 116–30.

Johnson, D. W. (1971). Role reversal: A summary and review of the research. *International Journal of Group Tensions, 1,* 318–34.

Johnston, R. W. (1982, March–April). Negotiation strategies: Different strokes for different folks. *Personnel, 59,* 36–45.

Jones, E. E. (1964). *Ingratiation.* New York: Appleton-Century-Crofts.

Jones, E. E. & Nisbett, R. E. (1976). The actor and the observer: Divergent perceptions of causality. In J. W. Thibaut, J. T. Spence, & R. C. Carson (Eds.), *Contemporary topics in social psychology* (pp. 37–52). Morristown, NJ: General Learning Press.

Jones, M. & Worchel, S. (1992) Representatives in negotiation: "Internal" variables that affect "external" negotiations. *Basic and Applied Social Psychology, 13* (3), 323–36.

Jones, S. B. & Burgoon, M. (1975). Empirical investigations of language intensity: 2. The effects of irrelevant fear and language intensity on attitude change. *Human Communication Research, 1,* 248–51.

Joseph, M. L. & Willis, R. H. (1963). An experimental analog to two-party bargaining. *Behavioral Science, 8,* 1117–27.

Kahneman, D., Knetsch, J. L., & Thaler, R. H. (1990). Experimental tests of the endowment effect and the Coase Theorem. *Journal of Political Economy, 98,* 1325–48.

Kahneman, D. & Tversky, A. (1979). Prospect theory: An analysis of decisions under risk. *Econometrica, 47,* 263–91.

Kaplan, R. (1984). Trade routes: The manager's network of relationships. *Organizational Dynamics, 12,* 37–52.

Karambayya, R. & Brett, J. M. (1989). Managers handling disputes: Third party roles and perceptions of fairness. *Academy of Management Journal, 32,* 263–291.

Karambayya, R., Brett, J. M., & Lytle, A. (1992). Effects of formal authority and experience on third-party roles, outcomes, and perceptions of fairness. *Academy of Management Journal, 35,* 426–438.

Karrass, C. L. (1974). *Give and take.* New York: Thomas Y. Crowell.

Kellerman, J. L., Lewis, J., & Laird, J. D. (1989). Looking and loving: The effects of mutual gaze on feelings of romantic love. *Journal of Research in Personality, 23,* 145–61.

Kelley, H. H. (1966). A classroom study of the dilemmas in interpersonal negotiation. In K. Archibald (Ed.), *Strategic interaction and conflict: Original papers and discussion* (pp. 49–73). Berkeley, CA: Institute of International Studies.

Kelley, H. H. & Schenitzki, D. P. (1972). Bargaining. In C. G. McClintock (Ed.), *Experimental social psychology* (pp. 298–337). New York: Holt, Rinehart & Winston.

Kelley, H. H. & Thibaut, J. (1969). *Group problem solving.* In G. Lindzey & E. Aronson (Eds.), *Handbook of social psychology* (2nd ed.), (Vol. 4, pp. 1–101). Reading, MA: Addison-Wesley.

Kemp, K. E. & Smith, W. P. (1994). Information exchange, toughness, and integrative bargaining: The roles of explicit cues and perspective-taking. *International Journal of Conflict Management, 5,* 5–21.

Kim, P. H. (1997). Strategic timing in group negotiations: The implications of forced entry and forced exit for negotiators with unequal power. *Organizational Behavior and Human Decision Processes, 71,* 263–86.

Kimmel, M. J., Pruitt, D. G., Magenau, J. M., Konar-Goldband, E., & Carnevale, P. J. D. (1980). Effects of trust aspiration and gender on negotiation tactics. *Journal of Personality and Social Psychology, 38,* 9–23.

Kipnis, D. (1976). *The powerholders.* Chicago: University of Chicago Press.

Kleinke, C. L. (1986). Gaze and eye contact: A research review. *Psychological Bulletin, 100,* 78–100.

Koehn, D. (1997). Business and game playing: The false analogy. *Journal of Business Ethics, 16,* 1447–52.

Koh, T. T. B. (1996). American strengths and weaknesses. *Negotiation Journal, 12,* 313–17.

Kolb, D. (1985). *The mediators.* Cambridge, MA: MIT Press.

Kolb, D. M. & Putnam, L. L. (1997). Through the looking glass: Negotiation theory refracted through the lens of gender. In S. Gleason (Ed.), *Frontiers in dispute resolution in labor relations and human resources* (pp. 231–57). East Lansing, MI: Michigan State University Press.

Komorita, S. S. & Brenner, A. R. (1968). Bargaining and concessions under bilateral monopoly. *Journal of Personality and Social Psychology, 9,* 15–20.

Kopelman, S., Rosette, A. S., & Thompson, L. (2006). The three faces of Eve: An examination of strategic positive, negative, and neutral emotion in negotiations. *Organization Behavior and Human Decision Processes, 99* (1), 81–101.

Kozan, M. K. & Ergin, C. (1999). The influence of intra-cultural value differences on conflict management processes. *International Journal of Conflict Management, 10,* 249–67.

Krackhardt, D. & Hanson, J. R. (1993). Informal networks: The company behind the chart. *Harvard Business Review, 71,* 104–11.

Kramer, R. (1994) The sinister attribution error: Paranoid cognition and collective distrust in organizations. *Motivation and Emotion, 18,* 199–203.

Kramer, R. M. (1991). The more the merrier? Social psychological aspects of multiparty negotiations in organizations. In M. H. Bazerman, R. J. Lewicki, & B. H. Sheppard (Eds.), *Research on negotiation in organizations* (Vol. 3, pp. 307–32). Greenwich, CT: JAI Press.

Kramer, R. M., Pommerenke, P., & Newton, B. (1993). The social context of negotiation: Effects of trust, aspiration and gender on negotiation tactics. *Journal of Personality and Social Psychology, 38* (1), 9–22.

Kristensen, H. (2000) Does fairness matter in corporate takeovers? *Journal of Economic Psychology, 21* (1), 43–56.

Kristensen, H. & Garling, T. (1997). The effects of anchor points and reference points on negotiation process and outcome. *Organizational Behavior and Human Decision Processes, 71*, 85–94.

Kumar, R. (1997). The role of affect in negotiations: An integrative overview. *Journal of Applied Behavioral Science, 3* (1), 84–100.

Kumar, R. (2004). Brahmanical idealism, anarchical individualism, and the dynamics of Indian negotiating behavior. *International Journal of Cross Cultural Management, 4*, 39–58.

Landon, E. L., Jr. (1997). For the most fitting deal, tailor negotiating strategy to each borrower. *Commercial Lending Review, 12*, 5–14.

Lax, D. & Sebenius, J. (1986). *The manager as negotiator: Bargaining for cooperation and competitive gain*. New York: Free Press.

Lax, D. A. & Sebenius, J. K. (2002). Dealcrafting: The substance of three-dimensional negotiations. *Negotiation Journal, 18*, 5–28.

Le Poole, S. (1989). Negotiating with Clint Eastwood in Brussels. *Management Review, 78*, 58–60.

Leung, K., Tong, K., & Ho, S. S. (2004) Effects of interactional justice on egocentric bias in resource allocation decisions. *Journal of Applied Psychology, 89* (3), 405–15.

Levinson, J. C., Smith, M. S. A., & Wilson, O. R. (1999). *Guerilla negotiating*. New York: John Wiley.

Lewicki, R. J. (1983). Lying and deception: A behavioral model. In M. H. Bazerman & R. J. Lewicki (Eds.), *Negotiating in organizations* (pp. 68–90). Beverly Hills, CA: Sage.

Lewicki, R. J. (1992). Negotiating strategically. In A. Cohen (Ed.), *The portable MBA in management* (pp. 147–89). New York: John Wiley and Sons.

Lewicki, R. J. & Dineen, B. R. (2003). Negotiating in virtual organizations. In R. Heneman & D. Greenberger (Eds.), *Human resource management in virtual organizations*. New York: John Wiley and Sons.

Lewicki, R. J., Gray, B., & Elliott, M. (Eds.). (2003). *Making sense of intractable environmental disputes*. Washington, DC: Island Press.

Lewicki, R. J. & Hiam, A. (1999). *The fast forward MBA in negotiation and dealmaking*. New York: John Wiley and Sons.

Lewicki, R. J., Hiam, A., & Olander, K. (1996). *Think before you speak: The complete guide to strategic negotiation*. New York: John Wiley and Sons.

Lewicki, R. J., McAllister, D., & Bies, R. H. (1998). Trust and distrust: New relationships and realities. *Academy of Management Review. 23* (3), 438–58.

Lewicki, R. J. & Robinson, R. (1998). A factor-analytic study of negotiator ethics. *Journal of Business Ethics, 18*, 211–28.

Lewicki, R. J. & Spencer, G. (1990, June). Lies and dirty tricks. Paper presented at the annual meeting of the International Association for Conflict Management, Vancouver, B. C., Canada.

Lewicki, R. J. & Spencer, G. (1991, August). Ethical relativism and negotiating tactics: Factors affecting their perceived ethicality. Paper presented at the annual meeting of the Academy of Management, Miami, FL.

Lewicki, R. J. & Sheppard, B. H. (1985). Choosing how to intervene: Factors affecting the use of process and outcome control in third party dispute resolution. *Journal of Occupational Behavior, 6,* 49–64.

Lewicki, R. J. & Stark, N. (1995). What's ethically appropriate in negotiations: An empirical examination of bargaining tactics. *Social Justice Research, 9,* 69–95.

Lewicki, R. J. & Stevenson, M. (1998). Trust development in negotiation: Proposed actions and a research agenda. *Journal of Business and Professional Ethics, 16* (1–3), 99–132.

Lewicki, R. J., Weiss, S., & Lewin, D. (1992). Models of conflict, negotiation and third-party intervention: A review and synthesis. *Journal of Organizational Behavior, 13,* 209–52.

Liebert, R. M., Smith, W. P., & Hill, J. H. (1968). The effects of information and magnitude of initial offer on interpersonal negotiation. *Journal of Experimental Social Psychology, 4,* 431–41.

Lim, R. G. (1997). Overconfidence in negotiation revisited. *International Journal of Conflict Management, 8,* 52–70.

Lim, R. G. & Murnighan, J. K. (1994). Phases, deadlines, and the bargaining process. *Organizational Behavior and Human Decision Processes, 58,* 153–71.

Lin, X. & Miller, S. J. (2003). Negotiation approaches: Direct and indirect effects of national culture. *International Marketing Review, 20,* 286–303.

Lindskold, S., Bentz, B., & Walters, P. D. (1986). Trust development, the GRIT proposal and the effects of conciliatory acts on conflict and cooperation. *Psychological Bulletin, 85,* 772–93.

Loewenstein, J. & Thompson, L. (2000). The challenge of learning. *Negotiation Journal, 16,* 399–408.

Loewenstein, J., Thompson, L., & Gentner, D. (1999). Analogical encoding facilitates knowledge transfer in organizations. *Psychonomic Bulletin and Review, 6,* 586–97.

Loewenstein, J., Thompson, L., & Gentner, D. (2003). Analogical learning in negotiation teams: Comparing cases promotes learning and transfer. *Academy of Management Learning and Education, 2,* 119–27.

LoFasto, F. & Larson, C. (2001). *When teams work best.* Thousand Oaks, CA: Sage Publications.

Lytle, A. L., Brett, J. M., & Shapiro, D. L. (1999). The strategic use of interests, rights, and power to resolve disputes. *Negotiation Journal, 15* (1), 31–51.

Malhotra, D. K. (2003). Reciprocity in the context of trust: The differing perspective of trustors and trusted parties. *Dissertation Abstracts, 63* (11-B).

Malhotra, D. K. (2004) Trust and reciprocity decisions: The differing perspectives of trustors and trusted parties. *Organizational Behavior and Human Decision Processes, 94* (2), 61–73.

Mannix, E. A., Tinsley, C. H., & Bazerman, M. (1995). Negotiating over time: Impediments to integrative solutions. *Organizational Behavior and Human Decision Processes, 62,* 241–51.

Manz, C. C., Neck, C. P., Mancuso, J., & Manz, K. P.(1997). *For team members only.* New York: AMACOM.

Maxwell, S., Nye, P., & Maxwell, N. (1999) Less pain, some gain: The effects of priming fairness in price negotiations. *Psychology and Marketing, 16,* (7), 545–62.

Maxwell, S., Nye, P., & Maxwell, N. (2003) The wrath of the fairness-primed negotiator when the reciprocity is violated. *Journal of Business Research, 56,* (5), 399–409.

Mayer, J. D., Salovey, P., & Caruso, D. (2000). Emotional intelligence. In R. Sternberg (Ed.), *Handbook of intelligence* (pp. 396–420). Cambridge: Cambridge University Press.

Mayfield, M., Mayfield, J., Martin, D., & Herbig, P. (1997). Time perspectives of the cross-cultural negotiations process. *American Business Review, 15,* 78–85.

McAllister, D. J. (1995). Affect- and cognition-based trust as foundations for interpersonal cooperation in organizations. *Academy of Management Journal, 38*, 24–59.

McClelland, D. C. (1975) *Power: The inner experience*. New York: Irvington.

McClelland, D. C. & Burnham, D. H. (1976). Power is the great motivator. *Harvard Business Review, 43* (2), 100–10.

McCornack, S. A. & Levine, T. R. (1990). When lies are uncovered: Emotional and relational outcomes of discovered deception. *Communication Monographs, 57*, 119–38.

McCroskey, J. C., Jensen, T., & Valencia, C. (1973). Measurement of the credibility of mass media sources. Paper presented at the Western Speech Communication Association, Albuquerque, NM.

McDonald, J. W. (1996). An American's view of a U. S. negotiating style. *International Negotiation, 1*, 323–26.

McGuire, W. J. (1964). Inducing resistance to persuasion: Some contemporary approaches. In L. Berkowitz (Ed.), *Advances in experimental social psychology* (Vol. 1, pp. 191–229). New York: Academic Press.

McGuire, W. J. (1973). Persuasion, resistance and attitude change. In I. S. Poole, F. W. Frey, W. Schramm, N. Maccoby, & E. B. Parker (Eds.), *Handbook of communication* (pp. 216–52). Skokie, IL: Rand McNally.

Michener, S. K. & Suchner, R. W. (1971). The tactical use of social power. In J. T. Tedeschi (Ed.), *The social influence process* (pp. 235–86). Chicago: AVC.

Midgaard, K. & Underal, A. (1977). Multiparty conferences. In D. Druckman (Ed.), *Negotiations: Social psychological perspectives* (pp. 329–45). Beverly Hills, CA: Sage.

Milgram, S. (1974). *Obedience to authority: An experimental view*. New York: Harper & Row.

Miller, D. T. & Ross, M. (1975). Self-serving bias in the attribution of causality: Fact or fiction? *Psychological Bulletin, 82*, 213–25.

Miller, S. K. & Burgoon, M. (1979). The relationship between violations of expectations and the induction of the resistance to persuasion. *Human Communication Research, 5*, 301–13.

Mintzberg, H. & Quinn, J. B. (1991). *The strategy process: Concepts, contexts, cases* (2nd ed.). Englewood Cliffs, NJ: Prentice Hall.

Missner, M. (1980). *Ethics of the business system*. Sherman Oaks, CA: Alfred Publishing Company.

Moore, C. (1996). *The mediation process: Practical strategies for resolving conflict* (2nd ed.). San Francisco: Jossey-Bass.

Moran, R. T. & Stripp, W. G. (1991). *Dynamics of successful international business negotiations*. Houston, TX: Gulf Publishing.

Moran, S. & Ritov, I. (2002). Initial perceptions in negotiations: Evaluation and response to "logrolling" offers. *Journal of Behavioral Decision Making, 15*, 101–24.

Morley, I. & Stephenson, G. (1977). *The social psychology of bargaining*. London: Allen and Unwin.

Morris, M., Nadler, J., Kurtzberg, T., & Thompson, L. (2000). Schmooze or lose: Social friction and lubrication in e-mail negotiations. *Group Dynamics-Theory Research and Practice, 6*, 89–100.

Morris, M. W. & Gelfand, M. J. (2004). Cultural differences and cognitive dynamics: Expanding the cognitive perspective on negotiation. In (Eds.), In M. J. Gelfand & J. M. Brett (Eds.), *The handbook of negotiation and culture: Theoretical advances and cultural perspectives* (pp. 45–70). Palo Alto, CA: Stanford University Press.

Morris, W. N. (1989). *Mood: The Frame of Mind*. New York: Springer-Verlag.

Mosterd, I. & Rutte, C. G. (2000). Effects of time pressure and accountability to constituents on negotiation. *International Journal of Conflict Management, 11* (3), 227–47.

Murnighan, J. K. (1986). Organizational coalitions: Structural contingencies and the formation process. In R. J. Lewicki, B. H. Sheppard, & M. H. Bazerman (Eds.), *Research on negotiation in organizations* (Vol. 1, pp. 155–73). Greenwich, CT: JAI Press.

Myerson, D., Weick, K. E., & Kramer, R. M. (1996). Swift trust and temporary groups. In R. M. Kramer & T. Tyler (Eds.), *Trust in organizations: Frontiers of theory and research* (pp. 166–95). Thousand Oaks, CA: Sage Publications, Inc.

Nadler, J., Thompson, L., & Van Boven, L. (2003). Learning negotiation skills: Four models of knowledge creation and transfer. *Management Science, 49,* 529–40.

Naquin, C. E. (2002). The agony of opportunity in negotiation: Number of negotiable issues, counterfactual thinking, and feelings of satisfaction. *Organizational Behavior and Human Decision Processes, 91,* 97–107.

Naquin, C. E. & Paulson, G. D. (2003). Online bargaining and interpersonal trust. *Journal of Applied Psychology, 88* (1), 113–20.

Nash, J. F. (1950). The bargaining problem. *Econometrica, 18,* 155–62.

Natlandsmyr, J. H. & Rognes, J. (1995). Culture, behavior, and negotiation outcomes: A comparative and cross-cultural study of Mexican and Norwegian negotiators. *International Journal of Conflict Management, 6,* 5–29.

Neale, M. & Bazerman, M. H. (1983). The role of perspective-taking ability in negotiating under different forms of arbitration. *Industrial and Labor Relations Review, 36,* 378–88.

Neale, M. & Bazerman, M. H. (1991). *Cognition and rationality in negotiation.* New York: Free Press.

Neale, M. & Bazerman, M. H. (1992a). Negotiating rationally: The power and impact of the negotiator's frame. *Academy of Management Executive, 6* (3), 42–51.

Neale, M. A. & Bazerman, M. H. (1992b). Negotiator cognition and rationality: A behavioral decision theory perspective. *Organizational Behavior and Human Decision Processes, 51,* 157–75.

Neale, M., Huber, V., & Northcraft, G. (1987). The framing of negotiations: Contextual vs. task frames. *Organizational Behavior and Human Decision Processes, 39,* 228–41.

Neale, M. A. & Northcraft, G. B. (1986). Experts, amateurs, and refrigerators: Comparing expert and amateur negotiators in a novel task. *Organizational Behavior and Human Decision Processes, 38,* 305–17.

Nemeth, C. J. (1986). Differential contributions to majority and minority influence. *Psychological Review, 93,* 23–32.

Nemeth, C. J. (1989). The stimulating properties of dissent. Paper presented at the first annual Conference on Group Process and Productivity, Texas A & M University, College Station, TX.

Nierenberg, G. (1973). *Fundamentals of negotiating.* New York: Hawthorn Books.

Nierenberg, G. (1976). *The complete negotiator.* New York: Nierenberg & Zeif Publishers.

Nierenberg, G. & Calero, H. (1971). *How to read a person like a book.* New York: Simon & Schuster.

Northcraft, G. B. & Neale, M. A. (1987). Experts, amateurs, and real estate: An anchoring and adjustment perspective on property pricing decisions. *Organizational Behavior and Human Decision Processes, 39,* 228–41.

Northrup, H. R. (1964). *Boulwarism.* Ann Arbor, MI: Bureau of Industrial Relations, University of Michigan.

Novemsky, N. & Schweitzer, M. E. (2004). What makes negotiators happy? The differential effects of internal and external social comparisons on negotiator satisfaction. *Organizational Behavior and Human Decision Processes, 95,* 186–97.

O'Connor, K. M. (1997). Motives and cognitions in negotiation: A theoretical integration and an empirical test. *International Journal of Conflict Management, 8*, 114–31.

O'Connor, K. M. (1997). Groups and solos in context: The effects of accountability on team negotiation. *Organizational Behavior and Human Decision Processes, 72*, 384–407.

O'Connor, K. M. & Arnold, J. A. (2001). Distributive spirals: Negotiation impasses and the moderating role of disputant self-efficacy. *Organizational Behavior and Human Decision Processes, 84*, 148–76.

O'Connor, K. M. & Carnevale, P. J. (1997). A nasty but effective negotiation strategy: Misrepresentation of a common-value issue. *Personality and Social Psychology Bulletin, 23*, 504–15.

Ohanyan, A. (1999). Negotiation culture in a post-Soviet context: An interdisciplinary perspective. *Mediation Quarterly, 17*, 83–104.

Ohbuchi, K. & Takahashi, Y. (1994). Cultural styles of conflict management in Japanese and Americans: Passivity, covertness, and effectiveness of strategies. *Journal of Applied Social Psychology, 24*, 1345–66.

O'Keefe, D. J. (1990). *Persuasion: Theory and research*. Newbury Park, CA: Sage.

Oldmeadow, J. A., Platow, M. J., Foddy, M., & Anderson, D. (2003). Self-categorization, status, and social influence. *Social Psychology Quarterly, 66*, 138–44.

Olekalns, M. (2002). Negotiation as social interaction. *Australian Journal of Management, 27*, 39–46.

Olekalns, M. & Smith, P. (2001). Metacognition in negotiation: The identification of critical events and their role in shaping trust and outcomes. Melbourne Business School Working Paper 2001–15.

Olekalns, M., Lau, F., & Smith, P. (2002). The Dynamics of Trust in Negotiation. Paper presented at the International Association of Conflict Management, Park City, Utah. Melbourne Business School Working Paper 2002–09.

Olekalns, M., Smith, P. L., & Walsh, T. (1996). The process of negotiating: Strategy and timing as predictors of outcomes. *Organizational Behavior and Human Decision Processes, 68*, 68–77.

Oliver, R. L., Balakrishnan, P. V., & Barry, B. (1994). Outcome satisfaction in negotiation: A test of expectancy disconfirmation. *Organizational Behavior and Human Decision Processes, 60*, 252–75.

Ostermeier, T. H. (1967). Effects of type and frequency of reference upon perceived source credibility and attitude change. *Speech Monographs, 34*, 137–44.

Palich, L. E., Carini, G. R., & Livingstone, L. P. (2002). Comparing American and Chinese negotiating styles: The influence of logic paradigms. *Thunderbird International Business Review, 44*, 777–98.

Parrott, W. (1994). Beyond hedonism: Motives for inhibiting good moods and for maintaining bad moods. In D. M. Wegner & J. W. Pennebaker (Eds.), *Handbook of mental control* (pp. 278–305). Englewood Cliffs, NJ: Prentice Hall.

Parrott, W. G. (2001). Emotions in social psychology: Volume overview. In W. G. Parrott (Ed.), *Emotions in social psychology* (pp. 1–19). Philadelphia: Psychology Press.

Patterson, J. & Kim, P. (1991). *The day America told the truth*. New York: Prentice Hall.

Petty, R. E. & Brock, T. C. (1981). Thought disruption and persuasion: Assessing the validity of attitude change experiments. In R. E. Petty, T. M. Ostrom, & T. C. Brock (Eds.), *Cognitive responses in persuasion* (pp. 55–79). Hillsdale, NJ: Lawrence Erlbaum.

Petty, R. E. & Cacioppo, J. T. (1986a). Communication and persuasion: Central and peripheral routes to attitude change. New York: Springer Verlag.

Petty, R. E. & Cacioppo, J. T. (1986b). The elaboration likelihood model of persuasion. In L. Berkowitz (Ed.), *Advances in experimental social psychology* (Vol. 19, pp. 123–205). New York: Academic Press.

Petty, R. E. & Cacioppo, J. T. (1990). Involvement and persuasion: Tradition versus integration. *Psychological Bulletin, 107*, 367–74.

Pfeffer, J. (1992). *Managing with power.* Boston, MA: Harvard Business School Press.

Pfouts, R. W. (1994). Buying a pig when both buyer and seller are in a poke. *Atlantic Economic Journal, 22*, 80–5.

Phatak, A. V. & Habib, M. H. (1996). The dynamics of international business negotiations. *Business Horizons, 39*, 30–8.

Pillutla, M. M. & Murnighan, J. K. (1996). Unfairness, anger and spite: Emotional rejections of ultimatum offers. *Organizational Behavior and Human Decision Processes, 68* (3), 208–24.

Pinkley, R. L. (1995). Impact of knowledge regarding alternatives to settlement in dyadic negotiations: Whose knowledge counts? *Journal of Applied Psychology, 80*, 403–17.

Pinkley, R. L., Griffith, T. L., & Northcraft, G. B. (1995). "Fixed pie" a la mode: Information availability, information processing, and the negotiation of suboptimal agreements. *Organizational Behavior and Human Decision Processes, 62*, 101–12.

Pinkley, R. L., Neale, M. A., & Bennett, R. J. (1994). The impact of alternatives to settlement in dyadic negotiation. *Organizational Behavior and Human Decision Processes, 57*, 97–116.

Pinkley, R. L. & Northcraft, G. B. (1994). Cognitive interpretations of conflict: Implications for dispute processes and outcomes. *Academy of Management Journal, 37*, 193–205.

Polzer, J. T., Mannix, E. A., & Neale, M. A. (1995). Multi-party negotiations in a social context. In R. Kramer & D. Messick (Eds.), *Negotiation as a social process* (pp. 123–42). Thousand Oaks, CA: Sage.

Polzer, J. T., Mannix, E. A., & Neale, M. A. (1998). Interest alignment and coalitions in multiparty negotiation. *Academy of Management Journal, 41* (1), 42–54.

Provis, C. (1996). Interests vs. positions: A critique of the distinction. *Negotiation Journal, 12*, 305–23.

Pruitt, D. G. (1981). *Negotiation behavior.* New York: Academic Press.

Pruitt, D. G. (1983). Strategic choice in negotiation. *American Behavioral Scientist, 27*, 167–94.

Pruitt, D. G. & Carnevale, P. J. D. (1993). *Negotiation in social conflict.* Pacific Grove, CA: Brooks-Cole.

Pruitt, D. G. & Lewis, S. A. (1975). Development of integrative solutions in bilateral negotiation. *Journal of Personality and Social Psychology, 31*, 621–33.

Pruitt, D. G. & Rubin, J. Z. (1986). *Social conflict: Escalation, stalemate and settlement.* New York: Random House.

Pruitt, D. G. & Syna, H. (1985). Mismatching the opponent's offers in negotiation. *Journal of Experimental Social Psychology, 21*, 103–13.

Putnam, L. L. (1994). Productive conflict: Negotiation as implicit coordination. *International Journal of Conflict Management, 5*, 284–98.

Putnam, L. L. & Holmer, M. (1992). Framing, reframing, and issue development. In L. Putnam & M. Roloff (Eds.), *Communication and negotiation* (pp. 128–55). Newbury Park, CA: Sage.

Putnam, L. L. & Jones, T. S. (1982). Reciprocity in negotiations: An analysis of bargaining interaction. *Communication Monographs, 49*, 171–91.

Putnam, L. L. & Wilson, S. R. (1989). Argumentation and bargaining strategies as discriminators of integrative outcomes. In M. A. Rahim (Ed.), *Managing conflict: An interdisciplinary approach* (pp. 121–31). New York: Praeger.

Putnam, L., Wilson, S., & Turner, D. (1990). The evolution of policy arguments in teachers' negotiations. *Argumentation, 4,* 129–52.

Pye, L. W. (1992). *Chinese negotiating style.* New York: Quorum Books.

Quinn, J. B. (1991). Strategies for change. In H. Mintzberg & J. B. Quinn (Eds.), *The strategy process: Concepts, contexts, cases* (2nd ed., pp. 4–12). Englewood Cliffs, NJ: Prentice Hall.

Rahim, M. A. (1983). A measure of styles of handling interpersonal conflict. *Academy of Management Journal, 26,* 368–76.

Rahim, M. A. (1990). *Rahim organizational conflict inventory: Professional manual.* Palo Alto, CA: Consulting Psychologists Press.

Rahim, M. A. (1992). *Managing conflict in organizations* (2nd ed.). Westport, CT: Praeger.

Raiffa, H. (1982). *The art and science of negotiation.* Cambridge, MA: Belknap Press of Harvard University Press.

Rapoport, A. (1964). *Strategy and conscience.* New York: Harper & Row.

Rapoport, A., Erev, I., & Zwick, R. (1995). An experimental study of buyer-seller negotiation with one-sided incomplete information and time discounting. *Management Science, 41,* 377–94.

Raven, B. (1993). The bases of power: Origins and recent developments. *Journal of Social Issues, 49* (4), 227–51.

Raven, B., Schwartzwald, J., & Koslowski, M. (1998). Conceptualizing and measuring a power/interaction model of interpersonal influence. *Journal of Applied Social Psychology, 28* (4), 297–332.

Raven, B. H. & Rubin, J. Z. (1973). *Social psychology: People in groups.* New York: John Wiley and Sons.

Reardon, K. K. (1981). *Persuasion theory and context.* Beverly Hills, CA: Sage.

Richardson, R. C. (1977). *Collective bargaining by objectives.* Englewood Cliffs, NJ: Prentice Hall.

Ritov, I. (1996). Anchoring in simulated competitive market negotiation. *Organizational Behavior and Human Decision Processes, 67,* 16–25.

Robinson, R., Lewicki, R. J., & Donahue, E. (2000). Extending and testing a five factor model of ethical and unethical bargaining tactics: The SINS scale. *Journal of Organizational Behavior, 21,* 649–64.

Rogers, C. R. (1957). *Active listening.* Chicago, IL: University of Chicago Press.

Rogers, C. R. (1961). *On becoming a person: A therapist's view of psychotherapy.* Boston, MA: Houghton Mifflin.

Rosette, A., Brett, J. M., Barsness, Z., & Lytle, A. L. (2004). *When cultures clash electronically: The impact of e-mail and culture on negotiation behavior.* DRRC working paper. Evanston, IL: Northwestern University.

Roskos-Ewoldsen, D. R., Bichsel, J., & Hoffman, K. (2002). The influence of accessibility of source likability on persuasion. *Journal of Experimental Social Psychology, 38,* 137–43.

Rosnow, R. L. & Robinson, E. J. (1967). *Experiments in persuasion.* New York: Academic Press.

Ross, L., Green, D., & House, P. (1977). The false consensus phenomenon: An attributional bias in self-perception and social-perception processes. *Journal of Experimental Social Psychology, 13,* 279–301.

Ross, M. H. (2000). "Good-enough" isn't so bad: Thinking about success and failure in ethnic conflict management. *Peace and Conflict: Journal of Peace Psychology, 6,* 21–27.

Roth, A. E., Murnighan, J. K., & Schoumaker, F. (1988). The deadline effect in bargaining: Some empirical evidence. *American Economic Review, 78,* 806–23.

Roth, J. & Sheppard, B. H. (1995). Opening the black box of framing research: The relationship between frames, communication, and outcomes. *Academy of Management Proceedings*.

Rubin, J. Z. & Brown, B. R. (1975). *The Social psychology of bargaining and negotiation*. New York: Academic Press.

Rubin, J. Z. & Sander, F. E. A. (1991). Culture, negotiation, and the eye of the beholder. *Negotiation Journal, 7* (3), 249–54.

Rubinstein, R. A. (2003). Cross cultural considerations in complex peace operations. *Negotiation Journal, 19* (1), 29–49.

Russo, J. E. & Schoemaker, P. J. H. (1989). *Decision traps: The ten barriers to brilliant decision making and how to overcome them*. New York: Simon & Schuster.

Salacuse, J. (1998). So, what's the deal anyway? Contracts and relationships as negotiating goals. *Negotiation Journal, 14* (1), 5–12.

Salacuse, J. W. (1988). Making deals in strange places: A beginner's guide to international business negotiations. *Negotiation Journal, 4*, 5–13.

Savage, G. T., Blair, J. D., & Sorenson, R. L. (1989). Consider both relationships and substance when negotiating strategically. *Academy of Management Executive, 3* (1), 37–48.

Schatzski, M. (1981). *Negotiation: The art of getting what you want*. New York: Signet Books.

Schein, E. (1988). *Organizational culture and leadership*. San Francisco: Jossey Bass.

Schlenker, B. R., Helm, B., & Tedeschi, J. T. (1973). The effects of personality and situational variables on behavioral trust. *Journal of Personality and Social Psychology, 25* (3), 419–27.

Schlenker, B. R. & Riess, M. (1979). Self-presentation of attitudes following commitment to proattitudinal behavior. *Journal of Human Communication Research, 5*, 325–34.

Schneider, A. K. (2002). Shattering negotiation myths: Empirical evidence on the effectiveness of negotiation style. *Harvard Law Review, 7*, 143–233.

Schreisheim, C. & Hinkin, T. R. (1990). Influence strategies used by subordinates: A theoretical and empirical analysis and refinement of the Kipnis, Schmidt, and Wilkinson subscales. *Journal of Applied Psychology, 75*, 246–57.

Schurr, P. H. (1987). Effects of gain and loss decision frames on risky purchase negotiations. *Journal of Applied Psychology, 72*, 351–58.

Schwartz, S. H. (1992). Universals in the content and structure of values: Theoretical advances and empirical tests in 20 countries. In M. Zanna (Ed.), *Advances in experimental social psychology* (Vol. 25, pp. 1–65). Orlando, FL: Academic Press.

Schwartz, S. H. (1994). Beyond individualism and collectivism: New cultural dimensions of values. In U. Kim, H. C. Triandis, C. Kagitcibasi, S-C. Choi, & G. Yoom (Eds.), *Individualism and collectivism: Theory, method and application* (pp. 85–122). Thousand Oaks, CA: Sage Publications.

Schwartz, S. H. & Bilsky, W. (1990). Toward a theory of universal content and structure of values: Extensions and cross-cultural replications. *Journal of Personality and Social Psychology, 58*, 878–91.

Schweitzer, M. E. (1997). Omission, friendship and fraud: Lies about material facts in negotiation. Unpublished manuscript.

Schweitzer, M. E. & Kerr, J. L. (2000). Bargaining under the influence: The role of alcohol in negotiations. *Academy of Management Executive, 14*, 47–57.

Schweitzer, M. (2004). Promises and lies: Restoring violated trust. Wharton School of Business Administration, Unpublished Manuscript.

Schweitzer, M. E., Brodt, S. E., & Croson, R. T. A. (2002). Seeing and believing: Visual access and the strategic use of deception. *International Journal of Conflict Management, 13*, 258–75.

Schweitzer, M. E. & Croson, R. (2001). Curtailing deception: The impact of direct questions on lies and omissions. *International Journal of Conflict Management, 10* (3), 225–48.

Schweitzer, M. E. & Croson, R. T. A. (1998). Lying and deception in negotiations: The impact of direct questions. Unpublished manuscript.

Sebenius, J. K. (1983). Negotiation arithmetic: Adding and subtracting issues and parties. *International Organization, 37,* 1–34.

Sebenius, J. K. (1992). Negotiation analysis: A characterization and review. *Management Science, 38,* 18–38.

Sebenius, J. K. (2002a). The hidden challenge of cross-border negotiations. *Harvard Business Review, 80* (March), 76–85.

Sebenius, J. K. (2002b). Caveats for cross-border negotiations. *Negotiation Journal, 18* (2), 121–33.

Selekman, B. M., Fuller, S. H., Kennedy, T., & Baitsel, J. M. (1964). *Problems in labor relations.* New York: McGraw-Hill.

Selekman, B. M., Selekman, S. K., & Fuller, S. H. (1958). *Problems in labor relations.* New York: McGraw-Hill.

Seligman, C., Bush, M., & Kirsch, K. (1976). Relationship between compliance in the foot in the door paradigm and size of first request. *Journal of Personality and Social Psychology, 33,* 517–20.

Shah, P. P. & Jehn, K. A. (1993). Do friends perform better than acquaintances? The interaction of friendship, conflict and task. *Group Decision and Negotiation, 2,* 149–65.

Shapiro, D. L. (1991). The effects of explanations on negative reactions to deceit. *Administrative Science Quarterly, 36,* 614–30.

Shea, G. F. (1983). *Creative negotiating.* Boston, MA: CBI Publishing Co.

Shell, G. R. (1991). When is it legal to lie in negotiations? *Sloan Management Review, 32* (3), 93–101.

Sheppard, B. H., Lewicki, R. J., & Minton, J. W. (1992). *Organizational justice: The search for fairness in the workplace.* New York: Lexington Books.

Sheppard, B. H. & Tuchinsky, M. (1996). Micro-OB and the network organization. In R. Kramer & T. Tyler (Eds.), *Trust in organizations* (pp. 140–65). Thousand Oaks, CA: Sage.

Sherif, M., Harvey, L., White, B., Hood, W., & Sherif, C. (1988). *The Robbers' Cave experiment: Intergroup conflict and cooperation.* Middletown, CT: Wesleyan University Press. (Original work published 1961.)

Short, J., Williams, E., & Christie, B. (1976). *The social psychology of telecommunications.* London: John Wiley.

Sims, R. L. (2002). Support for the use of deception within the work environment: A comparison of Israeli and United States employee attitudes. *Journal of Business Ethics, 35,* 27–34.

Simons, T. (1993). Speech patterns and the concept of utility in cognitive maps: The case of integrative bargaining. *Academy of Management Journal, 36,* 139–56.

Simons, T. & Tripp, T. (1997, February). The negotiation checklist: How to win the battle before it begins. *Cornell Hotel and Restaurant Administration Quarterly, 38,* (1), 14–23.

Sitkin, S. B. & Bies, R. J. (1993). Social accounts in conflict situations: Using explanations to manage conflict. *Human Relations, 46,* 349–70.

Skarlicki, D. P. & Folger, R. (1997). Retaliation in the workplace: The roles of distributive, procedural and interactive justice. *Journal of Applied Psychology, 82* (3), 434–43.

Smith, P. & Schwartz, S. H. (1997). Values. In J. W. Berry, M. H. Segall., and C. Kagitcibashi (Eds.), *Handbook of cross-cultural psychology* (Vol. 3, pp. 77–118). Needham Heights, MA: Allyn & Bacon.

Song, F. (2004). Trust and reciprocity: The differing norms of individuals and group representatives. Unpublished paper.

Spitzberg, B. H. & Cupach, W. R. (1984). *Interpersonal communication competence.* Beverly Hills, CA: Sage.

Sproull, L. & Kiesler, S. (1986). Reducing social context cues: Electronic mail in organizational communication. *Management Science, 32,* 1492–512.

Stacks, D. W. & Burgoon, J. K. (1981). The role of non-verbal behaviors as distractors in resistance to persuasion in interpersonal contexts. *Central States Speech Journal, 32,* 61–80.

Staw, B. M. (1981). The escalation of commitment to a course of action. *Academy of Management Review, 6,* 577–87.

Stein, J. (1996). The art of real estate negotiations. *Real Estate Review, 25,* 48–53.

Stein, J. G. (1999). Problem solving as metaphor: Negotiation and identity conflict. *Peace and Conflict: Journal of Peace Psychology, 5,* 225–35.

Steinberg, L. (1998). *Winning with integrity.* New York: Random House.

Stillenger, C., Epelbaum, M., Keltner, D., & Ross, L. (1990). *The "reactive devaluation" barrier to conflict resolution.* Working paper. Stanford University, Palo Alto, CA.

Susskind, L., McKearnan, S., & Thomas-Larmer, J. (1999). *The consensus building handbook.* Thousand Oaks: Sage Publications.

Swenson, R. A., Nash, D. L., & Roos, D. C. (1984). Source credibility and perceived expertness of testimony in a simulated child-custody case. *Professional Psychology, 15,* 891–98.

Tajima, M. & Fraser, N. M. (2001). Logrolling procedure for multi-issue negotiation. *Group Decision and Negotiation, 10,* 217–35.

Tannen, D. (1998). How to turn debate into dialogue. *USA Weekend,* February 27–March 3, 4–5.

Taylor, S. E. & Brown, J. D. (1988). Illusion and well-being: A social-psychological perspective on mental health. *Psychological Bulletin, 103,* 193–210.

Tedeschi, J. T., Schlenker, B. R., & Bonoma, T. V. (1973). Conflict, power and games: The experimental study of interpersonal relations. Chicago: AVC.

Tenbrunsel, A. E. (1998). Misrepresentation and expectations of misrepresentation in an ethical dilemma: The role of incentives and temptation. *Academy of Management Journal, 4* (3), 330–39.

Tenbrunsel, A. E. (1999). Trust as an obstacle in environmental–economic disputes. *American Behavioral Scientist, 42,* 1350–67.

Thomas, K. W. (1992). Conflict and negotiation processes in organizations. In M. D. Dunnette and L. H. Hough, *Handbook of industrial & organizational psychology* (2nd ed., Vol. 3, pp. 651–718). Palo Alto, CA: Consulting Psychologists Press.

Thomas, K. W. & Kilmann, R. H. (1974). *Thomas-Kilmann conflict mode survey.* Tuxedo, NY: Xicom.

Thompson, L. (1990a). An examination of naïve and experienced negotiators. *Journal of Personality and Social Psychology, 59,* 82–90.

Thompson, L. (1990b). Negotiation behavior and outcomes: Empirical evidence and theoretical issues. *Psychological Bulletin, 108,* 515–32.

Thompson, L. (1991). Information exchange in negotiation. *Journal of Experimental Social Psychology, 27,* 161–79.

Thompson, L. (1995). They saw a negotiation: Partnership and involvement. *Journal of Personality and Social Psychology, 68,* 839–53.

Thompson, L. (1998). *The mind and heart of the negotiator.* Upper Saddle River, NJ: Prentice Hall.

Thompson, L. (2000). *Making the team: A guide for managers.* Englewood Cliffs, NJ: Prentice Hall.

Thompson, L. & DeHarpport, T. (1994). Social judgment, feedback, and interpersonal learning in negotiation. *Organizational Behavior and Human Decision Processes, 58,* 327–45.

Thompson, L., Gentner, J., & Loewenstein, J. (2000). Avoiding missed opportunities in managerial life: Analogical training more powerful than individual case training. *Organizational Behavior and Human Decision Processes, 82,* 60–75.

Thompson, L. & Hastie, R. (1990a). Social perception in negotiation. *Organizational Behavior and Human Decision Processes, 47,* 98–123.

Thompson, L. & Hastie, R. (1990b). Judgment tasks and biases in negotiation. In B. H. Sheppard, M. H. Bazerman, & R. J. Lewicki (Eds.), *Research on negotiation in organizations* (Vol. 2, pp. 31–54). Greenwich, CT: JAI Press.

Thompson, L. & Hrebec, D. (1996). Lose-lose agreements in interdependent decision making. *Psychological Bulletin, 120,* 396–409.

Thompson, L., Peterson, E., & Brodt, S. E. (1996). Team negotiations: An examination of integrative and distributive bargaining. *Journal of Personality and Social Psychology, 70,* 66–78.

Thompson, L., Valley, K. L., & Kramer, R. M. (1995). The bittersweet feeling of success: An examination of social perception in negotiation. *Journal of Experimental Social Psychology, 31,* 467–92.

Thompson, L. L., Wang, J. W., & Gunia, B. C. (2010). Negotiation. *Annual Review of Psychology, 61,* 491–515.

Thompson, L. L., Nadler, J., & Kim, P. H. (1999). Some like it hot: The case for the emotional negotiator. In L. L. Thompson, J. M. Levine, & D. M. Messick (Eds.), *Shared cognition in organizations: The management of knowledge* (139–61). Mahwah, NJ: Erlbaum.

Tinsley, C. H. (1998). Models of conflict resolution in Japanese, German, and American cultures. *Journal of Applied Psychology, 83,* 316–23.

Tinsley, C. H. (1997). Understanding conflict in a Chinese cultural context. In R. J. Bies, R. J. Lewicki, & B. H. Sheppard (Eds.), *Research on negotiation in organizations* (Vol. 6, pp. 209–25). Greenwich, CT: JAI Press.

Tinsley, C. H. (2001). How negotiators get to yes: Predicting the constellation of strategies used across cultures to negotiate conflict. *Journal of Applied Psychology, 86,* 583–93.

Tinsley, C. H. & O'Connor, K. (2004). Looking for an edge in negotiations? Cultivate an integrative reputation. Paper presented at the Academy of Management Meetings, New Orleans, LA.

Tinsley, C. H., O'Connor, K. M., & Sullivan, B. A. (2002). Tough guys finish last: The perils of a distributive reputation. *Organizational Behavior and Human Decision Processes, 88,* 621–42.

Tjosvold, D. (1986). *Working together to get things done: Managing for organizational productivity.* Lanham, ND: Lexington Books.

Tjosvold, D. (1997). The leadership relationship in Hong Kong: Power, interdependence and controversy. In K. Leung, U. Kim, S. Yamaguchi, and Y. Kashima (Eds.), *Progress in Asian social psychology,* Vol. 1. New York: John Wiley.

Tomlinson, E., Lewicki, B., & Dineen, R. J. (2003). The road to reconciliation: Antecedents of victim willingness to reconcile following a broken promise. *Journal of Management, 30* (2), 165–87.

Touval, S. (1988). Multilateral negotiation: An analytical approach. *Negotiation Journal, 5* (2), 159–73.

Tung, R. L. (1991). Handshakes across the sea: Cross-cultural negotiating for business success. *Organizational Dynamics, 19*, Winter. 30–40.

Tutzauer, F. (1991). Bargaining outcome, bargaining process, and the role of communication. *Progress in Communication Science, 10*, 257–300.

Tutzauer, F. (1992). The communication of offers in dyadic bargaining. In L. Putnam & M. Roloff (Eds.), *Communication and negotiation* (pp. 67–82). Newbury Park, CA: Sage.

Tversky, A. & Kahneman, D. (1981). The framing of decisions and the psychology of choice. *Science, 211*, 453–58.

Tyler, T. & Hastie, R. (1991). The social consequences of cognitive illusions. In M. H. Bazerman, R. J. Lewicki, and B. H. Sheppard (Eds.), *Research on negotiation in organizations* (Vol. 3, pp. 69–98). Greenwich, CT: JAI Press.

Ury, W. (1991). *Getting past no: Negotiating with difficult people.* New York: Bantam Books.

Ury, W. L., Brett, J. M., & Goldberg, S. B. (1988). *Getting disputes resolved.* San Francisco: Jossey-Bass.

Valley, K. L., Moag, J., & Bazerman, M. H. (1998). A matter of trust: Effects of communication on the efficiency and distribution of outcomes. *Journal of Economic Behavior and Organization, 34*, 211–38.

van de Vliert, E. (1985). Escalative intervention in small group conflicts. *Journal of Applied Behavioral Science, 21*, 19–36.

Van Pouke, D. & Buelens, M. (2002). Predicting the outcome of a two-party price negotiation: Contribution of reservation price, aspiration price, and opening offer. *Journal of Economic Psychology, 23*, 67–76.

Veitch, R. & Griffith, W. (1976). Good news–bad news: Affective and interpersonal affects. *Journal of Applied Social Psychology, 6*, 69–75.

Volkema, R. J. & Fleury, M. T. L. (2002). Alternative negotiating conditions and the choice of negotiation tactics: A cross-cultural comparison. *Journal of Business Ethics, 36*, 381–98.

Wade-Benzoni, K. A., Okumura, T., Brett, J. M., Moore, D. A., Tenbrunsel, A. E., & Bazerman, M. H. (2002). Cognitions and behavior in asymmetric social dilemmas: A comparison of two cultures. *Journal of Applied Social Psychology, 87*, 87–95.

Walcott, C., Hopmann, P. T., & King, T. D. (1977). The role of debate in negotiation. In D. Druckman (Ed.), *Negotiations: Social psychological perspectives* (pp. 193–211). Beverly Hills, CA: Sage.

Walton, R. (1987). *Managing conflict: Interpersonal dialogue and third-party roles* (2nd ed.). Reading, MA: Addison-Wesley.

Walton, R. E. & McKersie, R. B. (1965). *A behavioral theory of labor negotiations: An analysis of a social interaction system.* New York: McGraw-Hill.

Watkins, M. (2002) *Breakthrough business negotiations.* San Francisco: Jossey-Bass.

Weber, M. J. & Murnighan, J. K. (2008). Suckers or saviors: Consistent contributors in social dilemmas. *Journal of Personality and Social Psychology, 95*, 1340–53.

Weeks, H. (2001). Taking the stress out of stressful conversations. *Harvard Business Review*, July–August, 112–19.

Weingart, L. R., Bennett, R. J., & Brett, J. M. (1993). The impact of consideration of issues and motivational orientation on group negotiation process and outcome. *Journal of Applied Psychology, 78* (3), 504–17.

Weingart, L. R., Hyder, E. B., & Prietula, M. J. (1996). Knowledge matters: The effect of tactical descriptions on negotiation behavior and outcome. *Journal of Personality and Social Psychology, 70*, 1205–17.

Weingart, L. R., Prietula, M. J., Hyder, E. B., & Genovese, C. R. (1999) Knowledge and the sequential processes of negotiation: A Markov Chain analysis of response-in-kind. *Journal of Experimental Social Psychology*, *35*, 366–93.

Weingart, L. R., Thompson, L. L., Bazerman, M. H., & Carroll, J. S. (1990). Tactical behaviors and negotiation outcomes. *International Journal of Conflict Management*, *1*, 7–31.

Weiss, J. (2003). Trajectories toward peace: Mediator sequencing strategies in intractable communal disputes. *Negotiation Journal*, 109–15.

Weiss, S. E. (1994). Negotiating with "Romans": A range of culturally-responsive strategies. *Sloan Management Review*, *35* (1), 51–61; (2), 1–16.

Weiss, S. E. (1997). Explaining outcomes of negotiation: Toward a grounded model for negotiations between organizations. In R. J. Lewicki, R. J. Bies, & B. H. Sheppard (Eds.), *Research on negotiation in organizations* (Vol. 6, pp. 247–333). Greenwich, CT: JAI Press.

Weiss, S. E. & Stripp, W. (1985). *Negotiating with foreign business persons: An introduction for Americans with propositions on six cultures.* New York: New York University Graduate School of Business Administration, Working Paper 85–6.

Weldon, E. & Jehn, K. A. (1995). Examining cross-cultural differences in conflict management behavior: A strategy for future research. *The International Journal of Conflict Management*, *6*, 387–403.

Xing, F. (1995). The Chinese cultural system: Implications for cross-cultural management. *SAM Advanced Management Journal*, *60*, 14–20.

Yan, A. & Gray, B. (1994). Bargaining power, management control, and performance in United States–China joint ventures: A comparative case study. *Academy of Management Journal*, *37*, 1478–517.

Yankelovich, D. (1982, August). Lying well is the best revenge. *Psychology Today*, *71*, 5–6.

Yook, E. L. & Albert, R. D. (1998). Perceptions of the appropriateness of negotiation in educational settings: A cross-cultural comparison among Koreans and Americans. *Communication Education*, *47*, 18–29.

Yukl, G. (1974). Effects of the opponent's initial offer, concession magnitude, and concession frequency on bargaining behavior. *Journal of Personality and Social Psychology*, *30*, 323–35.

Yukl, G. & Tracey, J. A. B. (1992). Consequences of influence tactics used with subordinates, peers and the boss. *Journal of Applied Psychology*, *77*, 525–35.

Zand, D. (1972). Trust and managerial problem solving. *Administrative Science Quarterly*, *17*, 229–39.

Zand, D. (1997). *The leadership triad: Knowledge, trust and power.* New York: Oxford University Press.

Zarkada-Fraser, A. & Fraser, C. (2001). Moral decision making in international sales negotiations. *Journal of Business and Industrial Marketing*, *16*, 274–93.

Zartman, I. W. (1977). Negotiation as a joint decision making process. In I. Zartman (Ed.), *The negotiation process: Theories and applications* (pp. 67–86). Beverly Hills, CA: Sage.

Zartman, I. W. (1997). Conflict and order: Justice in negotiation. *International Political Science Review*, *18*, 121–38.

Zartman, I. W. & Berman, M. (1982). *The practical negotiator.* New Haven: Yale University Press.

Zebrowitz, L. A., Voinescu, L., & Collins, M. A. (1996). "Wide-eyed" and "crooked-faced": Determinants of perceived and real honesty across the life span. *Personality and Social Psychology Bulletin*, *22*, 1258–69.